A HISTORY
OF RELIGIOUS
IDEAS

Translated from the French by
Alf Hiltebeitel and Diane Apostolos-Cappadona

MIRCEA ELIADE

A HISTORY OF RELIGIOUS IDEAS

Volume **3** From Muhammad to the Age of Reforms

The University of Chicago Press

Chicago and London

The University of Chicago Press, Chicago 60637
The University of Chicago Press, Ltd., London

Library of Congress Cataloging in Publication Data
Eliade, Mircea, 1907–1986
   A History of religious ideas.
   Translation of Histoire des croyances et des
idées religieuses.
   Includes bibliographies and indexes.
   CONTENTS: 1. From the stone age to the Eleusinian
mysteries.—v.2.   From Gautama Buddha to the triumph
of Christianity.—v.3.   From Muhammad to the age of reforms.
   1. Religion—History.   2. Religions—History.
I. Title.
BL48.E3813   291   77-16784

ISBN: 0-226-20400-6 (vol. 1, cloth)   AACRI
        0-226-20401-4 (vol. 1, paper)
        0-226-20402-2 (vol. 2, cloth)
        0-226-20403-0 (vol. 2, paper)
        0-226-20404-9 (vol. 3, cloth)
        0-226-20405-7 (vol. 3, paper)

Originally published in French under the title *Histoire des
croyances et des idées religieuses*. Vol. 3: *De Mahomet à
l'âge des Réformes*. © Payot, Paris, 1983.

For Christinel

Contents

of Light   318. Current interest in Tibetan religious
creations

Preface

The delay with which this third volume appears is due to reasons of
health: as time goes by my vision continues to dwindle, and because of
a stubborn arthritis, I write with difficulty. This obliges me to complete the last part of *A History of Religious Ideas* with the collaboration
of several of my colleagues, selected from among my former students.

As the reader will not fail to notice, I have modified the plan announced in the Preface of volume 2. I have continued the history of the
Christian churches as far as the Enlightenment, and I have transferred
the chapters on the expansion of Hinduism, medieval China, and Japanese religions to the final volume. I have devoted four chapters to
the history of the beliefs, ideas, and religious institutions of Europe
between the fourth and seventeenth centuries. But I have concentrated
less on the familiar creations of Occidental thought (e.g., Scholasticism, Reformation) than on certain phenomena which have largely
passed into silence or been minimized in the manuals: heterodoxies,
heresies, mythologies, and popular practices such as sorcery, alchemy,
and esotericism. Interpreted in their proper spiritual horizon, these religious creations have their own special interest and occasionally their
grandeur. In any case, they have become integrated into the religious
history and culture of Europe.

An important section of the final volume of *A History of Religious
Ideas* will be a presentation of the archaic and traditional religions of
America, Africa, and Oceania. In fact, in the final chapter, I will un-
dertake to analyze the religious creativity of modern societies.

I wish to thank Professor Charles Adams, who had the kindness to
read chapters 33 and 35, and who communicated to me a number of
precise observations. It is I, however, who am responsible for the in-

terpretation of Shî'ism and Muslim mysticism, an interpretation grounded in the hermeneutic of my lamented late friend, Henry Corbin. I would like to acknowledge my colleague and friend, Professor André Lacocque, for the care with which he read and corrected the entire text of this present volume, and my publisher and friend, Jean-Luc Pidoux-Payot, for his patience and for the interest with which he has followed the elaboration of this work.

The presence, affection, and devotion of my wife have helped me to triumph over the fatigue and the discouragements provoked by my sufferings and infirmities. It is indeed thanks to her that this volume has been achieved.

31 The Religions of Ancient Eurasia: Turko-Mongols, Finno-Ugrians, Balto-Slavs

241. Hunters, nomads, warriors

The terrible invasions of the Turko-Mongols—from the Huns in the fourth century to the time of Tamburlaine in the fourteenth—were inspired by the mythic model of the primitive hunter of Eurasia: the carnivore pursuing his game on the steppes. In the suddenness and rapidity of their movements, their massacres of entire populations, and their annihilation of the external signs of sedentary cultures (towns and villages), the horsemen of the Huns, Avars, Turks, and Mongols were like packs of wolves hunting the cervidae on the steppes or attacking the herds of nomad shepherds. Certainly, the strategic importance and political consequences of this behavior were well known by their military chiefs. But the mystical prestige of the exemplary hunter, the carnivore, played a considerable role. A number of Altaic tribes claimed a supernatural wolf as their ancestor (cf. §10).

The flashing apparition of the "Empires of the Steppes" and their more or less ephemeral character still fascinate historians. In effect, the Huns in 374 crushed the Ostrogoths on the Dniester, provoking the precipitous migration of a series of other Germanic tribes, and then, leaving the Hungarian plains, ravaged several provinces of the Roman Empire. Attila succeeded in overwhelming a large part of central Europe, but shortly after his death (453), the Huns, divided and bewildered, disappeared from history. Similarly, the enormous Mongol Empire created by Genghis Khan in twenty years (1206–1227) and expanded by his successors (to Eastern Europe after 1241; to Persia, Iraq, and Anatolia after 1258; and to China in 1279) declined after the failure to conquer Japan (1281). The Turk Tamburlaine (1360–1404), who considered himself Genghis Khan's successor, was the last great conqueror inspired by the model of the carnivores.

We must insist that these various "barbarians" surging from the Central Asian steppes were not unaware of certain cultural and religious creations of civilized peoples. Moreover, as we will see in a moment, their ancestors, prehistoric horsemen and nomadic shepherds, had likewise benefited from the discoveries made in the diverse regions of southern Asia.

The populations speaking Altaic languages occupied a vast territory: Siberia, the Volga region, central Asia, north and northwest China, Mongolia, and Turkey. Three principal branches are distinguished: (1) common Turkish (Uigur, Chagataï); (2) Mongol (Kalmyk, Mongol, Buryat); and (3) Manchu-Tungus.[1] The primitive habitat of these Altaic peoples had in all likelihood been the steppes around the Altai and Ch'ing-hai mountains, between Tibet and China, extending to the north, as far as the Siberian taiga. These diverse Altaic groups, as well as the Finno-Ugrian populations, practiced hunting and fishing in the northern regions, nomadic shepherding in central Asia, and, in a very modest way, farming in the southern zone.

From prehistory, northern Eurasia had been influenced by cultures, skills, and religious ideas coming from the south. The breeding of reindeer in the Siberian regions had been inspired by the domestication of the horse, most probably effected on the steppes. The centers of prehistoric commerce (for example, the Island of the deer on Lake Onega) and metallurgy (Perm) had played an important role in the elaboration of Siberian cultures. Furthermore, central and northern Asia had gradually received religious ideas of Mesopotamian, Iranian, Chinese, Indian, Tibetan (Lamaism), Christian (Nestorianism), and Manichaean origin, to which it is necessary to add the influences of Islam and, more recently, of Russian Orthodox Christianity.

One must add, however, that these influences were not always successful in modifying the original religious structures. Certain beliefs and customs specific to the Paleolithic hunters still survive in northern Eurasia. In a number of cases, one recognizes these archaic myths and religious conceptions in Lamaist, Muslim, and Christian disguises.[2]

1. The hypothesis of an Uralo-Altaic linguistic family, including both Finnish and Hungarian, has been abandoned.

2. The written documents are few in number and late: several allusions in Chinese

As a result, despite the diverse syncretisms, one can distinguish certain characteristic conceptions: the belief in a celestial god, sovereign of mankind; a specific type of cosmogony; mystical solidarity with animals; shamanism. Nevertheless, the great interest in the religions of central and northern Asia resides chiefly in the syncretistic structure of their creations.

242. Tängri, the "Celestial God"

Of all the gods of the Altaic peoples, the most important and best known is indeed Tängri (Tengri among the Mongols and Kalmyks, Tengeri among the Buryats, Tängere among the Tatars of the Volga, and Tingir among the Beltirs). The vocable *tängri,* meaning "god" and "sky," belongs to the vocabulary of the Turks and the Mongols. Existing "from the prehistory of Asia, it has had a singular fortune. Its field of influence in time, in space, and across civilizations is immense; one knows of it over two millennia; it is or has been employed across all of Asia, from the borders of China to the south of Russia, from Kamchatka to the Sea of Marmara; it has served the Altaic 'peasants' by designating their gods and being their supreme God, and has been conserved in all the great universal religions which the Turks and the Mongols have embraced in the course of their history (Christianity, Manichaeanism, Islam, etc.)."[3]

The word *tängari* is used to express the divine. As applied to the great celestial god, it is attested among the Hsiung-nu in the second century B.C. The texts present him as "grand" (*üsä*), "white and heavenly" (*kök*), "eternal" (*möngkä*), and endowed with "strength" (*küc*).[4] In one of the Paleo-Turkic inscriptions of Orkhon (seventh to

---

Annals of the second century B.C., and by certain Latin and Byzantine historians of the fourth century A.D. (concerning the campaigns of Attila); the inscriptions of the Paleo-Turks of Orkhon in Mongolia (seventh to eighth centuries); and the literature elaborated following the conquests of Genghis Khan, to which one must add the accounts of the voyages of Marco Polo (thirteenth century) and of the first Catholic missionaries. It is only after the eighteenth century that the works of European authors supplied more coherent information about the beliefs and customs of Eurasia.

3. Jean-Paul Roux, "Tängri, essai sur le ciel-dieu des peuples altaïques" (first article), p. 49.

4. Cf. ibid., second article, p. 200.

eighth centuries), it is written: "When the blue sky on high, and the somber earth below were made, between the two were made the sons of men (=humankind)."[5] One can interpret the separation of the Sky and the Earth as a cosmogonic act. But as to a cosmogony proper, having Tängri as its author, there are only allusions. The Tatars of the Altai and the Yakuts, however, refer to their God as a "creator." And, according to the Buryats, the gods (*tengri*) created man and the latter lived happily up to the moment when the evil spirits spread sickness and death upon the earth.[6]

In such manner the cosmic order, and thus the organization of the world and society, and the destiny of mankind, depend upon Tängri. Accordingly, every sovereign must receive his investiture from heaven. One reads in the inscription of Orkhon: "Tängri who had elevated my father to Kaghan . . . Tängri who gave the empire, this Tängri has established me as Kaghan."[7] In effect, the Kaghan is the "Son of Heaven" according to the Chinese model (cf. §128). The sovereign is the envoy or representative of the Celestial God. The cult of Tängri is maintained in all its strength and integrity by the sovereign. "When anarchy reigns, when the tribes are scattered, when there is no longer an Empire (as in our times), Tängri, formerly so significant, tends to become a *deus otiosus,* to leave his place to secondary celestial divinities or to break apart into pieces (the multiplication of Tängris). . . . When there is no longer a sovereign, the celestial God is slowly forgotten, the popular cult is strengthened and tends to become primary."[8] (The Mongols knew 99 Tengris, most of them having their own names and precise functions.) The transformation of a celestial god and sovereign into a *deus otiosus* is a universally attested phenomenon. In the case of Tängri, his multiplication or his substitution by other divinities appears to have followed the breakup of the empire.

5. Ibid., p. 221.

6. Cf. the sources cited in my *Shamanism,* p. 69, n. 7. In the popular religious beliefs of the Mongols, Tengri "has created everything"; fire, milk, etc. Cf. W. Heissing, *La religion des Mongols,* p. 404. But it is not a question of a cosmogony in the proper sense of the word.

7. J.-P. Roux, "Tängri" (third article), p. 27. The same belief is attested in the Mongol epoch. "He was Khan by the power and force of eternal Heaven"; R. Grousset, *L'Empire des Steppes,* p. 182.

8. J.-P. Roux, "La religion des Turcs de l'Orkhon des VIIᵉ et VIIIᵉ siècles" (first article), p. 20.

But a similar process is verified in innumerable historical contexts (cf. *Patterns*, §§14ff.)

Tängri did not have temples, and it is unlikely that he was represented in the form of a statue. In his celebrated discussion with the Imam of Boukhara, Genghis Khan said to him: "The entire universe is the house of God, to what advantage is it to designate a particular place (for example, Mecca) in order to go there?" As everywhere else, the celestial god of the Altais is omniscient. In taking an oath, the Mongols would say, "May Heaven know it!" The military chiefs climbed mountain tops (images of the Center of the World) to pray to God, or, before their campaigns, they lived apart in their tents (occasionally for three days, as Genghis Khan did), while the troops invoked Heaven. Tängri manifested his discontent by cosmic signs: comets, famines, and floods. One would address him in prayers (for example, among the Mongols, the Beltirs, etc.) and one would sacrifice horses, cattle, and sheep to him. Sacrifice to celestial gods is universally attested, especially in cases of calamity or natural catastrophe. But, in central and northern Asia, as elsewhere, the multiplication of Tängri is followed by their assimilation to other gods (of the thunderstorm, cosmic fertility, etc.). Thus in Altaic, Bai Ülgän (the "Most Grand") is replaced by Tengere Kaira Kan ("the compassionate Heavenly Lord"), and it is to the latter that one performs the horse sacrifice (see below, §§248ff.).[9] Remoteness and passivity characterize other celestial gods. Thus Buga ("Heaven," "World") of the Tungus receives no cult; he is omniscient, but does not interfere in human affairs or punish evildoers. Urün Ai Toyon of the Yakuts inhabits the seventh heaven, governs all, but does only good (which is to say he doesn't bring punishment).[10]

243. The structure of the world

The cosmology and cosmogony of the Altaic peoples are of great interest. For one thing, they conserve archaic elements found in a

---

9. On divine names of Ouranian structure—"Chief," "Master," "Father," "Creator," "The Great," "Light," etc.—see Eliade, *Patterns in Comparative Religion*, §18; cf. Uno Harva, *Die religiösen Vorstellungen der altaischen Völker*, pp. 104ff.

10. See Eliade, *Patterns*, §18; Harva, *Rel. Vorstell.*, pp. 151ff.

number of traditional cultures. In addition, the forms by which they have been transmitted indicate a long syncretistic process of assimilation and reinterpretation of certain ideas received from other peoples. What is more: the cosmology does not always seem to account for the most widespread Asian cosmogonic myth. To be sure, we must take into account the heterogeneity of the evidence at our disposal: the cosmogonic myth has circulated above all in popular cultural contexts— an important point whose significance will soon be underscored.

In Asia, as in many other parts of the world, the structure of the universe is understood on the whole as having three tiers—Heaven, Earth, Hell—interconnected by a central axis. This axis passes through an "opening," a "hole," by which the gods descend to the Earth and the dead into the subterranean regions. It is through this opening that the soul of the shaman is able to fly away or descend during his celestial or infernal journeys. The three worlds—which are inhabited by gods, men, and the Sovereign of Hell with the dead—are thus imagined as three superimposed planes.[11]

A number of Altaic peoples have imagined that heaven is like a tent; the Milky Way is the "seam"; the stars, the "holes" for the light. From time to time, the gods open the tent to look out on the earth, thus causing meteors. Heaven is also conceived as a cover or lid which happens not to have been perfectly fitted to the edges of the earth; thus the great winds penetrate through the openings. And it is through this reduced space that heroes and other privileged beings are able to slip through and reach Heaven. In the middle of Heaven shines the polestar, which supports the celestial tent like a post. It is called "the Golden Pillar" (by the Mongols, Buryats, etc.), "the Iron Pillar" (by the Siberian Tatars, etc.), "the Solar Pillar" (by the Teleuts, etc.).[12]

As one would expect, this cosmology has found a model in the microcosm of the human world. The world axis is represented in a concrete fashion, whether by the pillars which support human habitations, or in the form of single, isolated posts, called "Pillars of the World."

11. This image is completed by the belief that the World is sustained by an animal (tortoise, fish) which prevents it from sinking into the ocean; cf. Harva, *Rel Vorstell.,* pp. 22ff.

12. See the sources cited in my *Shamanism*, pp. 260ff. The Buryats imagine the stars as a herd of horses and the polestar as the stake to which they are tethered. This idea is common to Altaic and Ugrian peoples. Cf. ibid., p. 261, n. 7.

When the form of the habitation is modified (from the hut with a conical roof one passes to the yurt), the pillar's mythico-religious function devolves upon the high opening for the removal of the smoke. This aperture corresponds to the similar orifice of the "House of Heaven," assimilated to the "hole" which the polestar makes in the canopy of heaven. This symbolism is extremely widespread.[13] The underlying idea is the belief in the possibility of direct communication with Heaven. On the macrocosmic level, this communication is represented by an axis (pillar, mountain, tree, etc.). On the microcosmic plane, it is signified by the central pillar of the dwelling-place or the highest opening of the tent. One may thus say that *every human habitation is projected as a "Center of the World,"* that every altar, tent, or home makes possible a rupture of levels and consequently communication with the gods, and even (in the case of the shamans) the ascent to Heaven.

As we have remarked several times before, the most widespread mythical images of the "Center of the World" (traceable even in prehistory; cf. §7) are the Cosmic Mountain and the World Tree. These images are encountered also among the Altaic populations and throughout Asia. The Tatars of the Altai imagined Bai Ülgän in the middle of Heaven, seated on the Golden Mountain. The Abakan Tatars called it "Iron Mountain." The fact that the Mongols, Buryats, and Kalmyks knew it under the name of Sumbur, Sumur, or Sumer, which clearly betrays an Indian influence (= Meru, the mythical mountain), does not necessarily imply that they were ever ignorant of this archaic and universal symbol.[14] As for the World Tree, it is attested to everywhere in Asia and plays an important role in shamanism. Cosmologically, the World Tree rises from the center of the earth, from the point of the earth's "navel," and its highest branches touch the palace of Bai Ülgän. The Tree unites the three cosmic regions, for its roots are sunk into the inmost depths of the earth. According to the Mongols and Buryats, the gods (Tengeri) feed off the fruits of the Tree. Other Altaic peoples believe that the souls of infants, before

13. It is attested among a number of archaic populations, as well as among more evolved cultures: Egypt, India, China, Mesopotamia, Greece, etc. Cf. the bibliographical citations in Eliade, *Shamanism*, pp. 262ff.

14. See the examples and bibliographies in *Shamanism*, pp. 266 ff.

birth, repose like little birds on the branches of the Cosmic Tree, and that it is there that the shamans go to look for them.[15] The shaman is supposed to fashion his drum from the wood of the World Tree. Replicas of this tree are found before and inside his yurt, and he also draws it on his drum. What is more, as we will see (§245), when the Altaic shaman climbs the ritual birch, he effectively climbs the Cosmic Tree.

244. The vicissitudes of creation

The cosmogonic myth best known among the peoples of central and northern Asia is almost universally dispersed, although in quite different forms. Its archaism (cf. §7), its considerable diffusion—outside of central and northern Asia, it is attested in Aryan and pre-Aryan India, in Southeast Asia, and in North America—and the multiple modifications that it has undergone in the course of the centuries are features of this myth that present the historian of religions with one of his most stimulating problems. In order to place the specific characters of these central Asian versions (and those of eastern Europe, §250) in relief, let us first present what appear to be the myth's earliest forms. The landscape is always the same: the Great Waters before the Creation. The scenario permits these variations: (1) God, in the form of an animal, himself plunges to the bottom of the abyss to bring up a little mud in order to fashion the Earth; (2) he dispatches an amphibious animal (an aquatic bird); or (3) he gets a creature (sometimes an ornithomorph) to dive, whose existence he was unaware of till that time and who, in what follows, turns out to be his adversary. The first version is found in Hinduism (a great god—Prajāpati, Brahmā, Viṣṇu—transformed into a boar descends to the bottom of the Waters and lifts up the Earth; cf. vol. 1, p. 441). The second is extremely widespread (pre-Aryan India, Assam, North America, etc.). Let us note that in this version the animal divers and the Creator are in no way opposed to each other. It is only in Asia and eastern Europe that the cosmogonic dive takes on "dualistic" overtones.

Among the different Turkish peoples one sometimes comes across

15. See ibid., pp. 39–40, 269ff.; one also finds this mythic motif in Africa and Indonesia; cf. p. 273, n. 56. Another theme, very probably of Mesopotamian origin, is that of the Tree-Book of Fates; cf. ibid., pp. 273–74.

the fusion of these last two versions. A Buryat myth presents Sombol-Burkan resting upon the primordial Ocean. Seeing an aquatic bird, he asks it to dive into the depths. With the mud carried back by the bird, he creates the Earth. According to other variations, Burkan then fashions man, always with the mud.[16] In a myth of the Lebed Tatars, a white swan dives on the command of God and brings back to him a bit of earth in its beak. God forms the Earth, flat and smooth. It is only afterwards that the Devil arrives, to make the marsh.[17] According to the Tatars of the Altai, in the beginning, when only the Waters existed, God and "man" swam together in the form of black geese. God sent "man" to find the mud. But the latter kept a bit in his mouth, and when the Earth began to grow larger, the mud began to inflate. He was obliged to spit it out, in this manner giving birth to the marsh. God said to him: "You have sinned, and your subjects will be evil. My subjects will be pious; they will see the Sun, the light, and I will be called Kurbystan (= Ohrmazd). You, you will be Erlik."[18] The syncretism with Iranian ideas is evident. But the scenario of the cosmic dive is almost entirely preserved. The identity between "man" and the Sovereign of Hell, Erlik Khan, is explained by the fact that the First Man, the mythic Ancestor, was also the first to die (a mytheme found in many traditions).

Among the Mongols, the variants are even more complex. Očirvani (= Vajrapani) and Tšagan-Šukurty descend from Heaven onto the primordial sea. Očirvani asks his companion to dive and bring him some mud. After having spread out this mud on a tortoise, they both fall asleep. Then comes the Devil, Šulmus, who endeavors to drown them, but as much as he rolls them over, the Earth expands. According to a second variant, Očurman, who lives in Heaven, wishes to create the Earth and seeks a companion. He finds one in Tšangan-Šukurty, and sends him to find the clay in his name. But Tšangan-Šukurty becomes

16. See my study "The Devil and God," pp. 103–104 (in *Zalmoxis, the Vanishing God*, pp. 76–130), analyzing certain Buryat and Yakut variants.

17. W. Radlov, cited in "The Devil and God," pp. 100–101.

18. Radlov, cited ibid. The myth next recounts the creation of man. Erlik Khan asks for as much of the earth as he can cover with the staff. He strikes the earth, and noxious animals appear. Finally, God sends him beneath the earth. The antagonism between Erlik and God does not necessarily indicate a "dualistic" conception. In the Paleo-Turkic inscriptions, Erlik is the God of Death; cf. Annemarie V. Gabain, "Inhalt u. magische Bedeutung der altturkischen Inschriften."

boastful: "Without me, you would not have been able to obtain the clay!" he cries. Then the clay slips out from between his fingers. Diving again, he takes the mud this second time in the name Očurman. After the Creation Šulmus comes by and demands a part of the Earth, exactly as much of it as he can touch with the tip of his staff. Šulmus hits the sun with his staff, and the serpents appear.[19] The myth unifies or juxtaposes two different dualistic motifs: (1) the identification of the adversary-rival with the protagonist of the dive; and (2) the Evil One who arrives from some unknown place when the Earth has already been created, and demands a part of it or seeks to destroy it.

The cosmogonic dive is also found among the Finno-Ugrians, the western Slavs, and in eastern Europe. We will soon return to the "dualistic hardening" of the myth, and examine the hypotheses advanced as to its origin (§250). For the moment, let us insist that it is from the third variant—in which the Creator gets an anthropomorphic auxiliary to undertake the dive—that the dramatic and, ultimately, the "dualistic" possibilities of the myth are developed. The vicissitudes of the dive and the cosmogonic work which follows it are invoked henceforth to explain the imperfections of Creation: advent of Death, the appearances of mountains and marshes, as well as the "birth" of the Devil and the existence of Evil. As it is no longer the *Creator himself* who plunges in order to procure the substance of the Earth, but one of his auxiliaries or servitors who carries out the task, it becomes possible to introduce into the myth, thanks precisely to this episode, an element of insubordination, of antagonism or opposition. The "dualistic" interpretation of the Creation has been made possible by the progressive transformation of the theriomorphic auxiliary of God into his "servitor," his "companion," and finally his Adversary.[20] We will have further occasion to appreciate the importance of this dualistic interpretation in "popular" theodicies (§251).

The myths about the creation of man also set in relief the baneful role of the Adversary. As in many mythologies, God forms man from clay and breathes a soul into him. But in central and northern Asia, the scenario includes a dramatic episode: after having fashioned the bodies of the first men, God leaves a dog to protect them and climbs to Heaven in order to seek souls for them. During his absence Erlik comes

19. Potanin, cited in Eliade, *Zalmoxis*, p. 105.
20. Cf. Eliade, *Zalmoxis*, pp. 125ff.

along and, promising the dog (still naked at this moment) a fleece if it allows him to approach, stains the bodies with his saliva. The Buryats believe that without the stain of Cholm (the Adversary), humans would never have known of sickness and death. According to another group of Altaic variants, it was Erlik, profiting from the absence of God and enticing the dog, who animated the bodies himself.[21] In this latter case, it is a question of a desperate effort not only to absolve God of the existence of illnesses and human mortality, but also of the wickedness of the human soul.

245. The shaman and shamanic initiation

A celestial sovereign god who becomes a *deus otiosus* or is indefinitely multiplied (Tängri and the 99 Tengri); a creator god, but one whose works (the world and man) are bungled by the shrewd intervention of a satanic adversary; the precariousness of the human soul; illness and death provoked by demons and evil spirits; a tripartite universe— Heaven, Earth, and Hell—which implies a mythic geography that can be quite complex (the numerous celestial and infernal levels demand the knowledge of the paths which lead to heaven or into the netherworld)—it suffices to have recalled these essential elements in order to appreciate the considerable role of the shaman in the religions of central and northern Asia. In effect, the shaman is at one and the same time theologian and demonologist, specialist in ecstasy and medicine-man, auxiliary of the hunt, protector of the community and the animal herds, psychopomp and, in certain societies, poet and man of erudition.

The term ''shamanism'' is used to designate an archaic (seemingly attested since the Paleolithic) and universally dispersed (though rather exceptional in Africa) religious phenomenon. But shamanism, in the strict sense of the term, prevails especially in central and northern Asia and in the Arctic regions. It is repeatedly in Asia that shamanism has endured influences of the greatest number (Irano-Mesopotamian, Buddhist, Lamaist), without losing its proper structure.

The multiple powers of the shaman are the result of his initiatory

21. Harva, *Rel. Vorstell.*, pp. 114ff. One finds similar legends among the Finno-Ugrians.

experiences. It is thanks to the ordeals of his initiation that the future shaman measures the precariousness of the human soul and learns the means to defend it. Likewise, he knows by experience the sufferings provoked by different maladies and is able to identify their causes. He undergoes a ritual death, descends to Hell, and, sometimes, ascends to Heaven. In short, all the powers of the shaman depend on his experiences and his knowledge of the ''spiritual'' order. He succeeds in familiarizing himself with all the ''spirits'': the souls of the living and the dead, the gods and the demons, the innumerable figures—invisible to the rest of mankind—who inhabit the three cosmic regions.

One becomes a shaman by one of three means: (1) by a spontaneous vocation (a ''calling'' or an ''election''); (2) by the hereditary transmission of the shamanic profession; or (3) by a personal decision or, more rarely, by the desire of the clan. But whatever has been the method of selection, a shaman is recognized as such only after he has received a double instruction: (1) of an ecstatic order (dreams, visions, trances, etc.), and (2) of a traditional order (shamanic techniques, names and functions of spirits, mythology and genealogy of the clan, secret language, etc.). This double instruction, which is presided over by the spirits and the old master shamans, constitutes the initiation. This might be done publicly, but the absence of such a ceremony does not imply by any means the absence of an initiation. The latter may very well be effected in a dream or in an ecstatic experience of the neophyte.

The syndrome of the mystical vocation is recognized easily. The future shaman singles himself out by strange behavior. He becomes a dreamer, seeks solitude, loves to saunter in the woods or in deserted places, has visions, sings during his sleep. Sometimes this period of incubation is characterized by rather grave symptoms. Among the Yakuts, the young man may become mad and fall unconscious easily, take shelter in the forest, feed on the bark of trees, throw himself into the water and fire, and hurt himself with knives.[22] Even when it is a matter of hereditary shamanism, the election of the future shaman is preceded by a change of behavior. The souls of the ancestor-shamans choose a young man of the family; he becomes absentminded and dreamy, is seized by a need for solitude, has prophetic visions, undergoes fits which leave him unconscious. During that time, according to

22. See the examples cited in Eliade, *Shamanism,* pp. 35ff.

the Buryats, the soul is carried away by the spirit. Received in the palace of the gods, it is instructed by the ancestor-shamans in the secrets of the profession, the forms and names of the gods, the names and cult of the spirits, and so on. It is only after this first initiation that the soul reintegrates with the body.[23]

Quite often the mystical vocation implies a profound crisis, which plays the role of an initiation. Now every initiation, of whatever order, includes a period of segregation and a certain number of tests and tortures. The illness unleashed upon the future shaman by the anguished feeling that he has been "chosen" takes on, by its very nature, the value of an "initiatory illness." The precariousness and solitude that are part of every illness become aggravated, in this precise case, by the symbolism of mystical death. For in taking upon oneself this supernatural "election," one feels that one has been abandoned by the divine or demonic powers and left to an imminent death. The "madness" of future shamans, their "psychic chaos," signifies that the profane man is about to "dissolve" himself and that a new personality is at the point of being born.

In many cases, the syndrome of "sickness" follows very closely the classic ritual of initiation. The sufferings of the "elect" bear a point by point resemblance with initiatory tortures. Just as, in rites of puberty, the novice is killed by demon-"masters of initiation," so the future shaman sees himself cut up and morselled out by the "demons of the illness." In his sickness, he experiences his ritual death in the form of a descent into Hell. He witnesses, in his dream, his own dismemberment. He sees the demons cut off his head and scratch out his eyes. According to the Yakuts, the spirits carry the future shaman to Hell and imprison him there for three years in a house. It is there that he undergoes his initiation: the spirits cut off his head, which they put aside (because the novice must look on with his own eyes as he is torn apart), and they cut him into little pieces, which they then distribute to the spirits of diverse illnesses. It is only by experiencing this condition

---

23. Since the middle of the last century, there have been several attempts to explain the phenomenon of Siberian and Arctic shamanism in terms of mental illness. The problem was posed poorly. On the one hand, future shamans are not always *neurotics;* on the other, those among them who had been sick *would become shamans precisely because they had succeeded in being cured.* The initiation was tantamount to a healing; among other things, it brought about a new psychic integration. See Eliade, *Shamanism,* pp. 33ff.; idem, *Myths, Dreams, and Mysteries,* pp. 75ff.

that the future shaman will obtain the power of healing. His bones are then covered over again with new flesh, and in certain cases he is also supplied with new blood. Other shamans tell that during their initiatory illness, the ancestral shamans pierce them with arrows, cut their flesh, and pull out their bones in order to clean them; or else they open up their stomach, eat their flesh and drink their blood; or cook their body and forge on their head with the use of an anvil. During this time, they lie unconscious, nearly inanimate, for three to nine days in the yurt or a solitary place. Some seem even to have stopped breathing and have nearly been buried. Finally, they are resuscitated, but with an entirely renewed body, and with the gift of the shaman.[24]

Generally, when the neophyte lies unconscious in the yurt, the family appeals to a shaman, and it is the latter, much later, who will have the role of instructor. In other cases, after his "initiatory dismemberment," the novice goes out in search of a master, in order to learn the secrets of the profession. The instruction is of an esoteric nature, and it is sometimes received in a state of ecstasy. In other words, the master shaman instructs his disciple in the same manner that the demons and the spirits would. Among the Yakuts, the master takes the soul of the novice with him on a long ecstatic journey. He begins by climbing a mountain. From the top, the master shaman shows the novice the fork in the path from which other trails lead towards the crests. That is where the various maladies that torment men reside. The master then leads his disciple into a dwelling. There, they put on shamanic costumes and shamanize together. The master reveals to him how to recognize and to heal the ills which attack the diverse parts of the body. Finally, he leads his disciples to the higher world, to the residence of the celestial spirits. The new shaman has at his command henceforth a "consecrated body" and he is able to practice his craft.[25]

One also finds public initiatory ceremonies, especially among the Buryats, the Goldi, the Altais, the Tungus, and the Manchus. Among the most interesting are those of the Buryats. The principal rite calls for an ascent. In the yurt one fixes a solid birch, the roots set in the hearth and the top emerging from the smoke-hole. This birch is named "the guardian of the door," for it opens for the shaman his passage to Heaven. The apprentice climbs up to the top of the birch and, going out by the

---

24. See the examples cited in *Shamanism*, pp. 43ff., 76ff., 110ff.
25. G. V. Ksenefontov, cited in *Shamanism*, p. 114.

smoke-hole, cries out with strength to invoke the aid of the gods. Then, all those in attendance are directed in procession toward a site set off from the village, where a great number of birches have been planted the previous evening for the ceremony. Near one birch, a goat is sacrificed and the apprentice, naked from the waist up, is anointed with blood on the head, eyes, and ears, while other shamans play the drum. The master-shaman then climbs up a birch and makes nine incisions at the top. The apprentice, followed by the other shamans, climbs up in turn. As they mount, they all fall—or feign to fall—into ecstasy. According to one informed source, the candidate must climb nine birches which, like the nine notches, symbolize the nine heavens.[26]

What must be kept in mind about this initiatory rite is that the apprentice shaman is supposed to go to Heaven in order to be consecrated. As we will see, ascent by means of a tree or post also constitutes the essential rite in the seances of Altaic shamans. The birch or the post is comparable to the Tree or the Pillar which stands at the Center of the World and connects the three cosmic zones. In sum, the shamanic tree has all the prestige of the Cosmic Tree.

246. Shamanic myths and rituals

The myths of the origin of shamans set two highly significant themes in relief: (1) the "First Shaman" was created by God (or by the celestial gods); (2) but on account of his maliciousness, the gods severely limited his powers. According to the Buryats, the Tengris decided to give a shaman to mankind so that he could struggle against sickness and death, which had been introduced by evil spirits. They dispatched the Eagle. The latter saw a woman asleep and had intercourse with her.

26. *Shamanism*, pp. 115–22, following N. N. Agapitov, M. N. Changalov, and Jorma Partanen. As was well perceived by Uno Harva (*Rel. Vorstell.*, pp. 492 ff.), this rite recalls certain ceremonies of the Mithraic mysteries. Thus, the purification of the candidate by the blood of the goat resembles the *taurobolium*, and his ascent of the birch recalls the Mithraic initiate climbing a ladder of seven steps representing the seven planetary heavens (cf. §217). As we have already remarked, the influences of the ancient Near East are evident throughout central Asia and Siberia, and the initiatory rite of the Buryat shaman must very likely be included among those influenced. But one must add that the symbolism of the World Tree and the rite of initiatory ascension of the birch *precede* the cultural elements that arrived from Mesopotamia and Iran.

The woman gave birth to a son who became the "First Shaman." The Yakuts share the same belief. But the Eagle also bears the name of Supreme Being, Ai (the "Creator") or Ai Toyon (the "Creator of Light"). The children of Ai are represented as bird-spirits posed on the branches of the World Tree; at the top is found the Eagle with two heads, which probably personifies Ai Toyon himself.[27] The ancestors of the shamans—whose souls play a role in the election and initiation of the apprentice—descended from this First Shaman created by the Supreme Being in the form of the Eagle.

Some, however, consider the role of the ancestors in current shamanism as a degeneration. According to the Buryat tradition, in former times the shamans held their powers directly from the celestial spirits; it is only in our day that they receive it from their ancestors.[28] This opinion reflects a belief found throughout Asia and the Arctic regions that shamanism has declined. Formerly, the "first shamans" really flew in the clouds on their "horses" (which is to say their drums); they were able to take any form whatsoever and perform miracles that their living descendants find unrepeatable. The Buryats explain this decline by the pride and wickedness of the First Shaman: when he entered into competition with God, the latter drastically reduced his power.[29] In this etiological myth one can decipher the indirect influence of dualistic beliefs.

The shaman plays a major role in the religious life of the community, but he does not account for all of it. He is not the sacrificer.[30] And in the Altai he intervenes in birth and marriage ceremonies only if something untoward happens, as, for example, in the case of sterility

27. Cf. the sources cited in *Shamanism,* pp. 68ff. When Ai Toyon created the First Shaman, he also planted a birch tree with eight branches in his celestial dwelling, on which were nests for the Creator's children. He also planted three trees on earth; it is in their memory that the shaman also possesses a tree, on whose life he is in certain regards dependent; cf. ibid., p. 70, nn. 11, 12. In their initiatory dreams, certain shamans are transported close to the Cosmic Tree, on the summit of which one finds the Lord of the World.

28. L. Sternberg, "Divine Election," p. 495. Likewise among the Mongols, the shamans depend exclusively upon their ancestors; cf. Heissig, "Les religions de la Mongolie," pp. 354ff.

29. Cf. *Shamanism,* p. 68.

30. As we will soon see, among Altaic peoples it is the shaman himself who sacrifices the horse, but he does this because he is called upon to conduct the soul of the victim up to Bai Ülgän.

or a difficult childbirth. On the contrary, the shaman is known to be irreplaceable in every ceremony that touches on the experience of the human soul as such: illnesses (soul loss or possession by evil spirits) and death (when the soul must be led to the other world). Elsewhere in Asia, one calls upon the shaman when game gets scarce, or for his mastery of ecstatic techniques (divination, clairvoyance, etc.).[31]

Radlov has given a by now classic description of the Altaic horse sacrifice. This sacrifice is celebrated from time to time by every family, and the ceremony lasts two or three consecutive evenings. In a meadow the *kam* (= shaman) installs a new yurt, inside of which he places a birch stripped of its branches and marked with nine notches. After a number of preliminary rites, he blesses the horse, and, with the aid of several assistants, he kills it by breaking the spinal column in a manner which allows no blood to flow. Then, having made offerings to the ancestors and to the protective spirits, the flesh is prepared and ritually eaten.

The second part of the ritual, the most important, is left until the following evening. Donning his shamanic costume, the *kam* invokes a multitude of spirits. This is a long and complex ceremony which he accomplishes by an "ascent." While striking his drum and crying out, the shaman makes movements to indicate that he elevates himself to Heaven. In "ecstasy" (?!), he climbs onto the first notches of the birch, penetrating successively into the different heavens, up to the ninth, or, if he is truly powerful, up to the twelfth and still higher. When he reaches the top, which affords him his power, the shaman stops and invokes Bai Ülgän.

You, Ülgän, you have created all humans . . .
You, Ülgän, you have endowed us, all of us, with herds!
Don't let us fall into trouble!
Make it so that we can resist the Evil One.
Do not show Körmös [the evil spirit] to us.
Do not abandon us into his hands . . .
Do not condemn my sins!

The shaman learns from Bai Ülgän whether the sacrifice has been agreeable and receives predictions about the weather and the new harvest. This episode marks the culminating point of the "ecstasy": the

31. See the references in *Shamanism*, p. 184ff.

shaman collapses exhausted. After some time, he rubs his eyes, and appears to waken himself from a profound sleep and hail those who are present as after a long absence.[32]

The shaman's celestial ascent has its counterpart in his descent into Hell. This ceremony is much more difficult. The descent may be vertical, or horizontal and then doubly vertical (ascent followed by descent). In the first class, the shaman seems to descend one after another the seven steps or subterranean regions called *pudak,* "obstacles." He is then accompanied by his ancestors and his auxiliary spirits. Once each "obstacle" is cleared, he describes a new subterranean epiphany. At the second "obstacle," he seems to allude to metallic noises; at the fifth, he listens to the waves and the whistling of the wind; finally, at the seventh he perceives the palace of Erlik Khan, built in stone and black clay, and defended on every side. The shaman pronounces a long prayer before Erlik (in which he also mentions Bai Ülgän, "the one who is above"). Then he returns to the yurt and tells his assistants the results of his journey.

The second type of descent—horizontal and then vertical—is much more complicated and more dramatic. The shaman rides through the deserts and the steppes, scales the Iron Mountain, and after a new excursion arrives before the "smoke hole of the earth," the entrance to the other world. In descending, he encounters a sea, passes over a bridge the width of a hair,[33] passes before the place in which sinners are tortured, and, riding on again, arrives before the residence of Erlik Khan. There he succeeds in entering despite the dogs who guard it and the doorkeeper. The meeting with the King of the Dead—laboriously mimed—includes numerous episodes that are at once both terrifying and grotesque. The shaman offers Erlik different gifts and finally alcohol. The god finally gets drunk and becomes benevolent, blesses him, grants the multiplication of livestock, and so on. The shaman returns joyously to the earth, sitting astride not a horse but a goose. He rubs his eyes as if he has just awakened. He is asked: "Did you have a good ride? Did you succeed?" And he responds, "I had an admirable voyage. I have been very well received!"[34]

32. See Radlov, *Aus Sibirien,* 2, pp. 20–50, summarized in *Shamanism,* pp. 190–97.

33. In order to give a striking image to his passage, he totters and almost falls. At the water's edge he perceives the bones of innumerable shamans who have fallen there, for a sinner cannot cross over the bridge.

34. Potanin, summarized in *Shamanism,* pp. 200–203.

As we shall soon see, these ecstatic descents into Hell have had a considerable importance in the religion and culture of the Altaic peoples. The shamans undertake them to obtain the blessing of the Sovereign of the Dead on the livestock and the harvests (as in the example cited above), but especially in order to conduct the deceased there, or to find and deliver the soul of the sick person when it is imprisoned by the demons. The scenario is always the same, but the dramatic episodes vary from one population to another. The shaman mimes the difficulties of the descent, alone or accompanied by his auxiliaries. On arrival, the souls of the dead refuse to enter their new abode, and he must offer them the water-of-life. The seance becomes animated and sometimes grotesque. In other cases, after many an adventure, the shaman arrives in the land of the dead and finds, among the crowd of the spirits, the close relatives of the soul which he brings to entrust to them. Once he returns, he brings each of his assistants greetings from their own dead relatives and even distributes small gifts on their behalf.[35]

But the principal function of the shaman is healing. In general, illnesses are attributed to the straying or "seizure of the soul." The shaman seeks it out, captures it, and sees to its reintegration with the sick person's body. Sometimes the illness has a double cause: the soul's flight is aggravated by the evil spirits' "possession" of it, and the shamanic cure includes the quest of the soul as well as the expulsion of the demons. Many times, the search for the soul consists in itself of an entire spectacle. The shaman first undertakes a horizontally defined ecstatic journey—in order to assure that the soul has not "strayed" somewhere in neighboring or distant regions—and then he descends to Hell, identifies the bad spirit who holds the soul prisoner, and succeeds in wresting it from him.[36]

247. The meaning and importance of shamanism

The shamans play an essential role in the defense of the psychic integrity of the community. They are the antidemonic champions *par excellence;* they combat not only demons and illnesses but black magic. The warrior elements which have great importance in certain types

35. See the examples cited in *Shamanism,* pp. 205–9.
36. See the examples cited ibid., pp. 215ff.

of Asiatic shamanism (cuirass, lance, bow, sword, etc.) are explained by the requirements of combat against the demons, the true enemies of mankind. In a general sense, it can be said that the shaman defends life, health, fecundity, and the world of "light" against death, illnesses, sterility, misfortune, and the world of "darkness." It is difficult for us to imagine what such a champion could represent for an archaic society. But first of all, there is the certitude that humans are not alone in a strange world, surrounded by demons and "forces of evil." Aside from the gods and supernatural beings to whom one addresses prayers and offers sacrifices, there exist "specialists of the sacred," men capable of "seeing" the spirits, of climbing to Heaven and meeting the gods, of descending to Hell and combatting demons, illnesses, and death. The essential role of the shaman for the defense of the psychic integrity of the community is maintained chiefly by this trait: men are assured that one of their own kind is capable of aiding them in the critical circumstances provoked by the inhabitants of the invisible world. It is comforting and soothing to know that one member of the community is capable of seeing that which is hidden and invisible to others, and of reporting direct and precise information about the supernatural world.

It is thanks to his capacity to travel into supernatural worlds and *see* superhuman beings (gods, demons) and spirits of the dead that the shaman is able to contribute in such a decisive manner to the *knowledge of death*. It is likely that many features of the "funereal geography," as well as certain themes of the mythology of death, are the result of the ecstatic experiences of the shamans. The lands which the shaman sees and the personages whom he meets in the course of his ecstatic journeys into the beyond are meticulously described by the shaman himself, during or after the trance. The unknown and terrifying world of death takes form: it organizes itself in conformity with specific types; it takes final shape as a structure; and, with time, it becomes familiar and acceptable. For their part, the residents of the world of the dead become *visible;* they assume countenances, take on personalities, even biographies. Little by little, the world of the dead becomes recognizable and death itself takes on value, above all as a rite of passage toward a *spiritual mode of being*. In the final account, the tales of the shamans' ecstatic journeys contribute to "spiritualizing" the world of the dead, all the while enriching it with images and prestigious figures.

The shaman's adventures into the other world, the tests which he undergoes in his ecstatic descents to Hell and in his celestial ascents, recall the adventures of personages in popular tales and of the heroes of epic literature. It is very probable that a great number of the "subjects," motifs, personages, images, and clichés of epic literature are, in the last analysis, of ecstatic origin, in the sense that they have been borrowed from the accounts told by shamans of their journeys and adventures in superhuman worlds. It is thus, for example, that one hears of the adventures of the Buryat hero Mu-monto, who descends to Hell in place of his father, and, returning to earth, describes the tortures of the sinners. The Tatars have a considerable literature on this subject. Among the Tatars of the Sayan steppe, a courageous girl, Kubaiko, descends into Hell in order to bring back the head of her brother, which had been cut off by a monster. After several adventures, and after having assisted in different tortures which punish diverse sins, Kubaiko finds herself before the King of Hell himself. He then allows her to bring back her brother's head if she emerges victorious in a certain test. Other heroes of Tatar epic literature have to pass similar initiatory tests, all of them implying a descent into Hell.[37]

It is equally likely that the shaman's pre-ecstatic euphoria is one of the sources of lyric poetry. When he prepares for his trance, the shaman beats a drum, calls upon his auxiliary spirits, speaks in a "secret language" or the "language of animals," and imitates the cry of animals and above all the song of birds. He thus brings himself into a "second state" which sets in motion linguistic creativity and the rhythms of lyric poetry. One must also recall the dramatic character of the shamanic seance, which constitutes a *spectacle* without equal in the world of everyday experience. The exhibition of magical feats (firehandling and other "miracles") unveils another world, the fabulous world of gods and magicians, the world where *everything seems possible*, where the dead return to life and the living die in order to be resuscitated, where one is able to disappear and reappear instantaneously, where the "laws of nature" are abolished and where a certain superhuman "freedom" is illustrated and rendered *present* in a stunning manner. One understands the resonance of such a *spectacle* in a "primitive" community. The shamanic "miracles" not only confirm and fortify the structures of the traditional religion but also stimulate

37. Ibid., pp. 213ff.

and nourish the imagination, abolish the barriers between dreams and immediate reality, and open the windows toward the world inhabited by the gods, the dead, and the spirits.[38]

248. The religions of the northern Asians and the Finno-Ugrians

The arrangement of this work—which proposes chiefly to analyze *religious creations*—permits only a summary presentation of the religions common to the peoples who belong to the Paleo-Siberian, Uralian, and Finno-Ugrian linguistic groups. Not that these religions lack interest, but a number of their characteristic elements (celestial deities and *dei otiosi,* the myth of the cosmic dive and its dualistic hardening, and shamanism) resemble those of the Altaic peoples.

Thus, for example, one can mention Es of the Yenisei (Kets), a name which signifies both "heaven" and "celestial god" (cf. Tängri). According to Anutchin, Es is "invisible" in the sense that no one has ever seen him; whoever sees him becomes blind. Es is the creator and master of the Universe, and he has also created man. He is good and omnipotent, but he has no interest in human affairs; "he leaves that to the spirits of the second rank, to the heroes and the great shamans." He has no cult. He is offered no sacrifices, and is addressed no prayers. Nevertheless, he protects the world and helps mankind.[39] Kudjū ("Heaven") of the Yukagirs is a beneficent god, but he plays no role in the religious life.[40] The Koryaks called their supreme god "The One of the Height," "The Master of the Height," "The Overseer," and "He who exists,"[41] but he is rather inactive.

More important, and better known, seems to be Num of the Samoyeds. According to the oldest information (A. M. Castren), Num inhabits the sky, rules the winds and rains, sees and knows all that happens on the earth, rewards the good and punishes the wicked.[42] Other observers emphasize his goodness and power, but add that after

---

38. Ibid., pp. 508–11.

39. Anutchin, translated and summarized by Paulson, "Les religions des Asiates septentrionaux," pp. 50ff.

40. Jochelson, cited with commentary by Paulson, ibid., pp. 53ff.

41. Cf. *Patterns,* p. 59. See *Patterns,* §18, for other examples of celestial theonyms (among the Cheremis, Ostyaks, etc.).

42. Castren, *Reiseerinnerungen,* 1, pp. 253ff.

creating the world, life, and man, Num delegated his powers to other divine beings who are inferior to him. More recently, Lehtisalo has brought out some supplementary information: Num lives in the seventh Heaven, the Sun is his eye, he is not represented in images, and he is offered sacrifices of reindeer.[43] During the evangelization of the Samoyeds (1825–1835), the missionaries destroyed thousands of anthropomorphic "idols," some with three or seven faces. Since most accounts agree that Num had no images, it has been justly concluded that these idols represented ancestors and different spirits. It is probable, however, that the polycephalic trait—which implies the faculty of seeing and knowing all—was finally conferred on the Sun, Num's principal manifestation.[44]

The most popular cosmogonic myth is, as everywhere in central and northern Asia, the "dive" by an ornithomorphic being, the auxiliary or adversary of God. One after another Num dispatches the swans, the geese, the "polar diver," and the *ljuru* bird to bring him back the earth. It is only this last one who succeeds in returning with a bit of mud in his beak. When Num had created the Earth, "from somewhere" an "old man" came and asked him for permission to rest. Num allowed him to do so, but in the morning he surprised the old man on the shore of the island and found him trying to destroy it. Summoned to leave, the old man asked for—and obtained—as much land as he could cover with the end of his staff. He disappeared into that hole, after having declared that henceforth he would live there, and carry men off. Dismayed, Num recognized his error: he had thought that the old man would want to install himself *on* the Earth, not *under* it.[45] In this myth, Num is no longer omniscient. He is ignorant of the existence and intentions of the "old man" (the *Evil One* who would introduce death). Certain variants, attested among the Cheremis and the Voguls, underline the "dualistic" character of the Creation.[46] But the "dualism" is still more strongly marked in Finnish, Estonian, and Mordvinian legends: it is the Devil himself who makes the dive, at

---

43. A. C. Schrenk and Lehtisalo, summarized by Paulson, "Les religions des Asiates septentrionaux," pp. 61ff.

44. Cf. Pettazzoni, *L'onniscienza di Dio*, p. 383. On the solarization of celestial gods, see Eliade, *Patterns*, §37.

45. Lehtisalo, summarized in Eliade, *Zalmoxis*, p. 98.

46. Cf. ibid., pp. 97–98.

God's command. But he hides a bit of mud in his mouth, and thus gives birth to the mountains and the marshes.[47]

As for the shamanism of these peoples, it presents in broad lines the same structure of Asiatic shamanism that we have just outlined (§§245–47). Let us note, however, that it is in Finland that the literary creations of shamanistic inspiration reach their culmination. In the *Kalevala*, the national epic compiled by Elias Lönnrot (first edition, 1832), the principal personage is Väinämöinen, the "eternal Sage." Of supernatural origin, Väinämöinen is an ecstatic-visionary endowed with innumerable magical powers. Moreover, he is a poet, singer, and harpist. His adventures, as well as those of his companions—the blacksmith Ilmarinen and the warrior Lemminkäinen—often recall the exploits of the Asiatic shamans and sorcerer-heroes.[48]

In the hunting and fishing societies, the protective spirits of different animal species and the Masters of Animals play a considerable role. The animals resemble men. Each animal possesses a soul, and certain peoples (e.g., the Ukagirs) think that one cannot kill an animal before capturing its soul.[49] The Ainus and the Gilyaks dispatch the soul of the bear, once it is beaten to death, to its "original homeland." The Master of Animals protects both the game and the hunters. The hunt in itself constitutes a ritual of considerable complexity, since the game is supposed to have supernatural power.[50] The interest of these beliefs and rituals resides in their extreme archaism (one encounters them also in the two Americas, in Asia, etc.). They inform us about the mystical solidarity between man and the animal world, a magico-religious conception already found among the Paleolithic hunters (cf. §2).

It is significant that the beliefs in protective spirits of animal species and in the Masters of Animals, beliefs which have all but disappeared in agricultural societies, still survive in Scandinavia. What is more, a number of supernatural figures and mythological themes that bring into relief the magico-religious powers of animals reappear in the beliefs

47. See the variants presented ibid., pp. 82–84.
48. Cf. Martti Haavio, *Väinämöinen, Eternal Sage*, esp. pp. 83ff., 140ff., 230ff. On Ugrian shamanism, see Eliade, *Shamanism*, pp. 220ff.
49. Cf. Paulson, *Die primitiven Seelenvorstellungen der nordasiatischen Völker*, pp. 174ff.; idem, "The Animal Guardian," passim.
50. Cf. Eveline Lot-Falck, *Les rites de chasse chez les peuples sibériens*, passim; Paulson, "Les religions des Asiates septentrionaux," pp. 71ff.; idem, "Les religions des peuples finnois," pp. 170ff.

of pastoralists and above all in the folklore of farmers, as much in the rest of Europe as in western Asia. This fact has considerable consequences. It confirms the survival of archaic conceptions in certain rural European societies at least up to the beginning of the twentieth century.

249. The religion of the Balts

Of the three Baltic peoples—the Lithuanians, the Letts, and the Old Prussians (or Pruthenes)—the last were decimated in a long war of conversion and conquest by the Teutonic knights, and ended up being absorbed into the mass of German settlers. The Letts and the Lithuanians were equally subjugated by the Germans and, at least nominally, converted to Christianity in the fourteenth century. But they succeeded in maintaining their religious traditions. It is only in the sixteenth century that Lutheran missionaries embarked upon an incessant campaign against paganism. Nonetheless, the ethnography and folklore of the Baltic peoples have partially conserved the archaic heritage. As a result, they constitute an unequalled source for knowledge of the traditional religion.[51] Particularly important are the *dainas* (short songs of four verses); the rituals related to agriculture, marriage, and death; and the popular stories. The geography of the Balts favored their conservatism (let us recall the numerous beliefs and archaic customs surviving in the Pyrenees, the Alps, the Carpathians, and the Balkans). Yet this in no way excludes the influences of their neighbors—Germans, Estonians, Slavs—and, in the last four centuries, of Christianity.

Although there exist certain differences between the pantheons, religious conceptions, and practices of the three Baltic peoples, we will present them together in order to facilitate our exposition. First of all, it is important to stress the fact that the Balts have conserved the name of the old Indo-European celestial god, *deiuos;* Lettish, *dievs;* Lithuanian, *dievas;* Old Prussian, *deivas.* After the conversion to Chris-

---

51. The written sources (*Chronicles,* accounts of missionaries and ecclesiastical dignitaries, etc.) occasionally contain useful information, but must be consulted cautiously. The majority of their authors were ignorant of Baltic languages; moreover, they presented the ethnic "paganism" in accordance with the clichés of Christian propaganda and historiography.

tianity, the same theonym was used to designate the God of the Bible. In Lettish religious folklore, Dievs, the father of the divine family, lives on his farm on a mountain in Heaven. He visits the earth, however, and participates in the work of the farmers and in the seasonal festivals which are consecrated to him. Dievs has instituted order in the world and it is he who determines the destiny of men and watches over their moral life.[52] However, Dievs is neither the supreme god nor the most important divinity.

The god of thunder, Perkūnas (Lithuanian) or Pērkuons (Lettish),[53] also lives in the sky, but descends often onto the earth in order to combat the Devil and the other demons (traits which betray the influence of Christianity). Redoubtable warrior and blacksmith of the gods, he controls the rain and thus the fertility of the fields. In the life of the peasants, Perkūnas/Pērkuons plays the most important role, and it is he who is offered sacrifices on the occasion of droughts and epidemics. According to a sixteenth-century account, he is worshipped during a thunderstorm by offering him a piece of meat and addressing him with this prayer: "O God, Perkūnas, do not strike me, I beseech you, o god! I give you this meat." One recognizes here an archaic ritual, practiced during the thunderstorm by primitive peoples in honor of celestial deities (cf. *Patterns*, §14).

A considerable place in the Baltic pantheon seems to have been occupied by the goddess of the sun, Saule (whose similarity with the Vedic Sūrya was indicated long ago). She is imagined as both a mother and a young girl. Saule likewise possesses a farm on the celestial mountain, near that of Dievs. Sometimes these two divinities fight one another, and the battle lasts for three days. Saule blesses the soil, aids those who suffer, and punishes sinners. Her most important festival is celebrated on the summer solstice.[54] In Lettish religious folklore, Saule is the wife of Mēness, the god of the moon, who seems to have the role of a warrior god. All these celestial divinities are associated

52. See Harold Biezais, *Die Gottesgestalt der lettischen Volksreligion*, above all pp. 90ff., 182ff.

53. Perkūnas is mentioned in the *Chronicle* of Malalas (1261), and several times by sixteenth-century Christian authors. On Pērkuons, see the documents and the critical analysis of H. Biezais, *Die himmlische Götterfamilie der alten Letten*, pp. 92ff., 103ff.

54. See Biezais, *Die himmlische Götterfamilie*, pp. 183ff., 303ff. (the cult of Saule).

with horses. They travel over the mountains of Heaven and descend to the earth on chariots.

The majority of the chthonian divinities are goddesses. The Earth Mother is called *Zemen māte* by the Letts and *Zemyna* by the Lithuanians. The latter also recognize the "Master of the Earth," *Zemēpatis.* But the number of "Mothers" is considerable: for example, the Mother of the Forest (*Meza māte;* Lithuanian, *Medeine*) multiplies herself by emanation into a Mother of Gardens, a Mother of Fields, of Berries, of Flowers, of Mushrooms, and so on. One encounters a similar process among the aquatic divinities (the Mother of Waters, Mother of Waves, etc.), among personifications of meteorological phenomena (Mother of Rain, of Winds, etc.), and with reference to human activities (Mother of Sleep, etc.). As has already been said by Usener,[55] the proliferation of such mythological entities recalls a phenomenon characteristic of Roman religion (cf. §163). Among the Letts, the most important goddess was Laima (from the root *laime,* "good fortune," "chance"). She is a divinity of destiny *par excellence;* she determines the lot of men from their birth. But Laima also rules over marriage, the bounty of the harvests, and the well-being of the animals. Despite the syncretism with the Virgin Mary, Laima represents an archaic religious figure, belonging probably to the highest stage of Lettish paganism.[56]

Before the conversion to Christianity, the public cult was practiced primarily in the forests. Certain trees, certain springs, and certain spots were considered sacred, inhabited by the gods. As a result, it was forbidden to approach them. The community performed sacrifices in the open air, in groves, and in other holy places. The wooden house likewise constituted a sacred space, as did the house's "sacred corner." As to temples proper, our information is rather minimal. Excavations have brought to light traces of sanctuaries, built of wood, in a circular form of about five meters in diameter. The statue of the god was installed in the center.

As regards the existence of a sacerdotal class, we are faced with similar uncertainties. The sources present us with "sorcerers," that is, diviners and ecstatics. Their prestige was considerable. The treaty,

---

55. Cf. Usener, *Die Götternamen,* pp. 79–122.

56. See the comparative study of Biezais, *Die Hauptgöttinen der alten Letten,* above all pp. 179–275. On the syncretism with the Virgin Mary, see ibid., pp. 279ff.

imposed in 1249 by the Knights of the Teutonic Order of Old Prussians—this being the first written document of Baltic religion—required the vanquished to give up burning or interring the dead with horses or servants, weapons, vestments, or other precious objects;[57] to renounce sacrificing to the idol Curche after the harvest, as well as to other gods; and to stop consulting the visionary bards (*tulissones* or *ligaschones*) who eulogized the dead at funerary banquets, and claimed to see them flying away on horseback into the air toward the other world.

One can recognize in these "visionary bards" a class of ecstatics and magicians similar to the shamans of Asia. Very probably, at the end of the "funerary banquets," they led the souls of the dead to the other world. Among the Balts, as everywhere else, the ecclesiastical authorities regarded ecstatic techniques and magical practices as inspired by the Devil. But ecstasy and ecstatic theriomorphy as usual constitute a religious operation (or an operation of "white magic"): the shaman takes the form of an animal to combat the evil spirits. An analogous belief is attested among the Lithuanians of the seventeenth century. Accused of lycanthropy, an old man admitted that he was a werewolf and that on the nights of Saint Lucy, Pentecost, and Saint John he and his companions, transformed into wolves, walked to the "end of the sea" (i.e., Hell) and gave battle to the Devil and the sorcerers. The werewolves, explained the old man, changed themselves into wolves and descended to Hell in order to reclaim the goods stolen by the sorcerers—livestock, wheat, and other fruits of the earth. At the hour of death, the soul of a werewolf ascends to Heaven, while a sorcerer's is taken by the Devil. The werewolves are the "dogs of God." Were it not for their active intervention, the devil would have devastated the earth.[58]

The similarity between the funeral rites and those of marriage constitutes further proof of Baltic archaism. Such a solidarity between the rituals of marriage and death was similarly maintained, at the beginning of this century, in Romania and in the Balkan peninsula. Archaic as well is the belief that Dievs, Saule, and Laima sometimes dress

57. This archaic custom (attested in the protohistory of Mesopotamia, China, Scythia, etc.) nevertheless persisted up to the fifteenth century.

58. See the sources in my *Occultism, Witchcraft, and Cultural Fashions*, p. 129.

themselves as peasants and join the latter in their fields, a belief found in southeastern European folklore.

In conclusion, the characteristic traits of the Baltic religion are: (1) the notion of several divine families; (2) the dominant role of the divinities of the sun and the thunderstorm; (3) the importance of the goddesses of childbirth and fate (Laima) and of telluric divinities and their hypostases; and (4) the conception of a ritual combat, effected in trance, between the "good magicians," devoted to God, and the sorcerers, servants of the Devil. Despite Christian syncretism, these religious forms are archaic. They were derived from either the Indo-European heritage (Dievs, Perkūnas, and Saule) or from the Eurasiatic substratum (Laima, Zemen māte). Baltic religion—as also that of the Slavs and the Finno-Ugrians—is of great interest precisely because its archaism can be illumined with the aide of ethnography and folklore. In effect, as Marija Gimbutas has said, the pre-Christian root of Baltic folklore "is so ancient that it undoubtedly derives from prehistoric times, at least from the iron age, or even, in certain elements, from several millennia before that."[59]

250. Slavic paganism

The Slavs and the Balts are the last Aryophonic peoples to penetrate into Europe. Dominated successively by the Scyths, the Sarmatians, and the Goths, the Slavs were forced to live for over a thousand years in the limited territory between the Dniester and the Vistula. But beginning in the fifth century, the devastation of Europe by the Huns, Bulgars, and Avars permitted the overflow of Slavic tribes and their progressive installation in central and eastern Europe.[60] Their name—*Sclavini*—is attested for the first time in the sixth century. Excavations have revealed a number of details about the material civilization, as well as about certain customs and religious beliefs of the Slavs living

59. M. Gimbutas, "The Ancient Religion of the Balts," p. 98. Such an interpretation of the folklore is not shared by certain scholars. See the controversy on the archaic character of the *dainas,* below, in Present Position of Studies, §249.

60. Certain Slavic groups formed part of Attila's hordes; cf. Gimbutas, *The Slavs,* pp. 98ff.

in Russia and the Baltic region. But the only written sources on the religion of the ancient Slavs are later than Christianity. Even where they are available, the ethnic paganism which they present has reached a decadent state. Nevertheless, as we will see a little later, an attentive analysis of their rites and popular beliefs allows us to grasp certain specific traits of the original Slavic religiosity.

One piece of precious information is furnished to us by Helmond in his *Chronica Slavorum,* written between 1167 and 1172. After having cited the names and functions of several gods, whom we will soon present, Helmond affirms that the Slavs do not dispute the existence "of one god in the heavens," but consider that this god "concerned himself only with celestial affairs," having abandoned the government of the world to inferior divinities whom he has procreated himself. Helmond called this God *prepotens* and *deus deorum,* but he is not a God of men: he reigns over the other gods, and has no longer any rapport with the Earth.[61] It is thus a matter of a celestial God becoming a *deus otiosus,* a process which we have just observed among the Altaic and Finno-Ugrian peoples, as well as among the Indo-Europeans (cf. the Vedic Dyaus, §65).

As for the other gods, a most complete list is found in the *Chronicle of Kiev,* called the *Chronicle of Nestor,* redacted in the twelfth century. The chronicler makes a quick (and indignant) reference to the paganism of the Russian tribes at the time of Great Prince Vladimir (978–1015). He cites seven gods—Perun, Volos, Khors, Dazhbog, Stribog, Simarglŭ, and Mokosh—and affirms that "people offered sacrifices to them . . . , they brought them their sons and daughters, and sacrificed them to these demons."[62]

Thanks to supplementary information, one can reconstitute, at least in part, the structure and function of some of these gods. Perun was known by all the Slavic tribes. One finds his traces in popular traditions and in toponymic features. His name is Indo-European (from the root *per/perk,* "to strike," "to shatter") and indicates a god of thunder, analogous to the Vedic Parjanya and the Baltic Perkūnas. In all likelihood, he resembled Perkūnas, who was conceived of as a great and vigorous man, red bearded, with an axe or a hammer in his hand

---

61. Helmond (ca. 1108–1177), *Chronica Slavorum,* 1, chap. 83.
62. The passages are translated by Brückner, *Mitologia Slava,* pp. 242–243, and *Die Slawen,* pp. 16–17.

that he threw at wicked spirits. One Germanic tribe identified Perun as Thor. A number of Slavic terms and expressions are etymologically related to his name, such as *piorum*, Polish for thunder and lightning.[63] The oak was consecrated to him, as to the other thunder gods of pre-Christian Europe. According to the Byzantine historian Procopius, cocks were sacrificed to him and, on the occasion of the great festivals, bulls, bears, or goats. In Christian folklore, Perun has been replaced by St. Elijah, imagined as an old man with a white beard, traversing the Heavens in his fiery chariot.

Volos, or Veles, the god of horned livestock, finds parallels in Lithuanian (*Velnias*, who now signifies "the devil," and *vēlē*, "the shadow of death") and in Celtic (Tacitus speaks of Veleda, the prophetess of the Celts).[64] According to Roman Jakobson,[65] he derives from the common Indo-European pantheon, and can be compared to Varuṇa. Khors is a theonym borrowed from the Iranian Khursid, the personification of the sun. Also of Iranian origin is Simarglŭ; Jakobson compares him to the Persian Sîmourg, the divine griffin. The Slavs have probably borrowed him from the Sarmatians, who knew him by the name Simarg.

Etymologically, Dazhbog signifies the "dispenser of riches" (Slavic *dati*, "to give," *bogŭ*, "riches," but also "god," the source of riches). This god has also been identified with the sun. As for Stribog, one knows practically nothing about him. An old Russian text, *The Poem of Igor*, affirms that the winds are his grandsons.[66] Mokosh, the last divinity mentioned by the *Chronicle of Nestor*, was probably a fertility goddess. In the seventeenth century, the Russian priests asked the peasants: "Have you gone to Mokosh?" The Czechs invoked her during droughts.[67] Certain medieval sources mention the god Rod (a theonym connected with the verb *roditi*, "to engender")

63. See the examples cited by Gasparini, *Il matriarcato slavo*, pp. 537ff.

64. Veles is attested in Christian demonology of the fifteenth and sixteenth centuries, and persists in toponymy; Gimbutas, *The Slavs*, pp. 167ff.; idem, "The Lithuanian God Velnias," pp. 87ff.

65. See his "The Slavic God Veles and his Indo-European Cognates"; but see also Jaan Puhvel, "Indo-European Structure of the Baltic Pantheon," p. 85.

66. His etymology is not assured; the Slavic root *srei*, "color," has been proposed, as has the Iranian *srira*, "beautiful," a common epithet for the wind, but one which also suggests the radiance of the sun; cf. Gimbutas, *The Slavs*, p. 164.

67. Brückner, *Mitologia Slava*, pp. 141ff.

and the *rozhenitsa* ("mother, womb, fortune"), fairies analogous to the Scandinavian Norns. In all likelihood, the *rozhenitsa* are the epiphanies or hypostases of the old chthonic Mother-Goddess *Mati syra zemlja* ("the Humid Earth Mother"), whose cult survived into the nineteenth century.

One also knows of about fifteen names of the gods from the Baltic, a region where Slavic paganism continued up to the twelfth century. The most important was Svantevit (Svetovit), the patron god of the island of Rügen, who had his sanctuary at Arkona and whose statue there measured eight meters.[68] The root *svet* originally denoted "strength," "to be strong." Svetovit was both a warrior god and a protector of fields. On the same island, Jarovit, Rujevit, and Porovit were also venerated. The names of the first two indicate a calendrical function: *jaro* (connected with *jaru*, "young, ardent, reckless") signifies "springtime";[69] *ruenū* is the name of the autumnal month when the young animals mate; *pora* means "middle of summer."

Polycephalism is found among certain Indo-European peoples (e.g., the tricephalic figure of the Gauls, the "Thracian Knight" of two or three heads, etc.), but it is also attested among the Finno-Ugrians (§248), with whom the Proto-Slavs present a number of analogies. The significance of the polycephalus is evident: it expresses divine omniscience, an attribute specific to celestial gods, but also to solar divinities. One may presume that the supreme god of the western Slavs—in his different forms (Triglav, Svantevit, Rugievit)—was a solar divinity.[70] Let us recall that among the eastern Slavs, Khors and Dazhbog were identified with the sun. Another god, Svarog (among the western Slavs, Svarožic), was the father of Dazhbog; he was considered by Thietmar von Merseburg (at the beginning of the eleventh century) as the supreme god (*primus Zuararasici dicetur*). According to the tradition, fire—celestial as well as domestic—was the son of

68. The temple was destroyed in 1168. Other sanctuaries on the island of Rügen, as well as a temple erected on the hill of Riedegost (Rethra), were destroyed in the twelfth and thirteenth centuries during the campaigns of forced conversion to Christianity.
69. The priest of Jarovit proclaimed in his name, "I am your god who covers the fields with grass and the forests with leaves. The produce of the fields and the forests, and all other things useful to men, are in my power" (Helmold, *Chronica Slavorum*, 3, 4).
70. Cf. R. Pettazzoni, *L'onniscienza di Dio*, pp. 343ff. This hypothesis is reinforced by the sacred horse's role in divination.

Svarog. In the tenth century, the Arab traveler Al-Masudi wrote that the Slavs adored the sun; they had a temple with an opening in the dome to see the sun's rising.[71] However, in the beliefs and customs of the Slavic people, the moon (of masculine gender) plays a more important role than the sun (neuter, probably derived from a feminine name). One addresses prayers to the moon—called "father" and "grandfather"—to obtain abundance and health, and eclipses are occasions for lamentation.[72]

251. Rites, myths, and beliefs of the Old Slavs

It would be vain to attempt a reconstruction of the history of Slavic religion. One can, however, distinguish its principal layers and specify their contributions to the fabric of Slavic spirituality. Beyond the Indo-European heritage and the Finno-Ugrian and Iranian influences, one can identify still more archaic strata. The adoption of the Iranian term *bog* ("riches," but also "god") has replaced the Indo-European theonym *deivos*, conserved by the Balts (cf. §248). Other borrowings of Iranian origin have been mentioned above.[73] As to the similarities with the beliefs and customs of the Finno-Ugrians, they can be explained either by contacts during the protohistoric period, or by their derivation from a common tradition. For example, we have drawn attention to the analogies between the structure of the sanctuaries of the western Slavs and the Finno-Ugrians, and the resemblance between their polycephalic representations of divinities and spirits.[74] A pan-Slavic custom, unknown among the Indo-Europeans, is the double-sepulcher.[75] After three, five, or seven years, one disinters the bones, washes them, and wraps them in a napkin (*ubrus*); the napkin is brought

71. Cf. F. Haase, *Volksglaube und Brauchtum der Ostslaven*, p. 256.

72. See the documentation amassed by Evel Gasparini, *Il matriarcato slavo*, pp. 597ff.

73. We add the term *ray*, which, before it expressed the Christian notion of "paradise," had the same meaning as *bog* ("riches").

74. See the documentation in Gasparini, *Il matriarcato slavo*, pp. 553–579. But as we have seen (§250), polycephalism is also attested among other Indo-European peoples.

75. It is found uniquely among peoples influenced by the Slavs: the Germans, Romanians, and other populations of southeastern Europe.

into the house and placed provisionally in the "sacred corner," in the place where the icons are hung. The magico-religious value accorded to this napkin is due to its contact with the skull and bones of the dead. Originally, a portion of the exhumed bones was deposited in the "sacred corner." This extremely archaic custom (attested in Africa and Asia) is also found among the Finns.[76]

Another Slavic institution which is not known by the Indo-Europeans is the *snochačestvo*, that is, the right of the father-in-law to sleep with the fiancées of his pubescent sons and with his daughters-in-law when their husbands go away for a long time. Otto Schrader has compared the *snochačestvo* with the Indo-European practice of the *adiutor matrimonii*. But among the Indo-Europeans, the temporary transfer of the girl or wife was effected by the father or husband, who thus exercised his paternal or marital authority. The transfer was not accomplished without the husband's knowledge, or against his wishes.[77]

No less characteristic is the equality of rights in the ancient Slavic societies. The entire community was invested with full powers. Decisions thus had to be made unanimously. Originally, the word *mir* designated both the communal *assembly* and the *unanimity* of its decisions. This explains why *mir* came to signify both *peace* and the *world*. According to Gasparini, the term *mir* reflects a period when every member of the community—*the women as well as the men*—possessed the same rights.[78]

As with other European ethnic groups, Slavic religious folklore, beliefs, and customs conserve a great part of the more or less Christianized pagan heritage.[79] Particular interest is attached to the pan-Slavic concept of the Spirit of the Forest (Russian *leshy;* Byelorussian *leshuk,* etc.) who assures the hunters the necessary quantity of game. The type of divinity is an archaic one: the Master of the Animals (cf.

76. Cf. Gasparini, "Studies in Old Slavic Religion: Ubrus"; idem, *Il matriarcato Slavo*, pp. 597–630.

77. Cf. *Il matriarcato Slavo*, pp. 5ff. Gasparini recalls other non-Indo-European traits: matrilocal weddings (pp. 232ff.); the existence—at least among the southern Slavs—of a maternal clan (pp. 252ff.); the authority of the maternal uncle (pp. 277 ff.); the periodic return of the wife to her paternal home (pp. 299ff.).

78. Ibid., pp. 472ff.

79. See the documents presented and analyzed by Gasparini, ibid., pp. 493ff., 597ff.

§4). The *leshy* becomes subsequently the protector of herds. Equally ancient is the belief that certain spirits of the forest (*domovoi*) penetrate into dwellings while they are being constructed. These spirits, good or bad, install themselves especially in the pillars of wood which sustain the houses.

The popular mythology illustrates still more clearly the survival of the old pre-Christian conceptions. We will cite only one example, but the most famous and most significant one: the myth of the cosmogonic dive that we have found diffused through all of central and northern Asia. In a more or less Christianized form it is found again in the legends of the Slavic peoples and southeastern Europeans. The myth follows the well-known schema: on the primordial sea, God recognizes Satan and orders him to dive to the bottom of the waters and bring back to him some mud in order to create the Earth. But the Devil keeps a little mud (or sand) in his mouth or hand, and when the Earth begins to grow, these several particles become the mountains and the marshes. A characteristic of the Russian versions is the appearance of the Devil, and in certain cases of God, in the form of the aquatic bird. Now the ornithomorphy of the Devil is a trait of central Asiatic origin. In the "Legend of the Tiberiad Sea" (an apocryphal story found in fifteenth and sixteenth century manuscripts), God, who flies through the air, perceives Satan in the form of an aquatic bird. Another version presents God and the Devil in the form of white and black diving ducks.[80]

Compared with the central Asiatic variants of the same cosmogonic myth, the Slavic and southeastern European versions accentuate the God-Satan dualism. Certain scholars have interpreted this conception of a god who creates the world with the aid of the Devil as being an expression of Bogomil beliefs. But this hypothesis runs into difficulties. First of all, this myth is not found in any Bogomil text. What is more, it is not attested in the regions where Bogomilism was maintained for centuries (Serbia, Bosnia, Herzegovina, and Hungary).[81] Beyond this variants have been collected in the Ukraine, in Russia, and in the Baltic regions, where Bogomil beliefs never penetrated. Finally,

80. See Eliade, *Zalmoxis,* pp. 94ff.

81. It is equally unknown in Germany and the West, even though the Cathars and Patarini have diffused a number of folkloric motifs of Manichaean and Bogomil origins into southern France, Germany, and the Pyrenees. Cf. *Zalmoxis,* pp. 90ff.

as we have seen, the densest concentration of versions of this myth is found among the peoples of central and northern Asia. An Iranian origin has been presumed, but the myth of the cosmic dive is not known in Iran.[82] Besides, as we have already indicated (§244), the myth has variants from North America, Aryan and pre-Aryan India, and southeast Asia.

In sum, it is a matter of an archaic myth, several times reinterpreted and revalorized. Its considerable circulation in Eurasia and in central and southeastern Europe proves that it met profound needs of the popular spirit. On the one hand, in accounting for the imperfection of the world and the existence of evil, the myth dissociates God from the gravest defects of the Creation. On the other hand, it reveals aspects of God which had already haunted the religious imagination of archaic man: his character as *deus otiosus* (made evident especially in the Balkan legends). One thus explains the contradictions and sufferings of human life, and the camaraderie, or even friendship, of God and the Devil.

We have insisted on this myth for several reasons. First of all—in its European versions—it constitutes a *total myth:* not only does it recount the creation of the world, but it explains also the origin of death and of evil. Moreover, if one takes into account all the variants, this myth illustrates a process of "dualistic" hardening which one can compare with other analogous religious creations (cf. India, §195; Iran, §§104, 213). However, this time it is a matter of *folkloric* legends, whatever their origins may be. In other words, the study of this myth allows us to grasp certain conceptions of popular religiosity. For a long time after their conversion to Christianity, it was through the lens of this myth that the peoples of eastern Europe still justified the actual situation of the world and our human condition. The existence of the Devil has never been contested by Christianity. But the role of the Devil in the cosmogony was a "dualist" innovation, one which assured these legends their enormous success and prodigious circulation.

It is hard to be certain whether the ancient Slavs shared other dualistic notions of the Iranian or Gnostic type. For our purposes, we

---

82. However, one also finds two constitutive motifs in the Iranian traditions which pass for Zurvanite (cf. §213): the fraternity of God (Christ) and Satan, and, in Balkan legends, the mental inertia of God after having created the world; cf. *Zalmoxis,* pp. 109ff.

must content ourselves with having shown, on the one hand, the continuity of archaic mythico-religious structures in the beliefs of the peoples of Christian Europe, and, on the other hand, the importance, for the general history of religions, of the revalorizations, effected at the folkloric level, of an immemorial religious heritage.

32 The Christian Churches up to the Iconoclastic Crisis
(Eighth to Ninth Centuries)

252. *Roma non pereat . . .*

"The end of Antiquity," writes Hugh Trevor-Roper, "the final failure of the great Mediterranean civilization of Greece and Rome, is one of the chief problems of European history. Nobody can agree why it happened, or quite when. All that we can see is a slow, fatal, apparently irreversible process which seems to begin in the third century A.D. and is completed, at least as far as western Europe is concerned, in the fifth."[1]

Among the causes of the decline of the Empire and the ruin of the ancient world, it is Christianity that is most repeatedly mentioned; more exactly, its promotion as the official religion of the state. We will not digress here on this difficult and delicate problem. It is sufficient to remember that, if Christianity did not encourage either military vocation or martial virtues, the anti-imperial polemic of the first apologists had lost its raison d'être after the conversion of Constantine (cf. §239). What is more: Constantine's decision to adopt Christianity and to build a new capital on the Bosporus made possible the conservation of the classical Greco-Roman culture.[2] But, as is evident, these beneficial consequences of the Christianization of the Empire eluded certain con-

1. Hugh Trevor-Roper, *The Rise of Christian Europe*, p. 33.
2. "Who can even guess what would have happened to the world, or to Christianity, if the Roman Empire had not become Christian, or if Constantinople had not preserved Roman law and Greek culture during the years of the barbarian and the Muslim conquest? The rediscovery of Roman law in the twelfth century marked an important stage in the revival of Europe. But the Roman law which was rediscovered was the law preserved in the great Byzantine compilation of Justinian" (ibid., p. 34). Likewise, the fifteenth-century rediscovery of Greek learning resulted in the Renaissance.

temporaries: above all when Alaric, Chief of the Goths (himself a Christian who followed the Arian heresy), captured and ravaged Rome in August of 410, massacring part of the population. From a military and political perspective, this event, despite its gravity, was not a catastrophe, since the capital was in Milan. But the news of it shattered the Empire from one end to the other. Reacting to it as a sign of things to come, the religious elite and the cultural and political centers of paganism interpreted this unprecedented disaster by abandoning the traditional Roman religion and adopting Christianity.[3]

It is in response to this accusation that Augustine, Bishop of Hippo, wrote between 412 and 426 his most important work, *De civitate Dei contra paganos*. It was, above all, a critique of paganism, in other words a repudiation of Roman mythologies and religious institutions combined with a theology of history that has profoundly influenced Western Christian thought. In fact, Augustine did not concern himself with the universal history that was currently understood in his period. Among the empires of antiquity, he mentions only Assyria and Rome (e.g., *Civ. dei* 18. 27, 23). Despite the variety of subject matter which he took up, and despite his considerable erudition, Augustine is obsessed solely with those two events which for a Christian like himself began and oriented history: the sin of Adam and the redemption of man by Christ. He rejects theories of the eternity of the world and the eternal return, but goes to no trouble to refute them. The world has been created by God and will have an end, since time is linear and finite. After the original fall, the only important new event has been the Incarnation. The truth, both historic and salvific, has been revealed in the Bible, for the destiny of the Jewish people shows that History has a meaning and pursues a precise objective: the salvation of mankind (4. 3; 5. 12, 18, 25, etc.). In sum, History consists in the struggle between the spiritual descendants of Cain and Abel (15. 1).

Augustine distinguished six epochs: (1) from Adam to the Flood; (2) from Noah to Abraham; (3) from Abraham to David; (4) from David to the Babylonian Captivity; (5) from the Exile to Jesus. The sixth epoch continues until the second coming of Christ.[4] All these historic periods

---

3. See P. de Labriolle, *La réaction païenne;* Walter Emil Kaegi, *Byzantium and the Decline of Rome,* pp. 59ff., 99ff.

4. But Augustine refrained from speculating on the date of the Parousia, which his compatriot Lactantius (240–300) had announced for the year 500.

participate in the *civitas terenna,* which is inaugurated by the crime of Cain, and opposed by the *Civitas Dei.* In full bloom under the sign of *vanitas,* the City of Man is temporal and mortal, and perpetuated by natural generation. Eternal, immortal, and illumined by *veritas,* the City of God is the place where spiritual regeneration is effected. In the world of history (*saeculum*), the just like Abel are pilgrims on the way to salvation. Ultimately, the mission—and the justification—of the Roman Empire is to maintain peace and justice so that the Gospel can be universally propagated.[5] Augustine did not share the opinion of certain Christian authors who drew a connection between the prosperity of the Empire and the progress of the Church. He continually repeats that Christians must only await the final triumph of the City of God over the civilization of men. This triumph will not take place in historical time, as the chiliasts and millenarists thought. In other words, even if the entire world should convert to Christianity, the Earth and history would not be transfigured. It is significant that the last book of the *City of God* (22) is dedicated to the resurrection of the body.

As for the devastation of the city by Alaric, Augustine recalls that Rome has known other disasters in the past; he insists that the Romans have likewise subjugated and exploited innumerable peoples. In any case, as Augustine proclaims in his famous sermon: *Roma non pereat si Romani non pereant!* In other words, it is the quality of men which assures the permanence of an institution, and not the inverse.

When Augustine finished the *City of God* in 425, five years before his death, Alaric's "sacrilege" had been forgotten, but the Western Empire was approaching its end. It is above all for the Christians, who, during the following four centuries, had to take part in the disappearance of the Empire and the "barbarization" of western Europe, that Augustine's work proved most salutary. The *City of God* had radically severed the historical solidarity between the Church and the moribund Roman Empire. Since the true vocation of the Christian is the pursuit of salvation, and the only certainty is the final and definitive triumph of the *Civitas Dei,* all historic disasters are, in the last analysis, devoid of spiritual significance.

During the summer of 429 and the spring of 430, the Vandals, cross-

5. *Civ. dei* 18. 46. According to Augustine, the states and the emperors are not the work of the Devil; nevertheless, they are the consequence of original sin.

ing the Strait of Gibraltar, devastated Mauritania and Numidia. They still occupied Hippo on 28 August 430 when Augustine died there. One year later, the city was evacuated and partially burned. Roman Africa had ceased to exist.

253. Augustine: From Tagaste to Hippo

As with a number of founders of religion, saints, or mystics (e.g., the Buddha, Muhammad, Saint Paul, Milarepa, Ignatius of Loyola, etc.), Saint Augustine's biography helps us to understand certain dimensions of his genius. Born to a pagan father and a Christian mother in 354, in the small village of Tagaste in Roman Africa, Augustine was first drawn to rhetoric. Subsequently, he embraced Manichaeanism, to which he remained faithful for nine years, and took a concubine who gave him his only son, Adeodatus. In 382, he moved to Rome in the hope of finding a professorial position. Two years later his protector Symmachus, leader of the pagan intellectual elite, sent him to Milan. Meanwhile, Augustine had abandoned the religion of Mani and dedicated himself with fervor to the study of Neoplatonism. In Milan he approached the bishop, Ambrose, who enjoyed a considerable prestige in the Church as well as in the Imperial Court. For some time, the organization of communities had adopted the structures which it would maintain until the twentieth century: the exclusion of women from the priesthood and spiritual activities (distribution of the sacraments, religious instruction); separation between the clergy and the laity; and the preeminence of bishops.

Soon Augustine's mother, Monica, came to join him. It is probably she who persuaded him to separate from his concubine (although soon enough Augustine would take another one). The sermons and the example of Ambrose, as well as Augustine's deep study of Neoplatonism, ended by convincing him that he must deliver himself from concupiscence. One day in the summer of 386, he heard in a neighboring garden the voice of a child saying: "Take and read!" (*tolle, lege!*). Augustine opened the New Testament and his eyes fell on a passage from the Epistle to the Romans (13:13–14): "not in reveling and drunkenness, not in debauchery and licentiousness, not in quarreling and jealousy. But put on the Lord Jesus Christ, and make no provision for the flesh, to gratify its desires."

He was baptized by Ambrose on Easter of 387, and decided to return to Africa with his family. But Monica died in Ostia (Adeodatus would die three years later). In Tagaste, Augustine had formed with his friends a semimonastic community dedicated to meditation and study. However, when he visited the town of Hippo in 391, he was ordained a priest and designated coadjutor of the bishop, whom he succeeded in 396. Until his death, Augustine dedicated himself in his sermons, letters, and innumerable works to the defense of the unity of the Church and the strengthening of Christian doctrine. He is justly considered to be the greatest and most influential of all Western theologians. However, he did not enjoy the same prestige in the Eastern Church.

One can recognize in Augustine's theology the deep marks of his temperament and his interior biography. Despite his rejection of Manichaeanism, he still retains, as we shall see, a materialist conception of the "evil nature" of man, the consequence of original sin that is transmitted by sexuality. As to Neoplatonism, its influence has been decisive. For Augustine, man is "a soul who is caught in a body. When he speaks as a Christian, Augustine takes care to recall that man is the unity of body and soul; philosophically, he falls within Plato's definition."[6] But it is his sensual temperament and his persistent but largely unsuccessful struggle against concupiscence that have contributed to his inordinate exaltation of divine grace and the hardening of his ideas on predestination (cf. §255).

Finally, in renouncing the contemplative life and in accepting all the responsibilities of priest and bishop, Augustine lived his religious life in a community of the faithful. More than any other great theologian, Augustine identified the path toward salvation with the life of the Church. It is for this reason that he strove to the last of his days to maintain the unity of the Great Church. For Augustine, the most monstrous sin was schism. And he did not hesitate to affirm that he believed in the Gospels because the Church had enjoined him to believe.

254. The great predecessor of Augustine: Origen

When Augustine contemplated his works, Christian theology was in full flight. The second half of the fourth century comprises a sort of

---

6. Etienne Gilson, *Christian Philosophy in the Middle Ages*, p. 74. This definition given by Plato in *Alcibiades* was repeated by Plotinus, where Augustine found it.

Golden Age of the Fathers of the Church. The great and the less great among the Fathers—Basil of Caesarea, Gregory Nazianzus, Gregory of Nyssa, John Chrysostom, Evagrius Ponticus, and still others—were students and accomplished their work, like Ambrose, during the peace of the Church. Theology was still dominated by the Greek Fathers. Against the Arian heresy, it is Athanasius who had formulated the doctrine of the consubstantiality (*homoousia*) of the Father and the Son, a formula which was accepted by the Ecumenical Council of Nicaea (325). However, Origen (ca. 185–ca. 254), the most ingenious and daring theologian, the only one who can be compared to Augustine, enjoyed none of the authority he merited, although his prestige and influence increased after his death.

Born in Alexandria of Christian parents, Origen was distinguished by intelligence, fervor, and extraordinary creativity. He devoted himself with competence, zeal, and erudition to the service of the Church (first in Alexandria, then in Caesarea). But convinced that biblical revelation and the Gospel had nothing to fear from Platonic philosophy, he studied with the famous Ammonius Saccas (who twenty years later would be the teacher of Plotinus). Origen thought that the theologian must know and assume Greek culture in order to make himself understood by the pagan intellectual elite, and also by recently converted Christians who were imbued with classical culture. (He thus anticipated a process which became common by the end of the fourth century.)

His oeuvre is immense:[7] philology (he founded biblical criticism with the *Hexapla*), apologetics (*Contra Celsum*), exegesis (conserved in many great commentaries), homiletics, theology, and metaphysics. But this considerable work has, in large part, been lost. Except for *Contra Celsum* and several great commentaries and homilies, we have only his *Treatise on Prayer,* the *Exhortation of Martyrs,* and the theological treatise, *De principiis (Peri archôn),* which is beyond doubt his most important work. According to Eusebius, in order to deliver himself from concupiscence, Origen interpreted "in an extreme and over-literal sense" a passage from the Gospel of Matthew.[8] All his life, he exalted the ordeals and the death of the martyrs. During the

7. Jerome cites 800 works, but adds that Pamphilius gave a list of 2,000 titles.
8. "There are eunuchs who have made themselves eunuchs for the sake of the kingdom of heaven" (Matthew 19:12). This happened before 210.

persecution of Decius in 250, he was imprisoned; and he died after being tortured in 254.

With Origen, Neoplatonism definitively inseminates Christian thought. Origen's theological system is a construction of genius which has much influenced later generations. But as we shall see, certain speculations, the most audacious ones, were susceptible to malicious interpretations. According to Origen, God the Father, transcendent and incomprehensible, eternally engenders the Son, his Image, who is at once both incomprehensible and comprehensible. Through the Logos, God creates a multitude of pure spirits (*logikoi*) and favors them with life and knowledge. But with the exception of Jesus, all the pure spirits estrange themselves from God. Origen does not explain the precise cause of their estrangement. He speaks of negligence, boredom, and forgetfulness. In sum, the crisis is explained by the pure spirits' innocence. In withdrawing from God, they became "souls" (*psychai;* cf. *De principiis* 2. 8. 3) and the Father provides them with concrete bodies in accord with the gravity of their faults: with bodies of angels, of men, or of demons.

Then, thanks to their free choice, but also to divine providence, the fallen souls begin the pilgrimage which will end in their return to God. Indeed, Origen thinks that the soul has not lost the freedom to choose between good and evil as a result of original sin (an idea which will be repeated by Pelagius; see below §255). By his omniscience, God knows in advance the acts of our liberty (*On Prayer,* 5–7). In emphasizing the redemptive function of freedom, Origen rejects the fatalism of the Gnostics and certain pagan philosophers. To be sure, the body constitutes a prison, but it is at the same time the means by which God reveals himself and which allows for the elevation of the soul.

The universal drama might be defined as the passage from innocence to experience, through the tests of the soul during its pilgrimage towards God. Salvation amounts to a return to the original perfection, the *apokatastasis* ("restoration of all things"). But this final perfection is superior to that original one since it is invulnerable, and therefore definitive (*De prin.* 2. 11.7). At this moment, souls will have "bodies of resurrection." The spiritual itinerary of the Christian is described admirably by the metaphors of voyage, natural growth, and combat against evil. Finally, Origen estimated that the perfect Christian could know God and join himself with him through love.[9]

9. See the edition and translation of *De principiis* in "Sources Chrétiennes," vols.

Already criticized during his lifetime, Origen was attacked for some time after his death by certain theologians and, at the demand of the Emperor Justinian, he was definitively condemned at the Fifth Ecumenical Council in 553. It was especially his anthropology and his conception of the *apokatastasis* that troubled numerous theologians. He was accused of being more of a philosopher and gnostic than a Christian theologian. *Apokatastasis* implies a universal salvation, thus including the salvation of the Devil; moreover, it integrates the work of Christ into a cosmic type of process. But one must take into account the time in which Origen was writing, and above all the provisional character of his synthesis. He considered himself at the exclusive service of the Church; that he was so is proved by many clear and firm declarations,[10] as well as by his martyrdom. Unfortunately, the loss of a number of Origen's works makes it sometimes difficult to distinguish between his own ideas and those of the "Origenists." Despite the suspicion voiced by an element of the ecclesiastical hierarchy, he did, however, exercise an influence on the Cappadocian Fathers. Thanks to Basil the Great, Gregory Nazianzus, and Gregory of Nyssa, the essentials of Origen's theological thought have been preserved inside the Church. Through the Cappadocians, he also influenced Evagrius Ponticus, the Pseudo-Areopagite, and John Cassian, most especially in their ideas of mystical experience and Christian monasticism.

But the definitive condemnation of Origen deprived the Church of a unique possibility of reinforcing its universalism, notably in opening Christian theology to dialogue with other systems of religious thought (e.g., Indian religious thought). With all its audacious implications, the vision of *apokatastasis* ranks among the most magnificent of eschatological creations.[11]

252, 253, 268, 269. A selection of these translated texts and commentaries has been made recently by Rowan A. Greer, *Origen*. On his theological system, see ibid., pp. 7–28.

10. For example in *First Principles* (1, para. 2): "we maintain that that only is to be believed as the truth which in no way conflicts with the tradition of the Church and the Apostles."

11. A thousand years later, the Western Church will resist the audacious speculations of Joachim of Floris and Meister Eckhart, thus denying these men's contemporaries the opportunity to benefit from their teachings.

255. The polemical positions of Augustine: His doctrine of Grace and Predestination

A few years after having been consecrated as bishop in 397, Augustine drafts his *Confessions*. He is depressed by the vivid memories of his youth, "terrified by my sins and the dead weight of my misery" (10. 43. 10). He remarks that "the enemy held my will in his power and from it he had made a chain and shackled me"(8. 5. 1). The composition of this work has a therapeutic purpose: it is his effort at self-reconciliation. Simultaneously, it is also a spiritual autobiography and a long prayer through which Augustine tries to penetrate the mystery of the nature of God. "But, dust and ashes though I am, let me appeal to your pity, since it is to you in your mercy that I speak, not to a man, who would simply laugh at me" (1. 6. 7). He addresses God with words of prayer: "God of my heart." "Oh, my late joy! *Deus dulcedo mea.*" "Ordain that which you wish." "Give that which I love."[12] Augustine evokes his sins and his youthful dramas—the theft of the pears, the abandonment of a concubine, his despair after the death of a friend—not for their anecdotal interest, but in order to open his heart to God and to better realize the gravity of his actions. The emotional tone of the *Confessions* still strikes the reader just as it impressed Petrarch and other writers of later centuries.[13] It is the only work of Augustine which can still be read with interest anywhere in the world, even today. As has often been repeated, the *Confessions* is the "first modern book."

But for the Church of the fifth century, Augustine was much more than just the author of the *Confessions*. He was above all else the great theologian and prestigious critic of heresies and schisms. His first polemics were directed against the Manichaeans and the Donatists. In his youth, Manichaeanism appealed to Augustine because its dualism allowed him to explain the origin and the apparently unlimited power of Evil. After some time, he rejected Manichaeanism, but the problem of

12. See the references in Peter Brown, *Augustine of Hippo,* pp. 167, 180. Even the title, *Confessions,* is itself important; for Augustine, *Confessio* signifies "accusation of oneself; praise of God" (ibid., p. 175).

13. It is above all after Petrarch that one cites the famous passage: "I was no longer in love but was in love with love. . . . I began to seek an occasion to fall in love because I madly loved the Idea of Love" (3. 1.1).

evil always troubled him. Beginning with Basil the Great, Christian theologians resolved this problem by denying the ontological reality of evil. Basil defined evil as "the absence of the good. Consequently, evil is not inherent in one substance proper to it, but appears through the mutilation of the soul" (*Hexameron* 2. 5). Likewise, for Titus of Bosra (d. 370) and for John Chrysostom (ca. 344–407), evil was "the absence of good" (*steresis, privatio boni*).

Augustine returns to similar arguments in the five treatises he wrote against Manichaeanism between 388 and 399. All that God has created is *real*, participates in being, and is therefore *good*. Evil is not a substance, for it contains not the least trace of good. This is a desperate effort to save the unity, omnipotence, and goodness of God while dissociating him from the existence of evil in the world. We have remarked on a similar effort to dissociate God from the appearance of evil in east European and central Asiatic cosmogonic legends (cf. §251). The doctrine of the *privatio boni* has preoccupied Christian theologians down to our own day; but it was never understood nor taken up by the masses of the faithful. In Augustine, the anti-Manichaean polemic[14] contributed to a hardening of his conception of the total fall of man; certain traces of pessimism and Manichaean materialism reappear in his theology of grace (cf. this §, below).

The schism of Donatus, a bishop in Numidia, began between 311 and 312 during the period of peace that followed the persecutions of Diocletian. The Donatists had excluded from their churches the members of the clergy who had deviated, in one manner or another, during the persecution. They thought that the mediation of grace by the sacraments was compromised if the one who administered them had sinned. Augustine, however, responded that the holiness of the Church depended not upon the perfection of the clergy and the faithful, but on the grace transmitted by the sacraments; so, too, the salvific virtue of the sacraments did not depend on the faith of those who received them. For a number of years, Augustine strove to avoid schism by reconciling the Donatists with the larger Church, but all to no avail.

The longest of Augustine's polemics, with its considerable repercussions, was the one against Pelagius and his disciples. An elderly British monk, Pelagius arrived in Rome in 400. He was displeased with the

14. The essential texts are reproduced and commented on by Claude Tresmontant, *La métaphysique du christianisme*, pp. 528–49.

conduct and morality of the Christians, and strove to reform them. His ascetic rigor and erudition secured him very quickly a considerable prestige. In 410, he took refuge with several disciples in North Africa, but did not meet with Augustine. He made his way to the eastern provinces, where he had the same success he had had in Rome, and where he died between 418 and 420.

Pelagius had an unlimited confidence in the possibilities of human intelligence and especially of man's will. He taught that by practicing virtue and asceticism, every Christian is capable of attaining perfection, and thus sainthood. Man alone is responsible for his sins, since he is disposed of the capacity to do good and avoid evil; in other words, he enjoys liberty or "free will." This is the reason why Pelagius did not accept the idea that original sin is automatically and universally shared by the descendants of Adam. "If sin is innate, it is not voluntary; if it is voluntary, then it is not innate." The goal of infant baptism is not to wash away original sin but to sanctify the new life in Christ. For Pelagius, grace consists in God's revelations through the Law, and especially, through Jesus Christ. The teaching of Christ constitutes a model that can be imitated by Christians. In sum, in Pelagian theology man appears in some way to be the author of his own salvation.[15]

The history of Pelagianism was short but eventful. Pelagius was excommunicated and exonerated several times by different synods and councils. Pelagianism was not definitively condemned until 579 at the Synod of Orange, and then it was the refutations drawn up by Augustine between 413 and 430 that were finally decisive. Just as in his polemic against the Donatists, Augustine attacked first the rigorous asceticism and moral perfectionism proposed by Pelagius. His victory was above all the victory of the average lay community of the Church over an ideal of austerity and reform.[16] The decisive importance which Augustine accorded to grace, and thus to God's omnipotence, reclaimed the biblical tradition and was not hampered by popular piety.

15. It is probable that his most brilliant disciple, Coelestius, further hardened Pelagius's theses. According to Paulinus of Milan, who refuted this heresy in 411 or 412, Pelagius maintained that Adam had been created mortal and that he would have known death even without having sinned; only Adam was harmed by his fault, and not all of mankind; infants find themselves in the same situation as Adam before the Fall; what is more, before Jesus Christ, there existed men who were perfectly pure, without any sin.

16. Cf. Brown, *Augustine of Hippo*, p. 348.

As to the doctrine of predestination, it was of greatest interest to the elites.

Origen had already held that divine providence (that is, God's prescience) is not the cause of man's acts; human acts are undertaken in complete liberty, and man is responsible for them (cf. §254). The passage from the dogma of divine prescience, which does not prevent human freedom, to the theology of predestination, is achieved by the theologoumenon of original sin. Ambrose had remarked on the causal relationship between the virginal conception of Jesus Christ on the one hand and the idea that original sin is transmitted by sexual union on the other. For Cyprian (200–258), infant baptism was necessary precisely because it effaced original sin.

Augustine retrieves, prolongs, and deepens the reflections of his predecessors. He insists particularly on the fact that grace is God's freedom to act without any external necessity. And since God is sovereign—*all* was created by him from *nothing*—grace is sovereign also. This understanding of divine sovereignty, omnipotence, and grace finds its most complete expression in the doctrine of predestination. Augustine defined predestination as "the organization by God of his future works, which can neither be deceived nor changed" (*Perseverantia* 17.41). But Augustine adds that predestination has nothing to do with the fatalism of the pagans: God punishes to manifest his anger and demonstrate his power. Universal history constitutes the arena where his acts take place. Certain men receive eternal life, others eternal damnation—and among the latter are unbaptized dead infants. This double predestination—to heaven and hell—is incomprehensible, as Augustine recognizes. Since it is transmitted by sexual propagation,[17] original sin is as universal and inevitable as life itself. In the final reckoning, the Church consists of a fixed number of saints predestined even before the creation of the world.

Carried away by the polemic, Augustine formulates certain theses which, although not integrally accepted by the Catholic Church, have provoked interminable controversies in Western theological circles. This rigid theology has been compared to pagan fatalism. Moreover, Augustinian predestination compromised Christian universalism, according to which God desired the salvation of *all* men. It was not the

---

17. Like a venereal disease, remarks Jaroslav Pelikan, *The Emergence of the Catholic Tradition (100–600)*, p. 300.

doctrine of grace which was objected to but the identification of grace with a particular theory of predestination; it was justly pointed out that the doctrine of God's prescience avoided the objections raised by the Augustinian interpretation of predestination.[18]

Let us also quote the conclusions of a great contemporary Catholic theologian: "Augustine had defended human liberty and responsibility against Manichaeanism. Where Augustine reproached the Manichaeans, it was for rejecting, for pushing aside the responsibility of evil onto a mythical 'nature' or 'principle.' In this much, Augustine made a positive and Christian contribution. But is the theory that Augustine proposed instead fully satisfactory? Is not the representation of original sin which Augustine transmits to posterity susceptible to the same critique? The evil that man does today . . . is it, in the Augustinian view, still indeed the actual man who is responsible? Isn't it rather an evil and perverted 'nature' which has been 'transmitted' to him by the fault of the first couple? . . . Saint Augustine tells us that it is in the first man that humanity has taken on in the *flesh* the *habitude* of sin. Is this not a materialistic understanding of the heredity of sin, a physical and likewise deterministic conception? It is not biology which weighs upon man, and in the child who is born the sin is not found inscribed upon his tissues or his psyche. The child *will go to receive* the heredity of sin through the education he will receive . . . , the mental forms and moral schemes which he will adopt. The dreadful Augustinian theory of the damnation of unbaptized dead infants shows that the greatest geniuses and the greatest doctors in the Church are not without redoubtable ambivalence. . . . We have borne in the Church for sixteen centuries the fruits and weights of the greatness and weakness of Saint Augustine."[19]

256. The cult of the saints: *Martyria,* relics, and pilgrimages

For a long time, Augustine inveighed against the cult of martyrs. He did not much believe in the prodigies accomplished by the saints, and

18. See the pertinent observations of Pelikan, ibid., pp. 325–326, and in general, his chapter on "Nature and Grace," pp. 278–331.

19. Tresmontant, *La métaphysique,* p. 611; in note 40 he cites a text of Leibniz which attests that the problematic had scarcely evolved: "How could the soul have been infected by original sin, which is the root of actual sins, unless there had been injustice on God's part in exposing the soul to it" (*Essais de Théodicée,* p. 86).

stigmatized the sale of relics.[20] But the transfer of the relics of Saint Stephen to Hippo in 425 and the miraculous cures that they brought about made him change his opinion. In his sermons preached between 425 and 430, and in Book 22 of the *City of God,* Augustine explains and justifies the veneration of relics and carefully records their miracles.[21]

The cult of martyrs was practiced, and accepted by the Church, from the end of the second century. But it is above all during the great persecutions and after the peace instituted by Constantine that the relics of the "witnesses" of Christ took on a disturbing importance. Certain bishops saw in this excessive veneration the danger of a recrudescence of paganism. In fact, there is a continuity between pagan funeral practices and the Christian cult of the dead; for example, in the banquets celebrated near the tomb on the day of interment, and every year thereafter on the anniversary date. The "Christianization" of this archaic rite did not take long to find its expression: for the Christians, the banquet near the tomb anticipated the eschatological feast in Heaven. The cult of martyrs prolonged this tradition, with the difference that it is no longer a familial ceremony, but involved the entire community and took place in the presence of the bishop. Moreover, the cult of martyrs presented a new element, one unknown in non-Christian societies. The martyrs had transcended the human condition; sacrificed for Christ, they were both near to God in heaven and here on earth. Their relics incorporated the sacred. Not only were the martyrs able to intercede with God—for they were his "friends"—but their relics were capable of producing miracles and assuring spectacular healings. The tombs and relics of the martyrs constituted a privileged and paradoxical place where Heaven communicated with Earth.[22]

The comparison with the cult of heroes is not self-evident. Among the pagans, the two cults—of gods and heroes—were clearly distinct (cf. §95). By his death, the hero was definitively separated from the gods, whereas the martyr's body brought those who worshipped it—who offered it a cult—nearer to God. This religious exaltation of the flesh was in certain ways related to the doctrine of the Incarnation.

20. Around 401, he reproved certain monks who "sold the limbs of the martyrs, if indeed it is always a question of the martyrs" (*De opere monachorum,* cited by Victor Saxer, *Morts, martyrs, reliques,* p. 240).

21. Cf. ibid., pp. 255ff.

22. Peter Brown, *The Cult of the Saints,* pp. 3ff.

Since God had incarnated himself in Jesus Christ, each martyr, tortured and put to death for the Lord, was sanctified in his own flesh. The sanctity of the relics represented a rudimentary parallel to the mystery of the Eucharist. Just as the bread and wine were transubstantiated into the body and blood of Christ, the body of the martyr was sanctified by his exemplary death, a true *imitatio Christi*. Such a homologization was reinforced by the unlimited parcelling out of the martyr's body and by the fact that one could multiply the relics indefinitely: garments, objects, oil, or dust reputed to have been in contact with the saint's tomb or body.

This cult attained a considerable popularity by the sixth century. In the eastern Empire, this excessive devotion sometimes became embarrassing for the ecclesiastical authorities. In the fourth and fifth centuries, there existed in Syria two types of churches: basilicas and *martyria,* the "churches of the martyrs."[23] The latter, distinguished by their dome,[24] had a central altar dedicated to the saint whose relics it contained. For a long time, and despite the resistance of the clergy, these special ceremonies, notably the offerings, prayers, and hymns sung in honor of the martyr, were celebrated around this central altar (*mensa*). The cult also included long nocturnal vigils which carried on until dawn: a ceremony that was certainly moving, since the faithful were all in expectation of miracles. *Agapes* and banquets took place around the altar (*mensa*).[25] The ecclesiastical authorities strove tirelessly to subordinate the veneration of saints and the cult of relics to the service of Christ. Finally, in the fifth and sixth centuries, numerous basilicas procured relics; in certain cases, a special chapel, a *martyrium,* was built in the interior in honor of the relics. At the same time, this aided in the gradual transformation of the martyria into regular churches.[26]

In the same epoch—from the end of the fourth to the sixth century—the exaltation of relics spread everywhere in the western Empire. But the cult was generally controlled, indeed encouraged, by the bishops, the true *impresarios* (according to the expression of Peter

23. See above all H. Grabar, *Martyrium.*
24. Cf. E. Baldwin Smith, *The Dome,* pp. 95ff.
25. A tenacious custom, which persisted in spite of the Church's opposition. In 692, the Council of Trullo again prohibited the *agapes* and the preparation of the foods on the altar.
26. Baldwin Smith, *The Dome,* pp. 137, 151.

Brown) of this popular fervor. The tombs of the martyrs, always at their most imposing in the cemetery areas at the edges of the cities, became the center of the religious life of the region. The cemeteries enjoyed an unequalled prestige. Paulinus of Nola congratulated himself for having built around the tomb of Saint Felix a complex of buildings of such size that strangers would regard it as forming another city. The power of the bishops resided in these new "cities outside of cities."[27] As Saint Jerome wrote, in venerating the saints, "the city changed its address."[28]

As in the East, a number of ceremonies took place near the tombs, which became the objects *par excellence* of processions and pilgrimages. Processions and pilgrimages represent a singular innovation in the religious history of the Mediterranean. Indeed, Christianity made a place in its public ceremonies for women and the poor. The ritual corteges and processions provided illustrations of sexual and social desegregation; they reunited men and women, aristocrats and slaves, rich and poor, natives and strangers. When they were officially introduced in a city, the relics received the same honors that were otherwise reserved for the visits of emperors.

Every discovery (*inventio*) of relics (following a dream or vision) stirred up great religious fervor; each was considered an announcement of a divine pardon.[29] Such an event could play a decisive role in ecclesiastical controversies, as was the case of Ambrose's discovery of the relics of the martyred saints Gervase and Protaise. The Empress Justine reclaimed the new basilica for the use of the Arians; but Ambrose carried the day by placing the relics under the altar.

The cult of the saints flourished particularly in ascetic milieus (Brown, p. 67). For Paulinus of Nola, Saint Felix was *patronus et amicus;* the day of his death had become for Paulinus the day of his second birth. Next to the tomb one would read the *Passio* of the mar-

27. See the texts in Brown, *The Cult of the Saints,* p. 8.

28. *Movetur urbs sedibus suis* (*Ep.* 107, I); Brown, p. 42. One can compare these "cities outside of cities" with the megalithic metropolises of Malta, and above all the famous necropolis of Hal Salfieni (see vol. 1, p. 119). This analogy gains precision when one recalls that these megalithic ceremonial centers were not only necropolises, but included chapels, temples, and terraces which served for processions and other rituals. Let us add, however, that such a morphological analogy does not imply a similarity of beliefs.

29. Cf. Brown, *The Cult of the Saints,* p. 92.

tyr. By this reactualization of his exemplary life and death, time was abolished, the saint was present anew—and the crowd awaited new miracles: healings, exorcisms of demons, protection against enemies. But the ideal of every Christian was inhumation *ad sanctos*. One sought to place one's grave as near as possible to the tomb of the saint in the hope that the latter would defend the deceased before God on the Day of Judgment. Beneath the martyria, or in their immediate vicinity, a considerable number of tombs have been unearthed crowded against each other.

The unlimited parcelling out of the relics and their *translatio* from one end of the Empire to the other had contributed to the diffusion of Christianity and the unity of the collective Christian experience. To be sure, abuses, frauds, and ecclesiastical and political rivalries increased with time. In Gaul and in Germany, where relics were very rare, they were brought from elsewhere, and especially from Rome. During the reign of the first Carolingians (740–840), a great number of Roman saints and martyrs were transported into the West. Around the end of the ninth century, it was presumed that all the churches possessed (or ought to possess) relics.[30]

Despite the "popular" character which came to dominate it with the passage of time, the cult of relics was not without a certain grandeur. Taken to its conclusion, it illustrates the *transfiguration of matter,* anticipating in a certain sense the audacious theories of Teilhard de Chardin. Furthermore, in the fervor of the believers, the cult of relics not only reconciled Heaven and Earth, but also men and God. For it was always God who regulated the "discovery" (*inventio*) of relics and permitted the miracles. Besides, the contradictions implicit in the cult (for example, the presence of the martyr simultaneously in Heaven and in his tomb, or in a fragment of his body) familiarized the believers with the paradoxes of religious thought. Indeed, one can consider the veneration of relics as an "easy parallel" (that is to say accessible to the laity) of the dogmas of the Incarnation, the Trinity, and the theology of the sacraments.

---

30. Cf. Patrick J. Geary, "The Ninth Century Relic Trade," pp. 104ff. The Popes willingly accepted these transfers, for the Roman relics heightened the prestige of Rome as the capital of the Empire and the center of Christianity.

257. The Eastern Church and the flowering of Byzantine theology

In the course of the fourth century, certain differences between the churches of the West and of the East began to become clear. For example, the Byzantine Church established the institution of patriarchs, a hierarchy superior to the bishops and metropolitans. At the Council of Constantinople (381), the Eastern Church proclaimed itself composed of four regional jurisdictions, each having a patriarchal see. It occurred sometimes that the tension between Constantinople—or indirectly, the Emperor—and Rome became critical. Possessing the relics of Saint Andrew, "the first called" (thus having precedence over Saint Peter), Constantinople claimed at least an equality with Rome. In the following centuries, christological or ecclesial quarrels repeatedly brought the two churches into opposition. We will consider only those which provoked the schism (§302).

At the first ecumenical councils, only certain representatives of the "Pope" participated. That title was adopted by Siricius (384–99), who thus proclaimed himself the "father" and not the "brother" of the other bishops. But Rome had pressed for the new condemnation of Arius (at the second council in Constantinople in 381) and the condemnation of Nestorius (at the third council in Ephesus in 431). At the fourth council (in Chalcedon in 451) against monophysitism,[31] Pope Leo I presented a formula for the new symbol of the faith which was approved by the Eastern Fathers, since it accorded with the thought of Saint Cyril: "one and the same Christ, Son, Lord, Only-begotten, to be acknowledged in two natures, inconfusedly, unchangeably, indivisibly, inseparably; the distinction of natures being by no means taken away by the union, but rather the property of each nature being preserved, and concurring in one Person and one Subsistence, not parted or divided into two persons, but one and the same Son, and only begotten, God the Word, the Lord Jesus Christ" (Philip Schaff, *The Creeds of Christendom,* vol. 2, New York, 1919, p. 62).

The formula completed the classical christology, but certain difficulties raised by the Monophysites were left unanswered. The symbol

---

31. The Monophysites held that if Jesus Christ was formed "from two natures" (divine and human), there subsisted no more than one of them in the union; consequently, "unique is the nature of the Word Incarnate."

of Chalcedon provoked reaction before the end of the fifth century, and above all in the sixth. It had not been accepted *in toto* by one part of Eastern Christianity, and left the separation of the Monophysite churches inevitable.[32] The quarrels over Monophysitism, or over certain speculations suspected of Monophysitism, continued, sterile and tedious, through the centuries.

Let us mention several developments which contributed to give the Church of the East its own structure. First of all, the unequalled vitality of the Byzantine liturgy, its hieratic pomp, its ritual and at the same time artistic splendor. The liturgy unfolded as a "mystery" reserved for the initiated. The Pseudo-Areopagite warned those who had experienced the divine mystagogy, "Take care not to disclose in sacrilegious fashion the holy mysteries among all mysteries. Be prudent and honor the divine secret" (*Ecclesiastical Hierarchy*, 1. 1). The curtains of the iconostasis were pulled closed at certain moments; in the following centuries, the iconostasis would be completely isolated from the nave.

"The four parts of the interior of the church symbolize the four cardinal directions. The interior of the church is the universe. The altar is paradise, which is located to the east. The Imperial Door of the sanctuary, as it was properly called, was also called the 'Gate of Paradise.' During Easter week, this door remains open throughout the entire service; the meaning of this custom is explained clearly in the Paschal Canon: Christ is risen from the tomb and has opened to us the gates of Paradise. By contrast, the west is the region of the shadows of affliction, of death, of the eternal residence of the dead, who await the resurrection of the body and the last judgment. The middle of the edifice is the earth. According to the understanding of Cosmas Indicopleustes, the earth is rectangular and limited by four walls, which are surmounted by one cupola. The four parts of the interior of the church symbolize the four cardinal directions."[33] As the image of the cosmos, the Byzantine Church both incarnates and sanctifies the world.

Religious poetry and choral music found a unique splendor with the poet and composer Romanos Melodus (sixth century). Finally, it is important to emphasize the role of the deacon, who serves as an inter-

32. The fifth and sixth councils of Constantinople (held in 553 and 680, respectively) had made concessions to the Monophysites.

33. Hans Sedlmayr, *Die Entstehung der Kathedrale*, p. 119; W. Wolska, *La Topographie chrétienne de Cosmas Indicopleustès* (Paris, 1962), p. 131 and passim.

mediary between the celebrants and the faithful. It is the deacon who directs the prayers and signals to those in attendance the decisive moments of the liturgy.

But the most significant creations of Eastern Christianity appeared above all in theology, and primarily in mystical theology. It is true that the structure of Byzantine religious thought in some way veils its "originality." For every doctor strove to save, protect, and defend the doctrine transmitted by the Fathers. Theology was immutable. Novelties belonged to heresies; the words "innovation" and "blasphemy" were nearly synonyms.[34] This apparent monotony (in the repetition of the ideas elaborated by the Fathers) could be considered—as it has been for centuries—as a sign of sclerosis and sterility.

But the central doctrine of Eastern theology, notably the idea of the deification (*theosis*) of man, is of great originality, even though it depends on Saint Paul, the Gospel of John, and other biblical texts. The equivalence between salvation and deification derived from the mystery of the Incarnation. According to Maximus the Confessor, God created man endowed with a mode of divine and immaterial propagation; sexuality, like death, is the consequence of the original sin. The Incarnation of the Logos had made *theosis* possible, but it is always the grace of God which effectuates it. It is this which explains the importance of the interior prayer (later "uninterrupted prayer"), the contemplation, and the monastic life in the Eastern Church. Deification is preceded or accompanied by an experience of mystical light. Already among the Desert Fathers, ecstasy manifested itself through phenomena of light. The monks "shone with the light of Grace." While the recluse was deep in prayer, his cell was entirely illuminated.[35] One thousand years later, the same tradition (prayer, mystical light, *theosis*) is found again among the Hesychastic monks of Mount Athos. The polemic aroused by their assertion that they enjoyed the vision of the uncreated Light provided the occasion for the great thinker Gregory Palamas (fourteenth century) to elaborate a mystical theology around the Taboric light.

In the Eastern church, one finds two complementary tendencies, apparently opposed, which become accentuated with time: on the one

---

34. Cf. the texts cited and commented on in Jaroslav Pelikan, *The Spirit of Eastern Christendom*.

35. Cf. the texts cited and commented on in Eliade, *The Two and the One*, pp. 60ff.

hand, the role and *ecclesial* value of the community of the faithful; on the other, the prestigious authority of the ascetic monks and contemplatives. While in the West the hierarchy will show a certain reserve with regard to the contemplatives and the mystics, in the East these latter will enjoy a great respect in the eyes of the faithful and the ecclesiastical authorities.

The only significant Eastern influence on Western theology has been that of Dionysius the [Pseudo-]Areopagite. His true identity and biography are unknown. He was probably a fifth-century Syrian monk, but as he was believed to have been a contemporary of Saint Paul, he enjoyed an almost apostolic authority. The theology of the Areopagite is inspired by Neoplatonism and by Gregory of Nyssa. For Dionysius, the supreme principle—although ineffable, absolute, beyond the personal and the impersonal—is nonetheless in rapport with the visible world through a hierarchy of beings. The Trinity is above all the symbol of the ultimate unity between the One and the many. Dionysius thus avoids both Monophysitism and the formulae of Chalcedon. He examines the manifestations of divinity in the *Divine Numbers,* and their expressions through the angelic orders in the *Celestial Hierarchy.* But it is chiefly a small treatise named *Mystical Theology* that is the basis of his extraordinary prestige. For the first time in the history of Christian mysticism, one finds such expressions as ''divine ignorance'' and ''nescience'' used with reference to the soul's ascent towards God. The Pseudo-Areopagite evokes the ''superessential luminosity of the divine Shadows,'' the ''Darknesses which are beyond the Light''; he rejects all divine attributes, ''for it is no more true to affirm that God is Life and Goodness than to affirm that he is air or stone.'' Dionysius thus provides the basis for a negative theology (or apophatic) which recalls the famous Upanishadic formula, *neti! neti!* (cf. §81).

Gregory of Nyssa had presented certain of these ideas more profoundly and in a more systematic manner. But the prestige of Dionysius contributed enormously to make them popular among the monks. Soon translated into Latin, the works of the Pseudo-Dionysius were retranslated in the ninth century by the Irish monk Scotus Erigenus; it is through this version that Dionysius was known in the West. His ideas were taken up again and elaborated by Maximus the Confessor, ''the most universal spirit of the seventh century and perhaps the last original thinker among the theologians of the Byzantine

Church."[36] In the form of *scholia,* Maximus the Confessor wrote a commentary on the mystical treatises of Dionysius, which was also translated by Erigenus. In fact, this corpus—the original and the explications of Maximus the Confessor—comprised the text of the Pseudo-Areopagite which influenced the thought of numerous Western mystics and theologians, from Bernard of Clairvaux and Thomas Aquinas to Nicholas of Cusa.[37]

258. The veneration of icons and iconoclasm

The grave crisis provoked by iconoclasm (eighth to ninth centuries) had multiple causes: political, social, and theological. Following the ban proclaimed in the Decalogue, Christians of the first two centuries did not fashion images. But in the Eastern Empire, the ban was ignored from the third century on when a religious iconography (figures or scenes inspired by the Scriptures) made its appearance in cemeteries and in rooms where the faithful gathered together. This innovation followed upon the blossoming of the cult of the relics. In the fourth and fifth centuries, the number of images multipled and their veneration became more pronounced. It is in the course of these two centuries that the criticism and the defense of the icon both gained their precise contours. The principal argument of the iconophiles was the pedagogical function—especially for the illiterate—and the sanctifying virtues of the images. It is only toward the end of the sixth and during the seventh centuries that the images became objects of cultic devotion, in the Churches as well as in private homes.[38] One prayed, one prostrated oneself before the icons; one embraced them, and took them on procession during certain ceremonies. During this period, there is an increase in the number of miraculous images—sources of supernatural power—which protect cities, palaces, and armies.[39]

36. H. C. Beck, cited by Pelikan, *The Spirit of Eastern Christendom,* p. 8. "Probably the single creative thinker of the century," wrote Werner Elart; "the true father of Byzantine theology" (Meyendorff).

37. Deno John Geanakoplos, *Interaction of the 'Sibling' Byzantine and Western Cultures in the Middle Ages and Italian Renaissance,* pp. 133ff.

38. Cf. Ernst Kitzinger, "The Cult of Images in the Age before Iconoclasm," p. 89.

39. Among the most celebrated were the icon of Christ of the city of Edessa (also

As Ernst Kitzinger has remarked, this belief in the supernatural power of images, presupposing a certain continuity between the image and the personage it represents, is the most important trait of the cult of the icons in the sixth and seventh centuries. The icon is ''an extension, an organ of the divinity itself.''[40]

The cult of images was officially banned by the Emperor Constantine V in 726, and declared anathema by the iconoclastic Synod of Constantinople in 754—the principal theological argument being the implicit idolatry in the glorification of the icons. The second iconoclastic synod, that of 815, rejected the cult of the images in the name of christology. For it is impossible to paint the figure of Christ without implying that one is representing the divine nature (which is a blasphemy), or without separating the two inseparable natures in order to paint solely the human nature (which is a heresy.)[41] By contrast, the Eucharist represents the true ''image'' of Christ, since it is imbued with the Holy Spirit; thus the Eucharist, in contrast to the icon, possesses both a divine and a material dimension.[42]

As to the iconophile theology, the most systematic treatment was elaborated by John of Damascus (675–749) and Theodore the Studite (759–826). In relying upon the Pseudo-Areopagite, the two authors underlined the continuity between the spiritual and the material. ''How do you, as someone who is visible, worship the things that are invisible?'' writes John of Damascus. The excessive ''spiritualism'' of the iconoclasts places them in the same category as the ancient gnostics who claimed that the body of Christ was not physical, but heavenly.[43] As a result of the Incarnation, the likeness of God has been rendered visible, thus annulling the Old Testament ban on imaging the divine. Accordingly, those who deny that Christ can be represented by an icon deny implicitly the reality of the Incarnation. However, our two authors specify that the image is not identical in essence and in substance

---

known as the Mandylion of Edessa), considered capable of repulsing the attack of the Persian army, and the image of Christ affixed above the great bronze door of the Imperial Palace, whose destruction in 727 marked the beginning of iconoclasm.

40. Kitzinger, ''The Cult of Images,'' p. 104. The images of the saints were inhabited by the Holy Spirit; ibid., pp. 140ff.

41. See Pelikan, *The Spirit of Eastern Christendom*, p. 129. Cf. Stephen Gero, *Byzantine Iconoclasm during the Reign of Constantine V*, p. 74.

42. Gero, p. 78; Pelikan, p. 109.

43. Pelikan, p. 122.

with its model. The image constitutes a resemblance which, while reflecting the model, maintains a distinction from it. Consequently, the iconoclasts are guilty of blasphemy when they consider the Eucharist as an image; for being identical essentially and substantially with Christ, the Eucharist *is* Christ, and not his image.[44]

As regards the icons of the saints, John of Damascus writes: "As long as they lived, the saints were filled with the Holy Spirit, and after their death, the grace of the Holy Spirit is never far from their souls, their tombs, or their holy images."[45] To be sure, the icons ought not to be adored in the same manner in which one would adore God. But they belonged to the same category of objects sanctified by the presence of Jesus Christ—as, for example, Nazareth, Golgotha, or the wood of the Cross. These places and objects have become the "recipients of divine energy" because it is through them that God effects our salvation. In our day, the icons take the place of the miracles and other acts of Jesus Christ which his disciples had had the privilege of seeing and admiring.[46]

In sum, just as the relics made possible a communication between Heaven and Earth, the icons reactualized the prodigious *illud tempus,* when Christ, the Virgin, and the Holy Apostles lived among men. If not equal in power to the relics, the icons were at least more easily accessible to the faithful: one found them in the most modest churches and chapels and in private homes. Moreover, their contemplation allowed access to a universe of symbols. As a result, the images were able to complete and deepen the religious instruction of the illiterate. (In effect, the iconography filled this role for all the rural populations of eastern Europe.)

Beyond the political and social factors, the iconoclastic fervor was fed by faults on both sides. On the one hand, the iconoclasts were ignorant of or repulsed by the symbolic function of sacred images; on the other, a number of iconophiles utilized the cult of the icons for their own profit or to assure the prestige, preponderance, and riches of their favorite ecclesiastical institutions.

---

44. Cf. ibid., p. 119; N. Baynes, "Idolatry and the Early Church," p. 135.

45. This text has been aptly commented upon by G. Mathews, *Byzantine Aesthetics,* pp. 103ff.

46. See the texts analyzed by Pelikan, p. 121. Just as the Evangelists have written of Christ with *words,* it is possible to write of him in *gold* in the icons; cf. ibid., p. 135.

33 Muhammad and the Unfolding of Islam

259. Allah, *deus otiosus* of the Arabs

Muhammad is the only one of all the founders of universal religions for whom we have a detailed biography.[1] This is not to say that one also knows his interior biography. But the historical information at our disposal is doubly precious: first, on his life and on the religious experiences which prepared and decided his own prophetic vocation; and second, on the Arabic civilization of his time and on the sociological structures of Mecca. The documentation explains neither the personality of Muhammad nor the success of his preaching, but it does enable us to better appreciate the creativity of the Prophet. It is important to have such rich historic documentation for at least one of the founders of the universal religions. We can better understand the power of the religious genius. We can see how a religious genius can use historic circumstances to make his message triumph, in short, to radically change the course of history.

Born in Mecca between 567 and 572, Muhammad belonged to a powerful tribe, the Quraysh. Orphaned at the age of six, he was brought up at first by his grandfather and later by his maternal uncle, Abû Tâlib.[2] At the age of twenty-five, he entered the service of a

1. The most important sources are the Quran (in Arabic: *al-Qur'ân,* "the Preaching") and the oral information transmitted by the Tradition (in Arabic: *al-Hadîth,* "the Talk," "the Dicta"). Let us add, however, that the historicity of these sources is not always guaranteed.

2. The nativity and childhood of the Prophet were soon transfigured, in conformity with the mythological scenario of exemplary saviors. During her pregnancy, his mother heard a voice announcing that her son would be the lord and the prophet of his people. At the moment of his birth, a brilliant light illuminated the entire world (cf. the

rather well-off widow, Khadîja, and made several caravan voyages into Syria. A little later, around 595, he married his patron, despite their difference in age (at that time Khadîja was forty years old). The marriage was a happy one; Muhammad, who was to marry nine women after the death of Khadîja, did not take another spouse during her lifetime. They had seven children: three sons who died at a young age, and four daughters (the youngest, Fâtima, would marry 'Alî, Muhammad's cousin). Khadîja had a considerable place in the Prophet's life; it is she who encouraged him in his religious vocation during his trials.

Little is known of Muhammad's life before the first revelations, around 610. According to the tradition, these were preceded by long periods of "spiritual retreats" (*tahannuth*) in caverns and other solitary places, a practice unknown to Arabic polytheism. Most probably, Muhammad was inspired by the night vigils, prayers, and meditations of certain Christian monks whom he had known or heard speak during his journeys. One of Khadîja's cousins was a Christian. Moreover, certain echoes of Christian teaching, both orthodox and sectarian (Nestorian, Gnostic), as well as the ideas and practices of the Jews, were known in Arab cities. However, there were only a few Christians in Mecca, and the majority of them were in a humble state (probably Abyssinian slaves) and poorly educated. The Jews were found in large numbers in Yathrib (the future Medina), and we shall see (§262) at which point the Prophet counted on their support.

However, at the time of Muhammad the religion of central Arabia seems not to have been modified by Judaeo-Christian influences. Despite its decadence, it retained the structures of Semitic polytheism. Mecca (*Makkah*) was the religious center. This name is mentioned in

---

births of Zarathustra, Mahāvīra, and the Buddha; §§101, 147, 152). He was born like a lamb, circumcised and with his umbilical cord already severed. As soon as he was born, he took a handful of earth and looked to the heavens. A Jew from Medina knew that the Paraclete had come into the world, and communicated this to his co-religionists. At the age of four years, two angels threw Muhammad to the earth, opened his chest, took out a drop of black blood from his heart and washed his viscera with the melting snow that they carried in a cup of gold (cf. Quran, sura 94:1f., "Did We not expand thy breast for thee . . ." etc. This initiatory rite is characteristic of shamanic initiations). At the age of twelve, he accompanied Abû Tâlib on a caravan trip into Syria. At Bostra, a Christian monk recognized on Muhammad's shoulder the mysterious signs of his prophetic vocation. See the sources cited by Tor Andrae, *Mohammed: The Man and His Faith,* pp. 34–38; W. Montgomery Watt, *Muhammad at Mecca,* pp. 34ff.

the Ptolemaic *Corpus* (second century A.D.) as *Makoraba,* a word derived from the Sabaean *Makuraba,* "sanctuary." In other words, from its beginning Mecca was a ceremonial center around which a city progressively arose.[3] In the middle of the consecrated territory, *Hima,* was found the sanctuary of the *Ka'ba* (lit. "cube"), an edifice open to the sky which encased within its corners the famous Black Stone, considered to be of celestial origin. In pre-Islamic times, just as it does today, the circumambulation of the Stone comprised an important ritual of the annual pilgrimage (*Hajj*) to Arafat, which is located several kilometers from Mecca. The Lord of the *Ka'ba* was supposed to be Allah (lit. "God"; the same theonym used by the Jews and Arab Christians to designate God). But Allah had already become a *deus otiosus*; his cult had been reduced to certain offerings of firstfruits (grains and animals), which were brought to him conjointly with various local divinities.[4] More important were the three goddesses of central Arabia: Manat ("Destiny"), Allat (feminine form of Allah), and Al'Uzza ("the Powerful"). Regarded as the "daughters of Allah," they enjoyed so much popularity that, at the beginning of his preaching, Muhammad himself made the error (corrected later) of praising their function as intermediaries before Allah.

In short, the pre-Islamic religion resembled the popular religion of Palestine in the sixth century B.C., as that is reflected, for example, in the documents of the Judaeo-Aramaic colony of Elephantine on the Upper Nile: alongside of Jahweh-Jahu, one venerated Bethel and Harambethel, the goddess Arat, and a god of vegetation.[5] In Mecca, the service in the sanctuary was confined to the members of influential families; the responsibilities, well rewarded, were transmitted from father to son. No sacerdotal body, properly speaking, seems to have existed. Although the term *Kôhên,* which among the Hebrews designates a "priest," may be cognate with the Arab word *Kâhin,* the latter indicated a "seer" or "diviner" who, possessed by a *jinn,* was capable of predicting the future and retrieving certain lost objects or wandering camels.[6] The only monotheists among the contemporaries of

3. This is, moreover, a general process; see Paul Wheatley, *The Pivot of the Four Quarters* (Chicago, 1971), passim.
4. See J. Henninger, *Les fêtes de printemps chez les Sémites,* pp. 42ff.
5. Cf. A. Vincent, *La religion des Judéo-Araméens d'Éléphantine* (Paris, 1937), pp. 593ff., 622ff., 675ff.
6. From the beginning of his preaching, Muhammad was often accused of being inspired by a *jinn.*

Muhammad were several poets and visionaries known by the name of *hanîf*. Some were influenced by Christianity, but the eschatology characteristic of Christianity (and later of Islam) was foreign to them, as it seems to have been strange to the Arabs in general.[7]

The prophetic mission of Muhammad was launched after several ecstatic experiences, which in some sense constitute the prelude to the revelation. In sura 53:1–8, he recalls the first among them: "This is naught but a revelation revealed, taught him by one terrible in power, very strong; he stood poised, being on the higher horizon, then drew near and suspended hung, two bows'-lengths away or nearer, then revealed to his servant that he revealed" (4–10). Muhammad had seen him the second time near a jujube-tree: "Indeed, he saw one of the greatest signs of his Lord" (17–18). In sura 81:22–23, Muhammad returned to this vision: "Your comrade is not possessed; he truly saw him on the clear horizon!"[8]

It transpired that the visions had been accompanied by auditory revelations, the only ones that the Quran considered to be of divine origin. The first mystical experiences which determined his prophetic career are reported in a tradition transmitted by Ibn Ishâk (d. 768). When Muhammad was asleep in the cave where he was making his annual retreat, the angel Gabriel came to him, holding a book in his hand, and ordered him: " 'Read!' As Muhammad refused to read, the Angel pressed '. . . the book on his mouth and nostrils' so hard that he was almost suffocated. Finally for the fourth time the Angel repeated, 'Read!' Muhammad asked, 'What should I read?' Then the Angel answered: 'Recite: In the Name of thy Lord who created, created Man from a blood-clot. Recite: And thy Lord is the Most-Generous, who taught by the Pen, taught man that he knew not' " (96:1–5). Muhammad recited and the Angel ended by withdrawing from him. "I awoke," said Muhammad, "from my sleep, and it was as if they had written a message on my heart." Muhammad left the cave and had scarcely arrived on the mountain when he heard a celestial voice say to him: " 'O Muhammad, thou art Allah's Apostle, and I am Gabriel!' I looked up and saw Gabriel in the form of a man with crossed legs at the horizon of heaven. I remained standing and observed him, and moved

7. Cf. Tor Andrae, *Les origines de l'Islam et le christianisme*, pp. 41ff. The monotheistic tendency of the archaic Arabian religion has been long established by J. Wellhausen, *Reste arabischen Heidentums*, pp. 215ff.

8. Unless other wise indicated, citations of the Quran are taken from Arthur J. Arberry, *The Koran Interpreted*, vols. 1 and 2 (London and New York, 1955).

neither backwards nor forwards. And when I turned my gaze from him, I continued to see him on the horizon, no matter where I turned."[9]

The authenticity of these experiences seems assured.[10] Muhammad's initial resistance recalls the hesitation of shamans and numerous mystics and prophets before assuming their vocation. It is likely that the Quran did not mention the oneiric vision in the cavern in order to avoid the accusation that the Prophet had been possessed by a *jinn*. But other allusions of the Quran confirm the veracity of the inspiration.[11] The command to "recite" was often accompanied by violent trembling, attacks of fevers, or chills.

260. Muhammad, the "Apostle of God"

For nearly three years, Muhammad communicated the first divine messages only to Khadîja and to several intimate friends (his cousin 'Alî, his adoptive son Zaïd, and the two future caliphs, 'Uthman and Abû Bakr). Some time later, the revelations of the Angel were interrupted and Muhammad passed through a time of anguish and discouragement. But a new divine message restored his confidence: "Thy Lord has neither forsaken thee nor hates thee, and the Last shall be better for thee than the First. Thy Lord shall give thee, and thou shalt be satisfied" (93:3–5).

It is as a result of one vision in 612, which commanded him to make his revelations public, that Muhammad began his apostolate. From the beginning, he insists on the power and mercy of God, who has made men "from a blood-clot" (96:1; cf. 80:17–22; 87:1); who has taught him the Quran and who has "taught him the Explanation" (55:1–4); who created heaven, the hills, earth, and the camels (88:17–20). He evokes the goodness of the Lord, recalling of his own life: "Did he not

9. Ibn Ishâk, translated by Andrae, *Mohammed,* pp. 43–44. See another translation in Blachère, *Le problème de Mahomet,* pp. 39–40.

10. Certain modern historians suggest that the two phases—the oneiric vision in the cave and the vision of the angel Gabriel projected onto the horizon—did not belong to the same experience; cf. Andrae, *Mohammed,* pp. 45f. But this objection lacks force.

11. "Move not thy tongue with it to hasten it; Ours it is to gather, and to recite it, So when We recite it, follow thou its recitation" (75:16–18). In other words, all personal improvisation of the Quran is prohibited.

find thee an orphan and shelter thee?'' etc. (93:3–8). He contrasts the ephemeral character of all existence to the perenniality of the Creator: ''All that dwells upon the earth is perishing, yet still abides the Face of thy Lord, majestic, splendid'' (55:26–27). However, it is surprising that in these first proclamations, Muhammad mentions the unity of God only once (''And set not up with God another god!'' 51:51); this is probably a later interpolation.[12]

Another theme of his preaching is the imminence of the Judgment and the resurrection of the dead: ''For when the Trumpet is sounded that day will be a harsh day, for the unbelievers not easy'' (74:8–10). There are other such references and allusions in the oldest suras, but the most complete is found at the beginning of a later one: ''When heaven is rent asunder . . . , when earth is stretched out and casts forth what is in it [= her burden; cf. 99:2], and voids itself . . . , O Man! Thou art laboring unto thy Lord laboriously, and thou shalt encounter Him. Then as for him who is given his book in his right hand, he shall surely receive an easy reckoning. . . . But as for him who is given his book behind his back, he shall call for destruction and he shall roast at a Blaze'' (84:1–12). In a number of suras dictated later, Muhammad expands the apocalyptic descriptions: the mountains will be displaced and, mixed all together, will become ashes and dust; the heavenly vault will burst, and the moon and the stars will be extinguished and sink. The Prophet speaks also of a cosmic conflagration, and of jets of fire and heated brass that will be cast upon men (55:35).

At the second sound of the trumpet, the dead will resuscitate and go forth from their tombs. The resurrection will occur in the blink of an eye. From behind the broken sky, the throne of God will appear, supported by eight angels and surrounded by celestial troops. Men will be reassembled before the throne, the good to the right, the miscreants to the left. Then Judgment will begin on the basis of the notes written in the *Book of Acts (of Men)*. The prophets of the past will be called together to testify that they had proclaimed monotheism and that they had warned their contemporaries. The miscreants will be condemned to the tortures of Hell.[13] However, Muhammad gives more attention to

12. See Bell, *The Qur'an;* Watt, *Muhammed at Mecca,* p. 64. In the beginning, the suras were memorized, but they began to be committed to writing once opposition of the polytheists stiffened; cf. Blachère, *Le problème de Mahomet,* pp. 52ff.

13. Let us note, however, that they are less terrifying than certain Buddhist or

the blessings which attend the faithful in Paradise. They are above all of a material sort: the clear rivers, the trees whose branches are bent with fruits, meats of all sorts, the young men "beautiful as pearls" who serve a delicious drink, the houris, chaste virgins especially created by Allah (56:26–43, etc.). Muhammad does not speak of the "souls" or of the "spirits" which suffer in Hell or exult in Paradise. The resurrection of the body is in fact a new Creation. Since the interval between death and the Judgment constitutes an unconscious state, the resurrected person will have the impression that the Judgment has occurred immediately after his death.[14]

In proclaiming, "There is no god but Allah!," Muhammad did not envisage the foundation of a new religion. He wished simply "to awaken" his fellow citizens, to persuade them to venerate Allah alone: they already recognized him as the creator of Heaven and Earth and the bestower of fertility (cf. 29:61–63); they evoked him on the occasion of the great crises and great dangers (29:65, 31:31; 17:69); and they swore "by God the most earnest oaths" (35:42; 16:38). Allah was, besides, the Lord of the Ka'ba. In one of the oldest suras, Muhammad asks the members of his own tribe, the Quraysh, to "serve the Lord of this House who has fed them against hunger and hath made them safe from fear" (106:3–4).

However, opposition was not slow to appear. The causes and pretexts are multiple. Ibn Ishâk affirms that when the Prophet, on the order of Allah, proclaimed the true religion (Islam, "submission"), his fellow citizens did not oppose it for such time as he did not speak evil of their gods. The tradition tells that after verse 20 of sura 53, which concerns the three goddesses Allat, Al'Uzza, and Manat, there first followed three verses: "They are sublime goddesses and their intercession is certainly desirable." But later Muhammad took the stance that these words were inspired in him by Satan. He thus replaced them as follows: "They are naught but names yourselves have named, and your fathers. . . . And yet guidance has come to them from their Lord."

Christian descriptions. It is important to observe that the commonly accepted Muslim eschatology contains a number of motifs absent in the Quran (e.g., punishment in the tomb, the Bridge above Hell, the Lake of Fire, etc.).

14. Sinners will be ready for judgment whether they have remained in their tombs only a day or a single hour; cf. 10:46ff.; 4:34ff.; etc.

This incident is instructive for two reasons. First of all, it shows the sincerity of the Prophet: he recognized that, in reciting the words dictated by divine inspiration, he had been deceived by Satan.[15] In the second place, he justifies the annulment of the two verses by the omnipotence and absolute freedom of God.[16] In effect, the Quran is the only Holy Book which knows the freedom to annul certain passages of Revelation.

For the rich oligarchy of the Quraysh to renounce "paganism" was equivalent to the loss of their privileges. Moreover, to recognize Muhammad as the true Apostle of God also implied the recognition of his political supremacy. Graver still, the revelation proclaimed by the Prophet condemned their polytheistic ancestors to perpetual Hell, an unacceptable idea for a traditional society. For a large portion of the population, the principal objection was the "existential banality" of Muhammad: "They say: What ails this Messenger that he eats food, and goes in the markets? Why has an angel not been sent down to him, to be a warner with him?" (25:7). His revelations were mocked and considered either to have been his own inventions or to have been inspired by *jinns*. Above all, the announcement of the end of the world and the resurrection of the body provoked irony and sarcasm. Besides, time passed and the eschatological catastrophe delayed its coming.[17]

Muhammad was also reproached for the absence of miracles: "They say: We will not believe thee till thou makest a spring to gush forth from the earth for us, Or till thou possessest a garden of palms and vines, and thou makest rivers to gush forth abundantly; . . . or thou bringest God and the angels as a surety; . . . or till thou goest up into heaven; and we will not believe thy going up till thou bringest down on us a book that we may read!" (17:93–96).

15. Most probably Muhammad considered the three goddesses to be intercessory angels; in fact, the belief in angels was accepted by Islam, and, later, angelology would play an important role in Shi'ism (cf. §281). But taking into account the risk which the intercession of the goddesses (= angels) would represent for his strictly monotheistic theology, Muhammad abrogated the two verses.

16. "And for whatever verse We abrogate or cast into oblivion, we bring a better or the like of it; knowest thou not that God is powerful over everything?" (2:10).

17. Muhammad insisted on the inevitability of the end of the world; he did not specify when the event would take place, although certain suras lead one to think that it would be accomplished during his lifetime.

261. The ecstatic voyage to Heaven and the Holy Book

In sum, Muhammad was asked to demonstrate the authenticity of his vocation by rising to Heaven and bringing back a Holy Book. In other words, he had to conform to the model illustrated by Moses, Daniel, Enoch, Mani, and the other messengers who, in rising to Heaven, had met with God and received from his right hand the Book containing the Divine Revelation. This scenario was as familiar to normative Judaism and the Jewish apocalyptic as it was to the Samaritans, Gnostics, and Mandaeans. Its origin goes back to the fabulous Mesopotamian King Emmenduraki, and draws upon a traditional royal ideology.[18]

The retorts and the justifications of the Prophet developed and multiplied themselves in proportion to the accusations of the unbelievers. As with other prophets and apostles before him, including certain of his rivals, Muhammad considered and proclaimed himself the Apostle (= Messenger) of God (*rasûl Allah*):[19] he brought his fellow citizens a divine revelation. The Quran is "the Revelation . . . in a clear Arabic tongue" (26:194–95); it was thus perfectly intelligible to the inhabitants of Mecca; if they persisted in their disbelief, it was through their blindness before the divine signs (23:68), through pride and heedlessness (27:14; 33:68; etc.). Besides, Muhammad knew very well that similar trials had been undergone by the prophets sent by God before him: Abraham, Moses, Noah, David, John the Baptist, and Jesus (21:66ff., 76ff.).

The celestial ascension (*mî'râj*) is also an answer to the unbelievers: "Glory be to Him, who carried His servants by night from the Holy Mosque to the Further Mosque the precincts of which We have blessed, that We have blessed, that We might show Him some of Our signs! He is the All-hearing, the All-Seeing" (17:1). The tradition places this nocturnal voyage in 617 or 619; mounted on the winged mare, al-Boraq, Muhammad visits the terrestrial Jerusalem and ascends to the Heavens. The narration of this ecstatic voyage is amply

---

18. See G. Widengren, *The Ascension of the Apostle and the Heavenly Book*, pp. 7 ff. and passim; idem, *Muhammad, the Apostle of God, and His Ascension*, pp. 115 and passim.

19. Cf. Widengren, *Muhammad*, pp. 16ff. It is a matter of a formula used abundantly in the ancient Near East, and which will be reclaimed by the Shî'ite Imâms; cf. ibid., chap. 2.

documented in the later sources. The scenario is not always the same. According to certain versions, the Prophet, on his winged horse, contemplates Hell and Paradise, and approaches the throne of Allah. The voyage had lasted only an instant: the jar that Muhammad had turned upside down in leaving still had not spilled all its contents when he returned to his room. Another tradition supplies a stairway which Muhammad climbs, led on by the angel Gabriel, to the gates of Heaven. He arrives before Allah and learns from his mouth that he has been chosen before all the other prophets and that he, Muhammad, is his "friend." God confides to him the Quran and certain esoteric knowledge, which Muhammad must not communicate to the faithful.[20]

This ecstatic voyage will play a central role in later Muslim mysticism and theology. It illustrates a specific trait of the genius of Muhammad and of Islam, which it is well to note now: that is, the will to assimilate and integrate traditional mythico-ritual practices, ideas, and scenarios into a new religious synthesis. We have just seen how the Islamic tradition has revalued the archaic theme of the Holy Book, received by an apostle at the time of his celestial voyage. We will later see the results of Islam's confrontations with Judaism and with other religious traditions, and even with a "pagan" and immemorial tradition such as that of the *ka'ba.*

262. The Emigration to Medina

The position of Muhammad and his followers was constantly aggravated. The dignitaries of Mecca decided to exclude them from the rights belonging to their respective tribes. Now an Arab's sole protection was his membership in a tribe. Muhammad was nevertheless defended by his uncle, Abû Tâlib, even though the latter would not embrace Islam. But after Abû Tâlib's death, his son, Abû Lahab, succeeded in dispossessing the Prophet of his rights. The problem posed

20. See the texts translated and commented upon by Widengren, *Muhammad,* pp. 102ff. One will find the translation of long extracts of al-Baghawî and Suyûti in Arthur Jeffrey, *Islam,* pp. 35–46. Certain scholars suggest that, thanks to the Latin translation of the Arab text on the *mî-râj,* Dante was able to use a number of details in the writing of the *Divina Commedia (Divine Comedy).* See Asin Palacios, *La escatologia musulmana en la Divina Commedia;* E. Cerulli, *Il "Libro della Scala."*

by this persistently violent opposition on the part of the Quraysh was resolved on the theological level: it is Allah himself who had willed it. Their blind attachment to polytheism was decided, for all eternity, by Allah (cf. 16:39, 10:75; 6:39). The break with the unbelievers was thus inevitable: "I serve not what you serve and you are not serving what I serve" (109:1–2).

Around 615, in order to shelter them from the persecutions, but also because he feared a certain schism,[21] Muhammad encouraged a group of seventy or eighty Muslims to emigrate into a Christian country, Abyssinia. The Prophet, who considered himself from the beginning to be uniquely sent to convert the Quraysh, now approached the nomads and the dwellers of two oasis cities, Tâ'if and Yathrib. He was unsuccessful among the nomads and Bedouins of Tâ'if, but the contacts with Yathrib (the future Medina) were encouraging. Muhammad chose to exile himself to Yathrib, where the traditional religion was not debased by economic and political interests, and where many Jews—that is, monotheists—were found. Moreover, this oasis city had exhausted itself in a long internecine war. Certain tribes considered that a Prophet, whose authority was based not on blood, but on religion, could disregard tribal relations and fill the role of arbiter. In addition, one of the two principal tribes had in great part already embraced Islam, convinced that God had sent Muhammad with a message addressed to all the Arabs.

In 622, on the occasion of the pilgrimage to Mecca, a delegation of seventy-five men and two women from Yathrib met with the Prophet in secret and took upon themselves by a solemn oath the responsibility of fighting for him. The faithful then began to leave Mecca in small groups for Yathrib. The trip through the desert (more than 300 kilometers) lasted nine days. Muhammad was one of the last to leave, accompanied by his father-in-law Abû Bakr. On the twenty-fourth of September, they arrived at Qoba, a hamlet in the environs of Medina. The *Hijra,* or "Emigration" (in Arabic, *al Hîjra*), had just been successfully completed. A short time later, the Prophet entered Medina and allowed his camel to choose the site of his future dwelling. The house, which was also to serve as the place of assembly for the faithful to meet for their common prayers, was only ready a year later, since quarters had to be built for Muhammad's wives.

21. Watt, *Muhammad at Mecca,* pp. 115ff.

Muhammad's religious and political activity at Medina differentiates itself clearly from that of the Meccan period. The change is evident in the suras dictated after the *Hijra:* they deal above all with the organization of the community of the faithful (*ummah*)[22] and its socioreligious institutions. The theological structure of Islam had been given shape at the moment that the Prophet left Mecca. But it is at Medina that he specified the rules of the cult (the prayers, fasts, alms, and pilgrimages). From the beginning, Muhammad displayed an exceptional political intelligence. He brought about the fusion of the Muslims who had come from Mecca (the ''Emigrés'') with the converts of Medina (the ''Auxiliaries'') by proclaiming himself their sole leader. Tribal loyalties were thus abolished. Henceforth, there existed only a community of Muslims organized as a theocratic society. In the Constitution, probably established in 623, Muhammad decreed that the Emigrés and the Auxiliaries (that is to say, the *ummah*) formed a single people distinct from all the others; he specified, however, the rights and privileges of the other clans and also of the three Jewish tribes. No doubt certain of the inhabitants of Medina were dissatisfied with Muhammad's initiatives. But his political prestige increased in proportion to his military victories. Yet it was above all the new revelations communicated by the Angel which assured the success of his decisions.[23]

Muhammad's greatest disappointment at Medina was the reaction of the three Jewish tribes. Before the Emigration, the Prophet had chosen Jerusalem as the point of orientation (*quiblah*) for prayers, in agreement with the Jewish practice; and, once he was established at Medina, he borrowed from other Israelite rituals. The suras dictated in the first years of the *Hijra* bear witness to his efforts to convert the Jews: ''People of the Book, now there has come to you Our Messenger, making clear to you many things you have been concealing of the Book, and effacing many things'' (5:19). Muhammad would have permitted the

22. On the meaning and history of this term, see, most definitively, F. M. Denny, ''The Meaning of *Ummah* in the Qur'ân.''

23. On the occasion of the first foray of the ''Emigrés,'' the Medinans cried out that it was a sacrilege, since the truce of the sacred month (*rajab,* December 623) had been violated. But Muhammad received this divine message: ''Fighting in it is a heinous thing, but to bar from God's way, and disbelief in Him, and the Holy Mosque, and to expel its people from it—that is more heinous in God's sight; and persecution is more heinous than slaying'' (2:213).

Jews to retain their traditional rituals, if they had recognized him as the Prophet.[24] But the attitude of the Jews was consistently hostile. They pointed to the errors in the Quran, proving that Muhammad did not know the Hebrew Scriptures.

The break took place on 11 February 624, when the Prophet received a new revelation enjoining the Muslims to reorient their prayers, directing them no longer toward Jerusalem but toward Mecca (2:136). With his ingenious intuition, Muhammad proclaimed that the *Ka'ba* had been built by Abraham and his son Ishmael (2:127). It was only due to the sins of the ancestors that the sanctuary now found itself under the control of idolaters. Henceforth, "the Arab world has its Temple, one more ancient than that of Jerusalem. The world has its monotheism, *Hanifism.* . . . By this shift, Islam, momentarily diverted from its origins, returns to them forever."[25] The religious and political consequences of this decision are considerable: for one thing, the future of Arab unity will be assured; in addition, later reflections on the *Ka'ba*[26] will add to a theology of the Temple under the sign of the oldest, and thus the "truest," monotheism. For the moment, Muhammad detached himself not only from Judaism but from Christianity; these two "religions of the Book" had not known how to conserve their original purity. That is why God had sent his *final* messenger, and why Islam was destined to succeed Christianity as the latter had succeeded Judaism.

263. From exile to triumph

In order to subsist, Muhammad and the Emigrés had to undertake raids against Meccan caravans. Their first victory took place at Badr in March 627 (cf. 3:123); they lost fourteen men, the idolaters lost seventy, and forty others were taken prisoner. The booty, so important, as well as the prisoners, were distributed by Muhammad in equal parts to all the combatants. One month later, the Prophet forced one of the three Jewish tribes to depart from Medina, leaving behind their houses and goods. The following year, the Muslims were vanquished at Uhud by a Meccan army estimated at 3,000 men; Muhammad himself was

24. Cf. Watt, *Muhammad at Mecca,* pp. 199ff.
25. Blachère, *Le problème de Mahomet,* p. 104.
26. See, e.g., Henry Corbin, "La Configuration du Temple de la Ka'ba comme secret de la vie spirituelle."

wounded. But the decisive event in this religious guerilla war is represented by the so-called battle of the "Ditch," named because on the counsel of a Persian, trenches were dug in front of the entranceways to the oasis city. According to the tradition, 4,000 Meccans laid siege in vain to Medina for two weeks; a tornado dispersed them in disarray. During the siege, Muhammad noticed the suspect behavior of certain pseudo-converts and of the Qurayza, the last of the Jewish tribes remaining in Medina. After the victory, he accused the Jews of treason and ordered their massacre.

In April 628, a new revelation (48:27) gave Muhammad the guarantee that the faithful could undertake the pilgrimage to the *Ka'ba*. Although some were hesitant, the caravan of believers approached the holy city. They did not succeed in entering Mecca, but the Prophet transformed this partial defeat into a victory: he demanded, as the direct representative of God, that the believers swear their absolute fidelity (48:10). He needed such an oath, because a short time later he concluded a truce with the Meccans which might have appeared humiliating, but which permitted him to make the pilgrimage the following year. Moreover, the Quraysh assured the Muslims a peace of ten years.

In 629, accompanied by 2,000 faithful, the Prophet in effect entered the city which had been temporarily abandoned by the polytheists, and celebrated the ritual of the pilgrimage. The triumph of Islam appeared imminent; moreover, numerous Bedouin tribes, and even representatives of the Quraysh oligarchy, began to convert. The same year, Muhammad sent an expedition to Mu'ta, on the frontier of the Byzantine Empire. Though the expedition was checked, it did not diminish his prestige. Mu'ta indicated the principal direction toward which Islam should be preached; Muhammad's successors understood well.

In January 630, with 10,000 men (according to the tradition) and under the pretext that the Meccans had supported a hostile tribe, the Prophet suspended the truce and occupied the city without striking a blow. The idols in the *Ka'ba* were destroyed, the sanctuary purified, and all the privileges of the polytheists were abolished. Once he was master of the holy city, Muhammad demonstrated great tolerance; with the exception of six of his most implacable enemies, who were executed, he forbade his followers to exact vengeance against the inhabitants. Guided by his admirable political instinct, Muhammad did not set up the capital of his theocracy at Mecca; after the pilgrimage, he returned to Medina.

The following year, in 631, the Prophet did not undertake the pilgrimage himself, but sent Abû Bakr to represent him. It was on this occasion that Muhammad, spurred on by a new revelation, proclaimed a total war against polytheism: "God is quit, and His Messenger, of the idolaters. . . . Then, when the sacred months are drawn away, slay the idolaters wherever you find them . . . . But if they repent, and perform the prayer, and pay the alms, then let them go their way; God is All-forgiving, All-compassionate. And if any of the idolaters seeks of thee protection, grant him protection till he hears the words of God; then do thou convey him to his place of security—that, because they are people who do know not" (9:3–6).[27]

As if impelled by a presentiment, Muhammad returned to Mecca in February/March 632; this was his last pilgrimage. On this occasion, he meticulously prescribed the details of the ritual of the *Hajj,* which are still followed to this day. And the Angel dictated to him these words of Allah: "Today I have perfected your religion for you, and I completed My blessing upon you, and I have approved Islam for your religion" (5:5–6). According to the tradition, at the end of his "Pilgrimage of Farewell," Muhammad cried out: "Lord! Have I fulfilled my mission well?" And the crowd replied: "Yes, you have fulfilled it well!"

On his return to Medina, in the last days of May 632, Muhammad fell ill. On 8 June, he died in the arms of his favorite wife, Aïsha. There was great distress. Certain individuals refused to accept the Prophet's death; they believed that Muhammad had risen to heaven like Jesus. His body was not interred in a cemetery but in a room of Aïsha's apartment, where a funeral monument was erected that is still today almost as sacred for the Muslims as the *Ka'ba.* Abû Bakr, who was elected caliph, which is to say "successor" to the Prophet, addressed the faithful: "If one venerates Muhammad, Muhammad is dead; but if one venerates God, Muhammad is living and does not die!"

27. As to the monotheists, "the people of the Book," Muhammad reminded them on another occasion: "the Torah and the Gospel, and what was sent down to them from their Lord. . . . Surely they that believe, and those of Jewry and the Sabaeans and those Christians, whosoever believes in God and the Last Day, and works righteousness—no fear shall be on them, neither shall they sorrow" (5:68–69).

264. The message of the Quran

The history of religions and universal history know of no enterprise comparable to that of Muhammad. The conquest of Mecca and the foundation of a theocratic state proved that his political genius was not inferior to his religious genius. It is true that circumstances—most notably, the contradictions of the Meccan oligarchy—were favorable to the Prophet. But these explain neither the theology, the preaching, nor the success of Muhammad, any more than the perenniality of his creation: Islam and the Muslim theocracy.

Undoubtedly the Prophet knew, either directly or indirectly, certain religious ideas and practices of the Jews and Christians. Concerning Christianity, his information was rather approximative. He spoke of Jesus and Mary, but indicated that they are not of divine nature (5:16–20), since they have been created (3:59). On several occasions, he alluded to the infancy of Jesus, his miracles and his Apostles ("Auxiliaries"). Against the opinion of the Jews, and in agreement with the Gnostics and Docetists, Muhammad denied Jesus's crucifixion and death.[28] However, he ignored Jesus's role as Redeemer, the message of the New Testament, the sacraments, and the Christian Mystery. The Prophet evoked the Christian triad as God-Jesus-Mary; his informants probably knew the Monophysite Church of Abyssinia, where the Virgin was venerated in an excessive manner.[29] On the other hand, one also recognizes certain Nestorian influences; for example, his belief that death renders the soul completely unconscious, and that the martyrs of the faith are immediately transported to Paradise. Similarly, the idea of a series of successive descents of the Revelation was shared by many of the Gnostic Judaeo-Christian sects.

But no external influence can serve to explain Muhammad's vocation or the structure of his preaching. In proclaiming the imminence of the Judgment and in recalling that before the throne of God man would be alone, Muhammad had shown the religious inanity of the conflicts and complexities of tribal relations. He reintegrated his individual followers into a new community of a religious nature, the *ummah*. He

28. "They did not slay him, neither crucified him, only a likeness of that was shown to them; . . . God raised him up to Him" (4:157–58).

29. Cf. Andrae, *Les origines de l'Islam,* pp. 209–10. It is also necessary to consider that the word designating "Spirit" in Semitic languages is feminine.

thus created the Arab nation, while at the same time allowing for an expansion of Islam that could widen the community of believers beyond ethnic and racial frontiers. The energy that had been expended in interminable intertribal wars was channeled into exterior wars against the pagans, wars undertaken in the name of Allah and for the total triumph of monotheism. However, in his campaigns against nomad tribes, and above all against the Meccans, Muhammad won more by skillful negotiations than by arms, setting up an exemplary model for his successors, the caliphs.

Finally, in revealing the Quran, he promoted his fellow citizens to the same rank as the two other "peoples of the Book" and ennobled Arabic as a liturgical and theological language with a view to its becoming the language of an ecumenical culture.

From the viewpoint of religious morphology, Muhammad's message, such as it is formulated in the Quran, represents the purest expression of absolute monotheism. Allah is God, the only God; he is perfectly free, omniscient, and all-powerful; he is the Creator of the earth and the heavens, of all that exists, and "increasing creation as He wills" (35:1). It is thanks to this continual creation that nights follow days, that water descends from heaven, and that the ship "sails on the sea" (2:164). In other words, Allah rules not only the cosmic rhythms but also the works of men. All his acts are free, and ultimately arbitrary, since they depend solely on his decision. Allah is free to contradict himself; let us recall the annulment of certain suras (§260).

Man is weak, not because of an original sin but because he is only a creature; yet he finds himself in a resacralized world as a result of the revelations communicated by God to his final Prophet. *Every act—* physiological, physical, social, historic—by the simple fact that it takes place thanks to God, finds itself under his jurisdiction. *Nothing* in the world is free or independent of God. But Allah is compassionate, and his Prophet has revealed a religion much simpler than the two preceeding monotheisms. Islam does not constitute a church and there is no priesthood. The cult can be practiced anywhere; a sanctuary is not necessary for religious worship.[30] Religious life is ruled by institutions which are at the same time juridical norms, notably the five "Pillars of Faith." The most important "pillar" is the *shalât,* the canonical cult

---

30. However, it is recommended that the faithful congregate in a public place at midday on Friday; 62:9.

or prayer comprising the five daily prostrations; the second is the *zakât* or obligatory almsgiving; the third, *sawn,* designates fasting from dawn to dusk during the entire month of *Râmâdan;* the fourth is the pilgrimage (*hajj*); and the fifth comprises the "profession of faith" (*shahâdat*), that is, the repetition of the formula: "There is no God but Allah, and Muhammad is His Prophet!"[31]

Given man's fallibility, the Quran does not encourage either asceticism or monasticism. "O Children of Adam! Take your adornment at every place of worship; and eat and drink, but be you not prodigal!" (7:31). The Quran addresses itself neither to saints nor the perfected, but to all men. Muhammad limits the number of legitimate wives to four (4:3), without specifying the number of concubines and slaves.[32] As to social differences, they are accepted, but all the faithful are equal in the *ummah.* Slavery is not abolished; however, the condition of slaves was better than in the Roman Empire.

In his "politics," Muhammad's mission reminds one of certain figures and concepts in the various books of the Old Testament. His "politics" is inspired, directly or indirectly, by Allah. Universal history is the uninterrupted manifestation of God; even the infidels' victories fulfill God's will. Total and permanent war is thus indispensable in order to convert the entire world to monotheism. Whatever the case, war is preferable to apostasy and to anarchy.

The pilgrimage and rituals accomplished at the *Ka'ba*—considered as the "House of Allah"—appear to contradict the absolute monotheism preached by Muhammad. But as we indicated earlier (§262), the Prophet wished to integrate Islam into the Abrahamic tradition. Alongside other symbols and scenarios presented in the Quran—the Holy Book, Muhammad's celestial ascension, the role of the archangel Gabriel, etc.—the pilgrimage will be continually reinterpreted and revalorized by later theology and mysticism. One must also consider the oral tradition transmitted in the *hadîth* ("dicta" of the Prophet) which will likewise be legitimated by numerous interpretations and specula-

31. This formula is not literally attested in the Quran, but its sense is omnipresent there; cf. Watt, *Muhammad at Mecca,* p. 308.

32. In response to European criticisms, certain Orientalists answer that this was already a form of progress in comparison with the sexual anarchy of pre-Islamic paganism. This "justification" of Islam, while valid on the sociological and moral plane, is fruitless, and indeed sacrilegious, from the perspective of Quranic theology. No detail of the Revelation needs to be "justified."

tions. Allah will always keep his position as God, unique and absolute, and Muhammad will be the Prophet *par excellence*. But like Judaism and Christianity, Islam will come to accept a certain number of intermediaries and intercessors.

265. The irruption of Islam into the Mediterranean and the Near East

As with the Jews and the Romans, Islam—especially in its initial phase—saw in historic events the episodes of a sacred history. It is the spectacular military victories won by the first caliphs that assured first of all the survival, and then the triumph, of Islam. In fact, the death of the Prophet unleashed a crisis which could have been fatal to the new religion. According to a tradition which has come to be accepted by the majority of Muslims, when Muhammad died, he had not designated a successor. Abû Bakr, the father of his favorite wife Aïsha, was elected caliph before the Prophet's interment. However, Muhammad's predilection for 'Alî, the husband of his daughter Fâtima and the father of his only still-living grandsons, Hasan and Husayn, was well known; most likely, Muhammad would have chosen 'Alî as his successor. But to save the unity of the *ummah,* 'Alî and his partisans accepted the election of Abû Bakr; as the latter was elderly, 'Alî did not doubt that he would succeed him quickly. For the moment, the essential need was to avert a crisis fatal to Islam. The Bedouin tribes were already beginning to detach themselves. It was the expeditions immediately undertaken by Abû Bakr that succeeded in subduing them. Immediately afterward, the caliph then organized raids against Syria, a rich province under Byzantine suzerainty.

Abû Bakr died two years later in 634, but he had already named one of his generals, 'Umar, as his successor. During the caliphate of this great strategist (634–644), the Muslim victories unfolded at a staggering pace. Vanquished in the battle of Yarmuk, the Byzantines abandoned Syria in 636. Antioch fell in 637, and in the same year the Sassanid Empire collapsed. The conquest of Egypt took place in 642 and that of Carthage in 694. Before the end of the seventh century, Islam had come to dominate North Africa, Syria and Palestine, Asia

Minor, Mesopotamia, and Iraq. Only Byzantium still resisted, but its territory was considerably reduced.[33]

Nevertheless, despite these unprecedented successes, the unity of the *ummah* was gravely compromised. Fatally wounded by a Persian slave, 'Umar had the time to designate six companions of the Prophet to elect his successor. Overlooking 'Alî and his partisans (*shî'at 'Alî*, lit., "party of 'Alî" or Shî'ah, Shî-ism), the six chose the Prophet's other son-in-law, 'Uthman (644–656). Belonging to the aristocratic clan of the Ummayah, former adversaries of Muhammad, 'Uthman distributed the key posts of the Empire to the notables from Mecca. After 'Uthman was assassinated by Bedouins of the garrisons of Egypt and Iraq, 'Alî was proclaimed caliph by the Medinans. For the Shî'ites, who recognize no "successor" outside the family of the Prophet and his descendants, 'Alî was the first true caliph.

However, Aïsha and a number of Meccan chiefs accused 'Alî of complicity in the assassination of 'Uthman. The two parties confronted one another in the "Battle of the Camel," its name deriving from the tradition that it was fought around Aïsha's camel. 'Alî established his capital in a garrison town of Iraq, but his caliphate was contested in battle by the governor of Syria, Mu'âwiya, cousin of 'Uthman and controversially the father-in-law of the Prophet. Having seen that the fight was lost, Mu'âwiya's soldiers hoisted the Quran on the point of their lances. 'Alî accepted the arbitration of the Book, but, poorly defended by his delegate, he had to surrender his claims. As a result of this gesture of weakness, he was abandoned by certain militants known ever since as the Khârijites, the "Secessionists." 'Alî was assassinated in 661, and his partisans, few in number, proclaimed his eldest son Hasan as caliph. Already elected caliph in Jerusalem by the Syrians, Mu'âwiya succeeded in persuading Hasan to abdicate in his favor.

Mu'âwiya was a capable military chief and a crafty politician; he

33. This vertiginous irruption of the Arabs has justly been described as similar to the last wave of the barbarian invasions which shook the western Roman Empire. However, in distinction from the barbarians, the Arabs installed themselves in new garrison towns erected at the edge of the desert. By paying a certain tribute, the conquered populations could conserve their religion and customs. But the situation would change appreciably when a large part of the urban population, especially the functionaries and intellectuals, would embrace Islam.

reorganized the Empire and founded the first dynasty of the caliphs, the Umayyads (661–750). But the last opportunity to reunify the *ummah* was lost when Husayn, the second son of 'Alî, was massacred in 680 at Karbala in Iraq with nearly all the members of his family. This martyrdom was never forgiven by the Shî'ites, and for centuries it incited revolts that were fiercely put down by the reigning caliphs. It was not until the tenth century that Shî'ite communities obtained permission to celebrate public ceremonies commemorating the tragic death of Imâm Husayn during the first ten days of the month of Muharram.[34]

Thus thirty years after the death of the Prophet, the *ummah* found itself divided—and so it has remained to this day—into three parties: the majority of the believers, the Sunnis, that is, the partisans of the *Sunnah* (the ''practice,'' the ''tradition''), under the guidance of the reigning caliph; the Shî'ites, faithful to the lineage of the first ''true'' caliph, 'Alî; and the Khârijites (''Secessionists''), who considered that only the community has the right to elect its leader, and also the duty to depose him if he is guilty of grave sins. As we will see (cf. chap. 35), each of these parties will make its contributions, however great or small, to the development of Muslim religious institutions, theology, and mysticism.

As to the history of the Empire founded by the first caliphs, it is sufficient to recall the most important events. The military expansion continued until 715, when the Turks forced an Arab army to abandon the region of the Oxus. In 717, the second naval expedition against Byzantium failed with heavy losses. In 733, Charles Martel, King of France, crushed the Arabs near Tours and constrained them to withdraw to the other side of the Pyrenees. This marks the end of the military supremacy of the Arab Empire. The future irruptions and conquests of Islam will be the work of Muslims from other ethnic backgrounds.

Islam itself also began to modify certain of its original structures. For some time already, the objective of holy war as defined by Muhammad—the conversion of the infidels—had been less and less honored. Arab armies preferred to subjugate polytheists without converting them, in order to subject them to heavy tribute. Moreover, the

---

34. See finally Earle H. Waugh, ''Muharram Rites: Community Death and Rebirth.''

converts did not enjoy the same rights as the Muslims. From 715 on, the tension between Arabs and new converts was continually aggravated. The latter were ready to support every rebellion which promised them equality with the Arabs. After several years of disorder and armed conflicts, the Umayyad dynasty was overthrown in 750, and replaced by another important Meccan family, the Abbāsids. The new caliph emerged victorious thanks above all to the aid of the Shî'ites. But the situation of the partisans of 'Alî did not change, and the second Abbāsid caliph, al-Mansur (754–775), stifled in blood a Shî'ite revolt. On the other hand, the difference between Arabs and new converts was definitively effaced under the Abbāsids.

The first four caliphs had kept the seat of the caliphate at Medina. But Mu'âwiya established the capital of the Empire at Damascus. From this point on, Hellenistic, Persian, and Christian influences increased progressively through the entire Umayyad dynasty. These manifested themselves chiefly in religious and secular architecture. The first great mosques of Syria borrowed the cupola of the Christian churches.[35] The palaces, villas, gardens, mural decorations, and mosaics imitated the models of the Hellenistic Near East.[36]

The Abbāsids prolonged and developed this process of assimilation of the Oriental and Mediterranean cultural heritage. Islam created and organized an urban civilization based on bureaucracy and commerce. The caliphs renounced their religious function; they lived isolated in their palaces, confiding to the *ulamâ*—theologians and specialists in canon law—the care of handling the daily problems of the faithful. The construction in 762 of a new capital, Baghdad, marked the end of a preponderantly Arab Islam. The city, in the form of a circle divided by a cross, was an *imago mundi,* center of the Empire: the four gates represented the four directions of space. The most auspicious planet, Jupiter, presided at the ''birth'' of Baghdad, as the work had begun on a day fixed by a Persian astrologer.[37] Al-Mansur and his successors were installed with all the pomp of the Sassanid emperors. The Abbāsids depended above all on the bureaucracy, the majority of which was of Persian origin, and on the royal army recruited from the Iranian

---

35. Cf. E. Baldwin Smith, *The Dome,* pp. 41ff.

36. See U. Monneret de Villard, *Introduzione allo studio dell'archeologia islamica,* especially pp. 24ff., 105ff.

37. See the sources cited by Charles Wendell, ''Baghdad: *Imago Mundi,*'' p. 122.

military aristocracy. Converted en masse to Islam, the Iranians returned to Sassanid models for their politics, administration, and etiquette. Sassanid and Byzantine styles dominated architecture.

This is also the age of translations, by the intermediary of Syriac, of the works of the Greek philosophers, doctors, and alchemists. Under the reign of Harun-al-Rashid (788–809) and his successors, the Mediterranean civilization of late antiquity knew its first renaissance, one of Arab expression; it completes, sometimes by opposing itself to it, the process of assimilation of Iranian values encouraged by the Abbāsids.[38] We will see later (chap. 35) the consequences of these discoveries and confrontations for the development of Muslim spirituality.

38. It concerns, of course, creations of the inexhaustible Iranian syncretism (cf. §212).

34 Western Catholicism from Charlemagne to Joachim of Fiore

266. Christianity during the High Middle Ages

In 474, Romulus Augustulus, the last Roman emperor of the West, was deposed by Odoacer, a barbarian chief. For a long time, historians have considered 474 as the conventional date for the end of antiquity and the beginning of the Middle Ages. But the appearance in 1937 of Henri Pirenne's posthumous work, *Mohammad and Charlemagne,* put the problem in an entirely different perspective. The Belgian historian called attention to several significant facts. For one thing, the Empire's social structures persisted for two more centuries. In addition, the barbarian kings of the sixth and seventh centuries employed Roman methods, and were attached to imperial titles. What is more: commercial communications continued with Byzantium and Asia. According to Pirenne, the rupture between the East and the West occurred in the eighth century, and the cause was the irruption of Islam. Isolated from the centers of Mediterranean culture and ruined by uninterrupted invasions and internal wars, the West sank into "barbary." The new society which rose from these ruins would be founded on rural autonomy: its expression would be feudalism. It is this new world, the Middle Ages, which Charlemagne succeeded in organizing.

Pirenne's hypothesis has given rise to a long controversy,[1] and today his view is only partially accepted. But it had the merit of obliging scholars to reexamine the complex historical process which led to the crystallization of the western Middle Ages. Pirenne did not take into account the profound changes brought about in the West by Chris-

---

1. See the criticisms cited by William Carroll Bark, *Origins of the Medieval World,* pp. 7ff., 114ff.

tianity. For as W. C. Bark has shown, the history of Western Europe (from 300 to 600) is the joint result of two factors: first, Christianity; and second, the shocks and countershocks of events: the gradual debacle of the economy and of the local Roman government; the disorder created by the repeated invasions; and the progressive self-sufficiency of an agrarian type of society. In fact, had the West not been divided, poor, and badly governed, the influence of the Church would not have become so important.[2]

From its beginnings, medieval society was a community of pioneers. Its model was in some sense constituted by the Benedictine monasteries. Saint Benedict (ca. 480–ca. 540), the father of Western monasticism, had organized a series of small communities which were completely autonomous from an economic point of view. The destruction of one or several of the monasteries did not result in the ruin of the entire institution. The invasions of the barbarian nomads, and the later incursions of the Vikings, had annihilated the towns and, along with them, the last centers of culture. The remnants of the classical cultural heritage survived in the monasteries.[3] But few of the monks had the leisure to dedicate themselves to study. Their principal duty was to preach Christianity and assist the poor. But beyond this, they were also builders, doctors, metalworkers, and, above all, farmers. These monks considerably improved the tools and methods for cultivating the earth.[4]

This chain of monasteries, enjoying such perfect economic autarchy, has been compared to the feudal system of property, that is, to the lands assigned by the lord to his vassals either in recompense for their military services, or as a gift anticipating them.[5] These two "seeds," capable of surviving historical catastrophes, served to provide the foundations for a new society and culture. Charles Martel secularized numerous properties belonging to the church in order to distribute them to his subjects. This was the only way to establish a powerful and devoted army; at the time, no sovereign had the means to equip his army on his own.

As we shall presently see in our discussion of chivalry (§267), the

2. Ibid., pp. 26–27.

3. Around 700, Western culture took refuge in the monasteries of Ireland and Northumbria. It is from there that a century later the scholars, theologians, and artists emerged.

4. See the exposition of these innovations in Bark, *Origins*, pp. 80ff.

5. Cf. Hugh Trevor-Roper, *The Rise of Christian Europe*, pp. 98ff.

feudal system and its ideology are of Germanic origin.[6] It is thanks to this institution that the West was able to surmount the consequences of the innumerable crises and catastrophes which developed after the fifth century. Charlemagne's coronation as "Holy Roman Emperor" by the pope in Rome in 800 could not have been imagined fifty years earlier. Given the grave tension between the emperors and the popes, and the jealousy of certain kings and princes over the following centuries, the role and importance of the Roman Empire remained precarious and generally limited. It is not for us to summarize the political and military history of the High Middle Ages. But it is important to note that from now on all the institutions—feudalism, chivalry, and Empire—emerged as new religious creations unknown, or in any case less elaborated, in the Byzantine world.

We must, due to the economy of this work, pass over the liturgical and sacramental innovations[7] and the religious elements of what has been called the "Carolingian Renaissance" of the ninth century.[8] It is important, however, to remark that for five centuries the Western Church alternately experiences periods of reform and decadence, triumph and humiliation, creativity and sclerosis, openness and intolerance. To cite only one example: after the "Carolingian Renaissance," in the tenth century and the first half of the eleventh century, the Church is once again in regression. But with the "Gregorian Reform" begun by Gregory VII, elected pope in 1073, it enters into an age of glory and power. It is not easy to present in a few lines the profound reasons for this alternation. Let it suffice to remark that the periods of ascendance, as well as those of decline, are related for one thing to the fidelity to the apostolic tradition, and for another to various eschatological hopes and nostalgias for a more authentic and profound Christian experience.

From its beginnings, Christianity has developed under the sign of the apocalyptic. Saint Augustine excepted, the theologians and visionaries discoursed on the theme of the "End of the World" and calculated the date of its arrival. Myths of the Anti-Christ and the "Emperor

6. Cf. Carl Stephenson, *Medieval Feudalism*, pp. 1–14.

7. For example, the exchange of wedding rings, the importance of the Mass (which could henceforth be celebrated for the living and the dead), the "missal" in which prayers were collected, etc.

8. A more adequate formation of the clergy, deepened study of a correct Latin, different monastic reforms after the Benedictine model, etc.

of the Last Days" fascinated both the clergy and the mass of the faithful. On the eve of the first millennium, the old scenario of the "End of the World" took on dramatic actuality. To the typical eschatological terrors were added all sorts of disasters: epidemics, famines, sinister omens (comets, eclipses, etc.).[9] The Devil's presence was felt to be everywhere. Christians accounted for these scourges by their sins. The only defense was penitence and recourse to the saints and their relics. The penances are the same as those which the dying imposed upon themselves.[10] Moreover, the abbots and bishops set themselves, in the words of the monk Raoul Glaber, to reunite the people around the relics "for the reestablishment of peace and for the institution of the holy faith." Knights pronounced the oath of peace with their hands on the relics: "In no way will I invade a Church. . . . In no way will I attack cleric or monk. . . . In no way will I take ox, cow, pig, lamb. . . . I will seize neither peasant nor peasant woman," etc.[11] The "Truce of God" banned battles during the most sacred periods of the liturgical calendar.

The collective pilgrimages—to Jerusalem, Rome, and St. James of Compostella—took on prodigious appeal. Raoul Glaber interprets the "holy voyage" to Jerusalem as a preparation for death and the promise of salvation; pilgrims in great numbers announced the coming of the Anti-Christ and "the approach of the end of the world."[12]

But once past the year 1033, the millennium of Christ's passion, Christians felt that the penances and purifications had fulfilled their goal. Raoul Glaber evokes the signs and the divine benediction: "Heaven began to laugh, to become clear and enliven itself with favorable winds. . . . All the surface of the earth covered itself with lovely greenness and an abundance of fruits which entirely eliminated scarcity. . . . Innumerable sick people regained their health in these reunions to which so many saints were led. . . . The assistants held their hands up to God crying out in a single voice: 'Peace! Peace! Peace!' "[13] Concurrently, certain efforts were made toward the re-

9. See the texts reproduced by Georges Duby, *L'An Mil,* pp. 105ff.

10. "It is precisely in the millennial year that the western Church finally entertained the ancient beliefs in the presence of the deceased, in their invisible survival, which was, however, little different from their carnal existence," Duby, ibid., p. 76.

11. See the full text of this oath in Duby, pp. 171ff.

12. Text reproduced by Duby, p. 179.

13. See the text in Duby, pp. 183–84.

generation of the Church, especially at the Benedictine monastery at Cluny. Everywhere in the West, sanctuaries were rebuilt, basilicas renovated, and relics discovered. Missions multiplied to the north and the east. But still more significant were the changes which took place in Church practice, due in part to the pressures of popular piety. The eucharistic celebration won an exceptional importance. Monks were induced to become priests themselves in order to participate "in the preparation of the body and the blood of Christ," to increase "in the visible word the portion of the sacred."[14] Veneration of the Cross increased, since it was the sign *par excellence* of Christ's humanity. This exaltation of "God incarnate" would soon be complemented by the devotion to the Virgin.[15]

The religious complex that crystallized around the terrors and hopes of the millennium anticipates in some fashion the crises and creations which characterize the following five centuries.

267. The assimilation and reinterpretation of pre-Christian traditions: Sacred kingship and chivalry

For the majority of Germanic tribes, royalty had a sacred origin and character: the founders of royal dynasties descended from the gods, and above all from Wodan.[16] The "luck" of the king was the proof *par excellence* of his sacred nature. The sovereign himself celebrated the sacrifices for the harvests and military successes; he was a charismatic intermediary between the people and the divinity. Abandoned by his "luck," or in other words by the gods, the king could be deposed or even put to death, as happened in Sweden with Domaldr following a series of disastrous harvests.[17] Even after the conversion to Chris-

14. Duby, p. 219.

15. See the texts cited by Duby, pp. 216ff.

16. The majority of Anglo-Saxon kings claim their descent from Wodan; cf. the documents cited by William A. Chaney, *The Cult of Kingship in Anglo-Saxon England*, pp. 33ff. The Scandinavian sovereigns descend from the god Yngwi, assimilated to Frey; according to the *Lai de Rig*, Heimdal (or Rig) was the ancestor of all the kings (ibid., p. 19). On ancient German royalty, see my *History of Religious Ideas*, vol. 2, pp. 478–79.

17. See *Ynglingasaga*, chap. 15 (18); cf. ibid., chap. 43 (47), the story of this latter scion of the Ynglings who was sacrificed to Othin on account of poor harvests. For other examples, see Chaney, *The Cult of Kingship*, p. 86.

tianity, the genealogies of sovereigns (i.e., their descent from Wodan) retained a decisive importance.[18]

As was so often paralleled elsewhere, the ecclesiastical hierarchy strove to integrate these beliefs into Christianity's sacred history. Thus certain royal genealogies proclaimed Wodan to be Noah's son, born in the ark, or a descendant of a cousin of the Virgin.[19] Kings fallen on the battlefield—even peasant kings—were assimilated to martyred saints. Christian rulers conserved, at least partially, the magico-religious prestige of their ancestors; they affected the seeds of future harvests, as well as the sick and children.[20] Kings were interred in churches in order to discourage the veneration of royal mounds.

The most original revalorization of the pagan heritage was the promotion of the king as *Christus Domini,* "the Lord's Anointed." The king thereby becomes inviolable; every conspiracy against his person is considered a sacrilege. Henceforth, the sovereign's religious prestige no longer derives from his divine origin but from his consecration, which proclaims him the Lord's Anointed.[21] "A Christian King is Christ's delegate in the midst of his people," affirms an eleventh-century author. "By the wisdom of the king, the people become happy [*gesaelig*], rich and victorious."[22] Such an exaltation of the Lord's Anointed reminds one of the old pagan tradition. However, the king is only the consecrated protector of the people and the Church; his function as mediator between man and the divine is henceforth exercised by the ecclesiastical hierarchy.

An analogous process of influence and symbiosis is seen in the development of chivalry. Tacitus provides a brief description of the military initiation of the ancient Germans: in the middle of the assembly of armed warriors, one of the chiefs, or the father, delivers the shield and javelin to the young man. Since adolescence, he has prepared himself with the companions (*comites*) of a chief (*princeps*), but it is as a result of this ceremony that the young man is recognized as a warrior and a member of the tribe. On the battlefield, adds Tacitus, it is shameful for the chief to

18. Of the eight genealogies of the English royal houses, seven claim descent from Wodan; Chaney, p. 29.
19. See the examples cited by Chaney, p. 42.
20. Cf. Marc Bloch, *Les rois thaumaturges,* passim; Chaney, pp. 86ff.
21. This implies the sovereign's obedience to the bishop.
22. *Principes d'un régime politique chrétien,* a treatise attributed to the Archbishop Wulfstone (d. 1023); cited by Chaney, p. 257.

be surpassed in bravery—and for his companions to be less brave than he. Anyone who outlives the *princeps* by withdrawing from the battlefield is disgraced for life. The defense of the chief is the sacred duty of all his companions. "The chief fights for victory; his companions for the chief." In return, the chief assures their sustenance, and provides them with military equipment and a portion of the booty.[23]

After the conversion of the Germanic tribes to Christianity, this institution was preserved. It is found at the base of feudalism[24] and chivalry. In 791, Charlemagne's eldest son Louis, though not yet thirteen, received the warrior's sword from his father. Forty-seven years later, Louis gratified his fifteen-year-old son with "manly arms, the sword." This is the origin of dubbing, the initiatory ritual specific to chivalry.

It is not easy to specify the origin of this institution, which played such a major role in the military, social, religious, and cultural history of the West. In any case, chivalry could not assume its "classical" form before the ninth-century introduction into France of large and powerful horses capable of carrying armored horsemen (*cathafracti*). Although from the beginning the knight's essential virtue has been complete loyalty to his lord,[25] every knight was supposed to defend the poor and the Church. The dubbing ceremony included the benediction of the weapons (the sword was placed on the altar, etc.). But as we shall see, it is above all from the twelfth century on that the Church's influence became important.

Following a period of apprenticeship and diverse trials, a candidate for knighthood proceeded to the public ceremony of dubbing. The lord ritually presented the squire with his arms: sword, lance, spurs, hauberk, and shield. The latter stood before his sponsor with his hands held together, sometimes kneeling with his head bent down. At the conclusion, the lord struck him a forceful blow on the neck with his fist or palm. The origin and significance of this rite is still controversial.

Chivalry attains its most complete expression in the eleventh and the first half of the twelfth centuries. By the thirteenth century, its decline begins; and after the fifteenth century, chivalry is no more than cere-

23. *Germania*, 13–14. On ancient German military initiations, see §175.

24. Feudalism can be defined as the association of vassalage with the fief (that is to say, the revenue from land which the vassal administers in the name of his lord).

25. Roland was considered the hero *par excellence* since he unconditionally respected the rules of the vassalage, even at the cost of his life.

monial and a mark of the nobility. Paradoxically, it is during its period of decline and decadence that chivalry becomes the object of numerous cultural creations, whose origin and religious significance can be readily deciphered (§270).

The institution briefly described by Tacitus had, to be sure, a religious dimension: the promotion of the young man announced the completion of his military initiation; absolute loyalty to the chief constituted, in fact, a religious mode of being. Conversion to Christianity gave rise to many reinterpretations and revalorizations of such ancestral traditions. But it never succeeded in effacing the pagan heritage. For three centuries, the Church contented itself with a rather modest role in the consecration of knights. But from the twelfth century on, the ceremony, at least in appearance, unfolds under ecclesiastical control. After his confession, the squire would spend the night in prayer inside the church. In the morning, he would take communion and, while receiving his arms, swear an oath of respect for the code of chivalry,[26] and also say a prayer.

After the First Crusade, two military orders were established in the Holy Land to defend pilgrims and to care for the sick: the Templars and the Hospitalers. Henceforth, certain monks added a chivalric type of military instruction to their religious education. Antecedents of these religious military orders can be found in the "holy war" (*jīhād*) of Islam (§265), in the initiation into the Mithraic mysteries (§217), and in the language and metaphors of the Christian ascetics who considered themselves soldiers of a *militia sacra*. But one must also take into account the religious significance of war among the ancient Germans (§175).[27]

268. The Crusades: Eschatology and politics

Enlightenment historians and philosophers from Gibbon and William Robertson to Hume and Voltaire have characterized the Crusades as a

26. According to certain sources, the code included four laws: daily Mass; eventual sacrifice of his life for the holy faith; protection of the Church; and the defense of widows, orphans, and the poor. Other versions add that the knight must aid "ladies and damsels who have need of him" and "honor women and . . . defend their rights."

27. Let us add that the institution of a religious chivalry also develops in Islam; cf. Henry Corbin, *En Islam iranien*, vol. 2, pp. 168ff.

painful deflagration of fanaticism and folly. Although such a judgment is now usually toned down, it is still shared by a number of contemporary authors. Nevertheless, the Crusades constitute a central fact in medieval history. "Before their inception, the centre of our civilization was placed in Byzantium and in the lands of the Arab Caliphate. Before they faded out, the hegemony in civilization had passed to western Europe. Out of this transference modern history was born."[28] But this hegemony exacted a very high price, which was paid above all by Byzantium and by the peoples of eastern Europe.

It is, however, the religious significance of the Crusades that must now detain us. Their eschatological origin and structure have been duly clarified by Paul Alphandéry and Alphonse Dupront. "At the center of a crusade consciousness, among both the clergy and the non-clergy, was the duty to liberate Jerusalem. . . . What expresses itself most powerfully in the crusade is the double plenitude of a fulfillment of time and a fulfillment of human space. In this sense, as regards space, the sign of the fulfillment of time is the reunion of nations around the holy city and mother of the world, Jerusalem."[29]

The eschatological character accentuates itself in proportion to the partial defeats and debacles experienced by the Crusades of the barons and the emperor. The first and most spectacular Crusade, called for by the Byzantine Emperor Alexis and Pope Urban I, was preached in 1095 by Peter the Hermit. After many adventures (including the massacre of the Jews in towns on the Rhine and the Danube, and the reconvening of the three Frankish armies at Constantinople), the Crusaders crossed Asia Minor and, despite jealousies and intrigues among their leaders, conquered Antioch, Tripoli, Edessa, and finally Jerusalem. However, one generation later, these conquests were lost, and Saint Bernard preached the Second Crusade at Vézelay in 1145. A great army led by the kings of France and Germany came to Constantinople; but only a short time later, it was annihilated in Iconium and Damascus.

The Third Crusade, called for by the Emperor Frederick Barbarossa in Mayence in 1188, was both imperial and messianic in nature. The kings of France and England, Philip Augustus and Richard the Lion-Hearted, responded to the appeal, but without "the enthusiasm and

28. Steven Runciman, *A History of the Crusades,* vol. 1, p. xi.
29. A Dupront, "Croisades et eschatologie," p. 177.

eagerness of the Barbarossa."[30] The Crusaders took Acre and arrived before Jerusalem, which was defended by Saladin, the legendary sultan of Egypt and Syria. This time again, the Crusade ended in disaster. The emperor lost his life in an Armenian river; and Philip Augustus returned to France in order to undermine his ally, the king of England. Left alone before the walls of Jerusalem, Richard the Lion-Hearted obtained permission from Saladin for his troops to make their devotions at the Holy Sepulcher.

Certain contemporaries explained the princes' incapacity to liberate Jerusalem by the unworthiness of the great and the rich. Incapable of penitence, the princes and the rich were no more able to obtain the Kingdom of God than to conquer the Holy Land. The latter belonged to the poor, the elect of the Crusade. "The failure of the Imperial attempts, despite the assurances of the messianic legend, attested well that the work of liberation could not belong to the powerful of the earth."[31] When Innocent III proclaimed the Fourth Crusade (1202–1204), he wrote personally to Foulques de Neuilly, the apostle of the poor, "one of the most remarkable figures in the history of the Crusades," as Paul Alphandéry has written. Foulques vehemently criticized the rich and the princes, and preached penitence and moral reform as the essential condition of the Crusade. But he died in 1202, while the Crusaders were already engaged in the adventure that made of the Fourth Crusade one of the most painful episodes of European history. In effect, spurred on by material ambitions and divided by intrigues, the Crusaders occupied Constantinople, massacring part of the population and pillaging the treasures of the city, instead of directing themselves toward the Holy Land. King Baudoin of Flanders was named Latin Emperor of Byzantium, and Thomas Morosini Patriarch of Constantinople.

It is useless to tarry over the partial victories and numerous disasters of the final crusades. It must suffice to recall that notwithstanding the excommunication of the pope, Barbarossa's grandson, the Emperor Frederick II, arrived in the Holy Land in 1225 and obtained from the sultan the possession of Jerusalem, where he was crowned and pro-

30. Paul Alphandéry and A. Dupront, *La chrétienté et l'idée de Croisade*, vol. 2, p. 19. "Philip Augustus had little concern for the success of the expedition; his chief concern was for the kingdom he was going to leave behind" (ibid.).
31. Ibid., p. 40.

ceeded to live for fifteen years. But in 1244, Jerusalem fell into the hands of the Mameluks, and was never again reconquered. Several sporadic expeditions were undertaken before the end of the century, but without any success.

To be sure, the Crusades opened western Europe to the Orient and permitted contact with Islam. But the cultural exchanges could have taken place without these bloody expeditions. The Crusades reinforced the papacy's prestige and contributed to the development of western European monarchies. But they weakened Byzantium by allowing the Turks to advance deeply into the Balkan peninsula, and exacerbated relations with the Eastern Church. Moreover, the wild conduct of the Crusaders turned the Muslims against *all* Christians, and a number of churches which had survived six centuries of Muslim domination were at last destroyed.

Despite the politicization of the Crusades, this collective movement retained throughout an eschatological structure. Among the many proofs of this, one was the Children's Crusade, which surged forth abruptly in northern France and Germany in 1212. The spontaneity of these movements seems beyond question: "no one is inciting them, neither from abroad nor from the country," affirms a contemporary witness.[32] Children, "characterized both—these are the extraordinary traits—by their extreme youth and by their poverty, above all the little shepherds,"[33] began to march and were joined by the poor. There were perhaps 30,000 who advanced in procession, singing. When asked where they were going, they responded: "to God!" According to one contemporary chronicler, "their intention was to cross the sea, and there where the powerful kings had failed, they would retake the sepulcher of Christ."[34] The clergy was opposed to this levy of children. The French Crusade ended catastrophically: arriving in Marseilles, they embarked on seven large ships, two of which ran aground following a storm off Sardinia, and all the passengers drowned. As to the other five ships, two traitorous ship-owners led them toward Alexandria, where they sold the children to Saracen chiefs and slave merchants.

The "German" Crusade presents the same picture. A contemporary

32. Ibid., p. 118.
33. Ibid., p. 119.
34. Reinier, cited by Alphandéry and A. Dupront, ibid., p. 120.

chronicle recounts how in 1212 "there appeared a child named Nicholas, who gathered around him a multitude of children and women. He affirmed that, at the command of an angel, he must accompany them to Jerusalem and liberate the Lord's Cross, and that the sea, as it had formerly done for the people of Israel, would let them pass without wetting their feet."[35] Moreover, they bore no arms. Leaving from the region of Cologne, they went down the Rhine, crossed the Alps, and reached northern Italy. Some arrived at Genoa and Pisa, but were driven away. Those who succeeded in reaching Rome were forced to recognize that they were without authoritative support. When the pope disapproved of their project, the young Crusaders were forced to retrace their journey. As the commentator describes it in the *Annales Carbacenses,* "they returned barefoot and famished, one by one and in silence." No one helped them. Another witness wrote: "A great many of them fell dead of hunger in the villages, at public places, and no one buried them."[36]

Alphandéry and Dupront have justly recognized in these movements the election of the child in popular piety. It is simultaneously the myth of the Innocents, the exaltation of the child by Jesus, and the popular reaction against the Barons' Crusade, the same reaction which expressed itself in the legends that crystallized around the "Tafurs" of the first Crusades.[37] "The reconquest of the Holy Land could no longer be expected without a miracle—and henceforth the miracle could only happen in favor of the most pure, the children and the poor."[38]

The failure of the Crusades did not eliminate the eschatological expectations. In his *De Monarchia Hispanica* (1600), Tommaso Campanella entreated the King of Spain to finance a new crusade against the Turkish Empire and to found, after his victory, the Universal Monarchy. Thirty-eight years later, in his *Ecloga* intended for Louis XIII and Anne of Austria in celebration of the birth of the future Louis XIV, Campanella prophesied both the *recuperatio Terrae Sanctae* and the *renovatio saeculi.* The young king would conquer the entire earth in a thousand days, crushing the monsters (that is, the kingdoms of the

35. *Annales Scheftlearienses,* text cited by Alphandéry and Dupront, ibid., p. 123.
36. Texts cited by Alphandéry and Dupront, ibid., p. 127.
37. The "Tafurs" (= vagabonds) were the poor who followed the Crusaders armed with knives, clubs, and axes; cf. Norman Cohn, *The Pursuit of the Millennium,* pp. 67ff.
38. Alphandéry and Dupront, *La chrétienté,* p. 145.

infidels) and liberating Greece. Muhammad would be repulsed from Europe; Egypt and Ethiopia would again become Christian; the Tartars, Persians, Chinese, and the entire East would be converted. The world's diverse peoples would form a single Christianity, and this regenerated universe would have a single center: Jerusalem. "The Church," wrote Campanella, "began at Jerusalem, and it is to Jerusalem that it will return after having covered the world."[39] In his treatise *La prima e la seconda risurrezione,* Campanella no longer considered, as Saint Bernard had done, that the conquest of Jerusalem was a step toward the celestial Jerusalem, but rather that it would be the beginning of the messianic kingdom on earth.[40]

269. The religious significance of Romanesque art and courtly romance

The period of the Crusades is also an age of the most grandiose spiritual creations. It is the age of the apogee of Romanesque art and the flight of gothic art, of the flowering of erotic and religious poetry, of the romances of the Arthurian cycle and of Tristan and Iseult; it is the age of the triumph of Scholasticism and mysticism, of the foundation of the most glorious universities, of monastic orders and of itinerant preaching. But it is also the age of an exceptional proliferation of ascetic and eschatological movements, for the most part on the margins of orthodoxy, or frankly heterodox.

We cannot pause to examine all of these creations with the care they deserve. Let us recall for now that the greatest theologians and mystics (from Saint Bernard, 1090–1153, to Meister Eckhart, 1260–1327), as well as the most influential philosophers (from Anselm of Canterbury, 1033–1109, to Saint Thomas Aquinas, ca. 1223–1274), accomplished their work in this period, one that was filled with crises and transformations that would radically modify the spiritual profile of the West. Let us also recall the founding of the Carthusian Order in 1084 and the Cistercian Order at Citeaux near Dijon in 1098, followed by the canons established in 1120 at Prémontré. Along with the Orders founded by

39. Note of Campanella to verse 207 of his *Ecloga,* cited by Dupront, "Croisades et eschatologie," p. 187.
40. Critical edition of Romano Amerio (Rome, 1955), p. 72; Dupront, ibid., p. 189.

Saint Dominic (1170–1224) and Saint Francis of Assisi (1182–1221), these monastic organizations would play a decisive role in the religious and intellectual life of the following four centuries.

Let us attempt to retrace briefly certain structures of the symbolic universe familiar to Medieval society after the crisis of the millennium. We may note first that from the beginning of the eleventh century, a new societal schema begins to impose itself. While addressing his king in about 1027, Bishop Adalbert of Laon reminded him that "the society of the faithful forms only one body, but the State comprises three. . . . The House of God, which is believed to be one, is divided into three: one group prays, another fights, and the other labors. These three parts which coexist do not allow themselves to be separated. . . . Accordingly, this triple assemblage is no less than one, and so it is that the law has been able to triumph and that the world enjoys peace."[41]

This schema recalls the tripartition of Indo-European societies so brilliantly studied by Georges Dumézil (cf. §63). What interests us here is the religious, and more specifically Christian, symbolism that informs this social classification. Profane realities participate within the sacred. This conception characterizes all of the traditional cultures. To recall a familiar example, it informs religious architecture from its beginnings, and is found in the structure of the Christian basilicas (cf. the symbolism of the Byzantine church, §257). Romanesque art partakes of this symbolism and develops it further. The cathedral is an *imago mundi*. The cosmological symbolism both organizes and sacralizes the world. "The universe is envisaged in a sacral perspective, whether it is a question of the stone or the flower, the beast or the man."[42]

In effect, one finds all the modes of existing in the cosmos and all the aspects of life and human labor, as well as the personages and events of sacred history, the angels, monsters, and demons. Cathedral

---

41. See the text in Duby, *L'An Mil,* pp. 71–75. By the eleventh century, "this schema translated the remodeling of society: a clergy dominated by the monastic model and the *opus Dei;* a military aristocracy; an economic elite of landed peasants who earned through their labor the right of ideological promotion"; Jacques Le Goff, *Histoire des religions,* vol. 2, p. 817. See also, by the same author, *Pour un autre Moyen Age,* pp. 80–90; and G. Duby, *Les trois ordres ou l'imiginaire du féodalism,* pp. 62ff. and passim.

42. M. M. Davy, *Initiation à la symbolique romane,* p. 19.

ornamentation constitutes an inexhaustible repertory of cosmic symbols (sun, zodiac, horse, tree of life, etc.) along with biblical and fable themes (devil, dragons, phoenix, centaurs, etc.) and didactic themes (monthly labors, etc.).[43] Two opposing universes can be distinguished: on one side hideous beings, deformed, monstrous, and demonic;[44] on the other, Christ the King in Glory, the Church (represented as a woman), and the Virgin, who wins, in the twelfth century, a considerable place in popular piety. This opposition is real, and its objective is obvious. But the genius of Romanesque art rightly consists in its fiery imagination and in its will *to reunite in one ensemble* all the modalities of existing in the sacred, profane, and imaginary worlds.

What is of interest for our purposes is not only the importance of this iconography in the religious instruction of the people, but its role in awakening and giving flight to the imagination, and thereby to symbolic thought. The contemplation of such a fabulous iconography familiarizes the Christian with a number of religious and parareligious symbolic universes. The faithful enter progressively into a world of values and meanings which, for some, becomes more "real" and precious than the world of everyday experience.

The value of these ceremonial images, gestures, and activities, of the epic tales, the lyric poetry and music, is to introduce the subject into an alternate parallel world which allows for psychic experiences and spiritual illuminations that are otherwise inaccessible. In traditional societies, such a value is enhanced by the religious, or parareligious, dimension of literary and artistic creations.[45] It is not necessary for us to discuss the creations of the troubadours and their doctrine of courtly love. Let us note, however, that the radical innovations which they include, and above all the exaltation of the Lady and of extramarital love, are of interest not only for the history of culture. One must not forget the inferior position of women in the medieval aristocracy, the financial or political interests which determined marriages, or the brutal and indifferent conduct of husbands. The "true love" discovered and exalted in the twelfth century implied a superior

43. Cf. ibid., pp. 209ff.

44. This is what aggravated Saint Bernard, who responded: "What do these ridiculous monsters signify in our cloisters, these horrible beauties and these beautiful horrors?" *Apologia*, 12, 29, as cited by Davy, ibid., p. 210.

45. As depth psychology has shown, the same process, however impoverished and degraded it may be, is attested in contemporary desacralized societies.

and complex culture, indeed a mystique and asceticism which one could learn only in the service of refined and cultivated women.

One encounters examples of such erudition, above all at Poitiers in the chateau of the famous Aliénor (or Eleanor) of Aquitaine, granddaughter of the first known troubadour William of Poitiers (1071–1127), and queen successively of France and England. Hundreds of princes, barons, and knights as well as duchesses and countesses were ''educated'' in this privileged cultural milieu, which was presided over by Eleanor's daughter Marie de Champagne. There was even a Court of Love, a unique tribunal of which we know the code and several of its judgments.[46] Women felt that they could instruct men by ''exercising their power in novel and delicate ways. Men were to be captivated, guided, educated. Eleanor points the way to Beatrice.''[47]

The theme of the poems was always that of love, but expressed in a conventional form, at once exultant and enigmatic. The Lady (in Provençal, *dompna*) was married, conscious of her worth, and preoccupied with her reputation (*pretz*). This is the reason that the *secret* played a decisive role. The lover was separated from his Lady by a number of social and emotional taboos. While praising the qualities of his Lady, the poet sought to evoke his own solitude and sufferings, but also his hopes: to see her, even from afar, to touch her garments, to obtain a kiss, etc.

This long stage of amorous initiation is at once an ascesis, a pedagogy, and an ensemble of spiritual experiences. The discovery of the Lady as model and the exaltation of her physical beauty and spiritual virtues, threw the lover into a parallel world of images and metaphors in which the profane condition was progressively transformed. Such a transformation occurred even if, in certain cases, the poet received the total gift from his Lady.[48] For this possession was the crowning event

---

46. As preserved in André Le Chapelain's *De arte amandi*. This little treatise has been translated and commented upon by J. Lafitte-Houssat, *Troubadeurs et Cours d'Amour*, pp. 43–65.

47. Friedrich Heer, *The Medieval World, Europe, 1100–1350*, p. 137.

48. See the documentation and critical analysis of Moshe Lazar, *Amour courtois et Fin'Amors dans la littérature du XIIᵉ siècle*. Moreover, Marie de Champagne specified unequivocally the difference between conjugal union and the union of lovers: "The lovers agree fully mutually, and *freely*. Spouses are bound *by duty* to submit reciprocally to each other's wills and to never refuse each other."

Esotericism and literary creations

of an elaborate ceremonial, ruled jointly by ascesis, moral elevation, and passion.

The ritual character of this erotic scenario is incontestable. One can compare it to Tantric sexual techniques (cf. chap. 40), which would also be carried out not only to the letter, but in the context of a subtle physiology, or on a purely spiritual plane; or it can be compared to the devotion of certain Vishnuite schools (cf. ibid.) in which the mystical experience is illustrated by the love of a married woman, Rādhā, for the young god Krishna. This latter example is particularly significant. First of all, it confirms the authenticity and mystical value of "passionate love." But it helps us further to distinguish the *unio mystica* of the Christian tradition (employing nuptial terminology to represent the marriage of the soul with Christ) from that specific to the Hindu tradition, which, precisely to underline the *absoluteness* of the mystical experience and its total separateness from society and its moral values, uses images not of the venerable institution of *marriage* but those of its opposite, *adultery*.

270. Esotericism and literary creations: Troubadours, *Fedeli d'Amore*, and the Grail cycle

In courtly love, one exalts, for the first time since the Gnostics of the second and third century, the spiritual dignity and religious values of Woman.[49] According to numerous scholars, the troubadours of Provence were inspired by the model of the Arabic poetry of Spain, which glorified the Lady and the spiritual love that she awakened.[50] But it is equally necessary to take into account the Celtic, Gnostic, and

49. A number of Gnostic texts exalt the divine mother as the "Mystic Silence," the Holy Spirit, Wisdom. "I am the Thought that [dwells] in [the Light] . . . [she who exists] before the All. . . . I move in every creation. . . . I am the invisible One within the All" (text cited by Elaine Pagels, *The Gnostic Gospels,* pp. 55ff.). In a Gnostic poem, *Thunder, Perfect Mind,* a feminine power declares: "I am the first and the last . . . I am the wife and the virgin. I am [the mother] and the daughter," etc. (ibid., p. 56).

50. See especially Menéndez Pidal, *Poesía árabe y poesía europea;* García Gomez, "La lírica hispano-árabe y la aparición de la lírica romance" and the works cited by Claudio Sanchez-Albornoz, "El Islam de España y el Occidente," pp. 178–79, n. 56.

Oriental elements that were rediscovered or reactualized in the twelfth century. Moreover, devotion to the Virgin—which dominates this same epoch—also indirectly sanctifies the woman. A century later, Dante (1265–1321) would go even further: Beatrice—whom he had known as an adolescent and rediscovered as the wife of a Florentine lord—is divinized. She is proclaimed superior to the angels and saints, immunized against sin, and nearly comparable to the Virgin. She becomes a new mediatrix between humanity (as represented by Dante) and God. When Beatrice is ready to show herself in the terrestrial Paradise, someone cries: *"Veni, sponsa, de Libano"* (*Purgatorio*, 30, 11), the famous passage from the Song of Songs (4.8) which the Church had adopted, but which one intoned only for the Virgin or the Church herself.[51] One knows of no more striking example of the divinization of a woman. Evidently, Beatrice represented theology, and thus the mystery of salvation. Dante had written the *Divine Comedy* in order to save mankind, bringing about this transformation not by the aid of theories but by terrifying and fascinating the reader with visions of Heaven and Hell. Although he was not alone, Dante illustrated in an exemplary manner the traditional conception according to which art, and especially poetry, is a privileged means not only for communicating a metaphysic or theology, but for awakening and *saving* mankind.

The soteriological function of love and Woman is also clearly proclaimed by another movement which appeared to be essentially "literary," but which included an occult gnosticism, and probably an initiatory organization. This was the *Fedeli d'Amore*,[52] whose representatives are attested from the twelfth century on in Provence and Italy as well as in France and Belgium. The *Fedeli d'Amore* comprised a secret and spiritual militia whose goal was the cult of the "Unique Lady" and initiation into the mystery of "love." Its members employed a "secret language" (*parlar cruz*), so that their doctrine would be inaccessible to "la gente grossa," as the common man was termed by Francesco da Barberino (1264–1348), one of the most illustrious of the *Fedeli*. Another *fedele d'amore*, Jacques de Baisieux, composed a poem, *C'est des fiez d'Amours*, in which he enjoined: "let one not

51. Elsewhere (*Purgatorio*, 33, 10ff.), Beatrice applies to herself the words of Christ: "A little while, and you will see me no more; again a little while, and you will see me" (John 16:16).

52. Cf. Liuge Valli, *Il linguaggio segreto di Dante e dei Fedeli d'Amore;* R. Ricolfi, *Studi su i "Fedeli d'Amore,"* vol. 1.

reveal the counsels of Love, but conceal them very carefully."[53] That initiation by Love was of a spiritual order is affirmed by this author in his interpretation of the significance of the word "Love":

A signifies in its part
Without and *mor* signifies mort [death];
Let us now assemble it, we would have ourselves *without death*.[54]

"Woman" symbolizes the transcendent intellect, Wisdom. Love for a woman awakens the adept from the lethargy into which the Christian world has fallen due to the spiritual unworthiness of the pope. One meets in the texts of the *Fedeli d'Amore* allusion to a "widow who is not a widow": this is the *Madonna Intelligenza,* who has remained a "widow" because her husband, the pope, has died to the spiritual life by giving himself exclusively to temporal affairs.

This is not a matter of a heretical movement properly speaking, but of a group which no longer recognized the popes as having the prestige of Christianity's spiritual leadership. Nothing is known of their initiatory rites, but they must have existed, since the *Fedeli d'Amore* formed a militia and held secret reunions.

Moreover, from the twelfth century on, the secrets and arts of dissimulation imposed themselves in diverse milieus. "The lovers as well as the religious sects had their secret language, and the members of small esoteric circles were only recognized by the signs and symbols, colors and passwords."[55] The "secret languages" as well as the proliferation of legendary and enigmatic personages and prodigious adventures constituted in themselves a complex of parareligious phenomena. Such is what one finds, for example, in the romances of the Round Table, elaborated in the twelfth century around the figure of King Arthur. The new generations which were educated, directly or indirectly, by Eleanor of Aquitaine and Marie de Champagne, no longer appreciated the old *chansons de geste.* Charlemagne's place was now occupied by the fabulous King Arthur. The *Matière de Bretagne* put at the poet's disposal a considerable series of personages and legends of pre-

53. "D'Amur ne doivent reveler/Les consiaus, mais tres bien celer . . ." (*C'est des fiez d'Amours,* vv. 499–500, as cited by Ricolfi, *Studi,* pp. 68–69).
54. As cited by Ricolfi, ibid., p. 63.
55. F. Heer, *The Medieval World,* p. 258.

dominantly Celtic origin[56] but open to the assimilation of hetero-
geneous elements: Christian, Gnostic, and Islamic.

It is Chrétien de Troyes, a poetic protégé of Marie de Champagne,
who launches the general infatuation with the Arthurian cycle. Of most
of his life we know nothing, but we do know that he began to write
around 1170, and that he composed five long romances in verse, of
which the most celebrated are *Lancelot, Erec,* and *Percival.* From the
perspective of our research, we can say that the romances of the Round
Table establish a new mythology, in the sense that they reveal, to their
audience, a "sacred history" and the exemplary models which should
guide the conduct of knights and lovers. Let us add that the mythology
of knighthood has had a cultural influence that is more important than
its history, properly speaking.

Let us first note the number and importance of archaic elements, and
more precisely of initiatory motifs. It is always a matter of a long and
eventful "quest" for marvelous objects which implies, among other
things, the hero's penetration into another world. In the rules that de-
termine admission into the group of knights, one can decipher certain
tests of entry into secret confraternities of the *Männerbund* type. Percival must pass the night in a chapel where a dead knight lies; while the
thunder roars, he sees a black hand which extinguishes the only lit
candle.[57] This is typical of the initiatory nocturnal watch. The tests
which the hero confronts are innumerable: he must cross a bridge,
which plunges into the water, or is made of a sharp sword, or is guarded by lions and monsters; castle gates are guarded by automatons,
fairies, or demons. All such scenarios recall the passage to the beyond,
the perilous descents into Hell; and when such voyages are undertaken
by living beings, they always form part of an initiation. In assuming
the risks of such a descent into Hell, the hero pursues the conquest of
immortality or a similar extraordinary end. The innumerable ordeals
undertaken by the characters of the Arthurian cycle range in the same
category: at the end of their "quests," the heroes cure the mysterious
malady of the king and, in doing so, regenerate the "wasteland"; or
they even attain sovereignty for themselves.

Certain Christian elements reappear in these contexts, but not al-

---

56. Arthur, the Fisher-King, Percival, Lancelot; the theme of the "Wasteland," the
marvelous objects of the other world, etc.

57. See the analysis by Jean Marx, *La Légende arthurienne et le Graal,* pp. 218ff.

ways in an orthodox context. One finds above all the mythology of chivalric honor and, sometimes pushed to the extreme, the exaltation of Woman.[58] This entire literature, filled as it is with initiatory motifs and scenarios, is precious for our study, were it only in consideration of its public success. The fact that these romantic stories, filled with initiatory clichés, were heard with delight seems proof to us that such adventures met a profound need of medieval people.

But one must equally consider the intention of the authors to transmit, through the medium of their works, a certain esoteric tradition (as the *Fedeli d'Amore* had done), or a message aiming at the "reawakening" of the reader according to the model established later by Dante. Such is the case with the symbolism and scenario of the Grail, a theme unknown to the first romances of the Arthurian cycle, which were of Breton origin. It is not until about 1180 that the Grail makes its appearance in the work of Chrétien de Troyes. As J. Vendryès has written, "there exists in no Celtic literature, however rich it may be, any account which could have served as the model for compositions as varied as those our medieval literature has drawn from this subject" (that is, the Grail).[59]

However, it is not Chrétien de Troyes who presents the most complete story and coherent mythology of the Grail, but a German knight named Wolfram von Eschenbach. In his *Parzival,* written between 1200 and 1210, Wolfram admits that he has followed the accounts of a certain Kiot, the Provençal. The structure of the work is composite: books 2–12 and a segment of book 13 are based on Chrétien, but in book 14, Wolfram disagrees with his illustrious predecessor, probably because he was disappointed in Chrétien's manner of treating the Grail. What is surprising in Wolfram's romance is the number and importance of its Oriental elements.[60] Parzival's father Camuret had served in the army of the caliph of Baghdad. His uncle, the hermit Trevrizent, had made youthful travels to Asia and Africa. Parzival's nephew will become Prester John, the famous and mysterious Priest-King who ruled in "India." The first person to have written the story of the Grail and to have communicated it to Kiot was the "pagan" (Muslim-Jewish) sage Flégétanis.

58. For example, Chrétien de Troyes' *Lancelot.* As for the beautiful and tragic story of Tristan and Iseult, according to R. S. Loomis it constitutes "by far the most popular secular story of the Middle Ages" (*The Development of Arthurian Romance,* p. 90).

59. J. Vendryes, "Le Graal dans le cycle breton," p. 74.

60. Moreover, 60 percent of the text has the East for its setting.

Today it is accepted that Wolfram von Eschenbach had access to precise and sufficiently extended information on Oriental realities, from Syria and Persia to India and China. He had probably collected it from the crusaders and from Italian merchants returning from the Orient.[61] For our purposes, still more precious are the myths, beliefs, and rites which Wolfram presents or even just evokes in relation to the Grail.[62] In contrast with Chrétien de Troyes, Wolfram exalted the dignity and role of Amfortas, the Fisher-King. The latter is the chief of an order of knights called Templeisen who, like the Templars, have taken the vow of chastity. They are chosen by God and undertake dangerous missions. Twenty-five noble Ladies serve the Grail.

Recently, two American scholars have sought to derive the term *graal* (cup, vase, basin) from the Greek word *krater*.[63] This etymology has the merit of explaining the Grail's redemptive function. In effect, according to the fourth treatise of the *Corpus Hermeticum*, "God has filled with intellect a great crater which he has sent upon the earth, and has appointed a herald with the order to proclaim to the works of man these words: Dive, you who can, into this crater which is before you, you who believe that you will reascend towards Him who has sent the crater onto the earth, you who know why you have come to be.—Thus all those who pay attention to the proclamation and who have been baptized by this baptism of the intellect, they have partaken of knowledge (*gnosis*), and they have become perfect men because they have received the intellect."[64] A Hermetic influence on *Parzival* seems plausible, for Hermeticism begins to become known in twelfth-century Europe following the massive translations of Arabic works.[65] As to the initiatory function of the gnosis revealed in the Hermetic texts, we

61. See Hermann Goetz, "Der Orient der Kreuzzüge in Wolframs *Parzival*." According to this author, the romance includes new and important data for the history of art; for example, what Wolfram indicates about the silk route to China (a century before Marco Polo); about the palaces of the late caliphs at Baghdad and the *stūpa* of Kanishka, etc.

62. Even the etymology of the three enigmatic names—Kiot, Flégétanis, and Trevrizent—is significant; see Present Position of Studies, §270.

63. Henry and Renée Kahane, *The Krater and the Grail: Hermetic Sources of the Parzival*, pp. 13ff. Henry Corbin has accepted this hypothesis; see his *En Islam iranien*, vol. 2, pp. 143–54.

64. *Corpus Hermeticum* 4, 3–6, trans. by Festugière, vol. 1, p. 50.

65. Cf. Kahane and Kahane, *The Krater and the Grail*, pp. 130ff.

have examined it elsewhere in the present work (§210), and will have further occasion to return to it.

From another perspective, in a work published in 1939, the Parsi scholar Sir Jahangir C. Coyajee has also remarked upon the analogy between the Grail and the royal Iranian Glory, *xvarenah* (cf. vol. 1, pp. 315ff.), and the similarities between the legends of Arthur and those of the fabulous King Kay Khosraw.[66] Henry Corbin has also examined the two ensembles, the Iranian and the Western, most pertinently comparing their scenarios, chivalric institutions, and initiatory wisdoms while avoiding the hypothesis of historical contacts proposed by Coyajee.[67] Among the numerous resemblances, let us single out the structure of the two Spiritual Chivalries and the occultation of Kay Khosraw and King Arthur.[68] Let us add that in the cycle of compositions posterior to Wolfram von Eschenbach, the Grail is won in India by Lohengrin, Parzival's son, accompanied by all the knights.

Whatever the general interpretation one makes of the works of Wolfram and his successors, it is evident that the symbolism of the Grail and the scenarios which it inspires represent a new spiritual synthesis that draws upon the contributions of diverse traditions. Behind this passionate interest in the Orient, one detects the profound disillusionment aroused by the Crusades, the aspiration for a religious tolerance that would have encouraged a rapprochement with Islam, and the nostalgia for a "spiritual chivalry" that would follow the model of the *true* Templars (the *Templeisen* of Wolfram).[69] It is certainly a matter of a synthesis, as is proved by the integration of Christian symbols (the Eucharist, the lance) with the presence of elements of Hermetic origin. Even irrespective of the validity of the etymology proposed by H. and R. Kahane (*graal* = *krater*), the rediscovery of Hermeticism through Arab translations seems beyond doubt. Alexandrian Hermeticism al-

66. Cf. Coyajee, in *Journal of the K. R. Cama Institute*, pp. 37–194; this comparison has been accepted by Jean Marx, *La légende arthurienne*, p. 244, n. 9.

67. Corbin, *En Islam iranien*, pp. 155–210.

68. Cf. Corbin, ibid., pp. 177ff.

69. The Templars, who had become the leading bankers during the period of the Crusades, had accumulated considerable riches; moreover, they enjoyed great political prestige. In order to appropriate their treasures, King Philip IV held a scandalous trial in 1310, accusing them of immorality and heresy. Two years later, Pope Clement V definitively suppressed the order of the Templars.

lowed for the hope of an initiation by the medium of gnosis, of the immemorial and universal wisdom (a hope which will know its apogee during the Italian Renaissance; cf. §310).

As is the case for all of Arthurian literature, it is impossible to know whether the initiatory trials undergone by the knights correspond to rituals properly speaking. Likewise, it would be vain to believe that one could use documents to confirm or deny the transfer of the Grail to "India" or elsewhere in the Orient. Just like the Island of Avalon to which Arthur has retired, or the miraculous Shambala of Tibetan tradition, the Orient where the Grail was transferred belongs to the domain of mythical geography. What matters here is the symbolism of the occultation of the Grail; it expresses a certain historical moment at which a secret tradition becomes henceforth inaccessible.

The spiritual message of the scenario elaborated around the Grail continues to excite the imagination and the reflection of our contemporaries. In sum, the mythology of the Grail is a part of the religious history of the West, even if, as sometimes happens, it confounds itself with the history of utopia.

271. Joachim of Fiore: A new theology of history

Born in Calabria around 1135, Joachim of Fiore (Gioacchino de Fiore) dedicated his life to God after a voyage to the Holy Land. He entered the Benedictine monastery of Corazzo, where he became abbot. For a long time, he struggled to incorporate his house into the Cistercian Order; but in 1188, when this was accepted, Joachim and his group had already separated themselves from Corazzo. In 1192, he founded a new mission at San Giovanni di Fiore.

Joachim had dealings with people at the highest levels: he had conversations with three popes (each of whom encouraged him to write his "prophecies"), and he met Richard the Lion-Hearted (to whom he announced, among other things, the birth of the Anti-Christ). At the time of his death on 30 March 1202, the Abbot of Fiore was one of the best known and most respected figures in the Christian world. But he also had powerful adversaries who, as we shall see, succeeded in deprecating him. His work, abundant but difficult, includes a series of exegetical treatises whose object is a new interpretation of the Scriptures.[70] But because of the legend which arose around Joachim's prophecies, numerous apocryphal texts began to circulate under his name.

Joachim, however, renounced the title of prophet. He recognized himself only as having the gift of deciphering the signs placed by God in history and preserved in the Scriptures. Indeed, he himself disclosed the source of his knowledge of sacred history: certain moments of illumination which were bestowed by God (once on Easter Eve, another at Pentecost).[71] According to Joachim, two numbers—2 and 3—dominate and characterize the ages of universal history:[72] the two Testaments, the two peoples chosen by God (the Jews and the Gentiles), and the three persons of the Trinity. The first age (he used the term *status*), that of the Old Testament, was dominated by God the Father and its religion was characterized by the fear which was inspired by the absolute authority of the Law. The second age, presided over by the Son, is the age of the New Testament and of the Church sanctified by grace; the keynote of its religion is faith. This age will last for forty-two generations of about thirty years each (just as according to Matthew 1:1–17, forty-two generations had passed between Abraham and Jesus Christ). According to Joachim's calculations, the second age would complete itself in 1260, at the dawn of the Third Age—this last dominated by the Holy Spirit—during which the religious life would know the fulness of love, joy, and spiritual freedom. But before the setting in of the third *status,* the Anti-Christ would rule for three and a half years, and the faithful would confront their final, and most terrible, trials.[73] A very holy pope and the *viri spirituales*—the latter composed of two groups among the religious: the preachers and the contemplatives—would resist the attack. The first age was dominated by married men, the second by the clergy, and the third would be guided by the spiritual monks. In the first age, work was primary; in the second age, science and discipline; the third *status* would accord the highest rewards to contemplation.

70. The most important were published in Venice at the beginning of the sixteenth century: *Concordia novi ac veteris Testamenti* (or *Liber Concordiae*), *Expositio in Apocalypsim,* and *Psalterium decem chordarum.*

71. Text reproduced by Bernard McGinn, *Visions of the End,* p. 130.

72. Cf. Marjorie Reeves, *The Influence of Prophecy in the Late Middle Ages: A Study of Joachimism,* pp. 7–11.

73. One finds here a well-known scenario of the Jewish and Christian apocalypse.

To be sure, this threefold schema of universal history and its relation to the Trinity are more complex than this, for Joachim reckoned equally with binary series (for example, the important events in Christian history were prefigured in the Old Testament). But the originality of his interpretation is incontestable. First of all, contrary to the view of Saint Augustine, the abbot estimates that after a number of tribulations, history could know an age of beatitude and spiritual freedom. Consequently, Christian perfection is before us in the *historical future* (an idea unacceptable to any orthodox theology). In effect, it is a matter of history and not of eschatology, one proof of which is the fact that the Third Age would also know degeneration and would come about through distress and ruin. For incorruptible perfection would be revealed only after the Last Judgment.

As one would expect, it is above all the concrete and historic character of the Third Age that aroused the strongest responses. These included not only the enthusiasm of the religious, and popular fervor, but ecclesiastical opposition. Joachim participated in the great movement of Church reform that had been underway since the eleventh century. He expected a true reform—a *reformatio mundi* conceived as a new irruption of divinity into history—and not a return to the past.[74] He did not reject traditional institutions, such as the papacy, sacraments, or clergy, but he accorded them a more modest role than they had had. The papacy's function and power were to be altered fundamentally.[75] The sacraments no longer seemed indispensable for the Church's future, which would be dominated by the Holy Spirit.[76] As to the priests, they would not disappear, but the direction of the Church would belong to the monks, the *viri spirituales:* a purely spiritual direction, and not a domination by the external institutions of the Church.[77]

The abbot determined that it was during the Third Age that Christ's work would be completed by the guidance of the Holy Spirit. But such a conception raised the question of Christ's central role in the history

74. Cf. McGinn, *Visions of the End*, p. 129.

75. McGinn, "Apocalypticism in the Middle Ages," p. 282, rectifying the opinion of Reeves, *The Influence of Prophecy*, pp. 395–97.

76. McGinn, "Apocalypticism," p. 282; cf. the bibliography cited in n. 82.

77. This is the reason why half a century after Joachim's death, the Spiritual Franciscans were dismayed that they were denied the freedom to practice the "new life"; McGinn, ibid., p. 282.

of salvation. In any case, the importance which Joachim accorded to the domination in the future Church of the *spiritual* over *institutions* clearly opposed forces which had emerged triumphant in the thirteenth-century Church. From this perspective, Joachim's conception constituted a radical critique of the Church of his own century.[78] The Abbot of Floris had announced the future foundation of two new orders, and the one created by Francis of Assisi probably reflects Joachimite ideas. In effect, the Franciscans believed that Saint Francis, through his exemplary existence of poverty, humility, and love for all living creatures, had realized in his own life a new "advent" of Christ. A great scandal erupted in Paris in 1254 when the Franciscan Gerardo di Borgo San Donnino published three texts of the Calabrian abbot under the title *Introduction to the Eternal Gospel,* adding an introduction and commentaries. He proclaimed that the Catholic Church's authority was nearing its end, and that soon (in 1280) the new spiritual Church, that of the Holy Spirit, would appear. The theologians at the University of Paris took advantage of this unexpected opportunity by denouncing the heresy and danger of the mendicant orders. Moreover, for some time already, Joachim had lost his welcome among the popes. In 1215, his Trinitarian doctrine was duly condemned. Following the "scandal" caused by the *Eternal Gospel,* Pope Alexander IV condemned the abbot's main ideas in 1263.

But Joachim was not to be without prestigious admirers, such as Dante, who placed him in Paradise. Manuscripts of his works multiplied and had a small circulation throughout western Europe. Directly or indirectly, Joachimism influenced the Fraticelli, the Beghards and the Beguines, and one rediscovers the Joachimite schema in the works of Arnold of Villanova and his disciples.[79] Later, toward the end of the sixteenth century and the beginning of the seventeenth, the first generations of Jesuits discovered the importance of the Joachimite conception of the third *status*. They felt, in effect, the drama of their own times, the approach of the decisive combat against Evil (identified with Martin Luther!).[80] One also detects certain unexpected prolongations of the Calabrian prophet's ideas in Ferdinand Lessing: in his *Education of the Human Race,* the latter philosopher develops the thesis of a

78. McGinn, *Visions of the End,* p. 129.
79. Cf. Reeves, *The Influence of Prophecy,* pp. 175–241.
80. Reeves, ibid., pp. 274ff.

continual and progressive revelation completing itself in a third age.[81]
The impact of Lessing's ideas was considerable. Through the Saint-
Simonians, he probably influenced August Comte in his doctrine of the
three stages. Fichte, Hegel, and Schelling have been marked, even if it
is for different reasons, by the Joachimite idea of an imminent third
age in which history will renew and complete itself.

81. Lessing, it is true, conceived of this third age as the triumph of reason, thanks to
education; but this was still no less, in his opinion, than the accomplishment of Christian revelation. He refers himself with sympathy and admiration "to certain enthusiasts of the thirteenth and fourteenth centuries" whose only error was to proclaim too
soon the "new eternal gospel"; cf. Karl Löwith, *Meaning in History,* p. 208.

35 Muslim Theologies and Mystical Traditions

272. The fundamentals of the mainstream theology

As we have seen (§265), the unity of the Muslim community (*ummah*) was destroyed following the rupture between the Sunnis (founded on the *sunna,* the "traditional practice") and Shî'ites (who claimed 'Alî as the first "true" caliph). Moreover, "from very early, it [Islam] diversified itself into an astonishing plurality of sects or schools, which often fought among themselves and sometimes even condemned each other, each of them presenting itself as the upholder *par excellence* of the revealed truth; many have disappeared in the course of history, and new disappearances always remain possible, but many (and often the most ancient) have also survived down to our own day with a remarkable vitality, thoroughly determined to perpetuate themselves and to continue to enrich with new contributions the sum of the beliefs and ideas bequeathed by their ancestors."[1]

Sunnism has represented, as it still continues to do, the Islamic mainstream. It is characterized first of all by the importance accorded to a literalist interpretation of the Quran and the tradition, and by the primary role of the Law, the *sharî'at*. But the domain of the *sharî'at* is larger than what one finds in western juridical systems. On the one hand, it regulates not only the faithful individual's relations with the community and the state, but also with God and with his own conscience. On the other hand, the *sharî'at* represents the expression of the divine will as it has been revealed by Muhammad. In effect, for Sunnism theology and the Law are inseparable. Its sources are as follows: the interpretation of the Quran; the *sunna* or tradition, based on

1. Henri Laoust, *Les schismes dans l'Islam,* pp. v–vi.

the activities and words of the Prophet; the *ijmâ*, or consensus of the testimonies of the Companions of Muhammad and their heirs; and *ijtihâd*, or personal reflection on issues where the Book and the *sunna* are silent. But certain authors include analogical reasoning (*ciyâs*) among the sources of the Law, and consider *ijtihâd* as the method by which such reasoning is effected.

For our purposes, it would be useless to study the four schools of jurisprudence recognized as canonical by the Sunni community.[2] All of the schools have used the rational method known as *kalâm*, an Arabic term meaning "speech" or "discourse," but which ends up by defining theology.[3] The oldest theologians are the Mo'tazilites, a group of thinkers who organized themselves at Basra in the first half of the second century following the Hijra. Their doctrine was rapidly imposed, and for some time became the official theology of Sunni Islam. Of the five fundamental theses of the Mo'tazilites, the most important are the first two. First is the *Tawhîd*, the divine Unity: "God is unique, nothing compares to him; he is neither body, nor individual, nor substance, nor accident. He is beyond time. He cannot reside either in a place or a being; he is not the object of any creaturely attributes or qualifications. He is neither conditioned nor determined, neither engendering nor engendered. . . . He has created the world without a pre-existent model and without assistance."[4] As a corollary, the Mo'tazilites deny the divine attributes and maintain that the Quran has been created. The second main thesis of the Mo'tazilites is that of divine justice, implying the free will which makes man responsible for his acts.

2. There are four schools: Hanafite, Malikite, Shafite, and Hanbalite. A brief study of their beginnings and several of their illustrative representatives has been made by Toufic Fahd, *L'Islam et les sectes islamiques,* pp. 31ff.

3. See especially H. A. Wolfson's monumental work, *Philosophy of the Kalâm*. Let us recall that the word *motakallim,* "he who speaks," gives rise to the term *motakallimûm,* "those who occupy themselves with the science of *kalâm,*" the "theologians." For certain philosophers like al-Fârâbî or Averroës, "the *motakallimûm* are above all apologists, attaching themselves not so much to a demonstrated or demonstrable truth, as to sustaining with all the resources of their dialectic theology, the articles of their traditional religious credo" (Henry Corbin, *Histoire de la philosophie islamique,* pp. 152–53).

4. Al-Ash'arî, as translated by Corbin, *Histoire,* p. 158. See Wolfson's exposition, *Philosophy,* pp. 129ff.; cf. also Laoust, *Les schismes,* s.v. *mu'tazilisme, mu'tazilite.*

The last three theses refer above all to the problems of individual morality and of the community's political organization.

At a certain moment, after the accession of the Caliph al Ma'mûn— who fully embraced Mo'tazilism and proclaimed it the doctrine of the state—the Sunni community underwent a particularly grave crisis. Unity was preserved by al-Ash'arî (260/873–324/935).[5] Although he had followed Mo'tazilite theology up to the age of forty, al-Ash'arî publicly abandoned it in the Great Mosque of Basra and dedicated the rest of his life to reconciling the different tendencies which competed with each other at the interior of Sunnism. Against the literalists, al-Ash'arî admitted the value of rational demonstration, but he criticized the absolute supremacy of reason such as it was professed by the Mo'tazilites. According to the Quran, faith in the *ghayb* (the invisible, the suprasensible, the mysterious) is indispensable to the religious life. Now, the *ghayb* exceeds rational demonstration. Always countering the Mo'tazilites, al-Ash'arî admits that God possesses the attributes and names mentioned in the Quran, but without "asking himself how"; he leaves "faith and reason face to face, without mediation." Similarly, the Quran is uncreated, since the divine word is eternal and not like "human enunciation [which is] manifested in time."[6]

Although it did not lack for criticism, especially as formulated by the Mo'tazilites and the literalists, the Ash'arite School has for centuries dominated almost all of Sunni Islam. Among its most important contributions, the profound analysis of the relations between faith and reason merits special attention. There is but one spiritual reality, and it is grasped by both faith and reason. "It is nonetheless a question in each case of a mode of perception whose conditions are so different that one can neither confuse them, nor substitute the one for the other, nor dispense with the one in order to keep only the other."[7] And yet, concludes Corbin, "in confronting the Mo'tazilites and the literalists at the same time, Ash'arism remains in fact on their own ground."[8] And on that ground, it would be difficult to develop a spiritual exegesis of the Revelation by passing from the exoteric meaning to the esoteric.

5. See Wolfson, pp. 248ff., etc.; Laoust, pp. 127ff., 177ff., 200ff.

6. Corbin, pp. 165ff.

7. Ibid., p. 177. See also Fazlur Rahman, *Islam,* pp. 91ff; Wolfson, pp. 526ff.

8. Corbin, p. 177. "If Ash'arism survived so many attacks and critiques, one must admit that the conscience of Sunni Islam recognized itself within it" (p. 178).

273. Shî'ism and the esoteric hermeneutic

Like Judaism and Christianity, Islam is a "religion of the Book." God has revealed himself in the Quran through his messenger the Angel, who dictated to the Prophet the divine word. From a legal and social perspective, the five "Pillars of Faith" (cf. §264) constitute what is essential for the religious life. But the Muslim ideal is to comprehend the "true" sense of the Quran, that is, what is true on the ontological plane (and is expressed by the term, *haqîqat*). The prophets, and above all the final one, Muhammad, have enunciated the Divine Law, the *sharî'at*, in their inspired texts. But the texts are susceptible to diverse interpretations, beginning with the most obvious, the literal. According to Muhammad's son-in-law, 'Alî, the first Imâm, "there is no Quranic verse which does not have four senses: the exoteric (*zâhir*); the esoteric (*bâtin*); the limit (*hadd*); and the divine project (*mottala'*). The exoteric is for oral recitation; the esoteric is for inner comprehension; the limit refers to proclamations regulating the licit and illicit; and the divine project is that which God offers in each verse for man's realization."[9] This conception, although specific to Shî'ism, is shared by numerous Muslim mystics and theologians. As the great Iranian philosopher, Nasîr-e Khosraw (fifth/eleventh century) wrote: "the positive religion (*sharî'at*) is the exoteric aspect of the Idea (*haqîqat*), and the *Idea* is the esoteric aspect of the positive religion. . . . The positive religion is the symbol (*mithâl*); the Idea is the symbolized (*manithûl*)."[10]

The Idea, *haqîqat,* requires Master Initiators to make it accessible to the faithful. For the Shî'ites, these master initiators, the spiritual guides *par excellence,* are the Imâms.[11] In fact, one of the most ancient spiritual exegeses of the Quran is found in the esoteric teaching given by the Imâms to their disciples. This teaching has been faithfully

9. Translated by Corbin, p. 30. Cf. the theory of the four senses in medieval Christian theology (literal, allegorical, moral, and analogical).

10. Translated by Corbin, p. 17. According to an *hadîth* considered as original to the Prophet himself, "the Quran has an exterior appearance and a hidden profundity, an exoteric sense and an esoteric sense; in its turn, this esoteric sense harbors an esoteric sense," and so on up to seven esoteric senses; cf. ibid., p. 21.

11. Let us recall that the Arabic term *Imâm* originally referred to one who led public prayer, that is, the caliph. For the Shî'ites, the Imâm has, in addition to his role as spiritual leader, the role of representing the highest politico-religious dignity.

transmitted and constitutes an imposing *corpus* (twenty-six folio volumes in the Majlisî edition). The exegesis practiced by the Imâms and the Shî'ite authors is founded on the complementarity of two key terms: *tanzîl* and *ta'wîl*. The first designates the positive religion, the letter of Revelation that has descended from the higher world thanks to the Angel's dictation. By contrast, *ta'wîl* involves a *return to the origin,* that is, to the true and original sense of the sacred text. According to an Ismaili text (cf. §274), "It is to make something arrive at its origin. The one who practices *ta'wîl* is thus someone who redirects what has been enunciated from its exterior (exoteric, *zâhir*) appearance, and makes it *return* to its truth, its *haqîqat.*"[12]

In opposition to the orthodox view, the Shî'ites believe that after Muhammad there began a new cycle, that of the *walâyat* ("friendship, protection"). God's "friendship" reveals to the prophets and the Imâms the secret meanings of the Book and of the tradition, and thereby makes it continually possible to initiate the faithful into the divine mysteries. "In this aspect, Shî'ism is the Gnosis of Islam. The cycle of the *walâyat* is thus the cycle of the Imâm succeeding the Prophet, that is, of the *bâtin* succeeding the *zâhir,* of the *haqîqat* succeeding the *sharî'at*" (Corbin, *Histoire,* p. 46). In fact, the first Imâms wished to maintain an equilibrium between positive religion and the "Idea" without dissociating the *bâtin* from the *zâhir.* But circumstances prevented them from maintaining this equilibrium, and with it, the unity of Shî'ism.

Let us briefly recall the highly dramatic history of this movement. Beyond the political persecutions of the Umayyad caliphs and the opposition of the Doctors of the Law, Shî'ism also suffered greatly from its own internal dissensions, giving birth to numerous sects and schisms. Since the religious leader was the Imâm, that is, a direct descendant of 'Alî, a crisis broke out on the death of the sixth Imâm, Ja'far al-Sâdik (d. 148/765). His son Isma'îl, already invested by his father, died prematurely. A segment of the faithful rallied to the latter's son, Muhammad ibn Isma'îl, whom they regarded as the seventh Imâm; these were the Ismailis, or the "Sevener" Shî'ites. Others of the faithful recognized Isma'îl's brother Mûsâ Kâzem as the seventh Imâm. This latter figure had also been invested by Ja'far. Mûsâ Kâzem's line continued down to a twelfth Imâm, Muhammad al-Mahdîq,

12. *Kalâm-e Pir,* translated by Corbin, *Histoire,* p. 27.

who disappeared mysteriously in 260/874 at the age of five on the same day that his young father, the next-to-last Imâm, died.[13] These are the "Twelver" Shî'ites or *Imâmîya,* who are also the most numerous. As for the numbers seven and twelve, they have been much commented upon by the theosophers of these two Shî'ite divisions.[14]

From a legal perspective, the most important differences from Sunni orthodoxy are the following: (1) temporary marriage, and (2) the right to conceal one's religious opinions, a vestige of the period of persecutions. The innovations of the two branches of Shî'ism are most evident on the theological plane. We have seen the importance of esotericism and gnosis. According to certain Sunni theologians and western authors, it is due precisely to the secret teaching of the Imâms that various foreign conceptions (above all, Gnostic and Iranian ones) have penetrated into Shî'ite Islam. One cites, for example, the idea of the divine emanation in successive stages and the insertion of the Imâms in this process. The same is said of the doctrine of metempsychosis, of certain cosmological and anthropological theories, and so on. Let us remember, however, that similar phenomena are found in Sufism (§275), in the Kabbala (§289), and in the history of Christianity. What one must account for in each case is not the fact in itself, and in particular the borrowing of foreign spiritual ideas and methods, but their reinterpretation and articulation within the systems that have assimilated them.

Moreover, the position which the Shî'ites accorded to the Imâm provoked criticism by the orthodox majority, especially when some Shî'ites compared their Master to the Prophet. We have already cited (§259, n. 2) several examples of the inevitable mythologization of Muhammad's biography. It would be easy to multiply them. For example, a light radiated from his father's head (an allusion to the "light

13. On the disappearance of the twelfth Imâm and its consequences (particularly the spiritual ones), see Henry Corbin, *En Islam iranien,* vol. 4, pp. 303–89. This disappearance marks the beginning of the "lesser occultation" which will last two years, during which the hidden Imâm secretly communicates several times through certain messengers. As he did not designate his successor, the Great Occultation, or the secret history of the twelfth Imâm, begins in 329/940.

14. One should also mention a third branch, the Zaidîya, named after the fifth Imâm, Zaid (d. 724). They are much less numerous and closer to Sunnism; in fact, they do not accord supernatural virtues to the Imâms, as is done above all by the Ismailis (cf. §274).

of Muhammad's glory''); Muhammad was the Perfect Man (*insân Kâmil*), having become the intermediary between God and mankind. One *hadîth* recalls that God had told him: "If you had not existed, I would not have created the spheres!" Let us add that for a number of mystical confraternities, the adept's final goal was union with the Prophet.

But for the Sunnis, the Imâm could not be placed beside Muhammad. They themselves recognized the excellence and nobility of 'Alî, but they rejected the idea that there existed no legitimate successors beyond 'Alî and his family. Above all, the Sunnis denied the belief that the Imâm is inspired by God, indeed that he is a manifestation of God.[15] In effect, the Shî'ites recognized in 'Alî and his descendants a particle of the divine Light—or according to some, a divine substance—but without thereby implying the idea of Incarnation. More correctly, one could say that the Imâm is a divine epiphany, a theophany (one finds a similar belief among certain mystics, but without it being related to the Imâm; cf. §276). As a consequence, for the Twelver Shî'ites as well as for the Ismailis, the Imâm becomes the intermediary between God and the faithful. He does not substitute himself for the Prophet, but completes his work and partakes of his prestige—an audacious and original conception, for it leaves open the future of the religious experience. Thanks to the *walâyat,* "the friendship of God," the Imâm can discover, and reveal to the faithful, still unsuspected dimensions of the spiritual Islam.

274. Ismailism and the exaltation of the Imâm; the Great Resurrection; the Mahdî

Thanks to the work of W. Ivanow, we are beginning to understand something of the Ismailis. Few texts remain from their first era. After the death of the Imâm Isma'îl, the tradition continued through three hidden Imâms. In 487/1094, the Ismaili community divided itself into two branches: the "orientals" (those from Persia), whose center was the "command post" of Alamût (a fortress in the mountains southwest of the Caspian Sea), and the "occidentals," those living in Egypt and

---

15. Rejected from Ismailism, the Nussaïrites of Syria considered 'Alî as superior to the Prophet; some even divinized him. But this conception was rejected by the Shî'ites.

Yemen. The scope of this present work does not allow for analysis, or even a summary, of the complex ensemble of Ismaili cosmology, anthropology, and eschatology.[16] Let us only specify that according to Ismaili authors, the Imâm's body is not a body of flesh; like that of Zarathustra (cf. §101), it is the result of a heavenly dewdrop absorbed by his parents. Ismaili gnosis understands the Imâm's "divinity" (*lâhit*) to refer to his "spiritual birth," which transforms him into the support of the "Temple of Light," a purely spiritual Temple. "His Imâmate, his 'divinity,' is the *corpus mysticum* composed of all the forms of the light of his adepts" (Corbin, *Histoire*, p. 134).

Still more audacious is the doctrine of the reformed Ismailism of Alamût.[17] On 17 Ramazan 559 (8 April 1164), the Imâm proclaimed to his followers the Great Resurrection. What the proclamation implied was nothing less than the advent of a pure spiritual Islam, freed of any legalistic spirit, of all servitude to the Law, a personal religion since it brought one to discover and make alive the spiritual sense of the prophetic Revelations" (ibid., p. 139). The capture and destruction of the Alamût fortress by the Mongols (in 654/1251) did not end the movement; this spiritual Islam perpetuated itself, camouflaged, in the confraternities of the Sufis.

According to reformed Ismailism, the person of the Imâm has precedence over that of the Prophet. "What Twelver Shî'ism thinks of as being at the end of an eschatological perspective, the Ismailism of Alamût accomplished 'in the present' by an anticipation of the eschatology which is an insurrection of the Spirit against all servitudes" (Corbin, *Histoire*, p. 142). With the Imâm being regarded as the Perfect Man, or the "Face of God," knowledge of the Imâm "is the sole knowledge of God which is possible for man." According to Corbin, it is the Eternal Imâm who speaks in the following sentences: "The

16. One speaks of the Primordial Principle or Organizer, of the Mystery of Mysteries, of the Procession of Being from the First Intelligence and from the Spiritual Adam, of two hierarchies—heavenly and earthly—which, according to Corbin's expression, "symbolize the one with the other," etc.; cf. Corbin, *Histoire*, pp. 110–36, summarizing the works cited in our bibliography (§274). The history of Ismailism is presented by Laoust, *Les schismes*, pp. 140ff., 184ff.

17. The castle-fort of Alamût and reformed Ismailism have inspired in the West an entire folklore about the "assassins" (a term derived, according to Sylvester de Sacy, from *hashshâshîn*, since it was supposed that the faithful had absorbed *hashish*). On these legends, see S. Olschki, *Marco Polo's Asia*, pp. 368ff., and the other works cited in our bibliography (§274).

prophets pass and change. We ourselves are Eternal Men.'' ''The Men of God are not God Himself; however, they are not separable from God'' (ibid., p. 144). Consequently, ''only the eternal Imâm as a theophany makes possible an ontology: being *the* revealed, he is *being* as such. He is the absolute Person, the eternal divine Face, the supreme divine Attribute who is the supreme name of God. In his earthly form, he is the epiphany of the Supreme Word, the true Gate of All Times, manifestation of the Eternal Man manifesting the Face of God'' (ibid., pp. 144–45).

Equally significant is the belief that for man, self-knowledge presupposes knowledge of the Imâm (this is, of course, a matter of spiritual knowledge, of the ''encounter,'' in the *mundus imaginalis,* with the hidden Imâm who is invisible and inaccessible to the senses). An Ismaili text affirms: ''He who dies without having known his Imâm dies the death of the unconscious.'' Corbin justly sees in the lines which follow a statement of what is perhaps the supreme message of Ismaili philosophy: ''The Imâm has said: 'I am with my friends wherever they seek me, on the mountain, in the plain and in the desert. He to whom I have revealed my Essence, that is, the mystical knowledge of myself, that one no longer has need of a physical proximity. And that is the Great Resurrection'' (ibid., p. 149).

The invisible Imâm has played a decisive role in the mystical experience of the Ismailis and other branches of Shî'ism. Let us add that analogous conceptions concerning the sanctity, indeed the ''divinity,'' of spiritual masters are also met in other religious traditions (India, Medieval Christianity, Hasidism).

It is proper to point out that the fabulous image of the hidden Imâm has been associated many times with the eschatological myth of the *Mahdî,* literally ''the Guide'' (that is, ''the one who is guided by God''). The term is not found in the Quran, and numerous Sunni authors have applied it to historical personages.[18] For some, the Mahdî was Jesus ('Isâ), but the majority of theologians make him descend from the family of the Prophet. For the Sunnis, although he unleashes the universal *renovatio,* the Mahdî is not the infallible Guide that the

18. See the references in the article by D. B. Macdonald in the *Shorter Encyclopedia of Islam,* p. 310. Among the most competent and detailed presentations of the legends and beliefs related to the figure of the Mahdî, cf. Ibn Khaldûn, *The Muqaddimah* (trans. by Rosenthal), vol. 2, pp. 156–206.

Shî'ites proclaim him to be; for the latter had identified the Mahdî with the twelfth Imâm.

The occultation and reappearance of the Mahdî at the end of time have played a considerable role in popular piety and in millenarist crises. For one particular sect (the Kaisânîya), the Mahdî will be Muhammad ibn al-Hanafîya, the son of 'Alî with a wife other than Fatima. Although ever alive, he lies in his tomb on Mount Radwa, where the faithful await his return. As in all of these traditions, the approach of the end of time is characterized by a radical degeneracy of men and by specific signs: the Ka'ba will disappear; copies of the Quran will become blank pages; those who speak the name of Allah will be killed, etc. The Epiphany of the Mahdî will inaugurate for the Muslims an age of justice and prosperity unequalled on earth. The Mahdî's reign will last five, seven, or nine years. Evidently, the expectation of his appearance reached its paroxysm during ages of disaster. Numerous political leaders have attempted to gain power (and have obtained it many times) by proclaiming themselves to be the Mahdî.[19]

275. Sufism, esoterism, and mystical experiences

Sufism represents the most well known of the mystical dimensions of Islam, and one of the most important traditions of Islamic esoterism. The etymology of the Arabic term *sufi* seems to derive from *suf*, "wool," an allusion to the woolen mantle worn by the Sufis. The term was widely used by the end of the third (ninth) century. According to the tradition, the spiritual ancestors of Sufism were found among Muhammad's Companions: for example, Salmân al-Fârisi, the Persian barber who lived in the Prophet's house and who became the model for spiritual adoption and mystical initiation, and Uways al Qaranî, whose devotion Muhammad exalted.[20] Less is known of the origins of ascetic tendencies,[21] but they probably developed under the Umayyad dynas-

19. An example is the Mahdî of Sudan, conquered by Lord Kitchener in 1885.
20. See L. Massignon, "Salman Pâk et les prémices de l'Islam iranien"; Anne-Marie Schimmel, *Mystical Dimensions of Islam*, pp. 28ff.
21. In the third century after the *Hijra*, the majority of Sufis were married; two centuries later, those married were only a minority.

ty. In effect, a great number of the faithful were disappointed by the religious indifference of the caliphs, who were solely preoccupied with the continued expansion of the Empire.[22]

The first mystic-ascetic is Hasan al-Basrî (d. 110/728), famous for his piety and profound melancholy, for he thought constantly of the Day of Judgment. Another contemplative, Ibrâhîm ibn Adham, is reputed to have defined the three phases of asceticism (*zuhd*): (1) renouncing the world; (2) renouncing the happiness of knowing that one has abandoned the world; and (3) realizing completely the world's lack of importance so that one no longer even regards it.[23] Râbî'a (d. 185/801), a slave set free by his master, introduced into Sufism the gratuitous and total love of God. Lovers of God should think neither of Paradise nor of Hell. Râbi'a is the first among the Sufis to speak of God's jealousy. "O, my Hope and my Repose and my Delight, the heart can love no other besides You!"[24] The nocturnal prayer becomes for Râbi'â a long and amorous conversation with God.[25] However, as recent research has shown,[26] Ja'far al-Sâdik, the sixth Imâm (d. 148/765) and one of the great masters of early Sufism, had already defined the mystical experience in terms of divine love ("a divine fire which devours man completely"). Here one sees evidence of the solidarity between Shî'ism and the first phase of Sufism.

In effect, the esoteric dimension of Islam (*bâtin*) that is specific to Shî'ism was at first identified in the *sunna* with Sufism. According to Ibn Khaldûn, "the Sufis were saturated in the theories of Shî'ism." Likewise, the Shî'ites considered their doctrines as the source and inspiration of Sufism.[27]

In any case, mystical experiences and theosophical gnoses were not

22. Later numerous Sufis identified the "government" with "evil"; cf. Schimmel, *Mystical Dimensions,* p. 30. One must also bear in mind the influences of Christian monasticism; cf. Marijan Molé, *Les mystiques musulmans,* pp. 8ff.

23. Schimmel, p. 37.

24. Translation by Margaret Smith, *Râbî'a the Mystic,* p. 55.

25. See the text translated ibid., p. 27.

26. Cf. Paul Nwyia, *Exégèse coranique et langage mystique,* pp. 160ff.

27. Cf. S. H. Nasr, "Shi'ism and Sufism," pp. 105ff. One must also recognize that in the first centuries of Islam, it was difficult to specify whether an author was Sunni or Shî'ite; ibid., pp. 106–7. The rupture between Shî'ism and Sufism occurred when certain Sufi masters presented a new interpretation of spiritual initiation and of the "divine friendship" (see below). Shî'ite Sufism vanished from the third/ninth century on, and didn't reappear until the seventh/thirteenth century.

easily received into orthodox Islam. The Muslim did not dare to conceive of an intimate rapport, born of spiritual love, with Allah. It sufficed for him to abandon himself to God, to obey the Law, and to complete the teachings of the Quran with the tradition (*sunna*). Strengthened by their theological erudition and their mastery of jurisprudence, the *ulamâ* considered themselves the sole religious leaders of the community. The Sufis, however, were staunchly antirationalist; for them, true religious knowledge was obtained by a personal experience ending in a momentary union with God. In the eyes of the *ulamâ*, the consequences of the mystical experience, and the interpretations given it by the Sufis, threatened the very foundation of orthodox theology.

Moreover, the "path" of Sufism necessarily implied "disciples," with their initiation and their long instruction by a master. This exceptional relationship between the master and his disciples resulted very quickly in the veneration of the *sheikh* and the cult of saints. As al-Hujwîri has written, "Know that the principle and foundation of Sufism, and the Knowledge of God, rest upon the Saints."[28]

These innovations disturbed the *ulamâ*, and this was not only because they saw their authority menaced or ignored. For these orthodox theologians, the Sufis raised suspicions of heresy. In effect, as we shall see, one can detect in Sufism the influences of Neoplatonism, Gnosticism, and Manichaeanism. To the orthodox, such influences were sacrilegious and harmful. Suspected of heresy, certain Sufis—such as the Egyptians Dhû'l-Nûn (d. 245/859) and al-Nûri (d. 295/907)—were placed on trial before the caliph, and the great masters al-Hallâj and Sohrawardî wound up being executed for heresy (cf. §§277, 280). All this obliged the Sufis to limit the communication of their experiences and conceptions to reliable disciples and to confine it to a restricted group of initiates.

The movement did, however, continue to progress, for it satisfied "the religious instincts of the people, instincts which were to some extent chilled and starved by the abstract and impersonal teachings of the orthodox and found relief in the more directly personal and emotional religious approach of the Sufis."[29] In effect, beyond the initiato-

---

28. *Kashf al-Mahjûb*, translated by R. A. Nicholson, p. 363; cf. H. A. Gibb, *Mohammedanism*, p. 138.
29. Gibb, *Mohammedanism*, p. 135.

ry instruction reserved for the disciples, the Sufi masters encouraged public "spiritual concerts." The religious chants, the instrumental music (reed flutes, cymbals, tambourines), the sacred dance, the untiring repetition of God's name (*dhikr*), touched the people as well as the spiritual elites. We will insist further on the symbolism and function of sacred music and dance (§282). The *dhikr* resembles an Eastern Christian prayer, the *monologistos,* which is limited to the continual repetition of the name of God or Jesus.[30] As we shall see (§283), the technique of the *dhikr* (as well as that of the Hesychastic practice) presents by the twelfth century an extremely complex morphology implying a "mystical physiology" and a method of yogic type (specific bodily positions, disciplined breathing, chromatic and acoustical manifestations, etc.). The possibility of certain Indian influences is not to be dismissed.

In the course of time, and with certain exceptions, the oppression exercised by the *ulamâ* would disappear completely. Even the most intransigent among the persecutors ultimately recognized the exceptional contribution of the Sufis to the expansion and spiritual renewal of Islam.

276. Several Sufi masters, from Dhû'l-Nûn to Tirmidhî

The Egyptian Dhû'l-Nûn (d. 245–859) practiced the art of dissimulating his mystical experiences. "O God! In public I tell you 'My Lord,' but whenever I am alone I call you 'O, My Love!'" According to tradition, Dhû'l-Nûn was the first to formulate the distinction between *ma'rîfa,* intuitive knowledge ("experience") of God, and *'ilm,* discursive knowledge. "The gnostic becomes more humble every hour, for every hour he is drawing nearer to God. . . . They are not themselves, but in so far as they exist at all, they exist in God. Their movements are caused by God and their words are the words of God, which are uttered by their tongues."[31] It is important to mention Dhû'l-Nûn's literary

30. Several centuries before the *dhikr,* this prayer is mentioned by a number of the Church Fathers (Saints Nils, John Cassian, John Climacus, etc.); it was practiced above all by the Hesychasts.

31. See Margaret Smith, *Readings from the Mystics of Islam,* no. 20. Cf. also Schimmel, *Mystical Dimensions,* pp. 43ff.

talent. His long hymns celebrating the Lord's glory inaugurated the mystical valorization of poetry.

One of the most controversial mystics of Islam, the Persian Abû Yazîd Bistâmî (d. 260/874), did not write any books. But his disciples have transmitted the essentials of his teachings in the form of sayings and maxims. By means of a particularly severe ascesis and a concentrated meditation on God's essence, Bistâmî obtained the "annihilation" of the self (fanâ), which he was the first to formulate; similarly, he was the first to describe his mystical experiences in terms of the mî'râj (the nocturnal ascension of Muhammad; cf. §261). He had realized "solitariness" and, at least momentarily—he believed—he had experienced the absolute unity between the beloved, the lover, and love. In ecstasy, Bistâmî had pronounced "theopathic expressions," while speaking as if he were God. "How is it you have arrived there? I cast off myself as a serpent casts off his skin; then I considered my essence: and I was myself Him!" Or again, "God considered every consciousness in the Universe, and He saw that they were all empty of Him, except for my own, where He saw Himself in plenitude."[32]

Following other Orientalists, Zaehner has interpreted Bistâmî's mystical experience as the result of Indian influence, and more precisely that of Shankara's Vedānta.[33] Considering the importance accorded to ascesis and meditation techniques, one would think rather of yoga. Be that as it may, certain Sufi masters doubted that Bistâmî had realized union with God. According to Junayd, he "made no progress, he did not attain the final and full state." Al-Hallâj believed that he "arrived at the very threshold of divine speech," and thought that "it was indeed from God that these words came to him"; but the route was blocked to him by the obstacle of his "self." "Poor Abû Yazîd," said Hallâj, "who did not know how to recognize where and how one should bring about the union of the soul and God."[34]

Abû'l Qâsim al-Junayd (d. 298/910) was the veritable master of the Sufis in Baghdad. He left numerous theological and mystical treatises, precious above all for their analysis of the spiritual experiences leading to the soul's absorption into God. In his teachings, Junayd emphasized

32. L. Massignon, trans., *Lexique technique de la mystique musulmane*, pp. 276ff. See also G.-C. Anawati and Louis Gardet, *Mystique musulmane*, pp. 32–33, 110–15.

33. R. C. Zaehner, *Hindu and Muslim Mysticism*, pp. 86–134.

34. Massignon, p. 280; Anawati and Gardet, p. 114.

the importance of sobriety (*sahw*), which he opposed to the spiritual intoxication (*sukr*) practiced by Bistâmî. After the ecstatic experience which annihilates the individual, it is important to gain a "second sobriety" in which the individual returns to consciousness of himself and an awareness that his attributes are restored to him, transformed and spiritualized by God's presence. The final goal of the mystic is not "annihilation" (*fanâ*) but a new life in God (*baqâ*, "that which remains").

Persuaded that the mystical experience could not be formulated in rationalist terminology, Junayd forbade his disciples to speak of it before the uninitiated (it is for having contravened this rule that he rejected al-Hallâj). His treatises and letters are composed in a sort of "secret language," inaccessible to the reader unfamiliar with his teaching.[35]

Another Iranian master, Husayn Tirmidhî (d. 285/898), was surnamed *al-Hakîm,* "the philosopher," since he was the first among the Sufis to draw upon Hellenistic philosophy. A prolific author (of some twenty-four tracts), Tirmidhî is known above all for his *Seal of Holiness* (*Khâtam al-walâya*),[36] in which he develops the terminology which Sufism continues to use henceforth. The leader of the Sufi hierarchy is the *qutb* ("pole") or *ghauth* ("aide"). The degrees of holiness which he describes do not make up a "hierarchy of love"; they refer to the saint's gnosis and illuminations. With Tirmidhî, the insistence on gnosis becomes more explicit, thus preparing the way for later theosophic speculations.[37]

Tirmidhî insisted persistently upon the notion of *walâyat* ("the divine friendship"; spiritual initiation). He distinguished its two degrees: a general *walâyat* accorded to all the faithful, and a particular *walâyat* reserved for the spiritual elite, the "intimates of God who converse and communicate with Him, since they are with Him in a state of effective and transcendent union." Now, as Corbin remarks, "the idea of the double *walâyat* is first postulated and established by Shî'ite doctrine."[38] In analyzing the relationship between *walâyat* and prophecy, Tirmidhî concludes that the former is supreme, since it is permanent

35. Schimmel, pp. 57ff. See also Zaehner, pp. 135–61.
36. One will find a list of the chapters in Massignon, pp. 289–92.
37. Schimmel, p. 57.
38. Corbin, *Histoire de la philosophie islamique,* p. 274. See also Nasr, "Shi'ism and Sufism" (= *Sufi Essays*), pp. 110ff.

and not tied to a historical moment like prophecy. In effect, the cycle of prophecy completes itself with Muhammad, while the cycle of the *walâyat* extends to the end of time.[39]

277. Al-Hallâj, mystic and martyr

Born in 244/857 in the southwest of Iran, al-Hallâj (Hussayn-ibn-Mansûr) received the teaching of two spiritual masters before he encountered the famous sheikh al-Junayd in Baghdad, and became the latter's disciple in 264/877. Hallâj undertook the pilgrimage to Mecca, where he practiced fasting and silence, and experienced his first mystic ecstasies. "My spirit blends itself with His Spirit as musk with amber, as wine with pure water."[40] On his return from the *hajj*, Hallâj was dismissed by Junayd, broke relations with the majority of the Sufis of Baghdad, and left the city for four years. Later, when he began his first public preaching, he irritated not only the traditionalists but also the Sufis, who accused him of disclosing "secrets" to the uninitiated. He was also reproached for "performing miracles" (like the Prophets!), in contrast with other sheikhs, who showed their powers only to the initiated. Al-Hallâj then rejected the Sufi habit in order to mingle freely with the people.[41]

Accompanied by four hundred disciples, Hallâj completed his second pilgrimage in 291/905. He then set off for a long voyage to India, Turkestan, and up to the frontiers of China. After his third pilgrimage to Mecca, where he stayed for two years, Hallâj finally took up residence in Baghdad (294/908) and devoted himself to public preaching (cf. Massignon, *Passion*, 1:268ff.). He proclaimed that the ultimate human goal is mystical union with God, effected by love (*'ishq*). In this union the acts of the faithful are sanctified and divinized. In ecstasy, he pronounced the famous words—"I am the Truth [= God]"—which led to his condemnation. This time, Hallâj had united against him the doctors of the Law (who accused him of pantheism), the politicians (who reproached him for agitating the crowd), and the Sufis. What is surprising is Hallâj's desire to die anath-

39. Corbin (p. 275) remarks on the analogy of this doctrine with Shî'ite prophecy.
40. *Dîw'ân*, translated by Massignon, *Lexique technique*, p. xvi.
41. L. Massignon, *La Passion d'al-Hallâj*, 2d ed., vol. 1, pp. 177ff.

ematized. "Wishing to provoke the faithful to make an end of this scandal of a man who dared to speak of himself as united with the Deity, as they were killing him he cried out in the Mosque of al-Mansûr: 'God, you have made lawful my blood. Kill me. . . . There is no more urgent duty on earth for the Muslims than my execution.' "[42]

This strange behavior of al-Hallâj recalls the *malâmtîya,* a group of contemplatives who for the love of God sought out the blame (*malâma*) of their coreligionists. They did not wear the Sufi habit, and they learned to hide their mystical experiences; what is more, they provoked the faithful by their eccentric and apparently impious behavior.[43] The phenomenon was known elsewhere among certain Eastern Christian monks from the sixth century on, and there are parallels in southern India.

Arrested in 301/915, and remaining in prison for nearly nine years,[44] Hallâj was executed in 309/922. Witnesses reported hearing these final words of supplication: "It is enough for the ecstatic when his Unique within him is alone there to witness Itself" (word for word: "what counts for the ecstatic is that the Unique reduces him to unity").[45]

His written work has been conserved only in part: some fragments of a commentary on the Quran, several letters, a certain number of maxims and poems, and a small book, *Kitâb at-tawasin,* in which Hallâj discusses divine unity and prophecy.[46] The poems are saturated with an intense nostalgia for ultimate union with God. One meets several times with expressions borrowed from alchemy (cf. Massignon, *Passion,* 3:369ff.) as well as references to the secret meaning of the Arabic alphabet.

An examination of these texts, all inventoried, edited, and exhaustively analyzed by Louis Massignon, brings out the integrity of al-Hallâj's faith and his veneration of the Prophet. The "way" of Hallâj

42. *Dîw'ân,* p. xxi.

43. Later certain *malâmatîya* groups pushed their contempt of norms to include orgiastic practices. See the texts translated by Molé, *Les mystiques musulmans,* pp. 73–76.

44. See Massignon, *Passion,* vol. 1, pp. 385ff. (the accusation); 502ff. (the trial); 607ff. (martyrdom).

45. *Dîw'ân,* pp. xxi–xxii.

46. A complete list, abundantly commented upon, can be found in Massignon, *Passion,* vol. 1, pp. 20ff.; vol. 3, pp. 295ff.

did not envisage the destruction of the human person, but sought out suffering in order to understand the ''impassioned love'' (*'ishq*) which reveals the essence of God and the mystery of Creation. The statement ''I am the Truth'' does not imply pantheism (of which some have accused him), for Hallâj always emphasized God's transcendence. It is only in rare ecstatic experiences that a creature's spirit can be united with God.[47]

The conception of the ''transforming union'' announced by al-Hallâj is summarized precisely enough by a hostile theologian, despite the latter's tendentious presentation. According to this author, ''[Hallâj maintained that] the one who dresses his body in obedience to the rites, fills his heart with pious works, endures privations of pleasures and possesses his own soul in forbidding himself desires—[such a one] raises himself up to the station of 'those who are reconciled' (to God); . . . then he does not cease to descend the degrees of distance until his nature is purified of what is carnal. And then . . . this Spirit of God descends upon him through which Jesus, the son of Mary, is born. Then he becomes 'one whom every thing obeys' (*Muta'*), and wishes nothing more than to put into execution the Commandment of God; from then on every act of his is an act of God, and each of his commandments is a Commandment of God.''[48]

After his martyrdom, Hallâj's sanctity did not cease to grow; indeed, it spread throughout the Muslim world.[49] Just as important has been his posthumous influence on the Sufis and on a strain of mystical theology.

278. Al-Ghazzâlî and the reconciliation between *Kalâm* and Sufism

Among other consequences, the martyrdom of al-Hallâj obliged the Sufis to demonstrate, in their public appearances, that they were not

47. Hallâj's theology has been analyzed by Massignon, *Passion*, vol. 3, pp. 9ff. (mystical theology); 63–234 (dogmatic theology). For a concise exposition, see Schimmel, *Mystical Dimensions*, pp. 71ff.
48. Text translated by Massignon, *Passion*, vol. 3, p. 48.
49. See in the Introduction to the *Dîw'ân*, pp. xxxviii–xlv, the brief exposition by Massignon on the gradual reincorporation of Hallâj into the Muslim community.

contradicting orthodox teachings. Some camouflaged their mystical experiences and theological ideas in eccentric behavior. This is the case, for example, with Shiblî (247/861–334/945), the friend who questioned Hallâj as he was hanging from the gallows on the meaning of the *unio mystica,* and who survived him by twenty-three years. In order to make himself look ridiculous, Shiblî compared himself to a toad. By his paradoxes and poetic effusions, he carefully managed a "privilege of immunity" (Massignon). He said: "He who loves God for His acts of Grace is a polytheist." Once Shiblî asked his disciples to abandon him, for no matter where they were, he would be with them and would protect them.[50]

Another mystic, Niffarî (d. 354/865) of Iraq, also used paradox but avoided the preciosity of Shiblî. He was probably the first to proclaim that prayer is a divine gift. "To me belongs the giving: if I had not answered thy prayer I should not have made thee seeking it."[51]

In the century following al-Hallâj's martyrdom, certain authors wrote about the doctrines and practices of Sufism. Let us note especially the theory, which becomes classical, of "steps" or "stations" (*maqâmât*), and the "states" (*ahwâl*) of the "path" (*tarîqah*). Three principal steps are distinguished: that of the novice (*murîd*); that of the individual who is progressing (*sâlik*); and that of the perfected (*kâmil*). On the advice of his sheikh, the novice must practice several ascetic exercises beginning with repentance and ending with the serene acceptance of all that happens to him. The ascesis and instruction constitute an inner combat carefully supervised by the master. Whereas the *maqâmât,* the "stations," are the result of personal effort, the "states" are a free gift of God.[52]

It is important to recall that in the third/ninth century, Muslim mysticism knew three theories of divine union. "Union is conceived: (a) as a conjunction (*ittisâl* or *wisâl*) which excludes the idea of an identity of the soul and God; (b) as an identification (*ittihâd*), which itself covers two different meanings: the one a synonym of the preceding, the other

50. See the texts cited by Schimmel, pp. 78ff.

51. Ibid., pp. 80ff. Schimmel emphasizes the similarity with Pascal's famous phrase.

52. Their number varies. One author, cited by Anawati, names ten of them, among them love, fear, hope, desire, peaceful tranquility, contemplation, certitude; cf. Anawati and Gardet, *Mystique musulmane,* pp. 42ff. See the texts translated and commented upon ibid., pp. 125–80, and by S. H. Nasr, *Sufi Essays,* pp. 73–74, 77–83.

evoking a union of natures; or (c) as inhabitation (*hulûl*): the Spirit of God resides, without confusion of natures, in the purified soul of the mystic. The doctors of official Islam allowed for union only in the sense of *ittisâl* (or its equivalent, the first sense of *ittihâd*), but rejected with vehemence every idea of *hulûl*."[53]

It is the famous theologian al-Ghazzâlî who is justly credited with making Sufism acceptable to orthodoxy. Born in 451/1059 in eastern Persia, Abû Hamîd al-Ghazzâlî studied *Kalâm* and became a professor in Baghdad. He then mastered the systems of Fârâbî and Avicenna that were inspired by Greek philosophy in order to be able to criticize and reject them in his *Refutation of Philosophies*.[54] Following a personal religious crisis, al-Ghazzâlî abandoned teaching in 1075 and traveled to Syria, and then visited Jerusalem and a part of Egypt. He studied Judaism and Christianity, and some have recognized in his religious thought certain Christian influences. For two years in Syria, he followed the way of the Sufis. After a ten-year absence, al-Ghazzâlî returned to Baghdad and resumed his teaching for a short time. But he finished by retiring with his disciples to his native village where he founded a seminary (*madrasa*) and a "convent" of Sufis. His numerous works made him a celebrity for a long time, but he continued to write. Unanimously venerated, he died in 505/1111.

One knows nothing of al-Ghazzâlî's spiritual guide or the type of initiation that he received. But it was no doubt after a mystical experience that he discovered the inadequacy of the official theology (*kalâm*). As he wrote with humor: "Those who are so learned about rare forms of divorce can tell you nothing about the simpler things of the spiritual life, such as the meaning of sincerity towards God or trust in Him."[55] After his mystical conversion and initiation into Sufism, al-Ghazzâlî felt that the teaching of the Sufis should not remain secret and reserved for a spiritual elite, but should become accessible to all the faithful.

The authenticity and vigor of his mystical experience[56] are confirmed by his most important work, *The Revivification of the Religious*

53. Anawati and Gardet, p. 43.
54. In its turn, this famous "refutation" was refuted by Averroës (cf. §280).
55. Cited by Schimmel, p. 93.
56. After his conversion, al-Ghazzâlî wrote a spiritual autobiography, *The Liberator from Errors*, but without revealing his intimate experiences; he insists above all on criticizing the philosophers.

Sciences. The work is a *summa* in forty chapters, in which al-Ghazzâlî successively studies ritual questions, customs, the message of the Prophet, "the things which lead to destruction," and those which lead to salvation. It is in this final section that certain aspects of the mystical life are discussed. However, al-Ghazzâlî makes every effort to keep things in a proper perspective, completing the Law and the Tradition with the teaching of Sufism, but without giving primacy to mystical experience. Thanks to this position, *The Revivification of the Religious Sciences* was adopted by orthodox theologians and obtained an unequalled authority.

An encyclopedic and prolific author, al-Ghazzâlî was also a great polemicist; he attacked Ismailism and all Gnostic tendencies relentlessly. Nevertheless, in certain of his writings the mystical speculations centering on Light betray a Gnostic structure.

According to a number of scholars, al-Ghazzâlî failed in his plan to "revivify" the religious thought of Islam. "As brilliant as he was, his contribution hardly succeeded in preventing the anchylosis which occurred two or three centuries later in Muslim religious thought."[57]

279. The first metaphysicians. Avicenna. Philosophy in Muslim Spain

It is the translations of Greek works of philosophy and science that have stimulated and sustained philosophic reflection in Islam. Toward the middle of the third/ninth century, writings depending directly on Plato and Aristotle (which were known besides through Neoplatonic interpretations) began to impose themselves alongside the theological disputes. The first philosopher whose works have partially survived is Abû Yûsof al-Kindî (185/796–ca. 260/873).[58] He studied not only Greek philosophy, but also the natural sciences and mathematics. Al-Kindî strove to prove the possibility and validity of a purely human

57. Anawati and Gardet, p. 51. See also a severe critique of Ghazzâlî in Zaehner, *Hindu and Muslim Mysticism,* pp. 126ff. But Corbin has shown that philosophic creativity did not end with the death of Averroës (1198); philosophy continued to develop in the East, above all in Iran, in the traditions of diverse schools and of Sohrawardî.

58. In the West, he was known by several works translated into Latin during the Middle Ages: *De intellectu, De Quinque Essentiis,* etc.

knowledge. To be sure, he admitted the knowledge of the supernatural order bestowed by God to His prophets; but at least in principle, human thought was capable of discovering the revealed truths by its own proper means.

Reflection on these two types of knowledge—human (notably that practiced by the Ancients) and revealed (*par excellence* in the Quran)—presents al-Kindî with a series of problems which will secure an essential place in Muslim philosophy. Let us concentrate on the most important: the possibility of a metaphysical (that is, rational) exegesis of the Quran and the tradition (*Hadîth*); the identification of God with Being in itself and the First Cause; Creation understood as a Cause of a different type from natural causes as well as from the emanations of the Neoplatonists; and finally, the immortality of the individual soul.

Certain of these problems are discussed and resolved in an audacious manner by al-Fârâbî (250/872–339/950), a profound philosopher doubling as a mystic. He was the first to attempt a rapprochement between philosophic meditation and Islam. He too had studied the natural sciences (such as Aristotle presented them), as well as logic and political theology. He developed the plan of the "Perfect City," inspired by Plato, and described the exemplary "Prince," assembling all the human and philosophic virtues like a "Plato reclothed in the prophetic mantle of Muhammad."[59] It could be said that this political theology allowed al-Fârâbî to show his successors how they should treat the relationship between philosophy and religion. His metaphysic is founded on the difference between the essence and the existence of created beings; *existence* is a predicate, an *accident of the essence.* Corbin justly points out that this thesis marks a watershed in the history of metaphysics. Equally original is his theory of Intelligence and the procession of Intelligences. But al-Fârâbî is passionately concerned with mysticism, and in his writings he uses the terminology of Sufism.

As he himself recognized, it is thanks to the writings of al-Fârâbî that the young Avicenna succeeded in understanding Aristotle's *Metaphysics.* Born near Bukhara in 370/980, Ibn Sînâ became famous in the West under the name Avicenna, when certain of his works were translated into Latin in the twelfth century. His preciosity and universal culture have hardly been equalled. His great *Canon* dominated Eu-

59. As cited by Corbin, *Histoire de la philosophie islamique*, p. 230.

ropean medicine for centuries, and is still influential in the East. An indefatigable worker (his bibliography contains 292 titles!), Ibn Sînâ composed, among other things, the following: commentaries on Aristotle; a *summa* (*Kitab al-Shifâ*) treating of metaphysics, logic, and physics; two works in which he presented his philosophy;[60] an enormous encyclopedia of twenty volumes which, with the exception of several fragments, disappeared when Isfahan was conquered by Muhammad of Ghazna; and so on. His father and brother were Ismailis. Ibn Sînâ, according to Corbin (p. 239), probably was a follower of Twelver Shî'ism. He died at age fifty-seven (in 426/1037) near Hamada, where he had accompanied his prince.

Avicenna acknowledged and prolonged the metaphysic of essence elaborated by al-Fârâbî. Existence is the result of the Creation, that is, "of the divine thought thinking of itself, and this consciousness that the divine Being has eternally of itself is none other than the First Emanation, the First *nous* or First Intelligence" (Corbin, p. 240). The plurality of being unfolds, by a series of successive emanations, from this First Intelligence.[61] From the Second Intelligence derives the motive Soul of the first Heaven; from the Third, the ethereal body of this Heaven; and thus it continues. What results is the Ten "cherubinic" Intelligences (*Angeli intellectuales*) and the celestial Souls (*Angeli caelestes*), "who have no sense faculties, but possess Imagination in its pure state" (Corbin, p. 240).

The Tenth Intelligence, designated the Agent or Active Intelligence, plays an important role in Avicenna's cosmology, for it is through it that the earthly world[62] and the multitude of human souls[63] derive. The soul, since it is an indivisible substance, immaterial and incorruptible, survives the death of the body. Avicenna was proud to have demonstrated with philosophical arguments that individual souls were immortal, even though they were created. For him, religion's principal function was to assure the happiness of every human being. But the true philosopher is also a mystic, for he dedicates himself to the love of

60. *Le livre des directives et remarques* and *Le livre de Science*, translated by A. M. Goichon. On the translation of other works of Avicenna, see below.

61. The process is described in *La métaphysique de Shifâ* (9, 6), translated by Anawati.

62. See Goichon, *Le livre des directives*, pp. 430ff.

63. According to Corbin (*Histoire*, p. 243), it is because of this Active Intelligence, which has the form and role of an Angel, that what is called "Latin Avicennism" was held in check.

God and seeks the inner truths of religion. Avicenna mentions several times his work on "eastern philosophy," of which only brief references remain, nearly all concerning life after death. His visionary experiences constitute the material of three *Mystical Accounts;*[64] it is a matter of an ecstatic journey to a mystical East accomplished under the direction of the Illuminating Angel, a theme which would be repeated by Sohrawardî (§281).

The plan of this work forces us to pass rapidly over the first theosophists and mystics of Andalusia. Let us mention Ibn Massara (269/883–319/931), who in his travels to the East had several contacts with esoteric circles, leading him eventually to withdraw himself with several disciples into a hermitage near Cordoba. It is Ibn Massara who organized the first mystical (and secret) confraternity in Muslim Spain. One has been able to reconstruct the basic outlines of his doctrine—at once both Gnostic and Neoplatonic—thanks to the long citations made by Ibn Arabî.

Also born in Cordoba was Ibn Hazm (403/1013–454/1063), jurist, thinker, poet, and author of a critical history of religions and philosophical systems. His celebrated book of poems, *The Dove's Neck-Ring,* is inspired by the Platonic myth of the *Symposium.* The analogy between his theory of love and "The Gay Science" of the first troubadour, William IX of Aquitaine, is obvious.[65] Much more important is the treatise on religions and philosophies. Ibn Hazm describes the diverse types of skeptics and believers, insisting on the peoples who possess a revealed Book, and above all those who have best conserved the idea of Divine Unity (*tawhîd*) and the original text of the Revelation.

Particularly important for the influence he exerted upon Averroës and Albert the Great is Ibn Bajja (Avempace in the scholastic Latin), the thinker who lived in the fifth/twelfth century. He commented upon many of Aristotle's treatises, but his principal metaphysical works remain unfinished. Let us note, however, that "the words which Ibn Bajja favored, those such as *solitary* and *stranger,* are none other than the typical words of mystical gnosis in Islam."[66] As for Ibn Tofayl of

64. Translated and pertinently commented upon by Corbin, *Avicenne et le récit visionaire.*

65. See A. R. Nykl, *A Book Containing the Risâla.*

66. Corbin, *Histoire de la philosophie islamique,* p. 320.

Cordoba (fifth/twelfth century), he mastered the same encyclopedic erudition which the age required; but he owes his renown to a philosophical romance entitled *Hayy Ibn Yaqzân,* which was translated into Hebrew in the twelfth century, but remained unknown among the Latin Scholastics. A contemporary of Sohrawardî (§281), Ibn Tofayl returns to "oriental philosophy" and the initiatory accounts of Avicenna. The action of his romance unfolds successively on two islands. The first is inhabited by a society practicing a completely exterior religion, ruled by a rigid Law. A contemplative, Absâl, decides to emigrate to the next island. He meets the sole inhabitant, Hayy Ibn Yaqzân; this philosopher had learned all alone the laws of life and the mysteries of the spirit. Wishing to communicate the divine truth to men, Hayy and Absâl return to the first island. But they quickly understand that human society is incurable and return to their hermitage. "Does the return to their island signify that the conflict between philosophy and religion in Islam is desperate and without resolution?"[67]

280. The last and greatest thinkers of Andalusia: Averroës and Ibn Arabî

Considered the greatest Muslim philosopher, Ibn Roshid (Averroës to the Latins) enjoyed an exceptional renown in the West. In fact, his total work is considerable. Averroës wrote pertinent commentaries on the majority of Aristotle's treatises, wishing to restore the authentic thought of the master. It is not a question of presenting here the broad lines of Averroës' system. It suffices to recall that he knew the Law well; he thus upheld that the faithful are bound to practice the fundamental principles of religion such as they are found in the Quran, the *Hadîth,* and the *ijmâ* (consensus). But those endowed with the greatest intellectual capacity had the obligation to pursue a higher science, that is, to study philosophy. Theologians did not have the right to intervene in this activity, nor to judge its conclusions. Theology was necessary as an intermediary discipline, but it must always be under the control of philosophy. However, neither philosophers nor theologians should unveil to the people their interpretations of the ambiguous verses of the

67. Ibid., p. 333.

Quran. (This in no way implies a "double truth," as certain Western theologians have interpreted it.)

Steadfast in this doctrine, Averroës criticized with severity and humor al-Ghazzâlî's *Refutation of Philosophies* (§278). In his famous *Refutation of the Refutation* (*Tahâfot al-Tahâfot,* translated into Latin as the *Destructio Destructionis*), Averroës demonstrates that al-Ghazzâlî had not understood the philosophical systems and that his arguments betrayed his incompetence. He also shows the contradictions between this work and the others written by the famous polygraph.

Averroës also criticized al-Fârâbi and Avicenna, accusing them of having abandoned the tradition of the ancient philosophers to please the theologians. Desirous of restoring a purely Aristotelian cosmology, Averroës rejected the Avicennian angelology, that of the *Animae coelestes,* and thereby the world of images perceived by the creative Imagination (cf. §279). The *forms* are not created by the Agent Intelligence, as Avicenna affirmed. *Matter in itself possesses in potentiality the totality of forms.* But since matter is the principle of individuation, the individual identifies himself with the corruptible; consequently, *immortality* can only be *impersonal.*[68] This last thesis provoked reactions not only among Muslim theologians and theosophers, but among Christian thinkers as well.[69]

Averroës had wished to know a very young Sufi, Ibn Arabî, and according to the latter's remembrance, he had paled at divining the inadequacy of his own system. Ibn al-Arabî is one of the most profound geniuses of Sufism and one of the most singular figures of universal mysticism. Born in 560/1165 at Murcia, he studied all the sciences and traveled continuously, from Morocco to Iraq, in search of sheikhs and companions. In good time, he had several supernatural experiences and certain revelations. His first teachers were two women, Shams, who was at the time ninety-five, and Fatima of Cordoba.[70] Later, finding himself in Mecca, he met the very beautiful daughter of

68. See the critical analysis of Corbin, ibid., pp. 340ff.

69. The first Latin translation of Averroës' commentaries on Aristotle were completed around 1230–35. However, "Latin Averroism," so important in the Western Middle Ages, in fact represented a new interpretation worked out from the perspective of Saint Augustine.

70. See his autobiographical writings translated by R. W. J. Austin, in the latter's *Sufis of Andalusia.*

a sheikh and composed poems collected under the title *The Interpretation of Desires*. Inspired by an ardent mystical love, the poems were considered too straightforwardly erotic, although they rather recall the relationship between Dante and Beatrice.

Meditating before the Ka'ba, Ibn Arabî experienced a number of ecstatic visions (among others, that of "eternal youth"), and had the confirmation that he was the "Seal of Muhammadan Sainthood." One of his most important writings, a mystical work of twenty volumes, is entitled *The Meccan Revelations*. In 1205 at Mossul, Ibn Arabî was initiated for the third time.[71] But shortly afterward in Cairo, in 1206, he had some difficulties with the religious authorities and hastily retreated to Mecca. After other travels, which hardly diminished his prodigious creativity, Ibn Arabî died in Damascus in 638/1240 at the age of eighty-five.

Despite his exceptional position in the history of Muslim mysticism and metaphysics (the Sufis called him "The Greatest Sheikh"), the thought of Ibn Arabî is still poorly known.[72] It is true that he always wrote very quickly, as one possessed by a supernatural inspiration. One of his masterpieces, *The Bezels of Wisdom,* recently translated into English, abounds in dazzling observations but is totally lacking in plan and rigor. Nevertheless, this rapid synthesis will allow us to grasp the originality of his thought and the greatness of his mystical theology.

Ibn Arabî recognized that: "Knowledge of mystical states can be obtained solely by experience; human reason cannot define it, nor arrive at it by deduction."[73] Thus he explains the need for esotericism: "This type of spiritual knowledge must be hidden from the majority of men because of its sublimity. For its depths are difficult to attain and its dangers are great."[74]

The fundamental concept of Ibn Arabî's metaphysic and mysticism is the *Unity of Being,* or more precisely the unity at once of both Being and Perceiving. In other words, the total undifferentiated Reality con-

71. Cf. ibid., p. 157.

72. His books are also forbidden in Egypt and his work, voluminous and difficult, is insufficiently edited. There are also few translations.

73. *Les Révélations mecquoises*, text edited in Austin, *Ibn al-Arabî, The Bezels of Wisdom*, p. 25.

74. Text cited by Austin, ibid., p. 24. For what follows, we use especially Austin's translation (*The Bezels of Wisdom*) and his commentaries.

stitutes the Divinity's primordial mode of being. Animated by Love and desiring to know itself, this divine Reality divides itself into subject (the knower) and object (the known). When he speaks of Reality in the context of the Unity of Being, Ibn Arabî uses the term *al-Haqq* (the real, the truth). When he speaks of Reality divided into two poles—a spiritual or intellectual pole and a cosmic or existential pole—he designates the first as Allah or the Creator (*al-khâliq*), and the second pole as Creation (*Khalq*) or Cosmos.[75]

In order to explicate the process of Creation, Ibn Arabî shows a preference for utilizing the themes of the Creative Imagination and Love. Thanks to the Creative Imagination, the latent forms which exist in the Real are projected onto the illusory screen of otherness, in a fashion that enables God to perceive himself as an object.[76] Consequently, the Creative Imagination constitutes the point of union between the Real as subject and the Real as object of Consciousness, between the Creator and the creature. Called into existence by the Creative Imagination, objects are recognized by the divine Subject.

The second theme used to illustrate the process of Creation is that of Love, that is to say, God's yearning to be known by his creatures. Ibn Arabî first describes the labor pains undergone by the procreative Reality. But it is always Love which reunites creatures. Thus the division of the Real into a divine subject and a created object leads to reintegration in the primordial Unity, this time *enriched by the experience of the consciousness of Self.*[77]

Insofar as he is a creature, each human in his latent essence can be nothing else than God; inasmuch as he is the object of God's consciousness, man contributes to that which God knows as Himself, and thereby participates in the divine liberty.[78] The Perfect Human constitutes the "Isthmus" between the two poles of Reality. He is at once both male, that is, representative of Heaven and the Word of God, and female, that is, representative of the Earth of the Cosmos. In reuniting Heaven and Earth in himself, the Perfect Human at the same time

75. Austin, ibid., p. 153. Ibn Arabî specifies that each pole—spiritual and cosmic—implies the potential and latent presence of the other pole.

76. Ibid., pp. 28, 121. See above all the important work of Henry Corbin, *L'imagination créatrice dans le soufisme d'Ibn Arabî.*

77. *The Bezels of Wisdom,* p. 29.

78. Ibid., pp. 33, 84.

obtains the Unity of Being.[79] The saint partakes with God of the power to create (*himmah*); he is thus able objectively to realize his own interior images.[80] But no saint succeeds in maintaining these images as objectively real for more than a limited period of time.[81] Let us add that Islam, for Ibn Arabî, is essentially the experience and the truth known by the saint, whose most important functions are those of prophet (*nabi*) and apostle (*rasûl*).

Like Origen, Joachim of Floris, or Meister Eckhart, Ibn Arabî, although he had faithful and competent disciples and was admired by the Sufis, did not succeed in enriching and renewing the official theology. Yet in contrast to these three Christian masters, the genius of Ibn Arabî reinforced the Muslim esoteric tradition.

281. Sohrawardî and the mysticism of Light

Shihâboddin Yahyâ Sohrawardî was born in 549/1155 at Sohraward, a town in northwest Iran. He studied in Azerbaijan and Isfahan, stayed several years in Anatolia, and then went to Syria. It is there that he was condemned in a trial brought against him by the Doctors of the Law, and there that he died in 587/1191 at the age of thirty-six. Given the name Sheikh *maqtûl* (assassinated) by historians, he is known to his disciples as Sheikh *shahîd*, "the martyr."

The title of his principal work, *Oriental Theosophy* (= *Hikmat al-Ishrâk*), defines Sohrawardî's ambitious enterprise, and in particular his intention to reactualize ancient Iranian wisdom and Hermetic gnosis. Avicenna had spoken of a "wisdom" or "oriental philosophy" (cf. §279), and Sohrawardî was familiar with his famous precursor's ideas. But according to Sohrawardî, Avicenna could not realize this "oriental philosophy" since he was ignorant of its principle, the

79. Corbin, *L'imagination*, chap. 4, 2. Let us note that according to Ibn Arabî the Perfect Man constitutes an exemplary model that is difficult to actualize in a human existence.
80. See Corbin, ibid., chap. 4; Austin, *The Bezels*, pp. 36, 121, 158; on p. 36 Austin recalls the Tibetan meditation that achieves the materialization of interior images; see below, §315.
81. *The Bezels*, p. 102. Ibn Arabî insists besides on the great dangers confronted by the possessors of this power; ibid., pp. 37. 158.

"oriental source" itself. On this matter, Sohrawardî writes: "Among the Ancient Persians, there was a community of men who were guided by God, and who thus walked on the right path, eminent theosopher-sages, without resemblance to the Magi [*Majûs*]. It is their precious theosophy of Light, the very same which is attested in the mystical experience of Plato and his predecessors, which I have revived in my book entitled *Oriental Theosophy*, and I have had no precursor on the path of such a project."[82]

The vast *oeuvre* of Sohrawardî (forty-nine titles) arises from a personal experience, a "conversion which came upon him in his youth." In an ecstatic vision, he discovered a multitude of the "beings of light whom Hermes and Plato contemplated, and the heavenly radiation, sources of the *Light of Glory* and the *Kingdom of Light* (*Ray wa Khorreh*) which Zarathustra proclaimed, toward which a spiritual rapture lifted the most faithful king, the blessed Kay Khosraw."[83] The idea of Ishrâq (the splendor of the rising sun) refers (1) to wisdom, the theosophy whose source is the Light, and thereby (2) to a doctrine founded upon the appearance of intelligible Lights. But it also refers to (3) the theosophy of the *Orientals,* the Sages of Ancient Persia. This "auroral splendor" is the "Light of Glory," the *Xvarenah* of the *Avesta* (in Persian, *Khorrah;* cf. the Parsi form of Farr, Farrah). Sohrawardî describes it as the eternal emanation of the Light of Lights, from which proceeds the first Archangel, referred to by the Zoroastrian name *Bahman* (*Vohu Manah*). This relation between the Light of Lights and the First Emanation is found at every degree of the procession of Being, thus ordering each category of creation by pairings. "Engendering each other through their emanations and their reflections, the hypostases of Light attained to the innumerable. Beyond the heaven of the Fixed [Stars] of the Peripatetic or Ptolemaic astronomy are presented innumerable marvelous universes" (Corbin, p. 293).

This world of the Lights is too complex to be presented here.[84] Let us only mention that all the modalities of spiritual existence and all the cosmic realities are created and directed by different species of arch-

82. Text translated by Corbin, *En Islam iranien*, vol. 2: *Sohrawardî et les platoniciens de Perse*, p. 29; cf. also his *Histoire de la philosophie islamique*, p. 287.

83. Text translated by Corbin, *Histoire de la philosophie islamique*, pp. 288–89. Another version is found in Corbin, *En Islam iranien*, vol. 2, p. 100.

84. See Corbin, *En Islam iranien*, vol. 2, pp. 81ff.; idem, *Histoire de la philosophie islamique*, pp. 293ff.

angels emanated from the Light of Lights. Sohrawardî's cosmology is simultaneously an angelology. His physics recalls both the Mazdaean conception of the two categories of reality (the *mênôk:* heavenly, subtle, and the *gêtik:* earthly, dense), and the dualism of the Manichaeans (cf. §§215, 233–34). Of the four universes of Sohrawardî's cosmology, let us concentrate on the importance of the *Malakût* (the world of heavenly souls and human souls) and of the *mundus imaginalis,* "the intermediary world between this intelligible world of beings of pure Light and the sensible world; the organ which perceives it as the Active Imagination."[85] As Corbin says of this intermediary world: "Sohrawardî is indeed the first, it seems, to have justified the ontology of this interworld, a theme that will be taken up and amplified by all the Gnostics and mystics of Islam."[86]

The accounts of spiritual initiation drafted by Sohrawardî can be deciphered from the perspective of this intermediary world. It is a matter of spiritual events taking place in the Malakût, but unveiling the profound significance of parallel exterior events. *The Account of the Western Exile*[87] constitutes an initiation that escorts the disciple to the East; in other words, this brief and at many points enigmatic narrative helps the "exile" to return *to himself.* For Sohrawardî and the "eastern theosophers" (*Hokama Ishrâqîyûn*), philosophical reflection goes hand in hand with spiritual realization; they reunite the method of the philosophers, searching for pure knowledge, with the method of the Sufis who pursue an interior purification.[88]

The spiritual experiences of the disciple in the intermediary world

85. Corbin, *Histoire de la philosophie islamique,* p. 296.

86. "In effect, its importance is major. It is at the first plane of the perspective which opens itself to the posthumous development of the human being. Its function is trifold: it is through it that the resurrection is accomplished, since it is the place of the 'subtle bodies'; it is through it that the symbols configured by the prophets as well as all visionary experiences are really true; and as a result, it is through it that the *ta'wîl* is accomplished, that is, the exegesis which 'reconducts' the teachings of the Quranic Revelation back to their 'spiritual truth' " (Corbin, *Histoire de la philosophie islamique,* pp. 296–97).

87. Translated and commented upon by Corbin, *L'Archange empourpré,* pp. 265–88. See in the same work the translations of other mystical accounts of Sohrawardî. See also *En Islam iranien,* vol. 2, pp. 246ff.

88. In the spiritual genealogy which Sohrawardî provides for himself, mention is also made of the Ancient Greek philosophers, the wisdom of Persia, and certain great Sufi masters; cf. Corbin, *Histoire de la philosophie islamique,* p. 299.

constitute, as we have seen, a series of initiatory trials called forth by the Creative Imagination. Although situated on another plane, one can compare the function of these initiatory accounts to that of the romances of the Grail (§270). Let us also recall the magico-religious value of all narratives, or "exemplary histories" (cf. Hasidism, §292), of the traditional type. It may be added here that among Romanian peasants, the ritual narration of stories (that is, during the night) defends the house against the Devil and evil spirits. Still more, the narration leads to the presence of God.[89]

These various comparative indications allow us to better understand both Sohrawardî's originality and the ancient tradition which it prolongs. The creative imagination, which makes possible the discovery of the interworld, is one with the ecstatic visions of the shamans and the inspiration of the ancient poets. One knows that the epic and a certain type of fairy tale both derive from ecstatic journeys and adventures, both heavenly ones and especially infernal ones.[90] All of this helps us to understand on the one hand the role of narrative literature in "spiritual education," and on the other, the consequences for the twentieth-century Western world of the discovery of the unconscious and the dialectic of the imagination.

For Sohrawardî, the sage who excels both in philosophy and mystical contemplation is the true spiritual leader, the *pole* (*Qutb*), "without whose presence the world could not continue to exist, even should he only be there *incognito,* completely unknown to men" (Corbin, pp. 300–301). Now as Corbin remarks, one recognizes here a major Shî'ite theme, for the "*pole of poles*" is the Imâm. His *incognito* existence implies the Shî'ite conceptions of the occultation of the Imâm (*ghaybat*) and the cycle of the *walâyat*, the "esoteric prophecy" succeeding the "Seal of the Prophets." There is thus an accord between the *Ishrâqîyûn* theosophers and the Shî'ite theosophers. Furthermore, as Corbin writes, "the doctors of the Law at Aleppo were not deceived. During Sohrawardî's trial, the incriminating thesis which caused his condemnation was his profession that God can at all times, and even now, create a prophet. Even if it was not a matter of a

89. See the examples cited by Ovidiu Bîrlea, *Folclorul românesc,* 1 (Bucharest, 1981), pp. 141ff. It is a matter of an ancient widely diffused conception; cf. Eliade, *Myth and Reality,* chap. 2.

90. Cf. Eliade, *Shamanism,* pp. 508ff.

legislator-prophet but of 'esoteric prophecy,' the thesis betrayed at least a crypto-Shî'ism. Thus by his life's work and by his martyr's death for prophetic philosophy, Sohrawardî lived to the very end the tragedy of the 'western exile'" (Corbin, p. 301). But Sohrawardî's spiritual posterity—the *Ishrâqîyûn*—still survives, at least in Iran, in our own day.[91]

282. Jalâl al-Dîn Rûmî: Sacred music, poetry, and dance

Muhammad Jalâl al-Dîn, known most widely as Rûmî, was born 30 September 1207 in Balkh, a village of Khorasan. Fearing the Mongol invasion, his father, a theologian and Sufi master, left the city in 1219 and made a pilgrimage to Mecca. The family finally settled in Konya. After his father's death, the then twenty-four-year-old Jalâl al-Dîn studied at Aleppo and Damascus. Seven years later, he returned to Konya and from 1240 to 1249 he taught jurisprudence and canonical law. But on 29 November 1249, a sixty-year-old wandering dervish, Shams of Tabrîz, arrived in the city. There are several accounts of their meeting, each of which tells a more or less dramatic version of Rûmî's conversion: the famous jurist and theologian becomes one of the greatest mystics and perhaps the most ingenious religious poet of Islam.

Persecuted by Rûmî's disciples, who were jealous of his ascendancy over their master, Shams left for Damascus. He consented to return but on 3 December 1247, he disappeared, mysteriously assassinated. For a long time Rûmî remained inconsolable. He composed a collection of mystical odes which bear the name of his master (*Diwân-e Shams-e Tabrîzî*), "admirable songs of 'love and grief,' an immense work entirely dedicated to this love, earthly in appearance, but which is in reality a hypostasis of divine love."[92] Moreover, Rûmî began a spiritual concert (the *samâ*) in honor of Shams. According to his son, Sultân Walad, "he never ceased for an instant from listening to music and dancing; he rested neither day nor night. He had been a scholar: he became a poet. He had been an ascetic: he became inebriated with

91. One of the great achievements of Henry Corbin and his students is to have begun the study of this rich philosophic tradition, still unknown in the West.
92. Eva de Vitray-Meyerovitch, *Rûmî et le sufisme*, p. 20.

love, and not of the wine of the grape; the illuminated soul drinks only the wine of the Light."[93]

Toward the end of his life, Rûmî chose Husâm al-Dîn Chalabî to direct his disciples. It is in great part due to Chalabî that the master wrote his principal work, the *Mathnawî*. Until his death in 1273, Rûmî dictated its distichs to him, sometimes while walking in the streets, or even when he was in his bath. The result is a vast mystical epic of about forty-five thousand verses incorporating texts of the Quran and prophetic traditions as well as apologies, anecdotes, and themes and legends of Oriental and Mediterranean folklore.

Rûmî founded a brotherhood, the *Târiqa mâwlawîya*, as he was called *Mawlânâ*, "Our Master" (Turkish *Mevlâna*), by his disciples and companions. From very early, the brotherhood was known in the West by the name "whirling dervishes," since during the ceremony of *samâ* the dancers turned themselves rapidly round and round, and also around the room. "In the musical cadences, said Rûmî, is a hidden secret; if I were to reveal it, it would overturn the world." In effect, the music awakens the spirit by making it recall its true home and by reminding it of its final end.[94] "We have all descended from the body of Adam, writes Rûmî, and we have listened to these melodies in Paradise. We recall a little of them to ourselves, even though the water and the clay have covered us with doubt."[95]

Like sacred music and poetry, the ecstatic dance was practiced from the beginnings of Sufism.[96] According to certain Sufis, their ecstatic dance reproduced that of the angels (see the text translated by Molé, pp. 215–16). In the *târiqa* instituted by Rûmî (but organized above all by his son, Sultân Walad), the dance has both a cosmic and theological character. The dervishes are dressed in white (like a shroud), covered by a black mantle (symbolic of the tomb), and coiffed in a high felt hat (the image of a tombstone).[97] The sheikh represents the intermediary

93. From the French translation by de Vitray-Meyerovitch, ibid., p. 18.
94. See the texts translated by Marjan Molé, "La danse extatique en Islam," pp. 208–13.
95. *Mathnawî*, 4, 745–46, translated by Molé, ibid., p. 239. The memory of the sojourn in Paradise and the expectation of the trumpet of the Last Judgment are themes attested in the oldest of the Sufi traditions.
96. See Molé's study, ibid., passim; cf. the critiques of theologians and even Sufi authors, ibid., pp. 176ff., etc.
97. Present since the beginnings of the *samâ*, this symbolism is made precise by the

between Heaven and Earth. The musicians play the reed flute (*ney*) and strike the drums and cymbals. The room where the dervishes turn symbolizes the universe, "the planets turning around the sun and around themselves. The drums evoke the trumpets of the Last Judgment. The circle of dancers is divided into two semi-circles of which the one represents the arc of descent, or the involution of souls into matter, and the other the arc of the ascent of souls to God."[98] Whenever the rhythm becomes very rapid, the sheikh enters into the dance and turns about in the center of the circle, for he represents the sun. "This is the supreme moment of realized union."[99] Let us add that the dances of the dervishes only rarely lead to psychopathic trances, and this occurs only in certain marginal areas.

Rûmî has an immense role in the renewal of Islam. His works have been read, translated, and commented upon from one end of the Muslim world to the other. This exceptional popularity proves once again the importance of artistic creativity, and especially that of poetry, in the deepening of religious life. As with other great mystics, but with a passionate ardor and poetic power that are unequalled, Rûmî never ceased to exalt divine love. "Without Love the world would be inanimate" (*Mathnawî*, 5, 3844). His mystic poetry abounds in symbols borrowed from the worlds of music and dance. Despite certain Neoplatonic influences, his theology is quite complex, at once personal, traditional, and audacious. Rûmî insists upon the necessity of attaining nonbeing in order to be able to *become* and to *be;* moreover, he makes numerous allusions to al-Hallâj.[100]

Human existence develops according to the will and plan of the Creator. Man has been charged by God to become the intermediary between Himself and the world. It is not in vain that man has "traveled from the seed up to reason" (*Mathnawî*, 3, 1975). "From the moment when you came into the world of existence, a ladder was placed before you in order to allow you to escape." Man was at first mineral, then plant, then animal. "Then you were made man, endowed with knowl-

---

Dîvân of the great Turkish poet Mehmed Tchelebi; see the French translation by Molé, ibid., pp. 248–51. On the *mawlawî* dance, see also the texts of Rûmî and of Sultân Walad translated ibid., pp. 238ff.

98. De Vitray-Meyerovitch, *Rûmî*, p. 41. Cf. Molé, "La danse," pp. 246ff.

99. De Vitray-Meyerovitch, *Rûmî*, p. 42. See the description of a *mawlawîya* seance in Molé, "La danse," pp. 229ff.

100. Cf. the texts cited by Schimmel, *Mystical Dimensions*, pp. 319ff.

edge, reason, and faith.'' Finally, man will become an angel and his residence will be in heaven. But even this is not the final stage. ''Surpass the angelic condition, penetrate into this ocean (the Divine Unity) so that your drop of water can become one sea.''[101] In a famous passage of the *Mathnawî* (2, 1157f.), Rûmî explains the original theomorphic nature of man created in God's image: ''My image dwells in the King's heart: the King's heart would be ill without my image. . . . The light of the intelligences comes from my thought; Heaven has been created on account of my original nature. . . . I possess the spiritual Kingdom. . . . I am not the congener of the King. . . . But I receive His Light from Him in His Theophany'' (from the French translation by de Vitray-Meyerovitch).

283. The triumph of Sufism and the reaction of the theologians. Alchemy

Once the theologian al Ghazzâlî's work had brought it respectability and acceptance among the Doctors of the Law, Sufism experienced great popularity. This was at first the case in the regions of the Near East and northern Africa, but soon it was so everywhere that Islam had penetrated: India, Central Asia, Indonesia, and East Africa. With time, the limited groups of disciples living around their sheikhs became veritable orders with numerous branches and hundreds of members. The Sufis were the best missionaries of Islam. Gibb suggests that the eclipse of Shî'ism was the result of the popularity and missionary spirit of the Sufis.[102] Such success explains their prestige and their protection by the civil authorities.

The tolerance of the *ulamâ* encouraged the adaptation of foreign conceptions and the utilization of exotic methods. Certain Sufi mystical techniques had been deepened and modified through contact with foreign environments. It suffices to compare the *dhikr* practiced by the first Sufis (cf. §275) with the one elaborated under Indian influence from the twelfth century on. According to one author, ''One begins the

101. *Odes Mystiques,* 2 (= *Dîvân-e Shams-e Tabrîz*), trans. by de Vitray-Meyerovitch, *Rûmî*, pp. 88–89. See ibid., p. 89, for the passages translated from *Mathnawî*, 9, 553, 3637.
102. Cf. Gibb, *Mohammedanism*, p. 143.

recitation from the left side (of the chest) which is like a niche enclosing the lamp of the heart, the hearth of spiritual clarity. One follows it by going from the base of the chest to the right side, and by ascending to the latter's top. One continues by returning to the initial position." According to another author, the *dhakîr* must "squat on the earth, legs crossed, arms thrown around the legs, head lowered between the two knees, and eyes closed. One raises the head, saying *lâ ilâh* for the time which passes between the arrival of the head at the height of the heart and its position on the right shoulder. . . . Whenever the mouth reaches the level of the heart, one articulates with rigor the invocation *illâ,* . . . and one says *Allah* in a more energetic manner while facing the heart."[103] One easily recognizes the analogies with yogico-tantric techniques, above all in the exercises which stimulate auditory phenomena and luminous concomitants, which are much too complex to be presented here.

Yet at least among the true *dhakîrs,* such influences do not deform the Muslim character of the *dhikr.* It is rather the contrary that transpires. A number of religious beliefs and ascetic methods have been enriched by borrowings or exterior influences. One could even say that, just as has occurred in the history of Christianity, such influences have contributed to a "universalizing" of Islam by giving it an ecumenical dimension.

Be that as it may, it is certain that Sufism has strongly contributed to the renewal of the Muslim religious experience. Sufism's cultural contribution was also considerable. In all the Muslim countries, one recognizes the Sufi influence in music, dance, and especially in poetry.[104]

But this victorious movement, which retains its popularity up to our own day,[105] has also had ambiguous consequences in the history of Islam. The antirationalism of certain Sufis sometimes becomes aggressive, and their invectives against philosophy regale the populace. Moreover, the excessive emotionalism, the trances, and the ecstasies during public seances amplified themselves. The majority of the Sufi

103. Texts cited by L. Gardet, "La mention du nom divin (*dhikr*) en mystique musulmane," pp. 654–55. On the analogies with yogico-tantric techniques, see Eliade, *Yoga, Immortality, and Freedom,* pp. 200ff., 362ff.

104. See *inter alia,* the texts translated by Schimmel, *Mystical Dimensions,* esp. pp. 287ff. Thanks to the mystical, or more exactly mystico-erotic poetry, a large number of non-Islamic themes and motifs entered into the different national literatures.

105. See ibid., pp. 403ff., and the bibliography cited in notes 1–7.

masters were opposed to such immoderate exaltations, but they could not always control them. Indeed, the members of certain orders, like those of the wandering dervishes or *fakirs* (= the "poor"), proclaimed their power to perform miracles and lived outside of the Law.

Although obliged to tolerate Sufism, the *ulamâ* continued to watch out for foreign elements, especially Iranian and Gnostic ones which, through the teachings of certain Sufi masters, threatened what the Doctors of the Law regarded as the unity of Islam. (It was, then as now, difficult for the theologians—and not solely the Muslim theologians—to recognize the mystics' immense contribution to the deepening of the religious experience among the common man, notwithstanding the risk of "heresy," a risk which has existed for the theologians at every level of religious knowledge.) The response of the *ulamâ* was the multiplication of the *madrasas,* the colleges for theological education with their official status and salaried professors. By the eighth/fourteenth century, the hundreds of *madrasas* had concentrated the control of higher education in the hands of the theologians.[106]

It is regrettable that classical Sufism was not better known in the West during the Middle Ages.[107] The indirect information transmitted eventually through the erotico-mystical poetry of Andalusia did not constitute a true encounter between the two great mystical traditions.[108] As is well known, the essential influence of Islam has been the transmission, in Arabic translation, of the philosophical and scientific works of antiquity, especially those of Aristotle.

Let us add, however, that if Sufi mysticism was ignored, Hermeticism and alchemy have penetrated the West thanks to Arabic writings, a certain number of which are original works. According to Stapleton, the alchemy of Alexandrian Egypt developed first at Harran, in Mesopotamia. This hypothesis is controversial, but it has the merit of explaining the origin of Arabic alchemy. In any case, one of

106. See Gibb's observations (*Mohammedanism,* pp. 144ff., 153ff.) on the cultural consequences of this control of education.

107. Just as it is regrettable that Islam has been known in southeastern Europe almost exclusively through the Ottoman Empire, that is to say, through the Turkish occupation.

108. On the other hand, the contacts between certain Muslim and Christian esoteric groups are not to be excluded. But one cannot measure their consequences in the religious and cultural history of the Middle Ages.

the first and most famous alchemists to use the Arabic language is Jabîr ibn Hayyân, the celebrated *Geber* of the Latins. Holmyard estimates that he lived in the second/eighth century, and that he was a student of Ja'far, the sixth Imâm. According to Paul Kraus, who dedicated a monumental monograph to this figure, it is a matter of several authors (a collection of around three thousand titles circulates under his name!), living in the period between the third/ninth to fourth/tenth centuries. Corbin has justly brought to light the Shî'ite and esoteric environment in which "Jabîr's" alchemy was developed. In effect, his *Science of Balance* allows one to discover "in each body the rapport which exists between the manifest and the hidden (the *zâhir* and the *bâtin*, the exoteric and the esoteric)."[109] It seems, however, that the four treatises of *Geber* known in Latin translations are not the work of Jabîr.

The first translations from Arabic into Latin were completed around 1150 in Spain by Gerard of Cremona. A century later, alchemy was quite well known, since it was included in Vincent de Beauvais's *Encyclopedia*. One of the most famous treatises, *Tabula Smaragdina*, was excerpted from a work known under the title of the *Book of the Secret of Creation*. Equally celebrated are *Turba Philosophorum*, translated from the Arabic, and *Picatrix*, written in Arabic in the twelfth century. It is unnecessary to insist that all these books, despite the substances, instruments, and operations of the laboratory which they describe, are imbued with esotericism and gnosis.[110] Several mystics and Sufi masters, among them al-Hallâj and especially Avicenna and Ibn Arabî, have presented alchemy as a veritable spiritual technique. One is still insufficiently informed on the development of alchemy in Muslim lands after the fourteenth century. In the West, Hermeticism and alchemy will know their age of glory a little before the Italian Renaissance, and their mystical prestige will fascinate even Newton (cf. §311).

109. Corbin, *Histoire de la philosophie islamique*, pp. 184ff., and above all, "Le Livre du Glorieux de Jâbir ibn Hayyân."
110. See Eliade, *The Forge and the Crucible*, pp. 142ff.

36 Judaism from the Bar Kokhba Revolt to Hasidism

284. The compilation of the Mishnah

In discussing the first war of the Jews against the Romans (66–73) and the destruction of the Temple by Titus in 70, we have recalled an episode which had considerable consequences for Judaism: the famous Rabbi Yohanan ben Zakkai was evacuated in a coffin during the siege of Jerusalem, and, a little later, obtained permission from Vespasian to establish a school in the village of Jabneh (in Judea). Rabbi Yohanan was convinced that although they were crushed militarily, the people of Israel would not disappear so long as the Torah was studied (cf. §224).[1] Consequently, R. Yohanan organized a Sanhedrin of seventy-one members under the leadership of a "patriarch" (*Nasi*). The Sanhedrin was to be both the uncontested religious authority and the Court of Justice. For the next three centuries, the office of "patriarch" was transmitted from father to son with only one exception.[2]

Within only sixty years, however, the second war with the Romans, unleashed by Bar Kokhba in 132 and ending in the catastrophe of 135, placed the religious identity and indeed the very survival of the Jewish people in jeopardy. The Emperor Hadrian abolished the Sanhedrin and banned under penalty of death the study of the Torah and the practice of cultic acts. Several Jewish masters, among them the famous Rabbi Akiba, died under torture. But Hadrian's successor, Antoninus Pius,

---

1. In effect, when the sacerdotal party of the Sadducees lost its *raison d'être* after the destruction of the Temple, the direction returned to the doctors of the Law, that is, the Pharisees and their successors, the Rabbis ("masters, instructors"). See, *inter alia*, G. F. Moore, *Judaism in the First Centuries of the Christian Era*, 1, pp. 83ff.

2. See Hugo Mantel, *Studies in the History of the Sanhedrin*, esp. pp. 140ff. (on the displacement of the Sanhedrin from Jabneh to Usha and elsewhere).

reestablished the Sanhedrin's authority; in fact, he increased it. Henceforth, the Sanhedrin's decisions were recognized throughout the Diaspora. It is during this period—which begins with the disciples of Rabbi Yohanan ben Zakkai and ends around the year 200—that the fundamental structures of normative Judaism are elaborated. The principal innovation was the replacement of the pilgrimage and sacrifices that had been accomplished at the Temple by the study of the Law, prayer, and piety. These latter were religious acts which could take place in synagogues anywhere in the world. Continuity with the past was assured by the study of the Bible and the prescriptions concerning ritual purity.

To specify, explicate, and unify the innumerable oral traditions[3] that related to cultural practices and to the interpretations of scripture and juridical questions, Rabbi Judah "The Prince" (Patriarch of the Sanhedrin from ca. 175 to ca. 220) strove to collect them and organize them into a single corpus of legal norms. This vast compilation, known as the Mishnah ("repetition") contains the materials elaborated between the first century B.C.E. and the second century C.E.[4] The work includes six "divisions": agriculture, festivals, family life, civil law, sacrificial and dietary prescriptions, and ritual purity.

One finds certain allusions to the mysticism of the *Merkabah* (cf. §288). But there are, on the contrary, no echoes of the messianic hopes or apocalyptic speculations that were so popular in the period (as illustrated, for example, in the famous pseudepigraphic works of 2 Baruch and 4 Esdras). One has the impression that the Mishnah ignores contemporary history, or turns its back on it. (For example, it deals with the question of the tithes of the harvests which should be brought to Jerusalem; what sorts of coins can be changed, etc.).[5] The Mishnah evokes an exemplary ahistoric situation, in which the diverse acts of the sanctification of life and man are accomplished according to duly legislated models. Agricultural work is consecrated by the presence of God and by the (ritualized) labor of man. "The land of Israel is sanctified through its relationship to God. The produce of the Lord is sancti-

3. The idea of an "oral *Torah*," taught by Moses to Joshua and the priests, claims for itself an old and venerable tradition.

4. One of the great merits of Jacob Neusner's recent *Judaism: The Evidence of the Mishnah,* is the identification and analysis of the materials pertaining to the periods before, during, and after the two wars with Rome.

5. The tractate *Maaser Sheni,* as summarized in Neusner, ibid., p. 128.

fied by man, acting under God's commandment, through verbal designation and separation of the various offerings."[6]

Similarly, in the division of feasts, the cycles of sacred time are organized, classified, and named, and intimately connected to the structures of sacred space (cf. Neusner, pp. 132ff.). And the same objective is found in all the other divisions. It specifies down to the smallest detail not only the ritual means of sanctifying the cosmic and social, the familial and individual enterprise, but also the means to avoid impurity and to make it inoperative by specific purifications.

One is tempted to suggest affinities between this religious conception and the beliefs and practices of rural Christianity, which we have called "cosmic Christianity" (cf. §237). There is, however, the difference that in the Mishnah, the work of sanctification is accomplished exclusively thanks to God and to the acts of man carrying out God's commandments. But it is significant that in the Mishnah (and evidently in its complements and commentaries, which we will discuss shortly) God—who is till then the *God of History par excellence*—seems indifferent to the immediate history of his people: for the moment, messianic salvation is replaced by the sanctification of life under the direction of the Law.

In fact, the Mishnah prolongs and completes the sacerdotal code formulated in Leviticus. This amounts to saying that the laity comport themselves in the manner of the priests and Levites; they respect the prescriptions against impurity and maintain themselves in their homes as the officiants did in the Temple. Such ritual purity, respected beyond the Temple walls, separates the faithful from the rest of the population and assures their holiness. If the Jewish people wishes to survive, it must live as a holy people, in a holy land, by imitating the holiness of God.[7]

The Mishnah pursued the unification and reinforcement of Rabbinic Judaism. In the last analysis, its objective was to assure the survival of Judaism, and in the process, the integrity of the Jewish people wherever they found themselves dispersed. As Jacob Neusner formulates it, to the question, "What can a man do?" the Mishnah responds as follows: "Man, like God, makes the world work. If man wills it, nothing is impossible. . . . So does the Mishnah assess the condition of Israel,

6. Richard S. Sarason, as cited by Neusner, ibid., pp. 131–32.
7. Neusner, ibid., pp. 226ff.

defeated and helpless, yet in its Land: without power, yet holy; lacking all focus, in no particular place, certainly without Jerusalem, yet set apart from the nations.''[8]

285. The Talmud. The anti-rabbinic Reaction: The Karaites

The publication of the Mishnah opens the period known as that of the *amoraim* (lecturers or interpreters). The ensemble composed of the Mishnah and its commentaries, the Gemara, forms the Talmud (literally, "teaching"). The first redaction, edited in Palestine (around 220–400) and known as the Jerusalem Talmud, is more concise and shorter than the Babylonian Talmud (200–650); this latter consists of 8,744 pages.[9] The codes of conduct (*halakhah*), classified in the Mishnah, have been complemented in the Talmud by the *aggadah,* a collection of ethical and religious teachings, certain metaphysical and mystical speculations, and even folkloric materials.

The Babylonian Talmud played a decisive function in the history of the Jewish people: it showed how the Jews should adapt themselves to the different sociopolitical environments of the Diaspora. Already in the third century, a Babylonian master had formulated this fundamental principle: the legislation of the regular government constitutes the only legitimate law, and must be respected by the Jews. Thus the legitimacy of local governmental authorities receives a ratification of a religious order. In matters which concern civil law, the members of the community are obliged to present their litigations before the Jewish courts.

Taken as a whole, and given its contents and objectives, the Talmud does not seem to give importance to philosophic speculation. However, certain researchers have brought to light the Talmud's theology, at once subtle and simple, as well as certain esoteric doctrines and even practices of an initiatory order which are preserved in this corpus.[10]

8. Ibid., pp. 282–83.

9. Certain laws pertaining to agriculture, purification, and the sacrifice, as they had been practiced in Palestine, lost their actuality in the Babylonian Talmud.

10. See, *inter alia,* the old but still valuable book of Solomon Schechter, *Aspects of Rabbinic Theology: Major Concepts of the Talmud;* or Gerd A. Wewers, *Geheimnis und Geheimhaltung im rabbinischen Judentum.* See also the numerous theological texts translated and commented upon by Moore, *Judaism,* 1, pp. 357–442, etc.

For our purposes, it suffices to pass rapidly in review those events which contributed to establishing the structures of medieval Judaism. The patriarch, recognized officially as the homologue of a Roman prefect, sent messengers to the Jewish communities to collect taxes and to inform them of the calendar of festivals. In 359, the Patriarch Hillel II decided to fix the calendar in writing in order to assure the simultaneity of festivals in Palestine and throughout the Diaspora. This measure was to prove its importance when the patriarchate of Palestine was abolished by the Romans in 429. Thanks to the religious tolerance of the Sassanids, Babylon became during the Sassanid period (226–637) the most important center of the Diaspora. This privileged situation was maintained even after the Muslim conquest. All the Jewish communities of the eastern Diaspora recognized the supremacy of the *gaon,* the spiritual master, arbiter, and political leader who represented the people before God and before the secular authorities. The period of the *gaonim,* begun around 640, came to an end in 1038 when the center of Jewish spirituality was displaced to Spain. But by this date the Babylonian Talmud was recognized universally as the authorized teaching of Rabbinism, which is to say the Judaism that had become normative.

Rabbinic Judaism was promoted by means of schools (from the primary school up to the academy or Yeshiva), the synagogues, and the courts. The synagogue cult, which replaced the sacrifices in the Temple, included morning and afternoon prayers, the profession of faith ("Hear O Israel, The Lord Our God, The Lord Is One"), and eighteen (later nineteen) "benedictions," short prayers expressing the hopes of the community and its individuals. Three times a week—Monday, Thursday, and Saturday—Scripture was read in the synagogue. Public lectures on the Pentateuch and the Prophets took place on Saturdays and Holy Days, followed by the rabbi's homily.

In the ninth century, one *gaon* published the first collection of prayers in order to fix the order of the liturgy. Since the eighth century, a new synagogal poetry had developed in Palestine, which was quickly accepted. As a result, up to the sixteenth century, various liturgical poems were composed and integrated into the synagogue service.

There were, however, certain times when the severe and radical traditionalism imposed by the *gaonim* provoked anti-Rabbinic reactions. Some of these, inspired by old sectarian doctrines of Palestine or by Islam, were promptly rebuked. But in the ninth century, a dissident movement arose, directed by Anan ben David, which quickly took on menacing proportions. Known as the Karaites ("Scripturalists," those recognizing only the authority of Scripture),[11] they rejected the oral (rabbinic) law, which they considered as a simple product of men. The Karaites proposed an attentive and critical examination of the Bible in order to recover the authentic doctrine and legislation; moreover, they demanded the return of the Jews to Palestine in order to hasten the coming of the Messiah. Indeed, under the direction of Daniel al-Qumi-qi (ca. 850), a group of Karaites established themselves in Palestine and succeeded in spreading their ideas throughout northwest Africa and Spain. The reaction of the *gaonim* was quick enough: a certain number of codes and manuals confirming and reinforcing Rabbinism were written to counteract this heresy. The proselytization of the Karaites lost its impetus, but the sect survived in certain marginal areas. However, as we shall soon see, the discovery of Greek philosophy through Arabic translations, although it stimulated the Jewish philosophic genius, also encouraged certain extravagant, and indeed scandalous, doctrines. It suffices for us to recall that Hiwî al-Balkî, a skeptical author of the ninth century, attacked the morality of the Bible and published an expurgated edition for its use in his schools.

286. Jewish theologians and philosophers of the Middle Ages

Philo of Alexandria (ca. 13 B.C.–ca. 50 A.D.) endeavored to reconcile the biblical revelation with Greek philosophy, but he was ignored by Jewish thinkers and had influence only on the theology of the Christian Fathers. It was not until the ninth and tenth centuries that, thanks to Arabic translations, the Jews discovered Greek thought and concurrently the Muslim method of justifying faith by reason (*kalam*). The first important Jewish philosopher was the *gaon* Saadia ben Joseph (882–942). Born and educated in Egypt, he established himself in Baghdad, where he directed one of the celebrated Talmudic academies of Babylonia. Although he did not elaborate a system and did not create a school, Saadia established the model for the Jewish philosopher.[12] In his apologetic work, *The Book of Beliefs and Opinions,*

11. Like the Sadducees, in the second century.
12. Some of his works have been lost; among others, the Arabic translation, with commentary, on the Bible.

written in Arabic, he showed the relationship between revealed truth and reason. Both emanate from God, but the Torah is a special gift to the Jewish people. Deprived of an independent state, its unity and integrity are maintained solely by this people's obedience to the Law.[13]

At the beginning of the eleventh century, the center of Jewish culture was displaced to Muslim Spain. Solomon ibn Gabirol lived in Malaga between 1021 and 1058. He became celebrated above all for his poems, the most famous of which have been integrated into the liturgy of Yom Kippur. In his unfinished work, *The Source of Life* (*Makor Hayyim*), he borrowed the Plotinian cosmogony of emanations. But in place of the Supreme Thought, ibn Gabirol introduced the notion of the divine will; in other words, it remains Yahweh who creates the world. Ibn Gabirol explains matter as one of the first emanations; however, this matter was of a spiritual order, its corporeality being only one of its properties.[14] Neglected by the Jews, the *Makor Hayyim* was translated under the title *Fons Vitae,* and was highly appreciated by Christian theologians.[15]

We know next to nothing of Bahya ibn Paqûda, who probably lived in eleventh-century Spain. In his *Introduction to the Duties of the Heart,* an Arabic treatise on spiritual morality, ibn Paqûda insists above all on interior devotion. At the same time, his work is a spiritual autobiography. ''From the preamble, this Jewish doctor indicates how he is alone, and how he suffers in his solitude. He writes his book in reaction to his milieu, too legalistic for his taste, in order to give witness that a Jew has at least struggled to live, as the authentic Jewish tradition wishes of him, according to the heart as well as according to the body. . . . It is above all during the night that Bahya feels his soul open. Then, in those hours propitious for the love to which partners devote themselves in their embrace, Bahya becomes the Lover of God: on his knees, bowed down, he passes hours of ecstasy in silent prayer, thus attaining the heights towards which the ascetic exercises of the

13. Cf. *The Book of Beliefs and Opinions* (translated by S. Rosenblatt), pp. 21ff., 29ff. Saadia's arguments for demonstrating the existence of God are borrowed from the *Kalam;* cf. H. A. Wolson, *Kalam Arguments for Creation in Saadia, Averroes,* etc., pp. 197ff.

14. *Fons Vitae,* 4 8f.; abridged text, Munk, 4, p. 1.

15. They knew ibn Gabirol as Avicebron. It was only in 1845 that Salomon Munk identified the author.

day, the humility, the examination of conscience, and the scrupulous piety all lead.''[16]

Like ibn Gabirol, Judah Halevi (1080–1149) is both a poet and a theologian. In his *Defense of the Despised Religion,* he presents dialogues between a Muslim doctor, a Christian, a Jewish scholar, and the King of the Khazars: at the end of these discussions, the latter is converted to Judaism. Like al Ghazzâlî, Judah Halevi employs a philosophical method to contest the validity of philosophy. Religious certainty is not procured by the medium of reason, but by biblical revelation, such as it is bestowed upon the Jewish people. The election of Israel is confirmed by the prophetic spirit; no pagan philosopher has become a prophet. The rise of prophetism is closely linked to obedience to the commandments of the Law and the sacramental value of the Holy Land, the true ''Heart of the Nations.'' Asceticism plays no role in the mystical experience of Judah Halevi.

287. Maimonides between Aristotle and the Torah

Rabbi, doctor, and philosopher, Moses ben Maimon, or Maimonides (b. 1135, in Cordoba, d. 1204, in Cairo), represents the apogee of Jewish medieval thought. He enjoyed and still enjoys an exceptional prestige; but his multifaceted genius and the apparent absence of unity in his work have prompted interminable controversies.[17] Maimonides is the author of several important exegetical works (the most famous being *The Commentaries on the Mishnah* and the *Mishneh Torah*) and a famous philosophical treatise, *The Guide for the Perplexed,* written

16. André Neher, ''La philosophie juive médiévale,'' p. 1021. Most likely, Bahya had been influenced by Muslim mysticism, but the Jewish character of his spiritual life and theology is beyond doubt. As Neher has justly noted, Bahya recuperated the Hasidic Jewish tradition, attested in the Bible, at Qumran, and in the Talmud: ''ascesis, the nocturnal vigil in prayers and meditation''; in brief, the tradition which ''knew how to reconcile the most universal religious experience with the particularism of the religion of Israel'' (ibid., p. 1022).

17. As Isadore Twersky puts it: ''stimulating for some, irritating for others, he rarely provoked an attitude of indifference or nonchalance.'' He has been seen as a multifaceted but harmonious personality, or, by contrast, as strained and complex, an author riddled consciously or unconsciously with paradoxes and contradictions; *A Maimonides Reader,* p. xiv.

in Arabic in 1195. Still in our own day, certain historians and Jewish philosophers regard Maimonidean thought as marked by an insurmountable dichotomy: on the one hand, the principles which inspire his exegetical and legalistic works (the principles of *halakhah*); on the other hand, the metaphysic articulated in *The Guide for the Perplexed*, whose source is found in Aristotle.[18]

It must be insisted from the beginning that Maimonides had the highest esteem for "the prince of philosophers" ("the most sublime representative of human intelligence after the prophets of Israel"), and that he did not rule out the possibility of a synthesis between traditional Judaism and Aristotelian thought.[19] But instead of seeking a deft accord between the Bible and Aristotelian philosophy, Maimonides begins by separating them, "thus safeguarding the biblical experience, without always, as al-Ghazzâlî and Judah Halevi had done, isolating it from philosophical experience and radically opposing the one to the other. The Bible and philosophy are connected in Maimonides; they derive from the same roots, and strive towards the same goal. But in this common march, philosophy plays the role of the path, whereas the Bible directs the man who advances upon it."[20]

To be sure, philosophy comprises for Maimonides a discipline that is rash, and even dangerous when it is poorly understood. It is only after having attained moral perfection (by observance of the Law) that one can dedicate himself to the perfection of his intelligence.[21] The deepening study of metaphysics is not obligatory for all members of the community; but for all, the observance of the Law should be accompanied by philosophic reflection. Intellectual instruction constitutes a virtue that is superior to the moral virtues. Having concentrated into thirteen principles the essential propositions of metaphysics, Maimonides maintained that this minimum theoretic should be meditated upon and assimilated by each of the faithful. For he does not

18. See several recent examples, notably the opinions of Isaac Husik and Leo Strauss, in David Hartmann, ed., *Maimonides: Torah and Philosophic Quest*, pp. 20ff. By contrast, Hartmann attempts to demonstrate the unity of Maimonides' thought.

19. In this enterprise, he had had two predecessors but without his scope.

20. Neher, "La philosophie," pp. 1028–29.

21. In his Introduction to the *Guide*, Maimonides acknowledges that, among other precautions, he has deliberately introduced contradictory affirmations to lead the unsuspecting reader into error.

hesitate to affirm that knowledge of a philosophical order is a necessary condition for assuring survival after death.[22]

Like Philo and Saadia before him, Maimonides applied himself to translating into philosophical language the historic events and terminology of the Bible. After criticizing and rejecting a hermeneutic of the *kalam* type, he introduces and uses the approach of Aristotle. To be sure, no argument could reconcile the eternity of the world as affirmed by Aristotle and the creation *ex nihilo* proclaimed in the Bible. But for Maimonides, these two theses share a commonality, in that neither provides irrefutable proofs. According to the Jewish doctor, Genesis does not affirm "creation *ex nihilo* as a reality: it suggests it, but an allegorical exegesis could interpret the biblical text in the sense of the Greek thesis. The criterion by virtue of which the debate can be resolved is thus not an exterior one: it is the sovereignty of God, His transcendence in relation to nature."[23]

Despite his genius, Maimonides did not succeed in demonstrating the identity of Aristotle's Prime Mover with the free, omnipotent creator God of the Bible. Yet he affirms that truth ought to be, and can be, discovered only by the intelligence; in other words, by the philosophy of Aristotle. With the exception of Moses, Maimonides rejects the validity of prophetic revelations; he considers them as the work of the imagination. The Torah received by Moses is a monument that is unique and valid for all times. For the great majority of the faithful, it is sufficient to study the Torah and to respect its injunctions.

Maimonides' ethic is a synthesis of the biblical heritage and the Aristotelian model; in effect, he exalts intellectual effort and philosophic knowledge. His messianism is purely terrestrial: "a human city constructed on the acquisition of knowledge provoking a spontaneous exercise of virtue."[24] In place of a bodily resurrection, Maimonides believed in an immortality obtained through metaphysical knowledge. However, certain exegetes have drawn attention to what has been called Maimonides' "negative theology." "Between God and man,

22. *Guide for the Perplexed*, 3: 51, 54. Cf. Vajda, *Introduction à la pensée juive du Moyen Âge*, p. 145. In the last account, it is only the sum of metaphysical attainments, acquired during terrestrial existence, that is "immortal." Such a conception is attested in a number of esoteric traditions.

23. Neher, "La philosophie," p. 1031.

24. Ibid., p. 1032. See also the texts translated and commented upon by Hartmann, *Maimonides,* pp. 81ff.

there is nothingness and the abyss. . . . How does one cross this chasm? First of all, by accepting nothingness. The negativity of the approach to the divine, the ungraspableness of God in the philosophic perspective, are only images for man's abandonment to nothingness: it is by progressing through this nothingness that man approaches God. . . . In some of the most remarkable chapters of the *Guide,* Maimonides shows how every prayer should be one of silence, and how every observance should tend towards something more elevated, which is Love. Through Love, the abyss between God and man can be positively crossed: without losing anything of its austerity, the meeting between God and man is established.''[25]

It is important to observe from now on that despite the more or less superficial influence of Greek, Hellenistic, Muslim, or Christian philosophers, Jewish philosophical thought lacks neither power nor originality. Less than a matter of influences, it is rather one of a continual dialogue between Jewish thinkers and representatives of the diverse philosophic systems of pagan antiquity, and of Christianity and Islam. This dialogue is to be interpreted as one in which all of the speakers are reciprocally enriched. One finds an analogous situation in the history of Jewish mysticism (cf. §§288ff.). In effect, the Jewish religious genius is characterized at once by its fidelity to the biblical tradition and by its capacity to submit to numerous exterior "influences" without allowing itself to be dominated by them.

288. The first expressions of Jewish mysticism

The morphology of the Jewish mystical experience is rich and complex. In anticipating the analyses which will follow, it is fitting to single out several specific traits. With the exception of the Messianic Movement launched by Sabbatai Zwi (§291), no other school, despite the occasional and sometimes quite serious tensions with the rabbinical tradition, separates itself from normative Judaism. As for the esotericism which characterized Jewish mysticism from the beginning, it

---

25. Neher, p. 1032. See also Hartmann, p. 187, and the texts translated by Twersky, *A Maimonides Reader,* pp. 83ff., 432–33, etc. For our purposes, we can neglect the several philosophers of the post-Maimonides era: Gersonides (Levi Ben Gerson, 1288–1344), Hasdai Crescas (1340–1410), Joseph Albo (1370–1444), etc.

drew for a long time on the Jewish religious heritage (cf. volume 2, pp. 257ff.). Similarly, the Gnostic elements, to at least some degree detectable everywhere, derive in the last analysis from the older Jewish Gnosticism.[26] Let us add that the supreme mystical experience, the union with God, seems rather exceptional. In general, the mystical goal is the vision of God, the contemplation of his majesty and comprehension of the mysteries of Creation.

The first phase of Jewish mysticism is characterized by the importance accorded to the ecstatic ascension up to the Divine Throne, the *Merkabah*. Attested by the first century B.C.E., this esoteric tradition continues up to the tenth century of our era.[27] The site of the manifestation of divine glory, the World of the Throne, corresponds for the Jewish mystic to the *pleroma* (the "plenitude") of the Gnostic Christians and the Hermeticists. The brief and frequently obscure texts are called the "Books of the *Hekhaloth*" ("Heavenly Palace"). They describe the rooms and the palace which the visionary passes through in his journey, before he arrives in the seventh and last *hekhal* where the Throne of Glory is found. The ecstatic journey, known in the beginning as the "ascension to the *Merkabah*," was around 500 designated, for unknown reasons, as "the descent toward the *Merkabah*." Paradoxically, the descriptions of the "descent" use metaphors of ascent.

From the beginning, it seems that there were well-organized secret groups which disclosed their esoteric doctrines and their unique methods to the initiated. Beyond moral qualities, the novices had to possess certain physiognomic and chiromantic criteria.[28] The ecstatic journey was prepared for by twelve to forty days of ascetic exercises: fasting, ritual chants, repetition of names, special position (head between the knees).

26. In certain cases, it cannot be ruled out that these traditional Gnostic elements might have been revived following direct or indirect confrontations with the heretical Christian movements of the Middle Ages.

27. Scholem distinguishes three periods: the anonymous conventicles of the ancient apocalyptists; the speculations on the Throne by certain masters of the Mishnah; and the mysticism of the *Merkabah* in the late and post-Talmudic period; cf. *Major Trends in Jewish Mysticism*, p. 43; see also *Jewish Mysticism, Merkabah Mysticism and Talmudic Tradition*, passim. The oldest description of the *Merkabah* is found in the fourteenth chapter of the Ethiopian *Book of Enoch*.

28. Scholem, *Major Trends*, p. 48.

The soul's ascension through the heavens, and the perils that it confronts, comprised a theme that was common to the Gnosticism and Hermeticism of the second and third centuries. As Gershom Scholem has written, the mysticism of the *Merkabah* comprises one of the Jewish branches of Gnosis.[29] However, the place of the Archons, who according to the Gnostics defended the seven planetary heavens, is taken in this Jewish Gnosticism by the "doormen" posted to the right and the left of the entry into the heavenly room. In both cases, the soul needs a password: a magic seal, containing a secret name, which wards off the demons and the hostile angels. As long as the journey continues, the dangers become more and more formidable. The final test seems highly enigmatic. In a fragment conserved in the Talmud, Rabbi Akiba, addressing himself to three rabbis whose intention was to enter "Paradise," says to them: "When you come to the place of the shining marble plates, then do not say: water, water! For it is written: He that telleth lies shall not tarry in my sight."[30]

During the journey, the soul receives revelations concerning the secrets of Creation, the hierarchy of angels, and the practices of theurgy. At the highest heaven, upright before the Throne, the soul "contemplates the mystical figure of the divinity in the symbol of the 'figure having the appearance of a man,' whom the Prophet Ezekiel (1:26) had received permission to see on the Throne of the *Merkabah*. There the 'measure of the body,' in Hebrew *Shi'ur Qoma,* had been revealed to him; that is, the anthropomorphic representation of the divinity appearing as the First Man, but also as the lover of the Song of Songs. At the same time, [the soul] receives the revelation of the mystical names of its members."[31]

One is thus concerned with the projection of the invisible God of Judaism in a mystical figure, one in which is revealed the "Great Glory" of the Jewish Apocalyptic and Apocrypha. But this imaged representation of the Creator (of his cosmic mantle illumining the stars and the heavens, etc.) unfolds from "an absolutely monotheistic con-

29. Cf. *Les origines de la Kabbale,* p. 36. Scholem speaks also of "rabbinic gnosticism," that is, the form of Jewish Gnosticism which strives to remain faithful to the Halakhah tradition; cf. *Major Trends,* p. 65.

30. Scholem, *Major Trends,* p. 52ff. See ibid., p. 49, references to analogous images in Hellenistic literature.

31. Scholem, *Les origines de la Kabbale,* p. 29.

ception; it is entirely lacking the antinomic and heretical character that it takes on when the Creator God has been opposed to the true God.''[32]

Alongside the writings concerning the *Merkabah*, one also finds a text of only a few pages, the *Sefer Yetsirah* (Book of Creation), which spreads its fame in the Middle Ages and becomes celebrated throughout the Diaspora. Its origin and date of composition are unknown (probably the fifth or sixth century). It contains a laconic exposition of the cosmogony and cosmology. The author endeavors ''to align his ideas, which were certainly influenced by Greek sources, with the Talmudic disciplines concerned with the doctrine of the Creation and the *Merkabah*, and it is in the course of this enterprise that we meet in him, for the first time, with speculatively inclined reinterpretations of conceptions that touch upon the *Merkabah*.''[33]

The first section presents the ''thirty-two marvelous ways of Wisdom (*Hokhma* or Sophia) by which God has created the world [cf. §200]: the twenty-two letters of the sacred alphabet and the ten primordial numbers (the *Sephiroth*). The first *Sephira* is the *pneuma* (*ruah*) of the living God. From the *ruah* comes forth Primordial Air, from which are born Water and Fire, the third and fourth of the *Sephiroth*. From Primordial Air, God created the twenty-two letters; from the Water he created the cosmic Chaos; and from Fire, the Throne of glory and the hierarchies of angels. The last six *Sephiroth* represent the six directions of space.''[34]

Speculation on the subject of the *Sephiroth*, tinted with mystical numbers, probably has a Neopythagorean origin. But the idea of ''letters as the means by which Heaven and Earth have been created'' can find its explanation in Judaism.[35] ''From this cosmogony and cosmology founded on the mysticism of language, which still so clearly betrays its rapport with astrological ideas, there are direct paths which by all evidence lead to the magical conception of the creative and mi-

32. Ibid., p. 31.

33. Ibid., p. 34. One will find a recent translation in Guy Casaril, *Rabbi Siméon Bar Yochai et la Cabbale,* pp. 41–48.

34. Scholem, *Les origines de la Kabbale,* pp. 35ff. See also Scholem, *Major Trends,* pp. 76ff.

35. Scholem, *Les origines de la Kabbale,* pp. 37–38. Casaril, *Rabbi Siméon Bar Yochai,* p. 42, insists on the parallel with a certain Christian Gnosticism, such as that of the Clementine *Homilies.*

raculous force of letters and words.''[36] The *Sefer Yetsirah* was also used for thaumaturgical purposes. It became the *vade mecum* of the Kabbalists and was commented upon by the greatest Jewish thinkers of the Middle Ages, from Saadia to Sabbatai Donnolo.

Jewish medieval pietism is the work of the three "Pious Men of Germany" (*Hassidei Ashkenaz*): Samuel, his son Yehudah the Hasid, and Eleazar of Worms. The movement appeared in Germany at the beginning of the twelfth century and underwent its creative period between 1150 and 1250. Although it plants its roots in the mysticism of the *Merkabah* and the *Sefer Yetsirah,* Rhenish pietism is a new and original creation. One notes the return of a certain popular mythology, but the Hasids reject the apocalyptic speculations and calculations concerning the coming of the Messiah. Likewise, they are interested in neither rabbinic erudition nor systematic learning. They meditate above all on the mystery of divine unity and strive to practice a new understanding of piety.[37] In contrast to the Spanish Kabbalists (cf. §289), the Hasidic masters address themselves to the people. The chief work of this movement—the *Sefer Hasidim*—makes primary use of anecdotes, paradoxes, and edifying tales. Religious life centers upon asceticism, prayer, and love of God. For in its sublimest manifestation, the fear of God becomes identical with love and devotion for him.[38]

The Hasids endeavor to obtain a perfect serenity of the spirit: they accept imperturbably the injuries and threats of other members of the community.[39] They do not court power; however, they make use of mysterious magical capacities.[40] Their penances betray certain Christian influences, except where sexuality is concerned. For as is well known, Judaism never accepted that type of asceticism. On the other hand, a strong pantheistic tendency has been noted: "God is even closer to the universe and to man than the soul is to the body.''[41]

36. Scholem, *Les origines de la Kabbale,* p. 40.

37. Scholem, *Major Trends,* pp. 91–92.

38. Ibid., p. 95.

39. Scholem compares their serenity to the *ataraxia* of the Cynics and the Stoics; ibid., p. 96. Cf. also the comportment of al-Hallâj (§277).

40. It is in the writings of Eleazar of Worms that one finds the first mention of the *Golem,* the magic *homunculus,* animated during the ecstasy of his maker; cf. Scholem, "The Idea of the Golem," pp. 175ff.

41. Scholem, *Major Trends,* pp. 107ff. (quote from p. 108). It is probably a matter of a Neoplatonic influence through Scotus Erigenus (ninth century); ibid., p. 109.

The German Hasids did not elaborate a systematic theosophy. One can, however, distinguish three central ideas, each derived from different sources: (1) the "divine Glory" (*Kavod*); (2) the idea of a "Holy" Cherub holding himself before the throne; and (3) the mysteries of the divine holiness and majesty, and the secrets of human nature and of man's itinerary toward God.[42]

289. The medieval Kabbalah

An exceptional creation of Jewish esoteric mysticism was the Kabbalah, a term which approximately signifies "tradition" (from the root K B L, "to receive"). As we shall see, while remaining faithful to Judaism, this new religious creation reactualized, at different points, either a Gnostic heritage, sometimes tainted with heresy, or the structures of a cosmic religiosity[43] (awkwardly designated "pantheism"). Difficult tensions were thus provoked between the initiates of a particular Kabbalah and the rabbinic authorities. But let us insist at the outset that despite such tensions, the Kabbalah contributed, whether directly or indirectly, to the strengthening of the spiritual resistance of the Jewish communities of the Diaspora. Moreover, although it was insufficiently known and indifferently understood by certain Christian authors during and after the Renaissance, the Kabbalah played a role in the process of the "de-provincialization" of Western Christianity. In other words, it has a significant place in the history of European ideas between the fourteenth and nineteenth centuries.

The oldest exposition of the Kabbalah properly speaking is found in a book called the *Bahir*. The text, transmitted in an imperfect and fragmentary state and composed of several strata, is obscure and awkward. The *Bahir* was compiled in Provence in the twelfth century from older materials, among which one, the *Raza Rabba* ("the Great Mystery"), was regarded by certain Eastern authors as an important piece of esoteric writing.[44] The Eastern—or more precisely Gnostic—origin

42. Scholem, ibid., pp. 110ff., 118. Let us specify now that there is no continuity between this Jewish pietism of the thirteenth century and the Hasidic movement which arose in Poland and the Ukraine in the eighteenth century (cf. §292).

43. See especially Scholem, "Kabbala and Myth," passim.

44. Cf. Scholem, *Major Trends,* p. 75; *Les origines de la Kabbale,* pp. 66ff.

of the doctrines developed in the *Bahir* is beyond doubt. One sees the speculations of the old Gnostic authors reemerge in diverse Jewish sources: masculine and feminine Eons, the *pleroma* and the Tree of Souls, the *Shekhinah* depicted in terms analogous to those used for the double Sophia (daughter and wife) of the Gnostics.[45]

The question of a possible relation "between the crystallization of the Kabbalah, under the form of the redaction of the *Bahir,* and the Cathari movement remains, however, uncertain. This relation lacks precise demonstration, but one can no longer exclude the possibility. In the history of thought, the book of the *Bahir* represents the perhaps conscious recurrence, but in any case one perfectly corroborated by the facts, of an archaic symbolism that is without counterpart in medieval Judaism. With the publication of the *Bahir,* a Jewish form of mythical thought becomes concurrent with, and inevitably controversial to, the rabbinic and philosophical formations of Judaism."[46]

It is principally on the foundation of the *Bahir* that the Kabbalists of Provence develop their theories. They complete the old Gnostic tradition of Eastern origin with the elements of another spiritual universe, notably that of medieval Neoplatonism. "In the form in which the Kabbalah appears in broad daylight, it includes these two traditions, the accent being placed now on the one, now on the other. It is in this figure, or double figure, that it will be transplanted into Spain."[47]

Despite the Kabbalah's prestige for mystical technique, ecstasy does not play an important role in it. Indeed, in the enormous Kabbalistic literature, there are but few references to personal ecstatic experiences, and only rare ones to the *unio mystica*. Union with God is referred to by the term *devekuth,*[48] "adhesion," "to be united with God," a state of grace which exceeds ecstasy. It is this which explains why the author who placed the greatest value on ecstasy was the least popular. Such was the plight of Abraham Abulafia, born in Saragossa in 1240. He traveled at length in the Near East, Greece, and Italy, and produced numerous works which won scant promotion among the rabbis, precisely because of their too personal nature.

45. Scholem, *Les origines de la Kabbale,* pp. 78–107, 164–94, etc.

46. Ibid., p. 211.

47. Ibid., pp. 384–85. On the Kabbalists of Gerone, a small Catalan town situated between Barcelona and the Pyrenees, see Scholem's ample exposition, ibid., pp. 388–500.

48. See Scholem, "Devekuth, or Communion with God," passim.

Abulafia developed a meditative technique around the names of God by applying a science based on combinations of the letters of the Hebrew alphabet. To explain the spiritual undertaking which led to the liberation of the soul from the chains of matter, he used the image of a knot which must be undone but not cut. Abulafia also appealed to certain practices of a yogic type: rhythmic breathing, special postures, different forms of recitation.[49] By the association and permutation of letters, the adept succeeds in obtaining the mystical contemplation and the prophetic vision. But his ecstasy is not one of trance; it is described by Abulafia as an anticipated redemption. In effect, during his ecstasy the adept is filled with a supernatural light.[50] "What Abulafia called *ecstasy* is the *prophetic vision* in the sense in which Maimonides and the Jewish thinkers of the Middle Ages understood it; the ephemeral union of the human intellect with God, and the influx into the personal soul of the *agent intellect* of the philosophers."[51]

It is very likely that Abulafia's prestige and posthumous influence were radically limited by the appearance in Spain, a little after 1275, of the *Sefer Ha-Zohar*, "The Book of Splendor." This gigantic book (nearly 1,000 pages in the Aramaic version of Mantua) had an unequalled success in the history of the Kabbalah. The only text which was considered as a canonical book, it was placed for several centuries next to the Bible and the Talmud. Written in a pseudepigraphic form, the *Zohar* presents the theological and didactic discussions of the famous Rabbi Simeon bar Yochai (second century) with his friends and disciples. For a long time, scholars have considered the "Book of Splendors" as a compilation of texts of diverse origins, some even containing ideas going back to those of Rabbi Simeon himself. But Gershom Scholem has shown that the author of this "mystical novel" is the Spanish Kabbalist, Moses de Leon.[52]

---

49. Cf. Scholem, *Major Trends*, p. 139.

50. Scholem translates the very elaborate description of such an experience, written by an anonymous disciple, in Palestine, in 1295; ibid., pp. 143–55.

51. Casaril, *Rabbi Siméon Bar Yochai et la Cabbale*, p. 72. "The nearly heretical originality of Abulafia is to have assimilated the prophetic vision (which according to the tradition depends always on God) and the *devekuth*, the adhesion to God by the lone human will and the lone human love, thus affirming that the prophet's vision could be deliberately prepared and provoked by every pious and sincere mystic" (ibid.).

52. Cf. Scholem, *Major Trends*, pp. 157–204.

According to Scholem, the *Zohar* represents Jewish theosophy, that is, a mystical doctrine whose principal goal is the knowledge and description of the mysterious works of the divinity. The hidden God is devoid of qualities and attributes; the *Zohar* and the Kabbalists call him *En-Sof,* the Infinite. But since the hidden God is active throughout the universe, he manifests certain attributes which, in turn, represent certain aspects of divine nature. According to the Kabbalists, there are ten fundamental attributes of God, which are at the same time the ten levels through which the divine life flows. The names of these ten *Sephiroth* reflect the different modes of divine manifestation.[53] All together, the *Sephiroth* compose the "unified universe" of the life of God and are imagined in the form of a tree (God's mystical tree) or of a man (*Adam Kadmon,* the primordial Man). Beside this organic symbolism, the *Zohar* uses the symbolism of the word, the names that God has given to himself.

The Creation takes place within God; it is the movement of the hidden *En-Sof,* which passes from repose to the cosmogony and to self-revelation. This act transforms the *En-Sof,* the ineffable plenitude, into mystical "nothingness"; and from this emanate the ten *Sephiroth.* In the *Zohar,* the transformation of Nothing into Being is expressed by the symbol of the primordial point.[54] One passage (1, 240b) affirms that the creation occurs on two planes, "a superior plane and an inferior plane"; this refers to the world of the *Sephiroth* and the visible world. God's self-revelation and his unfolding in the life of the *Sephiroth* constitute a theogony. "Theogony and Cosmogony represent not two different acts of creation, but two aspects of the same."[55] "Originally, everything was conceived as one great whole, and the life of the Creator pulsated without hindrance or disguise in that of his

53. The "wisdom" of God (*Hokhmah*), the "intelligence" of God (*Binah*), the "love" or compassion of God (*Hessed*), etc. The tenth *Sephirah* is *Malkhuth,* the "royalty" of God, generally described in the *Zohar* as the mystical archetype of the community of Israel, or as the *Shekhinah;* cf. Scholem, *Major Trends,* pp. 212–13. On the *Sephiroth* in the *Sefer Yetsirah,* see above, §288.

54. Identified as the "wisdom" of God, *Hokmah* (the second *Sephirah*). In the third *Sephirah,* the "point" becomes a "palace" or "building," thus indicating the creation of the world. *Binah,* the name of this *Sephirah,* not only designates "intelligence" but also "differentiation"; cf. Scholem, *Major Trends,* pp. 219ff.

55. Ibid., p. 223. This doctrine has been elaborated above all by Moses de Leon.

creatures. . . . Only the Fall has caused God to become 'transcendent.' ''[56]

One of the most significant innovations of the Kabbalists is the idea of the union of God with the *Shekhinah;* this *hieros gamos* completes the true unity of God. According to the *Zohar,* in the beginning this union was permanent and uninterrupted. But the sin of Adam provoked the interruption of the *hieros gamos* and, by way of consequence, the "exile of the *Shekhinah.*" Only after the restoration of the original harmony in the Act of Redemption will "God be one and His name one."[57]

As we have already remarked, the Kabbalah reintroduces into Judaism several ideas and myths that relate to a cosmic type of religiosity. To the sanctification of life by the medium of the work and rites prescribed by the Talmud, the Kabbalists add the mythological valorization of Nature and Man, the importance of mystical experience, and even certain themes of Gnostic origin. One can discern in this phenomenon of "opening," and this effort at revalorization, the nostalgia for a religious universe where the Hebrew Scriptures and the Talmud coexist with a cosmic religiosity, and with Gnosticism and mysticism. An analogous phenomenon appears in the "universalist" ideal of certain Hermeticist philosophers of the Italian Renaissance.

290. Isaac Luria and the new Kabbalah

One of the consequences of the expulsion of the Jews from Spain in 1492 was the transformation of the Kabbalah: from an esoteric doctrine, it turned into a popular one. Until the catastrophe of 1492, the

56. Ibid., p. 224. The idea is already attested among "primitives"; cf. Eliade, *Myths, Dreams, and Mysteries,* pp. 59ff.

57. Scholem, *Major Trends,* p. 232. As Scholem notes (p. 235), the Kabbalists attempted to discover the mystery of sex in God himself. Another original feature of the *Zohar* is the interpretation of evil as a manifestation—or *Sephirah*—of God (Scholem, ibid., pp. 237ff., remarks upon the parallelism with the thought of Jakob Boehme). As to the idea of the transmigration of souls, originally a Gnostic idea, it is attested for the first time in the *Bahir* (see ibid., pp. 241ff.), but it will become popular with the success of the "new Kabbalah" of Safed, in the sixteenth century; cf. Scholem, "The Messianic Idea in Kabbalism," pp. 46ff.

Kabbalists concentrated their interest more on Creation than on Redemption: whoever knew the history of the world and of man could eventually return to the original perfection.[58] But after the expulsion, the pathos of messianism invaded the new Kabbalah; the "beginning" and the "end" were bound together. The catastrophe took on a redemptive value: it signified the birth pangs of the messianic era (cf. §203). Henceforward, life was to be understood as an existence in Exile, and the sufferings of the Exile were to be explained by certain audacious theories about God and man.

For the new Kabbalah, death, repentance, and rebirth are the three great events which can elevate man toward the beatific vision of God. Humanity is menaced not only by its own corruption, but also by the world's corruption. The latter was provoked by the first fissure in the creation, when the "subject" separated itself from the "object." In insisting on death and rebirth (interpreted as a reincarnation or spiritual rebirth obtained as a result of repentance), the Kabbalists' propaganda, through which the new messianism endeavored to open a path, gained widespread popularity.[59]

Some forty years after the expulsion from Spain, Safed, a Galilean city, became the home of the new Kabbalah. But even before this date, Safed was known as a growing spiritual center. Among the most famous masters, one must mention Joseph Karo (1488–1575), author of Rabbinic Orthodoxy's most important treatise, the *Shulkhan Arukh,* and also of a curious and passionate *Journal* in which he noted his ecstatic powers. Karo's example is particularly instructive: he shows the possibility of integrating rabbinic erudition (*halakhah*) with mystical experience of a kabbalistic type. In effect, Karo found in the Kabbalah both the theoretic foundations and the practical method for obtaining ecstasy, and thus the presence of the *maggid.*[60]

58. Scholem, *Major Trends,* pp. 244ff. Let us specify, however, that long before 1492 certain Kabbalists had proclaimed precisely this catastrophic year as the year of Redemption. The expulsion from Spain revealed that the Redemption signified both a liberation and a catastrophe; ibid., p. 246.

59. The horrors of the Exile would be revalorized by the doctrine of metempsychosis. The most tragic fate for the soul was to be "outcast" or "naked," a state precluding reincarnation or even entry into Hell; cf. ibid., p. 250.

60. See R. J. Zwi Werblowsky, *Joseph Karo, Lawyer and Mystic,* pp. 165ff. On the *maggid,* cf. ibid., pp. 257ff. See also chap. 4 ("Spiritual Life in Sixteenth Century Safed: Mystical and Magical Contemplation").

As for the new Kabbalah which triumphed in Safed, its most celebrated masters were Moses ben Jacob Cordovero (1522–70) and Isaac Luria. The first, a vigorous and systematic thinker, worked out a personal interpretation of the Kabbalah, and more particularly of the *Zohar*. His total work is considerable, whereas Luria, who died at the age of thirty-eight in 1572, left no writings. One knows his system through the notes and books of his disciples, above all an enormous treatise by Hayyim Vital (1543–1620). According to all the remembrances of him, Isaac Luria was a visionary who enjoyed a very rich and singularly varied ecstatic experience. His theology is founded upon the doctrine of the *Tsimtsum*. This term originally signified "concentration" or "contraction," but the Kabbalists used it in the sense of "retreat" or "withdrawal." According to Luria, the existence of the universe has been made possible by a process of divine "contraction." For could there be a world if God is everywhere? "How can God create the world *ex nihilo* if there is no nothing? . . . Thus, God was compelled to make room for the world by, as it were, abandoning a region within Himself, a kind of mystical primordial space from which He withdrew in order to return to it in the act of creation and revelation."[61] Consequently, the first act of the Infinite Being (the *En-Sof*) was not a movement *from outside* but an act of retreat *from inside* himself. As Gershom Scholem has remarked (p. 261), *Tsimtsum* is the deepest symbol of Exile; it could be considered as the Exile of God within himself. It is only in a second movement that God sends out a ray of light and begins his creative revelation.[62]

Before the "contraction," there existed in God not only the attributes of love and mercy, but also the divine severity which the Kabbalists call *Din,* "Judgment." However, *Din* becomes manifest and identifiable as a result of the *Tsimtsum,* for the latter signifies not only an act of negation and limitation, but also a "judgment." Two tendencies are distinguished in the process of creation: ebb and flow ("going out" in the kabbalistic lexicon). As with the human organism, the creation constitutes a gigantic system of divine inhalation and exhala-

61. Scholem, *Major Trends,* p. 261.
62. According to Jacob Emden as cited in Scholem, ibid., pp. 261–62, this paradox of the *Tsimtsum* is the only serious attempt at explaining the idea of Creation *ex nihilo*. Moreover, the conception of the *Tsimtsum* gives a sharp check to the pantheistic tendencies which began to influence the Kabbalah, especially from the Renaissance on.

tion. In following the tradition of the *Zohar,* Luria considers the cosmogonic act as taking place within God; in effect, a vestige of the divine light remains in the primordial space created by the *Tsimtsum.*[63]

This doctrine is completed by two equally profound and audacious conceptions: the "Breaking of the Vases" (*Shevirath Ha-Kelim*) and the *Tikkun,* a term signifying reparation for a mistake, or "restitution." The lights which emanated progressively from the eyes of the *En-Sof* were received and conserved in "vases" that correspond to the *Sephirot.* But with the last six *Sephirot,* the divine Light bursts forth all at once and the "vases" break into pieces. Thus Luria explains, on the one hand, the blend of the lights of the *Sephirot* with the "shells" (*Kelipoth*), that is, the forces of evil which lie in the "depth of the great abyss"; and on the other hand, the necessity of purifying the elements of the *Sephirot* by eliminating the "shells" in order to accord a separate entity to Evil.[64]

As for the *Tikkun,* the "restitution" of the ideal order, the reintegration of the primordial All, it is the secret goal of human existence, or in other words, the Redemption. As Scholem writes: "these sections of the Lurianic Kabbalah undoubtedly represent the greatest victory which anthropomorphic thought has ever won in the history of Jewish mysticism" (*Major Trends,* p. 268). In effect, man is conceived as a *microcosm* and the living God as a *macrocosm.* One could say that Luria arrived at a myth of God giving birth to Himself.[65] Still more, man plays a certain role in the process of the final restoration; it is he who achieves the enthronement of God in his heavenly Kingdom. The *Tikkun,* presented symbolically as the emergence of God's personality, corresponds to the process of history. The appearance of the Messiah is the consummation of the *Tikkun* (ibid., p. 274). The mystical element and the messianic element are fused together.

Luria and the Kabbalists of Safed—especially Hayyim Vital—see a direct relation between the accomplishment of man's mission and the doctrine of the metempsychosis, or *Gilgul.* This connection under-

63. The idea recalls the system of Basilides; see Scholem, *Major Trends,* p. 264. Cf. Eliade, *History of Religious Ideas,* vol. 2, pp. 375ff.

64. Scholem has underlined the Gnostic and above all Manichaean character (the fragments of scattered light in the world) of this doctrine; *Major Trends,* pp. 267ff., 280. Cf. Eliade, *History,* §§252–53.

65. For Luria, the *En-Sof* has little religious interest; cf. Scholem, *Major Trends,* p. 271.

scores the importance accorded to man's role in the universe. Every soul retains its individuality until the moment of spiritual restoration. The souls which have obeyed the Commandments await, each in its blessed place, their integration into Adam, when the universal restoration will occur. In sum, the true history of the world is that of the migrations and interrelations of souls. Metempsychosis (*Gilgul*) constitutes a moment in the process of the restoration, *Tikkun*. The duration of this process can be shortened by certain religious acts (rites, penitence, meditation, prayer).[66] It is important to note that after 1550, the conception of *Gilgul* became an integrated part of Jewish popular beliefs and religious folklore.

"The Lurianic Kabbalah was the last religious movement in Judaism the influence of which became preponderant among all sections of the Jewish people and in every country of the Diaspora, without exception. It was the last movement in the history of Rabbinic Judaism which gave expression to a world of religious reality common to the whole people. To the philosopher of Jewish history it may seem surprising that the doctrine which achieved this result was deeply related to Gnosticism, but such are the dialectics of history."[67]

It is fitting to add that the considerable success of the new Kabbalah illustrates once again a specific trait of the Jewish religious genius: the capacity to renew itself by integrating elements of exotic origin without thereby losing the fundamental structures of rabbinic Judaism. What is more, in the new Kabbalah a number of basically esoteric conceptions were made accessible to the uninitiated and sometimes became popular (as was the case with metempsychosis).

291. The Apostate Redeemer

Although it quickly miscarried, a grandiose messianic movement arose in September 1665 at Smyrna: before a frenzied crowd, Sabbatai Zwi (1626–76) proclaimed himself the Messiah of Israel. For some time

66. Ibid., pp. 281ff. The mystical prayer proves a powerful instrument of redemption; the doctrine and practice of the mystical prayer constitutes the esoteric part of Luria's Kabbalah; ibid., pp. 276, 278.
67. Ibid., pp. 285–86.

already, rumors had circulated about him and his divine mission, but it is due to his "disciple," Nathan of Gaza (1644–80), that Sabbatai was recognized as the Messiah. Actually, Sabbatai suffered periodically from spells of excessive sadness followed by great joy. When he learned that a visionary, Nathan of Gaza, "revealed to everyone the mysteries of his soul," Sabbatai went to him in the hope of being cured. Nathan, who seems to have had a gift of "seeing," succeeded in convincing him that he was truly the Messiah. And it was this exceptionally gifted "disciple" who organized the theology of the movement and assured its propagation. As for Sabbatai, he wrote nothing, and no original message or memorable saying is attributed to him.

Throughout the Jewish world, the news of the Messiah's coming aroused an unequalled enthusiasm. Six months after his proclamation, Sabbatai made his way to Constantinople, perhaps to convert the Muslims. But he was arrested and imprisoned by Mustafa Pasha (6 February 1666). In order to avoid martyrdom, Sabbatai Zwi renounced Judaism and embraced Islam.[68] But neither the apostasy of the Messiah nor his death eleven years later stopped the religious movement that he had set in motion.[69]

Sabbatianism represents the first serious deviation in Judaism since the Middle Ages, and the first of those mystical ideas that led directly to the disintegration of orthodoxy. In the final analysis, this heresy encouraged a sort of religious anarchy. In the beginning, the propaganda for the Apostate Messiah openly continued. It is only much later, when there emerged an expectation of the "triumphal return of Sabbatai Zwi from the spheres of impurity," that the propaganda became secret.

The glorification of the Apostate Redeemer, an abominable sacrilege for Jewish thought, was interpreted and exalted as the most profound and the most paradoxical of the mysteries. Already in 1667, Nathan of Gaza affirmed that it was precisely the "strange actions of Sabbatai [that] constituted proof of the authenticity of his messianic mission." For, "if he were not the Redeemer, these deviations would not occur to him." The true acts of Redemption are those which cause

68. See ibid., 286–324, and esp. Scholem's *Sabbatai Sevi, The Mystical Messiah,* pp. 103–460.
69. See Scholem, *Sabbatai Sevi,* pp. 461–929.

the greatest scandal.[70] According to the Sabbatian theologian Cardozo (d. 1706), only the soul of the Messiah is strong enough to sustain such a sacrifice, that is, to descend to the depths of the abyss.[71] In order to complete his mission (to deliver the last divine sparks imprisoned by the forces of Evil), the Messiah must condemn himself by his own actions. This is the reason why the traditional values of the Torah are henceforth abolished.[72]

Two tendencies are distinguished among the adepts of Sabbatianism: one of the moderates, the other of the radicals. The moderate group did not doubt the authenticity of the Messiah, since God could not so brutally deceive His people; but the mysterious paradox realized by the Apostate Messiah did not constitute a model to follow. The radicals thought otherwise: just as the Messiah did, so ought the faithful to descend into Hell, for Evil must be combatted by evil. In this way the soteriological value, or function, of Evil is thus proclaimed. According to some of the radical Sabbatians, every visibly impure and wicked act achieves contact with the spirit of holiness. According to others, now that the sin of Adam is abolished, one who does evil is virtuous in the eyes of God. Like the seeds buried in the earth, the Torah must rot in order to bear fruit, most notably in the messianic glory. All is permitted, hence also sexual immorality.[73] The most sinister Sabbatian, Jakob Frank (d. 1791), held what Scholem has termed a "mystique of nihilism." Some of his disciples expressed their nihilism in diverse political activities of a revolutionary nature.

In the history of the Kabbalah, as Scholem observes, the emergence of new ideas and interpretations is accompanied by the certainty that History is nearing its end and that the most profound mysteries of

70. See Scholem, *Major Trends*, p. 314; idem, *Sabbatai Sevi*, pp. 800ff.

71. As cited by Scholem, *Major Trends*, p. 310; see also his *Sabbatai Sevi*, pp. 614ff. Nathan of Gaza held that the soul of the Messiah finds itself, from the beginning, captive in a great abyss; *Major Trends*, pp. 297–98. The idea is of a Gnostic structure (attested among the Ophites), but the seed is found in the *Zohar* and the Lurianic writings (ibid.).

72. For Abraham Faez, those who remain faithful to the Law are sinners; Scholem, *Major Trends*, p. 212.

73. Ibid., p. 316. Some orgiastic practices, analogous to those of the Carpocratians, are attested in the years 1700–1760.

Divinity, obscured in the period of the Exile, will reveal their true significance on the eve of the New Age.[74]

292. Hasidism

It may appear paradoxical that the final mystical movement, Hasidism, should surge forth in Podolia and Volhynia, regions where the Apostate Messiah had exercised a profound influence. It is very likely that the founder of this movement, Rabbi Israel Baal Shem Tov (the "Master of the Good Name," or in short, the "Besht") was familiar with the moderate form of Sabbatianism.[75] But he neutralized the messianic elements of Sabbatianism, just as he renounced the exclusivism of the secret initiatory confraternity which characterized the traditional Kabbalah. The "Besht" (ca. 1700–1760) sought to make the spiritual discoveries of the Kabbalists accessible to the common people. Such a popularization of the Kabbalah—already initiated by Isaac Luria—guaranteed a social function for mysticism.

The enterprise's success was prodigious and persistent. The first fifty years following the death of the Baal Shem Tov—1760 to 1810—constituted the heroic and creative period of Hasidism. A considerable number of mystics and saints contributed to the regeneration of religious values that had petrified in legalistic Judaism.[76] In effect, a new type of spiritual leader made his appearance: in place of the erudite Talmudist or the initiate of the classical Kabbalah, there was now the "pneumatic," the illuminate, the prophet. The *zaddik* (the "Righteous"), or spiritual master, becomes the exemplary model *par excellence*. The exegesis of the Torah and the esotericism of the Kabbalah lose their primacy. It is the virtues and comportment of the *zaddik* that inspire his disciples and his faithful followers, a development which explains the social importance of the movement. The *existence* of the saint constitutes, for the entire community, the concrete proof that it is possible to realize the highest religious ideal of Israel. It is the

74. Ibid., pp. 320–21. The necessary apostasy of the Messiah is a new expression of a Gnostic type of dualism, notably the opposition between the hidden (transcendent) God and the God of Creation; ibid., pp. 322–23.

75. See Scholem's argumentation, ibid., pp. 331–32.

76. Ibid., pp. 336ff.

personality of the master, and not his doctrine, which matters. A famous *zaddik* says: "I did not go to the 'Maggid' of Meseritz to learn Torah from him but to watch him tie his boot-laces."[77]

Despite certain innovations in matters of ritual, this revival movement has always kept itself within the framework of traditional Judaism. But the public prayer of the Hasids was charged with emotional elements: chants, dances, enthusiasm, explosions of joy. Adding to the sometimes eccentric behavior of certain masters, this unaccustomed emotiveness irritated the adversaries of Hasidism.[78] But suddenly after 1810, the excesses of emotionalism lose their prestige and popularity, and the Hasids begin to recognize the importance of the rabbinic tradition.

As Scholem has shown, Hasidism, even in its late and exaggerated form of "Zaddikism," provided no new mystical idea.[79] Its most significant contribution to the history of Judaism consists in the means, at once simple and audacious, by which the Hasidic saints and masters succeed in popularizing—and making accessible—the experience of an inner renewal. The Hasidic tales, made famous by Martin Buber's translation, represent the most important creation of the movement. The retelling of the deeds done and the words spoken by the saints acquire a ritual value. Narration recovers its primordial function, notably that of reactualizing mythical time and making present supernatural and fabulous personages. The biographies of the saints and the *zaddikim* also abound in marvelous episodes, where certain magical practices are reflected. At the end of the history of Jewish mysticism, these two tendencies—mysticism and magic—draw together and coexist as in the beginning.[80]

Let us add that analogous phenomena are also met elsewhere; for example, in Hinduism or in Islam, where the recitation of the legends

77. As cited by Scholem, ibid., p. 344. In effect, the supreme aspiration of the *zaddik* is not to interpret the Torah in the most rigorous manner possible, but to become the Torah himself; ibid.

78. The most famous would be Rabbi Elijah, the *gaon* of Vilna, who directed a systematic persecution against the movement in 1772; see ibid., pp. 345–46.

79. Ibid., pp. 338ff. The single exception is that of the school established by Rabbi Shneur Zalman of Ladi (in the Ukraine), who was called *Habad* (abridged from *Hochmah-Binah-Daath*, the first three *Sephiroth*); cf. ibid., pp. 340ff. See esp. *Lettre aux hassidim sur l'extase* by R. Shneur's son, Dov Baer of Lubavitch (1773–1827).

80. Scholem, *Major Trends*, p. 349.

of the famous ascetics and yogins, or of the episodes from the different epics, plays a capital role in the popular religion. Here also one recognizes the religious function of oral literature, and primarily of *narration,* that is to say, the telling of fabulous and exemplary "histories." Equally striking is the analogy between the *zaddik* and the *guru,* the spiritual master of Hinduism (sometimes divinized by his faithful followers: *gurudev*). In its extreme form, Zaddikism knew certain aberrant cases, as when the *zaddik* fell victim to his own power. The same phenomenon is attested in India, from Vedic times up to the modern era. Let us finally recall that the coexistence of two tendencies, mysticism and magic, equally characterizes the religious history of India.

37 Religious Movements in Europe:
From the Late Middle Ages to the Eve of the Reformation

293. The dualist heresy in the Byzantine Empire: The Bogomils

From the tenth century on, lay and religious observers in Byzantium remarked upon the rise in Bulgaria of the sectarian movement of the Bogomils. The founder was Bogomil (''beloved of God''), a village priest, of whom we know nothing but his name. Around 930, he seems to have begun to preach poverty, humility, penitence, and prayer; for according to Bogomil, this world is evil; it has been created by Satan (Christ's brother and God's son), the ''wicked God'' of the Old Testament.[1] The sacraments, icons, and ceremonies of the Orthodox Church are vain, being the work of the Devil. The Cross should be detested, for it is on the Cross that Christ was tortured and put to death. The only valid prayer was the *Our Father,* which was to be said four times a day and four times at night.

The Bogomils neither ate meat nor drank wine, and advised against marriage. Their community had no hierarchy. Men and women confessed their sins and gave absolution to each other. They criticized the rich, condemned the nobility, and encouraged the common people to disobey their masters by practicing passive resistance. The success of the movement is explained by a popular devotion that was disillusioned with the pomp of the Church and the unworthiness of the priests; but it was also affected by the hatred of the Bulgarian peasants,

---

1. It is likely that Bogomil had known certain dualistic ideas diffused by the Paulicians and Messalians, heretics from Asia Minor (sixth to tenth centuries); for a brief study of their history and doctrine, see Steven Runciman, *The Medieval Manichee,* pp. 21–26.

poor and reduced to servitude, for the landowners and especially for the Byzantine agents.[2]

After the conquest of Bulgaria (1018) by Basil II, a number of Bulgarian nobles settled in Constantinople. Adopted by certain families of the local nobility and even by some Byzantine monks, Bogomilism shaped its theology. But it is probably as the result of theological disputes that the schism of the sect occurred. Those who maintained the autonomy of Satan, affirming that he is an eternal and omnipotent god, gathered in the Church of Dragovitsa (the name of a village on the border between Thrace and Macedonia). The old Bogomils, who regarded Satan as the fallen brother of God, kept the old name of "Bulgars." Although the "Dragovitsians" proclaimed an absolute dualism and the "Bulgars" a moderate one, the two churches mutually tolerated each other. For Bogomilism at this period experienced a new vigor. Communities were organized in Byzantium, Asia Minor, and Dalmatia, and the number of the faithful increased. Two categories were now distinguished: the priests and the believers. Prayer and fasting were strengthened; ceremonies multiplied and grew longer. "By the end of the twelfth century, the peasant movement of the tenth century had become a sect with monastic rites and a speculative teaching in which the estrangement between dualism and Christianity was more and more evident."[3]

When the repression of this movement began to organize itself, already at the beginning of the twelfth century, the Bogomils retreated to the north of the Balkans, and their missionaries made their way to Dalmatia, Italy, and France. At certain moments, however, Bogomilism succeeded in imposing itself at the official levels. This was the case, for example, in the first half of the thirteenth century in Bulgaria; and in Bosnia, it became the state religion under the Ban Kulin (1180–1214). But the sect lost its influence in the fourteenth century, and after the Ottoman conquest of Bulgaria and Bosnia (1393), most of the Bogomils converted to Islam.[4]

---

2. See esp. Robert Browning, *Byzantium and Bulgaria*, pp. 163ff. One will find a parallel in the Crusade against the Albigensians, in which the northern nobility expressed its envy for the riches of the southern nobles.

3. Arno Borst, *Les Cathares*, p. 63. See also the sources cited in the notes.

4. The movement's history is retraced by Runciman, *Medieval Manichee*, pp. 63ff.; Obolensky, *The Bogomils*, pp. 120ff. On the persistence of enclaves of Bogomils, in

We will soon follow the fortunes of Bogomilism in the West. Let us add that in southeastern Europe, certain Bogomil conceptions have been transmitted by Apocrypha and still survive in folklore. In the Middle Ages, a number of apocryphal books circulated in eastern Europe under the name of Jeremias, a Bogomil priest.[5] However, none of these texts is Jeremias' work. For example, *The Wood of the Cross,* whose subject was celebrated all over medieval Europe, derives from the *Gospel of Nicodemus,* a work of Gnostic origin. The theme of another apocryphal text, *How Christ Became a Priest,* was known for a long time by the Greeks. But the Bogomils added dualistic elements to these old legends. The Slavonic version of *The Wood of the Cross* begins with this phrase: "When God created the world, only He and Satanael were in existence."[6] Now, as we have seen (§251), this cosmogonic motif is widely diffused, but the southeastern European and Slavic variants emphasize the role of the Devil. In following the model of certain Gnostic sects, the Bogomils probably reinforced the dualism by enhancing the Devil's prestige.

Similarly, in the apocryphal *Adam and Eve,* the Bogomils introduced the episode of a "contract" signed by Adam and Satan according to which, since the Earth is the latter's creation, Adam and his descendants belong to him until the coming of Christ. This theme is found in Balkan folklore.[7]

The method of reinterpreting such Apocrypha is illustrated by the *Interrogatio Iohannis,* the only authentic Bogomil text, which was translated into Latin by the Inquisitors of southern France. It concerns a dialogue between John the Evangelist and Christ bearing on the creation of the world, the fall of Satan, the ascension of Enoch, and the Wood of the Cross. One finds passages borrowed from other Apocrypha, and the translation of a Slavic work of the twelfth century, *The Questions of John the Evangelist.* "But its theology is strictly Bogomil. Satan was next after God before he fell (though Christ sat by the Father's side). . . . But here again we cannot tell if this is an origi-

---

the Balkans and in Romania down to the seventeenth century, see N. Cartojan, *Cărtile populare,* 1, pp. 241ff.; Râvzan Theodorescu, *Bizant, Balcani, Occident,* pp. 241ff.

5. See Runciman, pp. 82ff.; E. Turdeanu, "Apocryphes bogomiles et apocryphes pseudo-bogomiles"; etc.

6. Cited by Runciman, p. 84. On the history and spread of this legend, see Cartojan, pp. 115ff.; E. C. Quinn, *The Quest of Seth for the Oil of Life,* pp. 49ff.

7. As regards these Romanian legends, see Cartojan, pp. 71ff.

nal Bogomil work or a translation from the Greek. Probably, to judge from its doctrine, it represents a compilation made by some Bogomil author or some Messalian author out of the apocryphal material at hand.''[8]

What engaged our interest is that these Apocrypha, and above all their oral variants, have for a number of centuries played a role in popular religiosity. As we shall see (§304), this was not the only source of European religious folklore. But the persistence of heretical dualistic themes in the imaginary universe of the common people is not without significance. To give only one example: in southeast Europe, the myth of the creation of the world with the aid of the Devil (who dives to the bottom of the primordial ocean to bring up the vessel) has one consequence: the physical and mental fatigue of God. In certain variants, God falls deeply asleep; in others, he does not know how to resolve a post-cosmogonic problem: the Earth does not happen to enter under the vault of Heaven, and it is the hedgehog who advises him to press the Earth a little, thus giving birth to the mountains and the valleys.[9]

The prestige of the Devil, the passivity of God and his incomprehensible forfeiture—these can be considered as a popular expression of the *deus otiosus* of "primitive" religions, where after having created the world and men, God takes no further interest in the outcome of Creation and withdraws to Heaven, abandoning the completion of his work to a Supernatural Being or a demiurge.

294. The Bogomils in the West: The Cathars

The first decades of the twelfth century give notice of the presence of Bogomil missionaries in Italy, France, and western Germany. In Orléans they succeeded in converting nobles and even priests, among whom were a counselor to King Robert and the queen's confessor. One recognizes the essential thrust of the heresy: God did not create the visible world; matter is impure; marriage, baptism, the Eucharist, and confession are useless; the Holy Spirit, descending upon the believer by the imposition of hands, purifies and sanctifies him; and so on. The king discovered the heretics, judged them, condemned them, and, on 28 December 1022, had them burned. These were the first heretics in

8. Runciman, p. 86. See also Edina Bozóky, *Le Livre Secret des Cathares.*
9. See the sources cited in Eliade, *Zalmoxis, The Vanishing God,* pp. 76ff.

the West to die on the pyre. But the movement continued to spread. The Cathar Church,[10] already established in Italy, sent missionaries into Provence, Languedoc, the Rhenish regions, and as far as the Pyrenees. Above all it was the weavers who propagated the new doctrine. The communities of Provence were grouped into four bishoprics. A council seems to have taken place in 1167 near Toulouse. It was on this occasion that the Bogomil Bishop of Constantinople succeeded in converting groups from Lombardy and southern France to the radical form of dualism.

But in penetrating into the West, Bogomilism adopted certain elements of the local protesting tradition, making the lack of doctrinal unity all the more embarrassing.[11] The Cathars believed in neither Hell nor Purgatory; Satan's domain was the *world;* moreover, he had created it in order to imprison spirit in matter. Satan was identified as Yahweh, the God of the Old Testament. The true God, good and luminous, is to be found far from this world. It is He who sent Christ to teach the means of deliverance. Being a Pure Spirit, the body of Christ was only an illusion.[12] The hatred of life recalls certain Gnostic sects and Manichaeanism (cf. §§232ff.). One could say that the Cathars' ideal was the disappearance of humanity, by suicide and by the refusal to have children; for the Cathars preferred debauchery to marriage.

The ceremony of entrance into the sect, *convenza (convenientia)*, was celebrated only after a long apprenticeship as an adept. The second rite of initiation, the *consolamentum,* by which one obtained the rank of "Perfect," was generally carried out just before death or, if the adept so desired, sooner; but in this latter case, the tests were quite severe. The *consolamentum* took place in the house of one of the faithful under the direction of the eldest of the Perfects. The first part, the *servitium,* consisted in a general confession, made by the assembly; during this time, the Presider held open before himself a copy of the Gospels.[13] Then the catechumen ritually received the *Pater Noster*

10. The name—from *Katharos,* the "pure"—gains usage only from around 1163.

11. Let us add that, thanks to the trials initiated by the Inquisition, the conceptions and ceremonies of the Cathars are better known than those of the Bogomils.

12. It would be vain to insist on the doctrinal divergences; certain Cathars deny Christ's divinity; others mention the Trinity in their ceremonies; still others admit an entire series of eons between God and the world, each of them penetrated by the divine essence; etc. Cf. Runciman, pp. 148ff.; Borst, *Les Cathares,* 124ff.

13. Apparently, the *servitium* contained no heretical affirmation. Only two traits indicate that the speakers professed dualism: one is the stress upon the sins of the flesh,

and, prostrating himself before the Presider, asked him to bless him and pray to God for him, a sinner. The Presider answered: "May God wish to bless you, to make you a good Christian, and to grant you a good end!" At a certain moment in the ceremony, the Presider asked the catechumen to renounce the Church of Rome and the cross drawn on his forehead by a Roman priest at the time of his baptism. Should one fall again into sin after having received the *consolamentum*, the ritual was annulled. That is why certain Perfects practiced the *endura*, deliberately allowing themselves to die of starvation.[14] Every ceremony ended with the ritual sign of "peace," a kiss exchanged by all those present. The Perfects—men and women—enjoyed a prestige superior to that of the Catholic priests. They led a more ascetic life than the rest of the faithful, and practiced three long annual fasts. Little is known about the organization of the Cathar Church, but each bishop was assisted by a *filius major* and a *filius minor* and when the bishop died, the *filius major* succeeded him automatically. The similarities with the Roman liturgy are not a parody; they are explained by the liturgical tradition of the ancient Christian Church, from its origins to the fifth century.[15]

In order to understand the success of the Cathars' propaganda and, in general, of the paramillenaristic movements which soon enough became heretical, one must be aware of the crisis of the Roman Church, and especially of the degradation of the ecclesiastical hierarchy. In opening the Fourth Lateran Council, Innocent III referred to bishops preoccupied exclusively with their "carnal pleasures," without spiritual instruction and deprived of pastoral zeal, "incapable of proclaiming the Word of God and of directing the people." Moreover, the immorality and venality of the clergy increasingly alienated the faithful. A number of priests were married or lived in public concubinage. Some kept taverns in order to be able to provide for their wives and children. Since they had to repay their patrons, the priests taxed all supplementary religious services: marriages, baptisms, Masses for the sick and the dead, etc. The refusal to translate the

---

and the other is the significant phrase: "Have no mercy on the flesh born in corruption but have mercy on the spirit held in prison"; Runciman, p. 154.

14. See the sources summarized and analyzed by Runciman, pp. 154ff., and Borst, pp. 163ff.

15. Runciman, pp. 161–62. On the cult and hierarchy, see Borst, pp. 162–81.

Bible[16] (as had been done in the East) made all religious instruction impossible; Christianity was accessible only through the priests and monks.

In the first decades of the twelfth century, Saint Dominic (1170–1221) endeavored to combat the heresy, but without success. At his request, Innocent III established the Order of Preachers. But like the legates sent previously by the pope, the Dominicans did not succeed in checking the spread of the Cathar movement. In 1204, the final public dispute between Cathar and Catholic theologians took place at Carcassonne. In January 1205, Peter of Castlemare, whom Innocent III had charged with exterminating the heresy in the south of France, wished to relinquish his commission and retire to a monastery. But the pope responded: "action ranks higher than contemplation."

Finally, in November 1207, Innocent III proclaimed the Crusade against the Albingensians, appealing above all to the great leaders of the northern nobility: the Duke of Burgundy and the counts of Bac, Nevers, Champagne, and Blois. He seduced them with the promise that the properties of the Albingensian nobles would become theirs after the victory. On his side, the king of France was enticed by the possibility of extending his domain toward the south. The first war lasted from 1208–9 to 1229, but it had to be resumed and prolonged for many years. It was not until around 1330 that the Cathar Church of France ceased to exist.

The sinister "Crusade against the Albigensians" is significant for several reasons. By an irony of history, it was *the only* Crusade that was victorious. Its political, cultural, and religious consequences have been considerable. Among its works one may count the unification and expansion of the kingdom of France and also the ruin of the meridional civilization (which notably included the work of Eleanor and her "Courts of Love" with their exaltation of the Lady and the poetry of the troubadours; cf. §269). As regards consequences of a religious order, the most grave was the increased and always more menacing power of the Inquisition. Established during the war, in Toulouse, the Inquisition obliged all women over the age of twelve and all men over the age of fourteen to adjure the heresy. In 1229, the Synod of

---

16. Friedrich Heer sees this refusal as an explanation of Catholicism's loss of Northern Africa, England, and Germany; cf. his *The Medieval World*, p. 200.

Toulouse forbade the possession of the Bible in Latin or the vernacular language; the only tolerated texts were the Breviary, the Psalter, and the Book of Hours of the Virgin, all in Latin. The smaller numbers of Albigensians who took refuge in Italy ended by being discovered by the Inquisition's agents. For with time, the Inquisition succeeded in establishing itself in nearly all the countries of western and central Europe. Let us add, however, that the war against the heretics prompted the Church to undertake reforms and encouraged the missionary orders of the Dominicans and the Franciscans.

The manner in which the Albigensians were annihilated constitutes one of the blackest pages in the history of the Roman Church. But the Catholic reaction was justified. The movement's hatred of life and the body, for example, the ban on marriage, the denial of the Resurrection, etc., and its dualism separated Catharism from both the Old Testament tradition and from Christianity. In fact, the Albigensians professed a religion *sui generis,* one displaying an eastern structure and origin.

The unequalled success of the Cathars' missionaries represents the first massive penetration of eastern religious ideas, as much into the rural environments as among the artisans, clergy, and nobility. One must wait until the twentieth century to witness a similar phenomenon, notably the enthusiastic welcome, all over western Europe, of a millenarism of eastern origin, Marxism-Leninism.

295. Saint Francis of Assisi

The twelfth and thirteenth centuries experienced an exceptional religious valorization of poverty. Heretical movements like the *Humiliati,* the Waldensians, and the Cathars, and also the Beguines, saw in poverty the primary and most efficacious means of realizing the ideal proclaimed by Jesus and the Apostles. It is in order to canonize these movements that the popes, in the beginning of the thirteenth century, recognized the two orders of mendicant monks, the Dominicans and the Franciscans. But, as we shall see, among the Franciscans the mystique of poverty provoked crises which threatened the existence of their order. For it was their own founder who had exalted absolute poverty, which became for him the *Madonna Povertà.*

Born in 1182, the son of a rich merchant of Assisi, Francis made his first pilgrimage to Rome in 1205 and for one day took the place of a beggar in front of St. Peter's Basilica. On another occasion, he embraced a leper. Back at Assisi, he lived for two years as a hermit near a church. Francis understood his true vocation in 1209 when he heard the famous passage from the Gospel of Matthew: "Heal the sick, raise the dead, cleanse lepers. . . . Take no gold, nor silver."[17] Henceforth, he followed to the letter the words spoken by Jesus to the Apostles. Several disciples joined him, and Francis wrote a *Rule* that was sufficiently short and concise. In 1210, he went again to Rome to ask for Innocent III's authorization. The pope agreed on the condition that Francis become the director of a minor order (from which the name Friars Minor or Minorites was given to the Franciscans). The monks dispersed and preached throughout Italy, reuniting once a year at Pentecost. In Florence in 1207, Francis came to know Cardinal Ugolino; a great admirer of his apostolate, the cardinal became his friend and the protector of the order. The following year, the *Poverello* met Dominic, who proposed to him that the two orders be united; but Francis refused.

At the reunion of 1219, Ugolino, following the suggestion of some of the more cultured monks, asked for a modification of the *Rule*. But the request was unsuccessful. During this time, Franciscan missionaries began to enter foreign lands. Accompanied by eleven friars, Francis embarked for the Holy Land and, determined to preach before the Sultan, he crossed into the Muslim camp where he was well received. Some time later, informed that the two vicars whom he had designated had changed the *Rule* and had obtained privileges from the pope, Francis returned to Italy. He learned that certain Friars Minor had been accused of heresy in France, Germany, and Hungary; it is this which persuaded him to accept the official patronage of the pope. Henceforth, the free community of monks became a regular order under the jurisdiction of canon law. A new *Rule* was authorized by Honorius III in 1223, and Francis relinquished the direction of the order. The following year, he retired to Verona. It is in the hermitage there that he received the stigmata. Very ill, almost blind, he succeeded, however, in writing the *Canticles to the Sun,* the *Admonitions* for his Friars, and his *Testament.*

17. Matthew 10:8–10—"Heal the sick, raise the dead, cleanse lepers, cast out demons. You received without paying, give without pay. Take no gold, nor silver, nor copper in your belts, no bag for your journey, nor two tunics, nor sandals, nor a staff, for the laborer deserves his food."

It is in this latter moving text that Francis endeavored for the last time to defend the true vocation of his Order. He evoked his love for manual labor and ordered his Friars to work, and when they received no payment to have recourse "to the Lord's table, by asking for alms from door to door." He enjoined the Friars not to accept "under any pretext either churches or dwellings or anything that one builds for them, if it does not conform to the Holy Poverty that we have promised in the *Rule;* that they sojourn always as guests, strangers, and pilgrims. I formally forbid all the Friars by obedience, wherever they may be, to dare to ask for some letter in the Court of Rome, by themselves or by an intermediary, for a church or for some other place, under the pretext of preaching, or on account of some corporeal persecution."[18]

Francis died in 1226, and less than two years later was canonized by his friend Cardinal Ugolino, who had become Pope Gregory IX. It was certainly the best way to attach the Franciscan Order to the Church. But the difficulties were not eliminated. The first biographies presented Saint Francis as being sent by God to inaugurate the reforms of the Church. Certain Friars Minor recognized in their patron the representative of the Third Age proclaimed by Joachim of Floris[19] (cf. §271). The popular histories collected and diffused by the Franciscans in the thirteenth century, and published in the fourteenth under the title *The Little Flowers of St. Francis,* compared Francis and his disciples to Jesus and his Apostles. Though Gregory IX sincerely admired Francis, he did not accept the *Testament* and ratified the *Rule* in 1223. The opposition came chiefly from the "observants," and much later from the Spirituals, who insisted on the necessity of absolute poverty. In a series of bulls, Gregory IX and his successors strove to prove that it was not a question of "possession" but of the "usage" of residences and other goods. John of Parma, the General of the Order from 1247 to 1257, tried to save the heritage of Saint Francis while avoiding an open conflict with the pope, but the intransigence of the Spirituals made his efforts vain. Happily, John of Parma was replaced by Bonaventure, who is justly considered as the second founder of the order. But the polemic concerning absolute poverty continued during Bonaventure's

---

18. From the French translation by Ivan Gobry, *Saint François d'Assise,* p. 139.
19. See the excellent exposition by Steven Ozment, *The Age of Reform,* pp. 110ff., with a recent bibliography.

life and on past his death (1274). The controversy was finally put to rest after 1320.

To be sure, the victory of the Church reduced the original fervor of the order and discouraged the hope for a reform by a return to the austerity of the Apostles. But it is thanks to these compromises that the Franciscan Order was able to survive. It is true that the only exemplary model was constituted by the everyday life of Jesus, the Apostles, and Saint Francis; that is to say, by poverty, charity, and manual labor. But for the monks, obedience to the supreme magistrate of the order—the Minister General—remained the primary, and the most difficult, obligation.

296. Saint Bonaventure and mystical theology

Born in 1217 near Orvieto, Bonaventure studied theology in Paris, where he began teaching in 1253. At one of the most critical moments in the Franciscan Order, in 1257, he was elected its Minister General. Bonaventure endeavored to reconcile the two extreme positions by recognizing the necessity of study and meditation alongside of poverty and manual labor. He also wrote a more moderate biography of Saint Francis (*Legenda Maior,* 1263); three years later, it was proclaimed officially as the only authorized biography.

While he was teaching in Paris, Bonaventure wrote a *Commentary on the Sentences* (of Peter Lombard), the *Breviloquium,* and the *Disputed Questions.* But it was after a brief retreat to Verna in 1259 that he wrote his masterpiece, *The Soul's Journey into God.*[20] One year before his death in 1274, Bonaventure was made Cardinal-Bishop of Albano. Canonized by Sixtus IV in 1482, he was named *Doctor Seraphicus* of the Church by Sixtus V in 1588.

There is growing recognition that Bonaventure's theological syn-

---

20. ''While I meditated on the elevations of the soul towards God, I remembered among other things the miracle that occurred in this place to St. Francis himself: the vision of the winged seraph in the form of the Cross. Now it seems to me at once that this vision represented the ecstasy of the blessed father and indicated the itinerary to follow in order to reach there'' (*Prologue,* trans. H. Duméry).

thesis is the most complete of the Middle Ages. Bonaventure endeavored to utilize Plato and Aristotle, Augustine and the Greek Fathers, the Pseudo-Dionysius and Francis of Assisi.[21] While Thomas Aquinas built his system on Aristotle, Bonaventure conserved the Augustinian tradition of medieval Neoplatonism. But the profound significance of his theology was eclipsed during the Middle Ages following the success of the Aristotelian-Thomistic synthesis (just as it was in modern times by the triumphant emergence of Neo-Thomism).

A contemporary scholar, Ewert H. Cousins, identifies the idea of the *coincidentia oppositorum* as the keystone of Bonaventure's thought.[22] The conception in question is evidently one that is attested in a more or less explicit form through the whole history of religions. It is clear in biblical monotheism: God is infinite and personal, transcendent and active in history, eternal and present in time, etc. These oppositions are still more striking in the person of Christ. But Bonaventure elaborated and organized the system of the *coincidentia oppositorum* by taking as his model the Trinity, where the Third Person represents the mediating and willing principle.

Bonaventure's masterpiece is undoubtedly the *Itinerarium Mentis in Deum.* Here again, the author employs a universally diffused symbol, and one that is recognized from the beginning of Christian mystical theology, the image of the ladder.[23] "In relation to our position in creation, the universe itself is a ladder by which we can ascend into God. Some created things are vestiges, others images; some are material, others spiritual; some are temporal, others everlasting; some are outside us, others within us. In order to contemplate the First Principle, who is more spiritual, eternal and above us, we must pass through his vestiges, which are material, temporal and outside us. This means *to be led in the path of God.* We must also enter into our soul, which is God's image, everlasting, spiritual and within us. *This means to enter in the truth of God.* We must go beyond to what is eternal, most spir-

21. See Ewert H. Cousins, *Bonaventure and the Coincidence of Opposites,* pp. 4ff., and the bibliographical references, pp. 229ff.

22. Ibid., passim. Cf. esp. chaps. 1, 3, 5, 7.

23. For the comparative documents see Eliade, *Shamanism,* pp. 430ff., 487ff.; on the "Ladder of Paradise" in the Christian tradition, see Dom Anselme Stolz, *Théologie de la mystique,* pp. 117–45; on the ladder in Muslim and Jewish mysticism, see Alexander Altman, "The Ladder of Ascension."

itual and above us.''[24] One thus finds God as a Unity (that is to say, the One which is beyond Time) and as the Holy Trinity.

The first four chapters of the *Soul's Journey* present meditations on the reflection of God in the material world and in the soul, and on the approach to God. The following two chapters are dedicated to the contemplation of God as Being (chap. 5) and as the Good (chap. 6). Finally, in the seventh and last chapter, the soul is seized by mystical ecstasy, and with the crucified Christ, passes from death to life. Let us underscore the audacious revalorization of ecstasy. In contrast to the mystical experience of Bernard of Clairvaux, which was dominated by the symbol of conjugal love, for Bonaventure the *unio mystica* is a *death with Christ* and, together with Him, the reunion with God the Father.

Moreover, as a good Franciscan, Bonaventure encourages a precise and rigorous knowledge of Nature. God's wisdom is revealed in the cosmic realities; the more one studies something, the more one penetrates into its individuality, and better comprehends it as the exemplary being situated in the spirit of God (*Soul's Journey,* chap. 2, sec. 4f). Certain authors have seen in the Franciscan interest in nature one of the sources of the rise of the empirical sciences; for example, the discoveries of Roger Bacon (ca. 1214–92) and of the disciples of Ockham. One can compare this solidarity, as defended by Bonaventure, between mystical experience and the study of Nature, with the decisive role of Taoism in the progress of the empirical sciences in China (cf. §134).

297. Saint Thomas Aquinas and scholasticism

In a general sense, ''scholasticism'' designates the diverse theological systems aiming at the accord between revelation and reason, faith and intellectual comprehension. Anselm of Canterbury (1033–1109) had taken up the formula of Saint Augustine: ''I believe in order to under-

24. Ewert H. Cousins, trans., *Bonaventure,* ''The Classics of Western Spirituality'' (New York: Paulist Press, 1978), p. 60 (*Itinerarium,* chap. 1, section 2; see also chap. 6). Cf. the commentary of Cousins in his *Bonaventure and the Coincidence of Opposites,* pp. 69–97. Let us add that these three stages of the ascension toward God— *without, within,* and *above* us—each include two phases which can be designated the immanent and the transcendent. It is thus a matter of six stages symbolizing the six wings of the Seraph who, in embracing Saint Francis, brought on the stigmata.

stand.'' In other words, reason begins its task where the articles of faith end. But it is Peter Lombard (ca. 1100–1160) who elaborates in his text, *The Four Books of Sentences,* the specific structure of scholastic theology. In the form of questions, analyses, and responses, the scholastic theologian must present and discuss the following problems: God, the Creation, the Incarnation, the Redemption, and the Sacraments.

In the twelfth century, the works of Aristotle and the great Arabic and Jewish philosophers (above all Averroës, Avicenna, and Maimonides) became partially accessible in Latin translations. These discoveries put the relations between faith and reason into a new perspective. According to Aristotle, the domain of reason is completely independent. Albertus Magnus, or Albert of Bollstadt, 1206/7–1280, one of the most universal spirits of the Middle Ages, enthusiastically accepted the reconquest, for reason, ''of the rights which reason itself had let fall into desuetude.''[25] By contrast, such a doctrine could only arouse the indignation of traditionalist theologians: they accused the scholastics of having sacrificed religion to philosophy, and Christ to Aristotle.

The thought of Albertus Magnus was deepened and systematized by his disciple, Thomas Aquinas (1224–74).[26] Thomas is at once both philosopher and theologian; but for him, the central problem is the same: Being, or in other words, God. Thomas radically distinguished Nature from Grace, the domain of reason from that of faith; however, this distinction implies their accord. The existence of God becomes evident as soon as man takes the trouble to reflect on the world as he

25. Étienne Gilson, *La philosophie au moyen âge,* p. 507. ''If the characteristic of modern thought is the distinction between what is demonstrable and what is not, it is indeed in the thirteenth century that modern philosophy was founded, and it is with Albert the Great that in setting its own limits, it became aware of its values and its rights'' (ibid., p. 508).

26. Thomas's life was quite brief, and devoid of dramatic events. Born near Agni at the end of 1224 or the beginning of 1225, he donned the Dominican habit in 1244 and the following year left for Paris to study under the direction of Albertus Magnus. Receiving his licentiate in theology in 1256, Thomas taught in Paris (1256–59), and then in several Italian cities. He returned to Paris in 1269, but left it again in 1272 and taught in Naples in 1273. Summoned by Gregory X to the Second General Council of Lyon, Thomas left in January 1274, but illness forced him to stop in Fossanova, where he died on March 7. Of his numerous writings, the most famous, in which Thomas shows his true genius, are the *Summa Theologica* and *Summa contra Gentiles.*

knows it. For example: in one manner or another, this world is in movement; every movement must have a cause, but this cause results from another. The series, however, cannot be infinite, and one must thus admit the intervention of a Prime Mover, who is none other than God. This argument is the first of a group of five which are designated by Thomas as the "five ways." The reasoning is always the same: taking the world of evident reality as the point of departure, one comes to God. (Every efficient cause presupposes another, and in tracing back through the series one comes to the first cause, God. And so on.)

Being infinite and simple, the God thus discovered by reason is beyond human language. God is the pure act of being (*ipsum esse*); thus he is infinite, immutable, and eternal. In demonstrating his existence by the principle of causality, one arrives at the same time at the conclusion that God is the creator of the world. He has created all freely, without any necessity. But for Thomas, human reason cannot demonstrate whether the world has always existed or, on the contrary, the Creation took place in time. Faith, founded on the revelations of God, asks us to believe that the world began in time. It is a question of revealed truth, like the other articles of faith (original sin, the Holy Trinity, the Incarnation of God in Jesus Christ, etc.), and thus an object of theological investigation and no longer of philosophy.

All knowledge implies the central concept of *being,* in other words the possession or presence of the reality that one wishes to know. Man has been created so that he may enjoy the full knowledge of God, but after original sin, he can no longer attain it without the aid of grace. Faith allows the believers, aided by grace, to accept the knowledge of God such as He has revealed it in the course of sacred history.

"Despite the resistances which it encountered, Saint Thomas's doctrine soon won numerous disciples, not only within the Dominican Order, but in still other contexts, both scholastic and religious. . . . The Thomist reform affected the entire field of philosophy and theology; there is thus not a single question relating to these domains in which history cannot note its influence and follow its traces, but it seems to have had particular effect on the fundamental problems of ontology, whose solution determined that of all the others."[27] For Gilson, the great merit of Saint Thomas is to have avoided not only "rationalism," but a "theologism" which admitted the self-sufficien-

27. Gilson, *La philosophie au moyen âge,* p. 541.

cy of faith. And the decline of scholasticism, according to the same author, began with the condemnations of certain of Aristotle's theses (above all as they were interpreted by his Arabic commentators) by the Bishop of Paris, Stephen Tempier, in 1270 and 1277.[28] From then on, the structural links between theology and philosophy were seriously compromised. The critiques of Duns Scotus (ca. 1265–1308) and William of Ockham (ca. 1285–1347) contributed to the ruin of the Thomist synthesis. In the last analysis, the constantly increasing distance between theology and philosophy anticipated the separation, evident in modern societies, between the sacred and the profane.[29]

Let us add that Gilson's interpretation is no longer accepted in its entirety. Thomas Aquinas was not the only medieval scholastic of genius. In the thirteenth and fourteenth centuries, other thinkers—Scotus or Ockham—enjoyed an equal if not greater prestige. But the importance of Thomism results from its having been proclaimed, in the nineteenth century, as the official theology of the Roman Church. What is more, the renaissance of Neo-Thomism in the first quarter of the twentieth century constitutes a significant moment in the history of Western culture.

Duns Scotus, known as the *doctor subtilis,* criticized Thomas's system by attacking it at its base: that is, by denying the importance accorded to reason. For Duns Scotus, with the exception of the identity of God as the first cause, which one discovers by logical reasoning, all religious knowledge is given by faith.

Ockham, the *doctor plusquam subtilis,* went much further in his critique of rationalist theologies. Since man can know only the particular facts he observes, the laws of logic, and divine revelation, every metaphysic is impossible. Ockham categorically denies the existence of "universals": it is a matter of mental construction without autonomous reality. Since God cannot be known intuitively and since reason is incapable of proving his existence, man must be content with that which faith and revelation teach him.[30]

---

28. See the discussion of these condemnations ibid., pp. 58ff. A large number of these theses were Averroist; some refer to the teachings of Thomas.

29. Cf. Ozment, *Age of Reform,* p. 16.

30. According to Gilson, "the study of Ockham allows one to establish an historical fact of capital importance, and one that is constantly misunderstood, that the internal criticism levelled against itself by what one calls, all too vaguely, scholastic philoso-

The originality and profundity of Ockham's religious thought can be grasped above all in his conception of God. Since God is absolutely free and omnipotent, he can do all; he can even contradict himself; for example, he can save a criminal and condemn a saint. One must not restrain the freedom of God according to the limits of reason, imagination, or human language. An article of faith teaches us that God has assumed human nature; but he would have been able to manifest himself in the form (that is, having the nature) of an ass, a stone, or a piece of wood.[31]

These paradoxical illustrations of divine liberty did not stimulate the theological imagination of later centuries. However, from the eighteenth century on, that is, after the discovery of "primitives," Ockham's theology would have allowed a more adequate understanding of what some called the "idolatry of the savages." For the sacred manifests itself in any form whatsoever, and even in the most aberrant. In the perspective opened by Ockham, theological thought would have been able to justify the hierophanies attested everywhere in archaic and traditional religions; indeed, one now knows that it is not the natural objects (stones, trees, springs, etc.) that are adored, but the supernatural forces that these objects "incarnate."

298. Meister Eckhart: From God to the Deity

Born in 1260, Eckhart studied among the Dominicans of Cologne and at Paris. He exercised the functions of professor, preacher, and administrator in Paris (1311–13), Strasbourg (1313–23), and Cologne (1323–27). In these latter two cities, he preached and led the religious as well as the Beguines. Among his numerous works, the most important are the *Commentary on the Sentences* of Peter Lombard, and the *Opus tripartitum*, an extensive theological *summa*, unfortunately for the most part lost. By contrast, a number of his writings in German

---

phy, had provoked its own ruin well before the so-called modern philosophy had succeeded in establishing itself" (p. 640).

31. *Est articulus fidei quod Deus assumpsit naturam humanam. Non includit contradictionem Deum assumere naturam asineam. Paris ratione potest assumere lapidem aut lignum.* See the discussion of this thesis in Eliade, *Patterns in Comparative Religion,* §9, pp. 26–30.

have been saved, including the *Spiritual Instructions*, several treatises, and many sermons. But the authenticity of certain sermons is not assured.

Meister Eckhart is an original, profound, and difficult author.[32] He is justly considered the most important theologian of Western mysticism. And, although he prolongs the tradition, he inaugurates a new epoch in the history of Christian mysticism. Let us recall that from the fourth to the twelfth century, contemplative practice implied the abandonment of the world, or in other words, a monastic life. It was in the desert or in the solitude of the cloister that the monk hoped to approach God and enjoy the divine presence. This intimacy with God amounted to a return to Paradise; the contemplative in some manner rediscovered the condition of Adam before the Fall.

In what can be considered as the first example of Christian mystical experience, Saint Paul alludes to his ecstatic ascension to the third heaven: "I know a man in Christ who fourteen years ago was caught up to the third heaven—whether in the body or out of the body I do not know, God knows. And I know that this man was caught up into Paradise—whether in the body or out of the body I do not know, God knows—and he heard things that cannot be told, which man may not utter" (2 Corinthians 12:2–4). The nostalgia for Paradise thus made itself felt from the beginnings of Christianity. During prayer, one turned towards the East, the direction of the earthly Paradise. Paradisical symbolism found expression in the churches and the gardens of monasteries. The early monastic Fathers (like Saint Francis later) were obeyed by wild animals; thus the primary syndrome of the paradisical life—the dominion over the animals—could be recaptured.[33]

In the mystical theology of Evagrius Ponticus (fourth century), the perfect Christian was the monk; he constituted the model of the man who had rediscovered his origins. The final goal of the solitary contemplative was union with God. However, as Saint Bernard, among others, put it: "God and man are separated from one another. Each retains his own will and his own substance. Such a union is for them a communion of wills and an accord in love."[34]

32. Besides, it is only in our own day that his Latin and vernacular texts are in the process of being carefully edited.

33. Cf. Eliade, *Myths, Dreams, and Mysteries*, pp. 681ff; Stolz, *Théologie*, pp. 18ff. and passim.

34. *Sermones in Cantica Canticorum*, number 70, in *Pat. Lat.*, vol. 183, p. 1126.

This almost conjugal valorization of the *unio mystica* is abundantly paralleled in the history of mysticism, and not only in Christian mysticism. Let us insist immediately that it was completely foreign to Meister Eckhart. The fact is all the more significant in that the Dominican, in his sermons, addresses himself not only to the monks and the religious, but also to the mass of the faithful. In the thirteenth century, spiritual perfection was no longer sought exclusively in monasteries. One hears of the "democratization" and "secularization" of the mystical experience, phenomena which characterize the age from 1200 to 1600. Meister Eckhart is the theologian *par excellence* of this new stage in the history of Christian mysticism; he proclaims and theologically justifies the possibility of reintegrating the ontological identity with God, while remaining in the world.[35] For him also, the mystical experience implies a "return to the origin," but an origin which precedes Adam and the creation of the world.

Meister Eckhart elaborated this audacious theology with the help of a distinction that he introduced in the very being of the divinity. By the word "God" (*Gott*), he designates God the creator, while he uses the term "deity" (*Gottheit*) to indicate the divine essence. The *Gottheit* is the *Grund,* the principle and matrix of "God." To be sure, it is not a question of anteriority or of an ontological modification which would have taken place in time, following after the creation. But because of the ambiguity and limits of human language, such a distinction could give rise to unfortunate misunderstandings. In one of his sermons, Eckhart affirms: "God and the deity are as different from one another as heaven and earth. . . . God effects, deity does not effect, it has nothing to effect. . . . God and the deity differ by action and inaction."[36] Dionysius the Areopagite (cf. §257) had defined God as "a pure nothingness." Eckhart prolongs and amplifies this negative the-

35. One can compare this conception with the message of the *Bhagavad Gītā* (cf. §§193–94).

36. From the French translation by Jeanne Ancelet-Hustache, *Maître Eckhart,* p. 55. A number of texts emphasize, however, the absolute identity between the trinitarian God and the *Gottheit.* See the references in Bernard McGinn, "Theological Summary" (in Edmund Colledge and Bernard McGinn, trans., *Meister Eckhart, the Essential Sermons, Commentaries, Treatises and Defense*), p. 36, notes 71–72. Cf. ibid., p. 38, n. 81, on the Eckhartian interpretation of the Father as *Unum,* creating the Son as *Verum,* and together engendering the Holy Spirit as *Bonum,* an interpretation based on the teaching of Saint Augustine.

ology: "God is without name, for no one can comprehend anything of him. . . . Thus if I say: God is good, this is not true. I am good, but God is not good. . . . If I say further: God is wise, this is not true; I am wiser than he. If I say again: God is a being, this is not true; he is a being above being and a superessential negation."[37]

Moreover, Eckhart insists on the fact that man is of "the race and kinship of God," and he urges the faithful to attain the divine principle (*Gottheit*), beyond the Trinitarian God. For, by its own nature, the *Grund* of the soul partakes of nothing other than divine Being, directly and without mediation. It is in His totality that God penetrates the human soul. Eckhart saw in the mystical experience not the *unio mystica* exalted by Saint Bernard and other illustrious authors, but the return to the unmanifested deity, *Gottheit;* through that the believer discovers his ontological identity with the divine *Grund*. "When I first was, I had no God and was merely myself. . . . I was pure being [*ein ledic sin*] and knew myself by divine truth. . . . I am my own first cause, both of my eternal being and of my temporal being. I was born to and for eternity and because of my eternal birth, I shall never die. By virtue of this eternal birth I have been eternally. I am now, and shall be forevermore. . . . I was the cause of myself and of everything else."[38]

For Eckhart, this primordial state before the creation will be equally that of the end; the mystical experience anticipates the reintegration of the soul into the undifferentiated deity. It is, however, not a question of pantheism nor of a Vedantic type of monism. Eckhart compares the union with God to a drop of water which, when dropping into the ocean, identifies itself with the latter; but the ocean by no means identifies with the drop of water. "So the soul becomes divine, but not God the soul." However, in mystical union, "the soul is in God as God is in Himself."[39]

While taking into consideration the difference between the soul and

37. From the French translation of Ancelet-Hustache, p. 55. Nevertheless, Eckhart specifies in another sermon: "When I said that God was not a being and was above being, I did not contest his being; on the contrary I attributed a higher being to him" (ibid.).

38. Text edited by Franz Pfeiffer and translated by Ozment, p. 128.

39. Text edited by Josef Quint, *Deutsche Predigten und Traktate,* number 55, p. 410, and translated by Ozment, p. 131; see also the references cited by McGinn in Colledge and McGinn, *Meister Eckhart,* pp. 45ff.

God, Eckhart had the great merit of showing that this difference is not definitive. For him, man's predestined vocation is *to be in God,* and not to live in the world as just a creature of God. For this *real* man— that is, his soul—is eternal; man's salvation begins with his retreat from *Time.*[40] Eckhart repeatedly praises "detachment" (*Abgeschiedenheit*), a religious practice necessary for reintegration with God.[41] Salvation is an ontological operation made possible by *true knowledge.* Man is saved in the measure that he discovers his own proper being; but he cannot attain his being before knowing God, the source of all being.[42] The fundamental religious experience which assures salvation consists in the birth of the Logos in the believer's soul. Since the Father engenders the Son in eternity, and since the Father's *Grund* is the same as that of the soul, God engenders the Son in the soul's *Grund.* Moreover, "He engenders me, his son [who is] the very Son." "He engenders me not only myself, his Son, but engenders me like himself [that is, the Father] and Himself like me."[43]

Nothing irritated Eckhart's adversaries more than his thesis on the birth of the Son in the believer's soul, a doctrine implying the identity of the "good and just" Christian with Christ. It is true that the analogies deduced by the Dominican were not always fortunate. At the end of sermon number 6, Eckhart speaks of man completely transformed in Christ just as the sacramental bread becomes the body of the Lord. "I

40. According to Eckhart, time is the greatest obstacle in the approach to God; and not only Time "but also temporal things, temporal affections, even the aroma of Time"; cf. the text translated by C. de B. Evans, *Meister Eckhart,* 1, p. 237.

41. In his treatise on detachment, Eckhart considers this practice superior even to humility and charity; cf. *On Detachment* (trans. Edmund Colledge), in Colledge and McGinn, pp. 285–87. But he stipulates that charity is one of the paths which lead to detachment (ibid., p. 292).

42. This interdependence between ontology and knowledge (*intelligere*) reflects in a certain manner a paradoxical, if not contradictory, aspect of Meister Eckhart's theology. In effect, he begins his systematic work, *Opus propositionum,* with an analysis of the proposition *Esse Deus est,* whereas in his *Parisian Questions,* Eckhart affirms that God is correctly defined as *intelligere;* the act of comprehension is thus above the *esse.* Cf. Bernard McGinn, "Theological Summary," in Colledge and McGinn, p. 32 and n. 32. Numerous other passages accord priority to God conceived as pure intellect or comprehension; cf. the references ibid., p. 300, n. 45.

43. Sermon no. 6, trans. by Colledge, in Colledge and McGinn, p. 187. See the other passages cited by McGinn, ibid., pp. 51ff., and by G. J. Kelley, *Meister Eckhart on Divine Knowledge,* pp. 126ff. This thesis had been condemned at Avignon, not as being heretical but as being "suspect of heresy."

am so completely changed in Him that He produces His being in me, the same being and not a similar one.''[44] But in his *Defense,* Eckhart specifies that he speaks "inasmuch as" (*in quantum*), that is, in a formal and abstract sense.[45]

The decisive importance accorded by Eckhart to detachment (*Abgeschiedenheit*) from all that is not God (i.e., *Gottheit*)—in short, his distrust with regard to temporal works—diminishes in certain eyes the actuality and efficacy of his mystical theology. He has been accused, wrongly, of a lack of interest in the sacramental life of the Church and in the events of the history of salvation. It is true that the Dominican did not insist on God's role in history or on Christ's Incarnation in Time. But he praised the one who interrupted his contemplation to give a little soup to a sick person, and he repeated that one could encounter God in the street as well as in church. Moreover, Eckhart held that the final object of contemplation, that is, the return to the undifferentiated deity, cannot satisfy the faithful in their search for emotional religious experience. For him, the true beatitude was not in the *raptus,* but in the intellectual union with God that is gained by contemplation.

In 1321, Meister Eckhart was accused of heresy, and during his final years he was obliged to defend his theses. In 1329 (one or two years after his death), Pope John XXII condemned twenty-eight articles by declaring seventeen of them to be heretical and the rest to be "scandalous, very rash, and suspect of heresy.''[46] It is likely that it was the ambiguity of his language and the jealousy of certain theologians that contributed to his condemnation. Be that as it may, its consequences were considerable. Despite the efforts of his disciples Henry Suso and Johann Tauler (cf. §300), and the fidelity of numerous Dominicans, the works of Meister Eckhart were over the centuries set aside. The theology and metaphysics of the Christian West did not benefit from his intuitions and ingenious interpretations. His influence was limited to Germanic lands. The cautious circulation of his writings encouraged the production of apocryphal texts. Nevertheless, the audacious

44. Colledge, in Colledge and McGinn, p. 180. Cf. also *In agro dominico,* article 10, translation by McGinn, ibid., p. 78.

45. See the texts edited by McGinn, ibid., pp. 53ff. In *Sermon* no. 55, he explains that it is a question of unity with the *Gottheit* and not with the creator God.

46. On Meister Eckhart's trial and condemnation, see Ancelet-Hustache, pp. 120ff.; McGinn, in Colledge and McGinn, pp. 13ff.

thought of Meister Eckhart continued to inspire certain creative spirits; among the greatest, Nicholas of Cusa (cf. §301).

299. Popular piety and the risks of devotion

From the end of the twelfth century, spiritual perfection was no longer sought only in monasteries. A growing number of the laity had chosen to imitate the life of the Apostles and the saints while remaining in the world. Thus, the Waldensians of Lyon, disciples of a rich merchant named Peter Waldo who in 1173 distributed his goods to the poor and preached voluntary poverty; or the *Humiliati* in northern Italy.[47] Most remained still faithful to the Church; but some, exalting their direct experience of God, dispensed themselves of the cult and even of the sacraments.

In the northern region—Flanders, the Netherlands, Germany— small communities of lay women known as the Beguines[48] were organized. They divided their life between work, prayer, and preaching. Less numerous but equally dedicated to the ideal of Christian perfection and poverty were the Beghards, communities of men.[49]

This movement of popular piety, inspired by nostalgia for a *vita apostolica,* recalls the religious ideal of the Waldensians. It betrays at the same time a contempt for the world and a discontent *vis-à-vis* the clergy. It is probable that some Beguines would have preferred to live in monasteries, or at least to benefit from the spiritual direction of the Dominicans. Such was the case of Mechthilde of Magdeburg (1207– 82), the first mystic to write in German. She called Saint Dominic "my beloved Father." In her book, *Flowing Light of the Godhead,* Mechthilde used the mystico-erotic language of the union between husband and wife. "You are in me, and I in you!"[50] Union with God

47. The two groups were declared anathema by Pope Lucius III in 1184.

48. According to certain authors, this name seems to be derived from "Albigeneses"; cf. Ozment, p. 91, n. 58; Gordon Leff, *Heresy in the Later Middle Ages,* 1, pp. 18ff.

49. See E. W. McDonnell, *The Beguines and Beghards in Medieval Culture,* passim.

50. Christ said to her: "Thou art so natured (*genaturt*) in me that absolutely nothing can stand between thee and me!" as cited by Robert E. Lerner, *The Heresies of the Free Spirit in the Late Middle Ages,* p. 19. The same experience of Love (*minne*) inspired the work of the Flemish Beguine Hadewijch, one of the greatest poets and mystics of the thirteenth century; cf. Hadewijch, *Complete Works,* pp. 127–58.

delivers man from sin, she wrote. For spirits who are forewarned and honest, this affirmation does not in itself comprise an heretical opinion. Moreover, certain popes and a number of theologians testified in favor of the orthodoxy and merits of the Beguines.[51] But especially from the fourteenth century on, other popes and theologians charged the Beguines and the Beghards with heresy[52] and, drawing on the traditional clichés, accused them of orgies carried out under the inspiration of the Devil. The true cause of the persecution was the jealousy of the clergy and the monks. They saw only hypocrisy in the *vita apostolica* of the Beguines and the Beghards and accused them of insubordinate zeal.[53]

Let us add, however, that piety led many times to heterodoxy and even, in the eyes of ecclesiastical authorities, to heresy. Besides, in the thirteenth and fourteenth centuries, the boundaries between orthodoxy and heterodoxy were rather in flux. Moreover, certain lay groups demanded a religious purity beyond human possibilities. The church, unable to tolerate the peril of such an idealism, reacted vehemently. It thus lost the opportunity to satisfy the need for a more authentic and profound Christian spirituality.[54]

In 1310, Marguerite Poret was burned in Paris, the first person identified as belonging to the movement of the brothers and sisters of the Free Spirit. (Despite significant resemblances, this movement must be distinguished from the communities of Beguines and the Beghards.) The partisans of the Free Spirit[55] had broken every tie with the Church. They practiced a radical mysticism, seeking union with the divine. According to their accusers, the brothers and sisters of the Free Spirit believed that in his earthly existence man could attain such a degree of perfection that he could no longer sin. These heretics dispensed with the intermediary of the Church, for "where the Spirit of the Lord is, there is freedom" (2 Corinthians 3:17). Nevertheless, there is no proof that they encouraged antinomianism; on the contrary, it was by austerity and ascesis that they prepared for the *unio mystica*. Finally, they

51. Cf. Lerner, pp. 38ff.

52. It is true nevertheless that certain groups shared the Cathar doctrines; cf. Denzinger, as cited by Ozment, p. 93, n. 63.

53. This unjust criticism is explained by the fact that toward the end of the thirteenth century, the monks had lost much of their initial zeal and enjoyed ecclesiastical privileges; cf. Lerner, pp. 44ff.

54. Ozment, p. 96; cf. also Leff, 1, pp. 29ff.

55. See Leff, 1, pp. 310–407; Lerner, passim.

no longer felt themselves separated from God and Christ. Some of them affirmed: "I am Christ, and I am still more!"[56]

Although she herself had been burned as a heretic, Marguerite Poret's work, *The Mirror of Simple Souls,* was widely copied and translated into several languages. It is true that it was unknown that she was the author (the identification dates from 1946), but this proves that the heresy was not evident. *The Mirror* includes a dialogue between Love and Reason concerning the direction of one soul. The author describes seven "states of Grace," which lead to union with God. In the fifth and sixth "states," the soul is "annihilated" or "delivered," and becomes akin to the angels. But the seventh state, the *unio,* does not complete itself until after death, in Paradise.[57]

Other works by authors belonging to the Free Spirit movement circulated under the name of Meister Eckhart. The most famous are the (pseudo-) *Sermons* numbers 17, 18, and 37.[58] The treatise *Schwester Katrei* tells of the relationship of a Beguine with her confessor, Meister Eckhart. At the end, Sister Catherine gives him this confession: "Lord, rejoice with me: I have become God!" Her confessor orders her to live for three days of solitude in the Church. As in *The Mirror,* the soul's union with God has no anarchic consequences. The great innovation introduced by the Free Spirit movement is the certitude that the *unio mystica* can be obtained *here,* on earth.[59]

300. Disasters and hopes: From the flagellants to the *devotio moderna*

Along with the great crisis that shook the Western Church,[60] the fourteenth century is characterized by a series of calamities and cosmic

56. See the texts reproduced by Lerner, pp. 116ff.

57. Marguerite Poret is "heretical" for her passivity; the Mass, sermons, fasts, and prayers are useless because "God is already there." But *The Mirror* is an esoteric text; it addresses itself only to those who "understand." See the texts and the analyses in Lerner, pp. 200ff.

58. In the latter one can read: "The person who has renounced the visible creation and in whom God fully executes His will . . . , is at once both man and God. . . . His body is so completely penetrated by the divine Light . . . that he can be called a divine man."

59. Cf. Lerner, pp. 215ff., 241ff.

60. The sojourn of the popes at Avignon, 1309–77; the Great Schism, 1378–1417, when two (or even three) popes governed at the same time.

scourges: comets, solar eclipses, floods, and, above all, from 1347 on, the terrible epidemic of the plague, "the Black Death." The processions of flagellants multiplied themselves in order to move God to pity.[61] It is a matter of a popular movement which follows the characteristic trajectory: from piety to heterodoxy. In effect, proud of their self-torture, and despite their theological ignorance, the flagellants believed their activities could substitute for the charismatic and thaumaturgical powers of the Church. That is the reason why from 1349 they were banned by Clement VI.

In order to expiate their sins and above all the sins of the world, itinerant lay groups traversed the countryside under the direction of a "master." On arrival in a city, the procession—sometimes as large as several thousand people—made its way to the cathedral, chanting hymns and forming several circles. While sighing and crying, the penitents called upon God, Christ, and the Virgin, and began to flagellate themselves with such violence that their bodies became a swollen mass of bruised flesh.[62]

Moreover, the entire age seemed obsessed with death and with the sufferings that awaited the deceased in the afterworld. Death impressed the imagination more powerfully than the hope in the resurrection.[63] Artworks (funerary monuments, statues, and especially paintings) presented with morbid precision the different phases of bodily decomposition.[64] "The cadaver is now everywhere, even on the tombstone."[65] The *danse macabre* ("dance of death"), in which a dancer represents Death himself, drawing along men and women of all

61. The phenomenon was not new. The Flagellants made their appearance in Perugia in 1260, the year—according to the prophecy of Joachim of Floris—when the seventh age of the Church was to begin. In the following decades the movement spread into central Europe, but with the exception of several fleeting eruptions it vanished, only to reappear with an exceptional power in 1349.

62. See the documents analyzed by Leff, 2, pp. 485ff. Each member of the group must be flagellated twice daily in public, and once in private during the night.

63. Francis Oakley, *The Western Church in the Later Middle Ages*, p. 117.

64. Cf. the excellent illustrated documentation in T. S. R. Boase, *Death in the Middle Ages*.

65. Jurgis Baltrušaitis, *Le Moyen Âge fantastique*, p. 236. "The end of the Middle Ages is full of these visions of decomposed flesh and skeletons. The jangling of skulls and the clacking of the bones overwhelmed it with their hubbub" (ibid.).

ages and classes (kings, monks, bishops, bourgeois, etc.) became a favorite subject in paintings and literature.[66]

This is also the age of bloody offerings, of manuals on the *ars moriendi*, of the development of the theme of the *Pietà*, and of the importance accorded to Purgatory. Although the pontifical definition of Purgatory dates from 1259,[67] its popularity developed later, thanks chiefly to the prestige of Masses for the dead.[68]

These times of crisis and despair accentuated and widened the desire for a more authentic religious life. The search for mystical experience sometimes became obsessive. In Bavaria, in Alsace, in Switzerland, fervent groups gathered to designate themselves "friends of God." Their influence made itself felt in diverse lay environments but also in certain monasteries. Meister Eckhart's two disciples, Tauler and Suso, strove to transmit his doctrine, but in a simplified form so as to make it accessible and shelter it from suspicions.

We know little enough of the life of Johann Tauler. He was born around 1300, and died in 1361. The texts attributed to him are not his [69] Tauler insisted on the birth of God in the soul of the believer: he must annihilate "every wish, every desire, every personal act; only a simple and pure attention to God must be allowed to subsist." The spirit is led into "the secret darkness of God without mode, and finally into a unity that is simple and without mode, where it loses all distinction, where it is without object or feelings" (from the French translation of Jeanne Ancelet-Hustache). But Tauler hardly encouraged the search for the blessings bestowed in the mystical experience.

We have more complete information on the life and work of Henry Suso (1296–1366). At a very young age, he entered the Dominican Monastery of Constance, and at about eighteen, he experienced his

66. Ibid., pp. 235ff. Although of Hellenistic origin, these conceptions and images came, in the Middle Ages, from Asia, and probably from Tibet; cf. ibid., pp. 244ff. Cf. also Boase, pp. 104ff., and especially Norman Cohn, *The Pursuit of the Millennium* (rev. ed.), pp. 130ff.

67. Cf. Jacques Le Goff, *La naissance du Purgatoire,* pp. 177ff., 381ff.

68. See the examples cited by Oakley, pp. 117ff. Also the Masses in honor of the healing saints multiplied: Saint Blaise for throat ailments, Saint Roche for prevention of the plague, etc. (ibid.).

69. It is only in 1910 that a certain number of sermons, complete or fragmentary, were successfully authenticated.

first ecstasy. In contrast to Meister Eckhart (to whom he was sent in 1320), Suso spoke of his ecstatic experience.[70] He thus outlined the stages of the mystical way: "He who has renounced himself must be detached from created forms, formed with Christ, and transformed in the divinity."

Perhaps as a result of his *Book of the Truth,* in which he defended Meister Eckhart's teachings, Suso had to abandon his lecturing position. He traveled to Switzerland, Alsace, and elsewhere, and met Tauler as well as a number of the "friends of God." As his preaching had made him popular, in monastic as well as in lay circles, Suso incited jealousies and was even malignly slandered. But after his death, his books were widely read.

Although he had severely criticized the Beguines and the adepts of the Free Spirit, the great Flemish mystic Jan van Ruysbroeck (1292–1381) did not escape the suspicion of the Magisterium.[71] The majority of his eleven authenticated writings concern spiritual guidance. Ruysbroeck insisted on the error of the "heretics" and the "false mysticisms" which confused spiritual vacuity with the union with God: one cannot know true contemplation without Christian practice and obedience to the Church; the *unio mystica* is not effected "naturally," but is a gift of divine grace.

Ruysbroeck was not unaware of the risk of being misjudged; that is why he did not encourage the circulation of certain works written exclusively for readers who were sufficiently advanced in contemplative practice.[72] Nevertheless, he was misunderstood, and was attacked by Jean Gerson, Rector of the University of Paris. Even his very sincere admirer, Gerhard Groote, recognized that Ruysbroeck's thought could

70. "I know a Preaching Brother who, in his beginnings, for perhaps ten years, generally received twice a day, morning and evening, an infused grace that lasted the time of two vigils. During this time, he was so absorbed in God, the eternal Wisdom, that he could not speak. It often seemed to him that he soared into the air and that he lost himself between time and eternity in the profound flood of the unfathomable marvels of God" (from the French translation by Ancelet-Hustache).

71. Ordained a priest in 1317, Ruysbroeck withdrew in 1343 with a group of contemplatives into a hermitage which quickly became a monastery according to the Augustinian rule; he died there at the age of eighty-eight.

72. Later he wrote *The Little Book of Enlightenment* to make the difficult *Kingdom of Love* more accessible. The essentials of Ruysbroeck's doctrines will be found in his long treatise, *The Adornment of the Spiritual Marriage* (his masterpiece), and in a little text, *The Sparkling Stone.*

give rise to confusions. In effect, while emphasizing the need for practice, Ruysbroeck affirmed that contemplative experience was accomplished on a higher plane. He made it clear that during this privileged experience "one cannot totally become God and lose our modality as a created being" (*The Sparking Stone*).[73] Nevertheless, this experience realizes "a unification in the essential unity of God," the soul of the contemplative "being embraced by the Holy Trinity" (*The Adornment of the Spiritual Marriage*, 3, Prologue; ibid., 3, 6). But Ruysbroeck recalls that God has created man in His image, "like a living mirror in which He imprints the image of His nature." He adds that in order to understand this deep and mysterious truth, man "must die unto himself and live in God" (ibid., 3, Prologue).

In the final analysis, the risk of ecclesiastical censure concerned the contemplatives instructed in theology no less than the enthusiasts of all types in their search for mystical experiences. Some spirituals well understood the uselessness of such a risk. Gerhard Groote (1340–84), founder of a new ascetic movement, the Brethren of the Common Life, had no interest in speculations and mystical experiences. The members of communities practicing what was called the *devotio moderna,* a simple, generous, and tolerant Christianity, did not estrange themselves from orthodoxy. The believer was invited to meditate on the mystery of the Incarnation, as reactualized in the Eucharist, instead of abandoning himself to mystical speculations. At the end of the fourteenth and during the fifteenth century, the movement of the Brethren of the Common Life attracted a large number of the laity. It is above all the general and deep need for a devotion accessible to everyone which explains the spectacular success of *The Imitation of Christ* written by Thomas à Kempis (1380–1471).

The significance and importance of this pietistic movement is still debated. Certain authors consider it as one of the sources of the reforms, whether they were Humanist, Catholic, or Protestant.[74] While recognizing that, in a certain sense, the *devotio moderna* anticipated and accompanied the Reform movements of the sixteenth century, Steven Ozment justly remarks that "its main achievement lay in the revival of traditional monasticism on the eve of the Reformation. It

73. See also Oakley, p. 279.
74. By contrast, R. R. Post insists upon the discontinuity between the *devotio moderna* and the spirit of the Reform; cf. *The Modern Devotion,* pp. 675–80.

demonstrated that the desire to lead a simple communal life of self-denial in imitation of Christ and the Apostles was as much alive at the end of the Middle Ages as it had been in the primitive church."[75]

301. Nicholas of Cusa and the twilight of the Middle Ages

Nicholas Krebs, born in Cusa in 1401, began his studies in a boarding school directed by the Brethren of the Common Life. Certain authors recognize the traces of this initial experience in the spiritual development of the future cardinal.[76] Nicholas of Cusa very soon discovered the works of Meister Eckhart and of the Pseudo-Areopagite; it is these two mystical theologians who oriented and nourished his thought. But his universal culture (he mastered mathematics, law, history, theology and philosophy), the profound originality of his metaphysic, and his exceptional ecclesiastical career make Nicholas of Cusa one of the most complex and attractive figures in the history of Christianity.[77]

It would be vain to attempt to present a condensed version of his system. For our purposes, it is most important to bring to mind the universalist perspective of his religious metaphysic, such as it appeared in his first book, *De Concordantia Catholica* (1433), in the *De Docta Ignorantia* (1440), and in *De pace fidei* (1453). Nicholas of Cusa was the first to recognize the *concordantia* as a universal theme, present as much in the life of the Church, and the development of the history and the structure of the world, as in the nature of God.[78] For

75. Ozment, p. 98.

76. Ernst Cassirer, *The Individual and the Cosmos in Renaissance Philosophy*, pp. 33, 49.

77. After having visited several famous universities (among others, that of Padua from 1417 to 1423), he was ordained a priest and, around 1430, was made Dean of the Cathedral of St. Florence at Koblenz. He was admitted to the Conciliary College of Basle in 1432; however, he rejoined the party of Pope Eugene IV, who sent him as a legate to Constantinople to invite the Eastern Patriarch and the Emperor John Palaeologus to the Council of Florence in order to prepare for the union of the Churches. In the interval which separates two of his most important works—*De Docta Ignorantia* (1440) and *De Visione Dei* (1453)—Nicholas of Cusa was elevated to the rank of Cardinal (1448) and Bishop of Brixen (1450). At Brixen, he entered into a conflict with Duke Sigismund of the Tyrol (1457) and retired to Rome, dedicating his last years to his writings. He died at Todi in 1464.

78. Cf. Jaroslav Pelikan, "Negative Theology and Positive Religion," p. 68.

him, the *concordantia* could fulfill itself not only between the pope and the Council, the Churches of East and West, but also between Christianity and the historical religions. He arrives at this audacious conclusion with the help of the negative theology of the Pseudo-Areopagite. And it is in continually utilizing the *via negativa* that he constructs his masterpiece on the "learned ignorance."

Nicholas of Cusa had the intuition of the *docta ignorantia* while crossing the Mediterranean (November 1437), heading toward Constantinople. Since it is a difficult work to summarize, let us point out only some of the central themes. Cusa recalls that knowledge (which is relative, complex, and finite) is incapable of grasping the truth (which is simple and infinite). All science being conjectural, man cannot know God (1:1–3). Truth, the absolute *maximum,* is beyond reason because reason is incapable of resolving contradictions (1:4). One must thus transcend discursive reason and imagination, and grasp the *maximum* by intuition. In effect, the intellect can elevate itself beyond differences and diversities by a simple intuition (1:10). But since the intellect cannot express itself in rational language, Cusa resorts to symbols, and first of all to geometric figures (1:1, 12). In God, the infinitely great (*maximum*) coincides with the infinitely small (*minimum,* 1:4), and virtuality coincides with the act.[79] God is neither one nor triune, but the unity which coincides with the trinity (1:19). In his infinite simplicity, God envelops (*complicatio*) all things, but at the same time he is in all things (*explicatio*); in other words, the *complicatio* coincides with the *explicatio* (2:3). In understanding the principle of the *coincidentia oppositorum,* our "ignorance" becomes "learned." But the *coincidentia oppositorum* must not be interpreted as a synthesis obtained through reason, for it cannot be realized on the plane of finitude but only in a conjectural fashion, on the plane of the infinite.[80]

Nicholas of Cusa had no doubt that the *via negativa,* which made possible the coincidence of opposites, opened a whole other horizon for Christian theology and philosophy, and further held the promise of encouraging a coherent and fruitful dialogue with other religions. Un-

79. Nicholas of Cusa recognizes that negative theology is superior to positive theology, but insists that they coincide as theological complements.

80. Let us note the difference between this conception—i.e., the *coincidentia oppositorum* effected on the infinite plane—and the archaic and traditional formulas relating to the real unification of opposites (e.g., *saṃsāra* and *nirvāṇa,* cf. §189). See also §296.

fortunately for Western Christianity, his intuitions and discoveries were not followed up. Cusa wrote *De pace fidei* in 1453 while the Turks came to conquer Constantinople and the Byzantine Empire ceased to exist. In fact, the fall of the "second Rome" provides a pathetic illustration of Europe's inability to conserve, or to reintegrate a unity on a religious and political plane. Notwithstanding this catastrophe, of which he was sadly aware, Cusa returned in *De pace fidei* to his arguments in favor of the fundamental unity of religions. He is not embarrassed by the problem of "particularities": polytheism, Judaism, Christianity, Islam. In following the *via negativa,* Cusa shed light not only on the discontinuities but also the continuities between the rituals of the polytheists and the true cult. For the polytheists "adored the divinity in all the gods."[81] As for the difference between the pure monotheism of the Jews and the Muslims and the trinitarian monotheism of the Christians, Nicholas of Cusa recalled that "inasmuch as He is the creator, God is triune and one, but as infinity, he is neither triune nor one, nor anything else that one can say. For the names attributed to God are derived from creatures; in Himself, God is ineffable and above all that one can name or say."[82] What is more, non-Christians who believe in the immortality of the soul presuppose, without knowing it, the Christ who was put to death and resurrected.

This resplendent and audacious book was nearly completely forgotten. As Pelikan recalls, *De pace fidei* was discovered by Lessing at the end of the eighteenth century. It is significant that Nicholas of Cusa's universalist vision inspired *Nathan the Wise.* It is no less significant that *De pace fidei* would again be ignored by the diverse ecumenists of recent years.

Nicholas of Cusa was the last important theologian-philosopher of the one and undivided Roman Church. Fifty years after his death, in 1517, Martin Luther published his famous Ninety-five Theses (cf. §309); several years later, the unity of Western Christianity was irremediably lost. And yet, from the Waldensians and the Franciscans of the twelfth century to John Hus and the adepts of the *devotio moderna* in the fifteenth, there were numerous efforts designed to "reform"

81. *De pace fidei,* 6:17, cited by Pelikan, p. 72. "It is You who gives life and being, You whom one seeks in the diverse cultic systems and whom one calls by diverse names, since, as you truly exist, You reside unknown to all and are ineffable" (*De pace fidei,* 7:21; Pelikan, ibid.).

82. *De pace fidei,* 7: 21; Pelikan, p. 74.

(''purify') certain practices and institutions, without the result of separation from the Church.[83]

With several rare exceptions, these efforts did not lead to significant changes. The Dominican preacher Girolamo Savonarola (1452–98) represents the last attempt at ''reform'' undertaken within the Roman Church; accused of heresy, Savonarola was hanged and his body burned at the stake. Henceforth, the reforms would be effected *against* the Catholic Church, or *apart from it.*

To be sure, all of these spiritual movements, sometimes on the border of orthodoxy, as well as the reactions which they provoked, were influenced, more or less directly, by transformations of the economic, political, and social order. But the hostile reactions of the Church, and above all the excesses of the Inquisition, had contributed to the impoverishment, indeed the sclerosis, of the Christian experience. As for the transformations of the political order, so important for the history of Europe, it is sufficient to recall the victories of the monarchies and the impetus of the new spiritual force which they supported: nationalism. It is more interesting for our purpose to observe that at the eve of the Reformation, the secular reality—the State no less than Nature—becomes independent of the domain of faith.

Perhaps contemporaries did not yet take it into account, but the theology and politics of Ockham found validation in the very course of history.

302. Byzantium and Rome. The *filioque* problem

The differences between the Eastern and Western church, evident already in the fourth century (cf. §251), continued to define themselves in the following centuries. The causes for them multiplied: different cultural traditions (Greco-Oriental on the one side, Romano-Germanic on the other); mutual ignorance not only of each other's language but also of the respective theological literatures; divergences of a cultural

---

83. Named Rector of the University of Prague in 1400, the Czech priest John Hus (1369–1415) criticized the clergy, the bishops, and the papacy in his sermons. Influenced by John Wycliffe (1325–84), Hus wrote his most important work, *De ecclesia* (1413). Summoned to Constance to defend himself (1414), he was accused of heresy and condemned to be burned.

or ecclesial order (the marriage of priests, prohibited in the West; the use of unleavened bread in the West, and of leavened bread in the East; water added to the wine of the Eucharist in the West, etc.). Pope Nicholas protests against the hasty elevation of Photius (a layman) to the rank of Patriarch, "forgetting" the case of Ambrose, who was directly consecrated as Bishop of Milan. Certain initiatives of Rome offended the Byzantines, as when, for example, in the sixth century the pope proclaimed the supremacy of the Church over the temporal power; or in 800, the papal confirmation of the coronation of Charlemagne as Roman Emperor, a title that had always belonged to the Byzantine Emperor.

Certain cultic developments and ecclesial institutions give Eastern Christianity its own physiognomy. We have seen the importance of the veneration of icons in the Byzantine Empire (cf. §258) and of the "cosmic Christianity" such as it was lived by the rural populations of southeastern Europe (cf. §236). The certitude that the whole of nature has been redeemed and sanctified by the Cross and the Resurrection justifies trust in life and encourages a certain religious optimism. Let us also recall the considerable importance accorded by the Eastern Church to the Sacrament of Chrismation, "the Seal of the Gift of the Holy Spirit." This rite immediately follows baptism, and transforms every layman (i.e., member of the *laos,* "people") into the bearer of the Spirit. This explains both the religious responsibility of all the members of the community, and the autonomy of such communities ruled by the bishop and grouped in metropolises. Let us add another characteristic trait: the certitude that the true Christian can attain divinization while here on earth (*theosis,* cf. §303).

The rupture was provoked by the addition of the *filioque* to the Nicene-Constantinopolitan Creed. The passage now reads: "The Spirit proceeds from the Father and the Son." The first known example of the *filioque* dates from the Second Council of Toledo, convoked in 589 to confirm the conversion of King Reccared from Arianism to Catholicism.[84] Closely analyzed, the two forms express two specific conceptions of the divinity. In Western trinitarianism, it is the Holy Spirit that guarantees the divine unity. By contrast, the Eastern Church empha-

---

84. Most probably, the *filioque* had been added to emphasize the different understanding of the second person of the Trinity between the Arians and the Catholics.

sizes the fact that God the Father is the source, the principle, and the cause of the Trinity.[85]

According to certain authors, it was the Germanic emperors who imposed the new formula of the Credo. "It is the constitution of the Carolingian Empire which generalized the *filioque* in Western usage and specified a properly *filioquist* theology. It was a matter of legitimating against Byzantium, until then the keeper of the Christian Empire, itself unique by definition, the foundation of a new State of universal pretensions."[86] But it is only in 1014—at the demand of the Emperor Henry II—that the Credo with the *filioque* was chanted in Rome[87] (this date can be considered as marking the beginning of the Great Schism).

Relations between the two churches were not, however, definitively broken. In 1053, Pope Leo IX sent an embassy to Constantinople led by his principal legate, Cardinal Humbert, in order to renew canonical relations and prepare an alliance against the Normans, who were advancing to occupy southern Italy. But the Byzantine Patriarch Michael Cerularius displayed sufficient wariness, refusing every concession. On 15 July 1054, the legates deposited on the altar of Hagia Sophia a sentence of excommunication against Cerularius, accusing him of ten heresies, including removal of the *filioque* from the Credo and approval of clerical marriages.

Following this rupture, the animosity of Occidentals against the Greeks increased. But the irreparable break finally occurred in 1204, when the armies of the Fourth Crusade attacked and pillaged Constantinople, breaking icons and throwing relics into filth. According to the Byzantine chronicler Nicétas Choniatès, a prostitute sang obscene songs on the patriarchal throne. The chronicler recalled that the Muslims "did not violate our women . . . , nor reduce the inhabitants to misery, nor strip them in order to march them naked through the streets, nor make them die by starvation or fire. . . . That, however, is how these Christian people who believe in the name of the Lord and shared our religion have treated us."[88] As we have noted earlier

85. Cf. the textual analysis in Jaroslav Pelikan, *The Spirit of Eastern Christendom*, pp. 196–97.

86. Olivier Clément, *L'essor du christianisme oriental*, p. 14.

87. The new formula was made a dogma in 1274 at the Council of Lyon.

88. Nicétas Choniatès, *Histoire*, Olivier Clément, trans., p. 81. See the other

(§268), Baudouin of Flanders was proclaimed Latin Emperor of Byzantium and the Venetian Thomas Morosini Patriarch of Constantinople.

The Greeks have never forgotten this tragic episode. Nevertheless, because of the Turkish menace, the Orthodox Church resumed ecclesiastical negotiations with Rome after 1261. It insistently demanded the convocation of an Ecumenical Council in order to settle the *filioque* controversy and arrange for union. For their part, the Byzantine emperors, who depended on military aid from the West, were impatient to see union with Rome realized. The negotiations dragged on for more than a century. Finally, at the Council of Florence (1438–39), the representatives of Orthodoxy pressed by the Emperor accepted Rome's conditions, but the union was immediately invalidated by the people and the clergy. Moreover, fourteen years later, in 1453, Constantinople was occupied by the Turks and the Byzantine Empire ceased to exist. Its spiritual structures survived, however, in eastern Europe and Russia for at least three more centuries. It was "Byzantium after Byzantium," according to the expression of the Romanian historian, N. Iorga.[89] This eastern heritage allowed for the vigor of a "popular" Christianity which has not only resisted the interminable terror of history, but has created an entire universe of artistic and religious values whose roots descend to the Neolithic (cf. §304).

303. The Hesychast monks. Saint Gregory Palamas

We have already alluded to deification (*theosis*)[90] and to the great doctors, Gregory of Nyssa and Maximus the Confessor, who systematized this doctrine of the union with God (cf. §257). In his *Life of Moses,* Gregory of Nyssa speaks of the "luminous darkness" where Moses "declares that he sees God" (2:163–64). For Maximus the

---

sources cited by Deno John Geanakoplos, *Interaction of the "Sibling" Byzantine and Western Cultures,* pp. 10ff., 307ff. (notes 17–22). Constantinople was reconquered by Michael Palaeologus in 1261.

89. See especially N. Iorga, *Byzance après Byzance* (Bucharest, 1933; new edition, 1971).

90. The idea is founded on the words of Christ: "The glory which thou hast given me I have given them, that they may be one even as we are one, I in them and thou in me, that they may become perfectly one"; John 17:22–23. Cf. 2 Peter 1:4.

Confessor, it is this vision of God in the darkness that effects *theosis;* in other words, the believer participates in God. Deification is thus a free gift, "an act of the all-powerful God freely emerging from his transcendence while remaining essentially unknowable."[91] Similarly, Simeon the New Theologian (942–1022), the only mystic of the Eastern Church to speak of his own experiences, describes the mystery of divinization in these terms: "You have granted to me, Lord, that this corruptible temple—my human flesh—unites itself with your holy flesh, that my blood melts itself into yours; and even now I am your transparent and translucent limb."[92]

As we have already observed (§257), *theosis* constitutes the central doctrine of Orthodox theology. Let us add that it is intimately connected with the spiritual disciplines of the Hesychasts (from *hesychia,* "quietude"), cenobites living in the monasteries of Mount Sinai. The preferred practice of these monks was the "prayer of the heart" or "Jesus prayer." This brief text ("Lord Jesus Christ, son of God, have mercy on me!"), had to be repeated endlessly, meditated upon, and "interiorized." From the sixth century on, Hesychasm spreads from Mount Sinai into the Byzantine world. John Climacus (sixth/seventh century), the most significant of the Sinai theologians, had already insisted upon the importance of *hesychia.*[93] But it is with Nicephorus the Solitary (thirteenth century) that this mystical current is implanted on Mount Athos and in other monasteries. Nicephorus recalls that the goal of the spiritual life is to make one aware of "the treasure hidden in the heart"; in other words of reuniting the spirit (the *nous*) with the heart, the "site of God." One achieved this reunion by making the spirit "descend" into the heart through the vehicle of the breath.

Nicephorus is "the first witness dated with certainty of the Jesus prayer combined with a respiratory technique."[94] In his treatise, *On the Care of the Heart,* Nicephorus exposes this method in detail. "As I have said to you, seat yourself, collect your spirit, introduce it—I say your spirit—into the nostrils; this is the path the breath takes in order to go the heart. Push it, force it to descend into your heart at the same time as the inhaled air. When it is there, you will see the joy which will

91. Jean Meyendorff, *Saint Grégoire Palamas et la mystique orthodoxe,* p. 45.
92. Translation cited in ibid., p. 57.
93. Cf. Colm Luibheid and Norman Russell, trans., *John Climacus: The Ladder of Divine Ascent,* "Introduction" by Kallistos Ware, pp. 48ff.
94. Jean Gouillard, *Petite Philocalie,* p. 185.

follow. . . . As the man who returns home after an absence no longer holds back his joy at being able to rejoin his wife and children, so the spirit, when it unites itself to the soul, overflows with joy and ineffable delight. . . . Know then that while your spirit finds itself there, you must neither fall silent nor remain idle. But have no other activities nor meditations than the cry: 'Lord Jesus Christ, son of God, have mercy on me!' No respite at any price.''[95]

Still more important for the rise of Hesychasm on Mount Athos was Gregory of Sinai (1255–1346). He insisted on the central role of the "Memory of God" ("You shall remember the Lord your God"; Deuteronomy 8:18) in order to make one aware of the grace bestowed by baptism, but then hidden on account of sin. Gregory prefers hermetic solitude to communal monasticism, for liturgical prayer seemed to him too exterior to release the "memory of God." But he drew the attention of the monks to the dangers of visions incited by the imagination.[96]

It is in great part due to the controversies raised by the Hesychasts that Byzantine theology ceased to be a "theology of repetition," as it had been since the ninth century. Around 1330, a Greek from Calabria named Barlaam came to Constantinople, won the confidence of the Emperor, and dedicated himself to the union of the churches.[97] After having met certain Hesychast monks, Barlaam strongly criticized their method and accused them of heresy, more precisely of Messalianism.[98] For the Hesychasts claimed to see God himself. Now the direct vision of God with corporeal eyes is held to be impossible. Among the defenders of the Hesychasts, Gregory Palamas is by far the most distinguished. Born in 1296, Palamas was ordained as a priest and spent twenty years in the monastery on Mount Athos before being consecrated Archbishop of Thessalonika. In responding to Barlaam in

95. From Gouillard, trans., ibid., p. 204. On the analogies with yogic practices and the *dhikr*, see Eliade, *Yoga, Immortality, and Freedom*, pp. 63, 216–19.

96. Meyendorff recalls that it is a matter of an "essential trait of the Orthodox mystical tradition: in all its voluntary and involuntary forms, the imagination is the most dangerous enemy of union with God" (Meyendorff, p. 71).

97. In 1339, he was entrusted with a confidential mission to Benedict XII in Avignon; see Barlaam's letter in Deno John Geanakoplos, *Byzantine East and Latin West*, pp. 90ff.

98. For the Messalians, the believer's final goal was ecstatic union with Christ's body of light.

his *Triads for the Defense of the Hesychast Saints,* Palamas went far to renovate Orthodox theology. His principal contribution consists in the distinction which he introduced between the divine essence and the "energies" through which God communicates and reveals himself. "The divine and unknowable essence, if it does not possess an energy distinct from itself, will be totally nonexistent and will have been only a spiritual conception."[99] The essence is the "cause" of the energies; "each of them truly signifies a distinct divine property, but they do not constitute different realities because all are the acts of a unique living God."[100] (The doctrine of energies was confirmed by the Byzantine Councils of 1341, 1347, and 1351.)

As regards the divine light seen by the Hesychasts, Palamas refers to the light of the Transfiguration. On Mount Tabor, there had been no change in Jesus, but a transformation in the Apostles: the latter, by divine grace, had recovered the ability to see Jesus such as he was, in the blinding light. Adam had this ability before the fall, and it will be restored to man in the eschatological future.[101] In addition, by way of developing the tradition of the Egyptian monks, Palamas affirms that the vision of the uncreated Light is accompanied by the objective luminescence of the saint. "He who participates in the divine energy . . . becomes, in some ways, light himself; he is united with the Light, and with the Light he sees in full consciousness all that remains hidden from those who have not had this grace."[102]

In effect, following upon the Incarnation, our bodies become "temples of the Holy Spirit who is in us" (1 Corinthians 6:19); by the Sacrament of the Eucharist, Christ is discovered within us. "We carry the light of the Father in the person of Jesus Christ" (*Triads,* 1:2, 2). This divine presence at the interior of our body "transforms the body and makes it spiritual . . . in such a way, that the entire man becomes

99. Text translated by Jean Meyendorff, *Introduction à l'étude de Grégoire Palamas,* p. 297.

100. Unedited text summarized by Meyendorff, ibid., p. 295.

101. This is to say that the perception of God in his uncreated Light is linked to the perfection of origins and of the end, of Paradise before History and of the Eschaton, which brings History to an end. But those who make themselves worthy of the Kingdom of God enjoy from now on the vision of the uncreated Light, like the Apostles on Mount Tabor. Cf. Eliade, "Experiences of Mystical Light," *The Two and the One,* pp. 60ff.

102. Sermon translated by Vladimir Lossky, "La Théologie de la Lumière," p. 110.

Spirit.''[103] But this ''spiritualization'' of the body by no means implies a detachment from matter. On the contrary, the contemplative, ''without separating himself or being separated from the matter which accompanies him, from the beginning,'' leads to God, ''through himself, the entire whole of creation,''[104] The great theologian revolts against Platonism which in the XIVth century (during the "Renaissance of the Paleologues") fascinated the Byzantine intelligentsia and certain members of the Church.[105] In returning to the biblical tradition, Palamas insisted upon the importance of the sacraments through which the material is "transubstantiated" without being annihilated.

The triumph of Hesychasm and of the Palamite theology provoked a renewal of the sacramental life, and provoked the regeneration of certain ecclesiastical institutions. Hesychasm spread very quickly into eastern Europe, into the Romanian principalities and penetrated Russia as far as Novgorod. The ''renaissance'' of Hellenism, with the exaltation of Platonic philosophy, did not, however, have a continuation. In other words, Byzantium and the Orthodox countries did not experience Humanism. Certain authors estimate that it is thanks to Palamas's twin victory—against the Ockhamism of Barlaam and against Greek philosophy—that Orthodoxy gave place to no movement of Reform.

Let us add that one of the most audacious theologians after Palamas was a layman, Nicolas Cabasilas (1320/25–1371), a high functionary in the Byzantine administration. Not only did Cabasilas brilliantly inaugurate a tradition which has been perpetuated among all the Orthodox peoples, but he considered the layman as superior to the monk. The latter's model is the angelic life, while that of the layman is the complete man. Moreover, it is for the laymen that Nicholas Cabasilas wrote so that they might become aware of the profound dimension of their Christian experience, and above all of the mystery of the sacraments.[106]

---

103. From *Triads*, 2: 2, 9; trans. by John Meyendorff.

104. Palamas takes up this theme at least three times; see Meyendorff, *Introduction à l'Étude de Grégoire Palamas,* p. 218.

105. Cf. Geanakoplos, p. 21 and n. 45. "In approving the thought of the Hesychast doctor, the Byzantine Church resolutely turned its back on the spirit of the Renaissance," Meyendorff, *Introduction,* p. 236.

106. His books, *Life in Jesus Christ* and *The Explanation of the Divine Liturgy,* are still read in contemporary Orthodox communities.

38 Religion, Magic, and Hermetic Traditions before and after the Reformation

304. The survival of pre-Christian religious traditions

As we have remarked at several points, the Christianization of the peoples of Europe did not succeed in effacing their different ethnic traditions. The conversion to Christianity has given place to symbioses and religious syncretisms which, many times over, provide brilliant illustration of the creativity specific to "popular," agrarian, or pastoral cultures. We have already recalled several examples of "cosmic Christianity" (cf. §237). Elsewhere, we have shown the continuity—from the Neolithic up to the nineteenth century—of certain cults, myths, and symbols relating to stones, water, and vegetation.[1] Let us add that, following their conversion, even where it was superficial, the numerous ethnic religious traditions, as well as the local mythologies, were homologized: that is, they were integrated into the same "sacred history" and expressed in the same language, as that of the Christian faith and Christian mythology. Thus, for example, the memory of storm gods has survived in the legends of Saint Elijah; a great number of heroic dragon slayers have been assimilated by Saint George; certain myths and cults relating to goddesses have been integrated into the religious folklore of the Virgin Mary. In sum, the innumerable forms and variants of the pagan heritage have been articulated in the same outwardly Christianized mythico-ritual corpus.

It would be vain to mention all the categories of "pagan survivals." It suffices to cite some particularly suggestive cases: for example, the *kallikantzari,* monsters who haunt Greek villages during the Twelve Days (between Christmas and Epiphany) and who prolong the myth-

---

1. Above all in Eliade, *Patterns in Comparative Religion,* chaps. 6, 8, and 9.

ico-ritual scenario of the centaurs of classical antiquity;[2] or the archaic ritual of the firewalk that is integrated into the *anastenaria* ceremony of Thrace;[3] or, finally, once again in Thrace, the Carnival feasts, whose structure recalls that of the "Dionysus of the fields" and the *Anthesteria* celebrated in Athens from the first millennium before the Christian era (cf. §123).[4] Let us also note, further, that a certain number of themes and narrative motifs attested in the Homeric poems are still current in Balkan and Romanian folklore.[5] What is more, in analyzing the agrarian ceremonies of central and eastern Europe, Leopold Schmidt was able to show that they are of the same stock as a mythico-ritual scenario that disappeared in Greece before the time of Homer.[6]

For our purposes, it is worth presenting several examples of pagan-Christian syncretism, illustrating both the resilience of the traditional heritage and the process of Christianization. We have chosen, to begin with, the complex ritual of the Twelve Days, for it submerges its roots in prehistory. Since there is no question of presenting it in its entirety (ceremonies, games, songs, dances, processions of animalian masks), we will concentrate on the ritual songs of Christmas. They are attested in all of eastern Europe, as far as Poland. Their Romanian and Slavic name, *colinde,* derives from *calendae Januarii.* Over the centuries, the ecclesiastical authorities strove to extirpate them, but without success. (In 692, the Council of Constantinople reiterated the ban in draconian terms.) In all, a certain number of *colinde* have been "Christianized," in the sense that they have borrowed mythological personages and themes from popular Christianity.[7]

The ritual customarily unfolds from Christmas Eve (24 December) to the morning of the following day. The group of from six to thirty young men (*colindători*) designates a leader familiar with the tradi-

2. See J.-C. Lawson, *Modern Greek Folklore and Ancient Greek Religion,* pp. 190–255. Their name derives from *Kentauroi,* ibid., pp. 233 ff. See also G. Dumézil, *Le problème des Centaures,* pp. 165ff.

3. Cf. C. A. Romaios, *Cultes populaires de la Thrace,* pp. 17–123.

4. Ibid., pp. 125–200.

5. Cf. C. Poghirc, "Homère et la ballade populaire roumaine"; Eliade, "History of Religions and 'Popular' Cultures," p. 7.

6. See L. Schmidt, *Gestaltheiligkeit im bäuerlichen Arbeitsmythos.*

7. We make use above all of the Romanian folkloric documents, but one finds the same scenario, with variants, everywhere in eastern Europe; see Eliade, "History of Religions and 'Popular' Cultures," pp. 11ff.

tional customs, and for forty or eighteen days they gather together four or five times a week in a house in order to receive the necessary instruction. On the evening of 24 December, dressed in new costumes and decorated with flowers and bells, the *colindători* first sing in the house of their host, and then visit all the homes of the village. In the streets they shout and play the trumpet and tambourine so that the uproar removes evil spirits and announces their approach to the householders. They sing the first *colinda* under the window, and after receiving permission they enter the house and continue their repertory, dance with the girls, and recite the traditional blessings. The *colindători* bring health and riches, represented by a small green branch of a fir tree set in a vase full of apples and peas. Except in poor families, they receive gifts: crowns, cakes, fruit, meat, drink, etc. After having passed through the village, the group organizes a feast in which the youth of the village participate.

The ritual of the *colinde* is quite rich and complex. The benediction (*oratio*) and the ceremonial banquet constitute the most archaic elements: they coincide with the festivities of the New Year.[8] The leader, followed by the other *colindători,* gives speeches (*urare*) in which he exalts the nobility, generosity, and wealth of the master of the house. Sometimes the *colindători* represent a group of saints (Saint John, Saint Peter, Saint George, Saint Nicholas). Among the Bulgarians, certain *colinde* have as their theme God's visit accompanied by the infant Jesus, or by a group of saints. Elsewhere, the *colindători* are those who are "invited" (*oaspeti buni*), sent by God to bring good fortune and health.[9] In a Ukranian variant, God comes himself to awaken the master of the house and tell him of the *colindători*'s approach. Among the Romanians of Transylvania, God descends from heaven on a wax ladder in a splendid vestment decorated with stars, on which the *colindători* are also painted.[10]

A certain number of *colinde* reflect the "cosmic Christianity" specific to the peoples of southeastern Europe. One finds in them reflections on the creation of the world, but without relation to the biblical cosmogony. God or Jesus has created the world in three days; but seeing that the earth is too large to be covered by Heaven, Jesus throws

8. Cf. Eliade, *Cosmos and History: The Myth of the Eternal Return,* pp. 51ff.
9. Among Ukranians, they are called the "little servants of God."
10. Cf. Monica Brătulescu, "Colinda românească," pp. 62ff.

three rings which transform themselves into angels, and produce from themselves the mountains.[11] According to other *colinde*, after having fashioned the earth, God put it on four silver pillars to sustain it.[12] A large number of songs present God as a flute-playing shepherd, with a large flock of sheep guided by Saint Peter.

But more numerous and more archaic are the *colinde* which open onto another imaginary universe. The setting for the action is the entire world: between the zenith and the deep valleys, or between the mountains and the Black Sea. Very far away, in the middle of the sea, is an island with a giant tree around which dance a group of young girls.[13] The personages of these archaic *colinde* are portrayed in a fabulous manner: they are beautiful and invincible; they carry the sun and the moon on their garments (like God in the Christian *colinde*). Very high in the sky, near the sun, a young hunter mounts a horse. The home of the householder and his family are mythologized: the master and his relatives are projected into a paradisical countryside, and resemble kings. The heroes of the most beautiful *colinde* are the hunters and shepherds, a point which confirms their archaism. At the emperor's request, the young hero fights with a lion, subdues and enchains it. Fifty cavaliers attempt to cross the (Black) Sea, but only one succeeds in reaching the island, where he marries the most beautiful of the girls. The other heroes pursue wild animals endowed with magical powers and triumph over them.

The scenarios of many *colinde* resemble certain initiatory rituals. Similarly, traces of initiation rites for girls have been recognized in some of them.[14] In the *colinde* sung by the girls and young women, as well as in other oral productions, one evokes the tribulations of a virgin lost or isolated in deserted places, her sufferings provoked by her sexual metamorphosis and the dangers of an imminent death. But in contrast to the male initiations, no precise ritual has been conserved. The feminine initiatory tests survive only in the imaginary universe of the

11. On this folkloric motif, see Eliade, *Zalmoxis, the Vanishing God,* pp. 76ff.

12. Al. Rosetti, *Colindele religioase la Români,* pp. 68ff.; Monica Brătulescu, "Colinda românească," p. 48.

13. In certain variants, the Cosmic Tree is situated in the middle of the sea or on the opposite side.

14. Let us add that under the direction of an old woman, the ceremonial group (*caeta*) of girls periodically reunites and receives traditional instruction concerning sexuality, marriage, funerary rituals, the secrets of medicinal plants, etc.; Monica Brătulescu, "Caeta feminină," *passim.*

colinde and other ceremonial songs. Nevertheless, these oral productions contribute, indirectly, to our knowledge of archaic feminine spirituality.

305. Symbols and rituals of a cathartic dance

The initiatory instruction of the *colindători*[15] is completed by the initiation into the closed group of cathartic dancers called *călușari*.[16] This time, the young men do not learn traditions and songs associated with the scenario of Christmas, but a series of specific dances and a particular mythology. The name of the dance, *căluș*, derives from the Romanian word *cal* ("horse"; Latin *caballus*). The group is composed of seven, nine, or eleven young men, selected and instructed by an older leader. They are armed with maces and sabers, and provided besides with a wooden horse's head and a "flag" with medicinal plants fixed to the end of the pole. As we shall see, one of the *călușari,* called "the Mute" or "the Masked One," plays a different role from the rest of the group.

The instruction unfolds over a period of two or three weeks in the woods or in other isolated places. Once they are accepted by the leader, the *călușari* gather together, on the eve of Pentecost, in a secret place. Hands on the "flag," they swear to respect the rules and customs of the group, to treat each other as brothers, to maintain chastity for the nine (or twelve or fourteen) days to come, to divulge nothing of what they will see or hear, and to obey their leader. When they take their oath, the *călușari* ask for the protection of the Queen of Fairies, Herodias (= *Irodiada*), raising their maces in the air and then striking them against one another. They keep a strict silence for fear that the fairies (*zîne*) might make them ill. After the oath and until the group's dispersal, the *călușari* remain constantly together.

Several elements recall the initiation into a men's society (*Männerbund*): the isolation in the forest, the vow of secrecy, the role of the "flag," the mace and the sword, the symbolism of the horse's head.[17]

---

15. Cf. Eliade, "History of Religions and 'Popular' Cultures," p. 17.

16. See Eliade, "Notes on the *Călușari*," passim; Gail Kligman, *Căluș.*

17. Prince Dimitri Cantemir provides some significant additional information, among which one finds certain points that were no longer confirmed in the nineteenth century. According to the author of the *Descriptio Moldaviae,* the *călușari* speak with

The central and specific attribute of the *călușari* is their adroitness as acrobat-choreographers, in particular their aptitude at giving the impression that they raise themselves into the air. By all the evidence, it is their leaps, jumps, gambols, and capers that evoke the horse's gallop and, at the same time, the flight and dance of the fairies (*zîne*). Furthermore, those whom the fairies are supposed to make ill set themselves to leaping about and crying, "like the *călușari,* appearing not to touch the earth." The relations between the *călușari* and the *zîne* are bizarrely ambivalent: the dancers ask for and count on the protection of Herodias, all the while running the risk of becoming the victim of her cortege of followers, the band of fairies. They imitate the flight of the *zîne,* but at the same time they exalt their solidarity with the horse, the masculine and "heroic" symbol *par excellence.* These ambivalent relations also manifest themselves in their activities and deportment. For nearly a fortnight, accompanied by two or three violinists, the *călușari* go into the villages and nearby hamlets dancing, playing, and trying to heal the victims of the fairies. One believes that during this period, which is the third week after Easter on Pentecost Sunday, the *zîne* fly, sing, and dance, especially in the night. One can hear their bells, tambourines, and other musical instruments because the fairies have at their service a number of violinists, bagpipers, and even a standard-bearer. The best protection against fairies is afforded by the magico-medicinal plants garlic and mugwort, the very plants that the *călușari* place in a pouch at the top of their flagstaff. And they chew as much garlic as possible.

The cure consists in a series of dances, completed by several ritual acts.[18] In certain regions, the patient is carried outside the village, near to the woods, and placed in the middle of the circle of *călușari.* During the dance, the leader touches one of the dancers with the "flag," and the one so touched falls to the ground. The faint, whether it is real or feigned, lasts for three to five minutes. At the moment the dancer falls, the patient is supposed to get up and flee; in any case, two *călușari* take him by the arms and depart as quickly as possible. The therapeutic

---

feminine voices and cover their faces with a linen cloth so as not to be recognized; they know more than a hundred different dances, some so extraordinary that the dancers seem not to touch the ground, "as if they flew in the air"; the *călușari* sleep solely in churches, in order not to be tormented by the fairies (the *zîne*). See *Descriptio Moldaviae* (critical ed., Bucharest, 1973), p. 314.

18. The invalid is touched with herbs and one then spits garlic onto his face; a pot of water is broken; a black chicken is sacrificed, etc.

intention of the faint is evident: the illness abandons the patient and penetrates into a *căluşar,* who "dies" instead, but then returns to life, for he is "initiated."

A series of burlesque scenes are played out in the interval between the dances and the end of the ceremony. The most important role devolves upon the "Mute." For example, the *căluşari* lift him in the air and let him fall down brusquely. Considered to be dead, the "Mute" is lamented by the entire group, and preparations are made to bury him, but not before skinning him, etc. The most comic and elaborate episodes are enacted on the last day, when the group returns to the village. Four *căluşari* personify certain familiar personages in a grotesque manner: the Priest, the Turk (or the Cossack), the Doctor, and the Woman. Each tries to make love with the Woman, and the pantomime is frequently licentious. The "Mute," provided with a wooden phallus, provokes general hilarity with his grotesque and eccentric gestures. Finally, one of the "actors" is killed and revived, and the "Woman" becomes pregnant.[19]

Whatever its origin,[20] the *căluş,* in its forms reported in recent centuries, is known only in Romania, and can be considered a creation of popular Romanian culture. What characterizes it is at once its archaism and its open structure (which explains the assimilation of elements belonging to other scenarios, for example the grotesque episodes). The eventual influences of a feudal society (the "flag," the saber, and, more rarely, spurs) have superimposed themselves on a quite archaic rural culture of which one finds proof in the ritual role of the mace, the pole modeled from a fir tree (a tree specific to pre-Christian ceremonies), to say nothing of the choreography itself. Although the taking of the oath is done in the name of God, the ceremony has nothing Christian about it. The ecclesiastical authorities reacted to it with violence, and with some success, since several archaic traits that were attested in the seventeenth century (cf. n. 17) have disappeared. Still at the end of the nineteenth century, in certain regions communion was prohibited to the *căluşari* for a period of three years. But the Church finally decided to tolerate them.

Thus, despite six centuries of Christianity and other cultural influences, one can still decipher the traces of initiatory scenarios in the

19. See Eliade, "Notes on the *Căluşari*" and "History of Religions and 'Popular' Cultures," pp. 17ff.
20. The origin remains obscure; cf. Eliade, "Notes on the *Căluşari*," pp. 129ff.

rural societies of southeastern Europe. These scenarios were articulated within the mythico-ritual systems of the New Year and the cycle of Spring. In certain cases, for example among the *călușari*, the archaic heritage is evident, especially in the dances and in the melodic structures associated with them. By way of contrast, in the mythico-ritual scenario of the *colinde*, it is the texts which have best conserved the initiatory elements. One might say that as a result of the different religious and cultural influences, a number of rituals connected with traditional initiations have disappeared (or have been radically camouflaged), while the choreographic and mythological (that is, narrative) structures have survived.

In any case, the religious function of the *dances* and the *texts* is clear. It thus follows that a correct analysis of the imaginary universe of the *colinde* is capable of revealing a type of religious experience and mythological creativity characteristic of the peasants of central and eastern Europe. Unfortunately, there does not yet exist a hermeneutic adequate to such rural traditions; in other words, one has yet to work out an analysis of mythico-religious *oral texts* comparable to the interpretation of *written* works. Such a hermeneutic would place in relief not only the profound sense of adherence to the traditional heritage, but the creative reinterpretations of the Christian message as well. In a "total" history of Christianity, the creations specific to rural populations deserve their own equal treatment. Beside the different theologies constructed on the basis of the Old Testament and Greek philosophy, it is important to consider the outlines of what may be called "popular theology": one will find, reinterpreted and Christianized, numerous archaic traditions, from the Neolithic to eastern and Hellenistic religions.[21]

306. "Witch hunts" and the vicissitudes of popular religion

The famous and sinister "witch hunts" undertaken in the sixteenth and seventeenth centuries, as much by the Reformed churches as by the Inquisition, pursued the destruction of a satanic and criminal cult which, according to the theologians, threatened the very foundations of the Christian faith. Recent research[22] has made clear the absurdity

21. Cf. "History of Religions and 'Popular' Cultures," pp. 24ff.
22. The bibliography is immense. See some of the citations in Eliade, *Occultism, Witchcraft, and Cultural Fashions,* pp. 69–70 and nn. 1–2, and the bibliography cited by Richard A. Horsley, "Further Reflections on Witchcraft and European Folk Culture." The most recent publications are indicated in the Critical Bibliographies, §306.

of the principal accusations: intimate relations with the Devil, orgies, infanticide, cannibalism, the practice of *maleficia*. Under torture, a considerable number of wizards and witches admitted to such abominable and criminal acts, and were condemned to the stake. This seems to justify the opinion of contemporary authors who have come to regard this mythico-ritual scenario of witchcraft as no more than an invention of the theologians and inquisitors.

This opinion, however, must be qualified. In effect, if the victims were not guilty of the crimes and heresies they were accused of, some of them confessed to having practiced magico-religious ceremonies of a "pagan" origin and structure—ceremonies long forbidden by the Church even if they were sometimes superficially Christianized. This mythico-ritual heritage was an ingredient of European popular religion. The examples which we will now discuss will permit us to understand the process through which certain adepts of this popular religion came to confess—and even to believe—that they practiced the cult of the Devil.

In the last analysis, the witch hunts pursued the liquidation of the last survivals of "paganism": that is, essentially, fertility cults and initiation scenarios. What resulted was the impoverishment of popular religiosity and, in certain regions, the decadence of the rural societies.[23]

According to the trials of the Inquisition in Milan in 1384 and 1390, two women had acknowledged belonging to a society led by Diana Herodias. Its members included not only the living but the dead. The animals which they ate in the course of their ceremonial meals were resuscitated (from their bones) by the goddess. Diana ("Signora Oriente") taught the faithful the use of medicinal herbs to cure diverse maladies, to discover the authors of thefts, and to identify sorcerers.[24] It is evident that Diana's faithful had nothing in common with the makers of satanic *maleficia*. Most likely, their rites and visions were prolongations of an archaic fertility cult. But as we shall see, the investigations of the Inquisition radically modified the situation. In the sixteenth and seventeenth centuries in Lorraine, the "magicians" called before the authorities acknowledged immediately that they were

---

23. In order to best indicate the complexity of the phenomenon, I will analyze only a few examples, of which some (the Romanian folkloric documents) are little known.

24. B. Bonomo, *Caccia alle streghe* (Palermo, 1959), pp. 15–17, 59–60; Richard A. Horsley, "Further Reflections on Witchcraft and European Folk Religion," p. 89.

"healer-diviners," but not sorcerers; only after being tortured did they finally admit that they were the "slaves of Satan."[25]

The case of the *benandanti* ("those who travel," "vagabonds") provides a moving illustration of the effects of the Inquisition in pressuring the transformation of a secret fertility cult into becoming a practice of black magic. On 31 March 1575, the Vicar General and the Inquisitor of Aquileia and Concordia learned of the presence in certain villages of magicians who, under the name *benandanti,* called themselves "good" witches because they did combat with sorcerers (*stregoni*). The investigation concerning the first group of *benandanti* brought to light the following facts: their reunions occurred in secret, during the night, four times a year (that is, during the weeks of the Ember days); they reached the site of their reunions on the back of a hare, cat, or other animal; these reunions presented nothing of the well known "satanic" characteristics proper to assemblies of sorcerers; they included neither abjuration nor vituperation of the sacraments or the Cross, nor any cult of the Devil. The basis of the rite remains rather obscure. Provided with branches of fennel, the *benandanti* confronted the sorcerers (*streghe* and *stregoni*) who were themselves armed with varieties of rushes used for brooms. They pretended to combat the evils of the sorcerers and cure their victims. Should the *benandanti* emerge victorious from these combats during the Four Seasons, the harvests would be adundant that year; if not, it would be a time for scarcity and famine.[26]

Later investigations revealed details on the recruitment of the *benandanti* and the structure of their nocturnal assemblies. They affirmed that a "heavenly angel" had asked them to join the association, and that they were initiated into the group's secrets between the ages of twenty and twenty-eight. Organized along military lines under the command of a captain, the association reunited when the captain convoked them to the sound of the tambourine. Its members were bound by the oath of secrecy. Their assemblies sometimes brought together up to five thousand *benandanti,* some from the same region but most of them not knowing each other. They had a flag of gilded white ermine, while the yellow flag of the sorcerers sported four devils. All the

---

25. Étienne Delcambre, as cited by Horsley, p. 93.
26. Carlo Ginzburg, *I Benandanti,* pp. 8ff.

benandanti had one trait in common: they were born "with the shirt." In other words, they were born clothed, with the membrane that was called a caul.

When the Inquisition, faithful to its stereotyped notion of the witches' sabbath, asked them if their "angel" had promised them delicate foods, women, and other salacious pleasures, they proudly denied these insinuations. Only sorcerers, they said, danced and amused themselves in their assemblies. The most enigmatic point concerning the *benandanti* remains their "voyage" toward the place of their reunions. They maintained that they brought themselves there *in spirito,* while they were sleeping. Before their "voyage," they fell into a state of deep exhaustion, an almost cataleptic lethargy, in the course of which their souls were able to leave their bodies. They used no unguents to prepare for their "voyage" which, though accomplished *in spirito,* was real in their own eyes.

In 1581, two *benandanti* were condemned to six months in prison for heresy, and required to abjure their errors. Other trials took place in the course of the following sixty years, and we will examine their consequences. For the moment, however, let us attempt to reconstitute, on the basis of the documents from the period, the structure of this popular secret cult. The central rite was, obviously, a ceremonial combat between sorcerers to assure the abundance of the harvests, the vineyards, and "all the fruits of the earth."[27] The fact that the combat took place on the four nights critical to the agricultural calender leaves no doubt as to its object. It is probable that the confrontation between the *benandanti* and the *stregoni* prolonged the scenario of an archaic rite involving tests and competitions between two rival groups, and designed to stimulate the creative forces of nature and to regenerate human society.[28] Although the *benandanti* had maintained that they were fighting for the Cross and "for faith in Christ," their ceremonial combats were only superficially Christianized.[29] Moreover, the *stregoni* were not accused of the usual crimes against the teachings of the Church; they were imputed to be responsible only for the destruction of harvests and the bewitchment of children. It is only in 1634

27. Ibid., p. 28.
28. On this mythico-ritual scenario, see Eliade, *La nostalgie des origines,* pp. 320ff.
29. Ginzburg, *I Benandanti,* p. 34.

(after 850 trials and denunciations presided over by the Inquisition of Aquileia and Concordia) that one meets for the first time an accusation charging the *stregoni* with guilt for celebrating the traditional diabolic sabbath. Nevertheless, the accusations of sorcery attested in northern Italy speak of no adoration of the Devil, but of a cult offered to Diana.[30]

As a result of these numerous trials, however, the *benandanti* began to conform to the demonological model that the Inquisition had so persistently attributed to them. At a given moment, it was no longer a question of what had traditionally constituted the cardinal point: *the fertility rite*. After 1600, the *benandanti* acknowledged only that they sought cures for victims of sorcerers. This avowal was not without danger, for the Inquisition considered the capacity for warding off evil as a clear proof of sorcery.[31] With time, the *benandanti*, having become more aware of their importance, multiplied the denunciations upon encountering people whom they themselves named as sorcerers. But despite this increased antagonism, they felt themselves unconsciously drawn toward the *streghe* and the *stregoni*. In 1618, a *benandante* acknowledged having been to a nocturnal sabbath presided over by the Devil; but he kept adding that this had been to obtain from him the power to heal.[32]

Finally, in 1634, after fifty years of inquisitional trials, the *benandanti* admitted that they and the sorcerers (*streghe* and *stregoni*) made common cause.[33] One of the accused made the following confession: having had his body anointed with a special unguent, he had gone to a sabbath where he had seen many sorcerers celebrate rites, dance, and engage in unrestrained sexual acts. He declared throughout, however, that the *benandanti* took no part in the orgy. Several years later, a *benandante* admitted having signed a pact with the Devil, abjuring Christ and the Christian faith, and having killed three children. Later trials then brought to light the inevitable elements of the already classic imagery of the witches' sabbath, the *benandanti* confessing that they frequented their dances, gave homage to the Devil, and kissed his rear end. One of the most dramatic confessions took place in 1644. The

30. It is only in 1532 that some of the initiates of Diana admitted under torture that they had profaned the Cross and the sacraments. See the documentation cited by Ginzburg, ibid., p. 36.
31. See ibid., pp. 87ff.
32. Ibid., p. 110.
33. Ibid., pp. 115ff.

accused made a meticulously detailed description of the Devil, told how he had given him his soul, and admitted having killed four children by bringing them bad fortune. But when he found himself alone in his cell with the episcopal vicar, the prisoner declared that his confession was false and that he was neither a *benandante* nor a *stregone*. The judges agreed that the prisoner "confesses whatever one suggests to him." The verdict is unknown to us, for the concerned party hanged himself in his cell. This was the last great trial brought against the *benandanti*.[34]

Let us look now more closely at the military character of the group, so important *before* the trials of the Inquisition. It is not a matter of an isolated example. We have cited above (§249) the case of an old Lithuanian from the seventeenth century who, with his companions, all transformed themselves into wolves, descended into Hell, and gave battle to sorcerers and the Devil, in order to reclaim the goods that had been stolen (cattle, wheat, and other fruits of the earth). Carlo Ginzburg has justly compared the *benandanti* and the Lithuanian werewolves with shamans, who descend, in ecstasy, into the subterranian world to assure the protection of their community.[35] One must also not forget the belief—general in northern Europe—that demonic forces are engaged in combat by dead warriors and the gods.[36]

Romanian popular traditions allow us to better understand the origin and function of this mythico-ritual scenario. Let us recall that the Romanian Church, like the other Orthodox churches, had no institution like that of the Inquisition. Thus, although heresies were not unknown to them, the persecution of sorcerers was neither massive nor systematic. I will limit my analysis to two terms that are decisive for our problem: *striga,* the Latin word for "sorcerer," and "Diana," the Roman goddess who had become the patroness of sorcerers in western Europe. In Romanian, *striga* has become *strigoï,* "sorcerers," whether they be living or dead (in the latter case, vampires). The

---

34. Ibid., pp. 148ff. However, as late as in 1661, the *benandanti* still had the courage to proclaim that they fought for the Christian faith against the *stregoni* (ibid., p. 115). J. B. Russell, *Witchcraft in the Middle Ages,* p. 212, finds certain traces of beliefs analogous to those of the *benandanti* in two cases of *maleficium* judged in Milan between 1384 and 1390.

35. Ginzburg, p. 40.

36. Cf., inter alia, Otto Höffler, *Verwandlungskulte, Volkssagen und Mythen* (Vienna, 1973), pp. 15, 234 and passim.

strigoï are born with the caul; when they reach maturity, they dress themselves in it and become invisible. They are said to be endowed with supernatural powers; for example, they can enter into houses with bolted doors, or play with impunity with wolves and bears. They give themselves over to all the misdeeds proper to sorcerers: they provoke epidemics among men and cattle, "subjugate" and disfigure people, bring on droughts by "subjugating" the rain, draw away the milk from cattle, and above all bring on bad fortune. They can transform themselves into monkeys, cats, wolves, horses, pigs, toads, and other animals. They are supposed to go abroad on certain nights, in particular on those of Saint George and Saint Andrew. Having returned home, they execute three pirouettes and recover their human form. Leaving their bodies, their souls bestride horses, brooms, or the thunder. The *strigoï* assemble together far from villages, in a given field or "at the end of the world, where not a blade of grass sprouts." Once assembled there, they assume their human form and *begin to engage in combat among themselves* with blows from cudgels, axes, scythes, and other instruments. The battle continues through the entire night, finishing with tears and a general reconciliation. They return exhausted, pale, not knowing what has happened to them, and then fall into a deep sleep.[37]

Unfortunately, one knows nothing as to the meaning and goal of these nocturnal battles. One thinks of the *benandanti,* and also of the *Wilde Heer,* the procession of the dead so common in central and eastern Europe. But the *benandanti* contested very specifically with the *striga,* while the Romanian *strigoï* fought among themselves and always ended their battles in tears and in a general reconciliation. As to the analogy with the *Wilde Heer,* it lacks the latter's most charac-

37. On the *strigoï,* see the rich documentation assembled by Ion Muşlea and Ovidiu Bîrlea, *Tipologia folclorului: Din răspunsurile la chestionarele lui B. P. Hasdeu* (Bucharest, 1970), pp. 224–70. Less frequent is the belief that the *strigoï* anoint themselves with a special unguent and go out through the chimney (pp. 248, 256). The deceased *strigoï* also gather together around midnight and fight amongst themselves with the same weapons as do their living counterparts (ibid., pp. 267ff.). As parallelled in many other European popular beliefs, garlic is considered the best defense against the dead or living *strigoï* (ibid., pp. 254ff., 268ff.). In the *Corrector* of Burchard of Worms (eleventh century), the defense is made to believe what certain women claim: that "they go out at night through closed doors and fly up into the clouds to do battle"; Russell, *Witchcraft,* p. 82. But we do not know whom these women fight against.

teristic trait: the horrible noise that terrorized the villagers. In any case, the example of the Romanian sorcerers illustrates the authenticity of a pre-Christian schema founded on oneiric voyages and an ecstatic ritual combat, a schema attested in many of the regions of Europe.

The history of Diana, goddess of ancient Dacia, is equally significant. It is highly probable that the name Diana had replaced the local name of an autochthonous Geto-Thracian goddess. But the archaism of the beliefs and rites relating to the Romanian Diana is beyond doubt. In effect, one can always suspect that among the peoples having Romance languages—Italian, French, Spanish, Portuguese—the medieval references touching on the cult and mythology of "Diana" reflect, on the whole, the opinions of lettered monks who were versed in Latin texts. One would not, however, be able to advance a hypothesis of this order when it comes to the history of Diana among the Romanians. The goddess's name has become *zîna* (<*dziana*) in Romanian, signifying "fairy." Moreover, there is another word that derives from the same root: *zînatec,* signifying "he who is heedless, flighty or crazy," that is to say, "taken" or possessed by Diana or the fairies.[38] Now, we have just observed (§304) the rapports, sometimes rather ambivalent, between the *zîne* and the *căluşari*. The *zîne* can be cruel, and it is imprudent to pronounce their name. One refers to them as "the Saints," "the Munificents," "the Rosalies," or simply as "they" in the feminine (*iele*). The fairies, who are immortal, have the air of beautiful girls, playful and fascinating. Dressed in white, their breasts bare, they are invisible by day. Provided with wings, they move about in the air, especially at night. They love to sing and dance, and wherever they dance the grasses of the fields look as if they were scorched by fire. They bring sickness upon those who see them dance, or who infringe upon certain interdictions, and these maladies can be cured only by the *căluşari*.[39]

38. The name of a special group of *zîne,* the *Sînziene,* probably derives from the Latin *Sanctae Dianae.* The *Sînzene,* rather benevolent fairies, have given their name to the important feast of Saint John the Baptist.

39. In the final analysis, the scenario actualized by the *căluşari* implies the *fusion of magico-religious ideas and techniques that are at once both opposed and complementary.* The astonishing persistence of this archaic scenario finds its most likely explanation in the fact that, pacified and reconciled, the "antagonistic" principles (sickness and death, health and fertility) are personified in one of the most exalting expressions of the primordial dyad of the female and the male: the fairy and the cathartic hero on his horse.

Thanks to their archaism, the Romanian documents are a major resource for our knowledge of European witchcraft. In the first place, there can no longer be any doubt as to the continuity of certain archaic rites and beliefs dealing above all with fertility and health. Secondly, these mythico-ritual scenarios implied a struggle between two groups of opposed although complementary forces, groups ritually personified by young men and women (*benandanti, striga, călușari*). Thirdly, the ceremonial struggle was sometimes followed by a reconciliation between the antithetical groups. Fourthly, this ritual bipartition of the collectivity implies a certain ambivalence, for, while expressing the process of life and cosmic fertility, one of the two rival groups always personifies its negative aspects. What is more, the personification of the negative principle can, according to the moment and the historical circumstances, be interpreted as a manifestation of *evil*.[40] Such seems to be what has happened in the case of the Rumanian *strigoï* and, to a lesser degree, among the *zîne,* the fairies who correspond to the "cortege of Diana." Under the constraints of the Inquisition, a similar interpretation took place concerning the *benandanti*. This process, thanks to the secular identification of the pre-Christian mythico-ritual survivals with satanic undertakings, and finally with heresy, has been much more complex in western Europe.

307. Martin Luther and the Reformation in Germany

In the religious and cultural history of western Europe, one of the most creative centuries was the one which preceded the intensification of the witch hunts. Its creativity resulted not only from the reforms brought about, despite numerous obstacles, by Martin Luther and John Calvin, but also because the period—which lasted approximately from Marsilio Ficino (1433–99) to Giordano Bruno (1548–1600)—is characterized by a series of discoveries (cultural, scientific, technological, geographical) which, without exception, took on a religious significance. There will be occasion to discuss the values and religious functions of the Neoplatonism that was reactualized by the Italian humanists, and also those of the new alchemy, the alchemical medicine of Paracelsus, and the heliocentrism of Copernicus and of Gior-

40. On the transformation of dichotomies and polarities in a religious dualism implying the idea of *evil,* see Eliade, *La nostalgie des origines,* pp. 345ff.

dano Bruno. But even a technological discovery such as printing has had important religious consequences: indeed, it played an essential role in the propagation and triumph of the Reformation. Lutheranism has been "from its beginning the child of book printing": with the help of this vehicle, Luther was able to transmit his message with force and precision from one end of Europe to the other.[41]

One is equally aware of the controversies of a theological order that were inspired by the discovery of America. But Christopher Columbus was already impressed by the eschatological character of his voyage. In "marvellous circumstances" (of which we know nothing), "God had shown his hand." Columbus considered his voyage as "an evident miracle." For it was not just a matter of the discovery of the "Indies," but of a transfigured world. "It is I whom God had chosen for his messenger, showing me on which side were to be found the new heaven and new earth of which the Lord had spoken through the mouth of Saint John in his Apocalypse, and of which Isaiah had made previous mention."[42] According to Columbus's calculations, the end of the world was due to occur in 155 years. But in the intervening years, thanks to the gold brought back from the "Indies," Jerusalem would be reconquered and the "Holy House" could be made "into the Holy Church."[43]

Like all his contemporaries, Martin Luther shared a number of ideas and beliefs common to the age. For example, he had no doubt of the terrible power of the Devil or of the necessity of burning witches, and he accepted the religious function of alchemy.[44] Like a great number

41. A. G. Dickens, *Reformation and Society in Sixteenth Century Europe*, p. 51: "For the first time in human history a great reading public judged the validity of revolutionary ideas through a mass-medium which used the vernacular languages together with the arts of the journalist and the cartoonist."

42. Letter to his Nurse, cited by Claude Kappler, *Monstres, Démons et merveilles à la fin du Moyen Age*, p. 108.

43. Letter to Pope Alexander VI, February 1502, trans. Claude Kappler, ibid., p. 109.

44. On the Devil, see the fragments of his *Commentary on the Epistle of Saint Paul to the Galatians*, reproduced in the anthology of A. C. Kors and Edward Peters, *Witchcraft in Europe*, pp. 195–201 (cf. ibid., pp. 202–12, several extracts from John Calvin's *The Institutes of the Christian Religion*). In one of his *Tabletalks*, Luther had said: "I would have no pity for witches: I would burn them all!" As for alchemy, again in his *Tabletalks* Luther acknowledges that it "pleases him much." "It pleases me not only for the numerous possibilities of utilization which there are in the decoc-

of theologians, of the religious, and of the laity who practiced a spiritual discipline (cf. §§299–300), Martin Luther found his "mystic"
consolation in the *Theologia deutsch,* a text which he ranked immediately after the Bible and Saint Augustine.[45] He had read and meditated
upon many books, and came quite soon under the influence of William
of Ockham. But his religious genius cannot be explained by the spirit
of his century. On the contrary, it is the personal experiences of Martin
Luther which have in great part contributed to the radical modification
of the period's spiritual orientation. Much as in the case of Muhammad, his biography helps us to understand the sources of his religious
creativity.

Born 10 November 1483 at Eisleben (Thuringia), Martin Luther enrolled in 1501 at the University of Erfurt and earned his licentiate in
1505. Some months later, during a terrible storm, he just missed being
struck by lightning and made the vow to become a monk. In that same
year, he entered the Augustinian monastery at Erfurt. Despite his
father's opposition, Martin did not renounce his decision. Ordained a
priest in April 1507, he taught moral philosophy at the universities of
Wittenberg and Erfurt. In November 1510, on the occasion of a trip to
Rome, he was dismayed at the decadence of the Church. Two years
later, after his doctorate in theology, he obtained the chair in holy
scripture at Wittenberg and opened his course with a commentary on
Genesis.

But his religious restlessness increased apace with his reflections on
the wrath and justice of God the Father, the Yahweh of the Old Testament. It was only in 1513 or 1514 that he discovered the true sense of
the expression "the justice of God": it is the act by which God makes
a just man; in other words, the act by which the believer receives,
thanks to his faith, the justice obtained by the sacrifice of Christ. This

---

tion of metals, in the distillation and sublimation of herbs and liquors, but also on
account of the allegory and secret significance, which is extremely seductive, on the
subject of the resurrection of the dead on the last day. For, just as in a forge the fire
extracts and separates one substance from the other parts, and removes the spirit, the
life, the sap, the force, while the impure materials, the dregs, remain at the bottom,
like a dead and worthless body, just so does God on the day of judgment separate all
things by fire, the just from the impious" (*Tischreden,* as cited by Montgomery,
"L'astrologie et l'alchimie luthérienne à l'époque de la Réforme," p. 337).

45. The edition of this anonymous work, written in Germany around 1350, was
moreover his first printed book.

interpretation of Saint Paul—"the just live by faith" (Romans 1:12)—constitutes the foundation of the theology of Martin Luther. "I felt that I was born anew," he said much later, "and that I had entered into Paradise by its open gates." In meditating on the Epistle to the Romans—according to him, "the most important document of the New Testament"—Luther understood the impossibility of obtaining justification (that is, an adequate relation with God) by his own works. On the contrary, man is justified and saved solely by faith in Christ. Like faith, salvation is accorded gratuitously by God. Luther elaborated this discovery in his course of 1515, developing what he called a "theology of the Cross."

His activity as a reformer began 31 October 1517; on that day, Martin Luther affixed his ninety-five theses against Indulgences[46] on the door of the church of the castle of Wittenberg, attacking the doctrinal and cultural deviations of the Church. In April 1518, he wrote respectfully to Pope Leo X. But he was summoned to Rome to exculpate himself. Luther asked Frederick the Wise, the Elector of Saxony, to allow him to be judged in Germany. The confrontation took place at Augsburg in October 1518 before Cardinal Cajetan. But the Augustinian monk refused to retract. For him, as for a great number of other prelates and theologians,[47] the matter of Indulgences had no dogmatic justification. In the following months, the conflict grew dangerously. At Leipzig in 1519, Luther contested the principle of papal primacy, declaring that the pope must also, like others, submit to the authority of the Bible. The response, in the form of the bull *Exsurge Domini,* came on 15 June 1520: Luther was ordered to retract in six months, under penalty of excommunication. The accused publically threw a copy of this bull into the fire, and published, one after another, four books which rank among the most brilliant and most important of his total work. In the manifesto *To the Christian Nobility of the German Nation* (August 1520), he rejected the supremacy of the pope over the

46. The Church was able to grant Indulgences by drawing on the "treasure of merits" accumulated by Christ, the Virgin, and the saints. The practice became popular at the time of the First Crusade, when in 1095 Pope Urban II announced that the crusaders would benefit from the temporal remission of their sins. But it was above all in Luther's time that certain unscrupulous ecclesiastics abused this practice, letting it be believed that with the Indulgences one obtained the permission to sin.

47. Innocent III had already tried to severely reduce this practice. But it is Pius V who in 1567 put an end to the abuses of the Indulgences.

councils, the distinction between clergy and laity, and the clergy's monopoly in the study of Scripture; to this end he recalled that all Christians, thanks to their baptism, are priests. Two months later, addressing himself to theologians, he published his *On the Babylonian Captivity of the Church,* attacking the clergy and the abuse of the sacraments. Luther accepted only three sacraments: baptism, the Eucharist, and confession. And later he also renounced confession. Thanks to the protection of the Elector of Saxony, he remained hidden in the Wartburg castle (1521), and did not return to Wittenberg until the following year.[48]

The definitive break with Rome was thus consummated, a break which could have been avoided if the Emperor Charles V had insisted before the Curia that it effect on all fronts the reforms demanded. Actually, as Steven Ozment has put it, the laity, as well as a number of the monks, "shared a common experience of unresolved religious oppression." The pamphlet presented in March 1521—*Grievances of the Holy Roman Empire and Especially the Entire German Nation*—expressed the resentments of the aristocratic class and the bourgeoisie, and repeated Luther's criticisms of the pope, the German high prelates, the Church, and the clergy in general.[49]

After his return to Wittenberg, the reformer had to preach against a certain "prophetic" movement and several innovations which had been effected during his absence. In the following years, he had to face other difficulties. After the peasant revolts which broke out in southern Germany in 1524, in less than a month, Luther published his *Against the Criminal Hordes and Pillaging of the Peasants* (1525), a pamphlet—diffused throughout the entire land—which was, and still is, much criticized.[50] It was during these peasant revolts that Luther married a former nun, Katherine van Bora, who bore him six children. It is also during this same period that he had his polemic with Erasmus (cf. §308). The organization of the Reformation proceeded with the help of Melanchthon (1497–1560) and other collaborators. Luther insisted on the importance of hymns chanted in the course of the service, and

48. During this period he translated the New Testament into German (the complete translation of the Bible was finished in 1534), and wrote *On Monastic Vows,* demanding clerical marriage and the freedom for monks to renounce their vows.

49. Ozment, *The Age of Reform,* p. 223.

50. The Peasant Wars (or Jacqueries) were suppressed with extreme cruelty by the coalition of princes.

wrote a number of them himself. As a result of his interpretation of the Mass, in which he recognized the real presence of Christ, a dispute broke out with the Swiss reformer Zwingli, the latter accepting only a symbolic presence.

Luther's last years were very difficult, above all because of political events. He had to accept the protection of the temporal power, for he preferred force to anarchy and chaos. He did not cease to attack the advocates of a radical Reform. In the final analysis, he elaborated in an ever more dogmatic manner the theology and cult of his evangelical movement, which had become the Lutheran Church. He died on 18 February 1546.

308. Luther's theology. The polemic with Erasmus

In a letter of June 1522, Martin Luther wrote: "I do not admit that my doctrine can be judged by anyone, even by the angels. One who does not receive my doctrine cannot come to salvation." Jacques Maritain cites this text[51] as a proof of pride and egocentrism. It is, however, a matter of a reaction specific to one *who did not dare to doubt* his own divine election or prophetic mission. Having received the revelation that it is the absolute freedom of God the Father which judges, condemns, and saves according to his own decision, Luther could no longer tolerate any other interpretation. His violent intolerance reflects the zeal of Yahweh and the latter's jealousy with regard to humankind. The revelation which so gratified Luther—that of justification, and thus of salvation, by faith alone, *sola fide*—is definitive and unalterable; even the angels cannot judge it.

This revelation, which had changed his life, was to be continually explicated and defended in Luther's theology. And indeed, he was a brilliant and erudite theologian.[52] Shortly before his theses against Indulgences, he attacked the theology of the end of the Middle Ages in

---

51. *Sämtliche Werke* (Erlangen, 1826–57), vol. 26, p. 144; J. Maritain, *Trois Réformateurs* (1925), p. 20. See ibid., a fragment from Moehler according to which "Luther's self was in his own opinion the center around which all humanity should gravitate; he made himself the universal man, in whom all should find their model."

52. Between 1509 and 1517 he had closely studied Aristotle, Saint Augustine, the Church Fathers, and the works of the great theologians of the Middle Ages.

his *Disputation against Scholastic Theology* (4 September 1517). According to the teaching of the medieval Church, illustrated above all by Thomas Aquinas, the faithful who do good deeds in a state of grace collaborate in their own salvation. Furthermore, the numerous disciples of Ockham considered that reason and conscience, being *gifts of God,* were not annulled by original sin; therefore, whoever practiced good according to their natural moral tendency received grace as recompense. For the Ockhamites, such a belief in no way implied Pelagianism (cf. above, §§255ff.), for, in the final reckoning, it is always God who wills man's salvation.

In his *Disputation against Scholastic Theology,* Luther vigorously attacked this doctrine. By its own nature, man's will is not free to do good. After the fall, one can no longer speak of ''free will,'' for that which henceforth dominates man is his absolute egocentrism and the furious pursuit of his own satisfactions. It is not always a question of immoral tendencies or actions; sometimes man seeks what is good and noble, practices religion, and tries to draw close to God. Yet even these actions are culpable, for their source is the same egolatry that Luther regarded as the fundamental model for all human activity (outside of grace).[53]

Luther equally condemned the *Ethics* of Aristotle, according to which the moral virtues are secured by education. In the final analysis, he saw in scholastic theology a new Pelagianism. For him, the good—whether it be accomplished in, or outside of, the state of grace—has never contributed to the salvation of the soul. From the autumn of 1517 (the season of his *Disputation*) on, Luther continually returned to the explanation of the *sola fide.* His insistence was not so much on the dogmatic content of faith; it was *his experience of faith* in itself that mattered, a *fiducia* naïve and total, like that of children.

As to the famous harmony between reason and faith, Luther considered it impossible, and included among the pagans those who affirmed it. Reason had nothing in common with the domain of faith. As he wrote later, the articles of faith are ''not against dialectical truth [Aristotelian logic], but rather outside, under, above, below, around, and beyond it.''[54]

---

53. See the texts assembled by B. A. Gerrish, ''De Libero Arbitrio,'' p. 188 and n. 10.

54. Cited by Ozment, *The Age of Reform,* p. 238.

Luther returned again to the fundamental theme of his theology—justification by faith—in responding to the criticisms formulated by Erasmus in his *De Libero Arbitrio*. The confrontation between these two great minds is at once significant, dispiriting, and exemplary. Erasmus (1469–1536) had for a long time attacked the abuses and corruption of the Church, insisting on the urgent need for reforms. What is more, he had reacted with sympathy to Luther's initial efforts.[55] But as a good Christian and sincere humanist, Erasmus refused to contribute to the breakup of the Christian community; he loathed war, verbal violence, and religious intolerance. He called for a radical reform of western Christianity and pronounced himself not only against Indulgences, the unworthiness of priests, the immorality of bishops and cardinals, and the imposture of monks, but also against the scholastic method and the obscurantism of the theologians. Erasmus believed in the need for a more rational education, and repeatedly recalled the great profit which Christianity could draw from the assimilation of classical culture.[56] His ideal was peace such as Christ had preached it: that alone could assure collaboration between the nations of Europe.

On 31 August 1523, Erasmus wrote to Ulrich Zwingli: "I believe I have taught nearly all that Luther taught, but not so harshly, and I have abstained from certain paradoxes and enigmas."[57] Although he did not accept certain of Luther's ideas, he had written letters in his favor, all the while knowing that these letters would be published.[58] When Luther's Theses were declared heretical, Erasmus retorted that an error is not necessarily a heresy,[59] and asked Catholic theologians to respond to Luther's interpretations rather than condemn them. Because he proclaimed the necessity of dialogue, Erasmus was accused—first by Luther, then by Rome—of "neutralism," indeed of a lack of

55. See several references and citations to this effect in Roland H. Bainton, *Erasmus of Christendom*, pp. 153ff. Erasmus also indicated his adherence in his *Letters* and in works that were in the course of preparation or reprinting.

56. See the texts summarized and commented upon in Bainton, ibid., pp. 113–114.

57. Gerrish, "De Libero Arbitrio," p. 191. The "enigmas" were Luther's famous affirmations that the works of the saints belonged to the sphere of sin, that freedom of choice is an empty name, that man can be justified by faith alone (ibid.).

58. See the texts cited by Bainton, *Erasmus*, pp. 156ff. Erasmus had even introduced passages that reflected some of Luther's criticisms in the new editions of his New Testament and *Ratio;* cf. ibid.

59. Cf. Gerrish, p. 191, n. 38.

244 RELIGION, MAGIC, HERMETIC TRADITIONS

courage. It is an accusation which was possibly true on the eve of a new and terrible religious war, when the sincerity of adherence to an article of faith was often enough publicly tested by martyrdom. But Erasmus's ideal—reciprocal tolerance and dialogue aimed at mutual understanding and the rediscovery of a common charismatic source—regained an almost touching actuality in the ecumenical movement of the last quarter of the twentieth century.

After many equivocations, Erasmus gave way to the pressures of Rome and agreed to criticize Luther. Moreover, he felt himself to be more and more removed from the new theology of Wittenberg. Still, he does not appear to have been in any great hurry. Completed in 1523, *De Libero Arbitrio* was not sent to the printer until August 1524 (the first copies came out in September). The criticism is rather moderate. Erasmus concentrates on Luther's affirmation that free will is in fact *a fiction*. In effect, while defending his Theses against the bull *Exsurge Domini*, Luther had written: "For I was wrong in saying that free choice before grace is a reality only in name. I should have said simply: 'free choice is in reality a fiction, or a name without reality.' For no one has it in his own power to think a good or bad thought, but everything (as Wyclif's article condemned at Constance rightly teaches) happens by absolute necessity."[60]

Erasmus defined his position clearly: "By free choice in this place we mean a power of the human will by which a man can apply himself to the things which lead to eternal salvation, or turn away from them."[61] For Erasmus, freedom of choice between good and evil was the condition *sine qua non* of human responsibility. "If the will had not been free, sin could not have been imputed, for sin would cease to be sin if it were not voluntary."[62] What is more, if man were not free to choose, God would be responsible for evil actions as well as good.[63] At several points, Erasmus insists on the decisive importance of divine grace. Man does not collaborate in his salvation, but as a little child learns to walk with the help of his father, so a person of faith learns to choose the good and avoid evil.

60. Cited by Erasmus, *De Libero Arbitrio* (*On the Freedom of the Will*, p. 64). We make use of the last translation with commentary by E. Gordon Rupp, in *Luther and Erasmus: Free Will and Salvation*.

61. *On the Freedom of the Will*, p. 47.

62. Ibid., p. 50.

63. Ibid., p. 53.

Luther responded in his *De Servo Arbitrio* (1525), a work for which he maintained great affection all his life. He recognized at the outset "the disgust, anger, and contempt" which Erasmus's work had inspired in him.[64] The response, four times the length of *De Libero Arbitrio*, is written with verve and vehemence, and theologically it goes beyond Erasmus's horizon. Luther reproached him for his preoccupations with universal peace. "You wish, like a peacemaker, to bring *our* battle to an end." But for Luther the matter was one of "a serious, vital, eternal truth, so fundamental that it must be maintained and defended at the price even of life itself, even if the entire world was not only thrown into tumult and combat, but was torn to pieces and reduced to nothing."[65] He then returned, with great haste but also with humor and sarcasm, to the defense of his theology.

Erasmus replied to him in a large work, *Hyperaspites*, in which he did not conceal his irritation and resentment. But the reformer no longer took the trouble to refute him. He was not mistaken: the tumult increased around him; in fact, the wars of religion had begun.

309. Zwingli, Calvin, and the Catholic Reformation

On 11 October 1531, the Swiss reformer Ulrich Zwingli fell, beside numerous companions, in the Battle of Kappel.[66] For several years, he had implanted the Reformation at Zurich and in other cities. Thanks to Zwingli, Zurich enjoyed a prestige equal to that of Wittenberg. But threatened with complete isolation, the Catholic cantons undertook a campaign against the Zurich forces. The former, with their greater

64. *De Servo Arbitrio,* translation and commentary by Philip S. Watson, in *Luther and Erasmus: Free Will and Salvation,* p. 103.

65. Ibid., pp. 112ff.

66. Born in 1489 near Zurich, Zwingli studied at Basle, Berne, and Vienna before being ordained a priest in 1506. He admired Luther, but did not consider himself a Lutheran, for he envisaged a still more radical Reformation. In 1522, he secretly married a widow, who bore him four children. The following year, Zwingli published his Sixty-seven Theses (*Schlussreden*), proclaiming the Gospel as the only theologically valid source; in 1525 appeared the first Protestant manifesto, the publication of his *Commentary on the True and False Religion.* The Council of Zurich accepted the Reformation: the Latin Mass was replaced by the service of the Eucharist in German; the images disappeared from the churches; the monasteries were secularized.

numbers and military superiority, were assured of victory. Zwingli's death arrested the expansion of the Reformation in Switzerland and fixed, until the beginning of the nineteenth century, the country's confessional boundaries. However, thanks to his successor, Henry Bullinger, Zwingli's work was continued and consolidated.

Zwingli is the author of several treatises, having written on Providence, Baptism, the Eucharist, and various other topics. It is above all the interpretation of the Eucharist which shows the Swiss reformer's originality. It is also because of this interpretation that it was impossible to realize a union with the movement led by Luther.[67] Zwingli insisted on the *spiritual presence* of Christ in the heart of the believer receiving the sacrament. Without faith, the Eucharist has no value. The formula "This is my body . . ." must be understood symbolically, as a commemoration of the sacrifice of Christ, which fortifies faith in redemption.

Luther was justly envious of the political liberties of the Swiss. But in Switzerland also, the religious Reformation had to take the political authority into account. Zwingli considered himself, with reason, to be more "radical" than Luther. But in Zurich no less than at Wittenberg, religious liberty encouraged extremist radical tendencies. For Zwingli, the hardest and most moving confrontation took place with Conrad Grebel, the founder of the Anabaptist movement (its name was provided by its adversaries). Grebel denied the validity of the baptism of children.[68] According to him, this sacrament could be administered only to adults, and more precisely to those who had freely chosen to imitate the life of Christ.[69] Zwingli attacked this doctrine in four treatises, but without great success. The first "rebaptism" was performed on 21 January 1528. In March, the civil authorities banned this heresy, and four Anabaptists were executed. Arrested in 1526, Grebel died the following year.

Despite persecutions,[70] Anabaptism spread, for the most part in

67. On this controversy, see Ozment, *The Age of Reform*, pp. 334ff.

68. Moreover, this baptism is not attested in the Gospels. By now, the respect for the unique and absolute authority of the Bible was generally held by the reformed communities.

69. From which comes the term "anabaptist," however improper it may be, for the converts did not recognize the sacramental value of the first baptism.

70. Historians have estimated the number of Anabaptists executed between 1525 and 1618 at between 850 and 5,000. They were burned, decapitated, and drowned; cf. Ozment, *The Age of Reform*, p. 332.

Switzerland and southern Germany after 1530. With time, this "radical Reformation" divided up into several groups, among which were the "Spiritualists" such as Paracelsus, Sebastian Franck, and Valentine Weigel.

Like Luther and Zwingli, John Calvin had to defend his theology against the Anabaptists.[71] Born in 1509 at Noyon, he studied in Paris at the Collège Montaigu (1523–28) and published his first book in 1532 (a commentary on Seneca's *De clementia*). Upon coming to know of the writings of Luther, his passion for humanism gave way to theology. Calvin was probably converted in 1533, and in 1536 he took refuge in Geneva. Named pastor, he applied himself fervently to the organization of the Reformation. However, after two years he was expelled by the city council. Calvin then established himself at Strasbourg, where the great humanist and theologian Martin Bucer (1491–1551) had invited him. It is at Strasbourg that Calvin experienced the best period of his life. He learned much, thanks to Bucer's friendship, and published in 1539 a revised edition of *The Institutes of the Christian Religion*[72] and, in 1540, a commentary on the Epistle to the Romans. Also in 1540, he married Idelette de Bure, the widow of an Anabaptist convert. The situation at Geneva became aggravated, however, and the cantonal council pleaded with him to come back. After ten months of hesitation, Calvin agreed to return in September 1541, and remained at Geneva until his death in May 1564.

Despite certain opposition, Calvin succeeded at Geneva in imposing his conception of the Reformation: the Bible is the sole authority in deciding all problems of faith and of the organization of the Church. Although he was constantly engaged in political, ecclesiastical, and theological controversies, Calvin's literary productivity was prodigious. In addition to a considerable correspondence, he wrote commentaries on the Old and New Testaments, a great number of treatises and pamphlets concerned with different aspects of the Reformation, sermons on the Epistles of Saint Paul, and more. His masterpiece, however, remains the *Institutes of the Christian Religion,* a work remarkable no less for its theology than for its literary perfection. The definitive edition of the Latin text appeared in 1559.[73]

71. For the first time, all the documentation has been gathered and analyzed in Willem Balke, *Calvin and the Anabaptist Radicals*.

72. Completed in France in 1535, the *Institutes* were continually revised and enlarged by Calvin in numerous later editions.

73. A painful episode was the execution in 1553 of Michael Servetus, a competent

Calvin's theology does not constitute a system. It is rather a summa, with commentary, on biblical thought. Calvin explores and reflects upon the two Testaments, read and understood at many points in the light of Saint Augustine. One also recognizes the influence of Luther, although it is not cited. Calvin discusses, in a quite personal manner, the essential problems of his theology: knowledge of God as Creator and Lord, the Decalogue and the Faith (according to the symbol of the Apostles), justification by faith and the merits of works, predestination and the providence of God, the two valid sacraments (baptism and the Eucharist), but also prayer, the ecclesiastical powers, the civil government. For Calvin, man never ceases to be a sinner; his "good works" become acceptable only through divine grace. The distance between the transcendent God and the human creature can be abolished by the revelation conserved in the Scriptures. Man, however, cannot know God in Himself, but only as the Lord *showing himself to humans*. The two sacraments constitute the means by which Christ communicates himself to the believer.

One may agree with the view of Calvin as the least original among the great theologians of the Reformation. For already, since the dogmatic stiffening of the later Luther, theological creativity loses its primacy in the reformed Churches. What matters is the organization of individual liberty and the reform of social institutions, beginning with public education. Luther had revealed—and had illustrated this principle in his own life—the importance of the creative capacity of the individual. More than the "human dignity" exalted by the humanists, it is the individual liberty to reject every authority outside of God that has made possible—by a slow process of desacralization—the "modern world" such as it emerges in the period of the Enlightenment, and defines itself with the French Revolution and the triumph of science and technology.

As for Calvin, he not only contributed, more than Luther, to the social and political progress of his Church, but he demonstrated by his example the function and theological importance of political activity. In fact, he anticipated the series of political theologies in vogue in the

---

Spanish doctor but amateur theologian, who had vigorously criticized Calvin; cf. Williams, *The Radical Reformation,* pp. 605ff. "For many, Calvin's role in the death of Servetus attached the same reactionary stigma to Protestantism that the Inquisition's later treatment of Galileo brought to the Catholic Church"; Ozment, p. 369.

second half of the twentieth century: theology of work, theology of liberation, theology of anticolonialism, etc. In this perspective the religious history of western Europe after the sixteenth century allows itself to become more integrated with the political, social, economic, and cultural history of the continent.

The last of the important Reforms, that effected by the Council of Trent (1545–63),[74] is quite ambiguous. Begun too late, and obsessed by the expansion of the evangelical movements, the Reform of Trent develops under the pressure of contemporary history and pursues above all the consolidation of the political power of the Holy See. However, numerous theologians and high-ranking members of the hierarchy had long demanded true reforms, and above all the limitation of the powers of the pope and the restoration of the authority of the bishops. Several years before the opening of the Council of Trent, and at the insistence of the Emperor Charles V, discussions took place at Regensburg in April 1541 between Protestant (among them Bucer and Melanchthon) and Catholic (John Eck, Johann Groper, etc.) theologians. In several weeks, the two parties reached an accord on certain essential problems (for example, the nature of salvation with respect to "double justification").

Unfortunately, the Council rendered this rapprochement useless. The pope and his Jesuit advisors were preoccupied with reforms designed to prevent the appearance of a new Luther, Zwingli, or Calvin in the Catholic lands. The Council's constitution was such that only the propositions of the pope were acceptable. As was to be expected, the reactionary tendency was triumphant. However, the Council did reestablish the authority of the bishops (on condition of living in their dioceses), reacted vigorously against the immorality and concubinage of the priests, and took important decisions in matters concerning the theological instruction of the clergy. More than this, the Council encouraged corrections of a cultural order, designed to satisfy the needs of the laity for a more authentic religious life.

What one now calls Post-Tridentine Catholicism is in part the result of such cleansing measures, but also of the work of several great mystics and apostles. The traditions of medieval mysticism and of the *devotio moderna* experienced a new flight with Theresa of Avila

74. The first session lasted from March 1545 to winter 1547; the second from May 1551 to May 1552; the last from April 1561 to December 1563.

(1515–82) and Saint John of the Cross (1542–91). The experience of the *unio mystica* expressed by Saint Theresa in terms of a marriage between the soul and Jesus gained an exceptional prestige,[75] despite the suspicions of the Inquisition. But it is above all Ignatius of Loyola (1491–1556), the founder of the Society of Jesus, who contributed to the success—moral, religious, and political—of the Counter-Reformation.[76] Although he had had mystical experiences, of which he has spoken, it was, according to a famous expression, an apostolate of "contemplation in action" that Ignatius of Loyola chose. It is above all for his works—orphanages, homes for former prostitutes, secondary schools and colleges, missions on three continents, etc.—that he has been admired.

The essentials of Ignatius of Loyola's doctrine can be summarized as follows: absolute obedience to God, and thus to His terrestrial representative, the Sovereign Pontiff, and to the General of the Society; the certitude that prayers, meditations, and the faculty of discernment which results from them can modify the human condition; the confidence that God encourages every effort to convert people, and thus also every effort to improve oneself; the assurance that good works—above all actions undertaken to help those who are in need—are favored by God.

Compared to the theologies of Luther and Calvin, that of Ignatius of Loyola is rather optimistic. This is possibly to be explained by Ignatius's mystical experiences, which oriented his method of contemplation and also the function and value which he attributed to action. The

75. We will return to these problems in a final chapter dedicated to the morphology and comparison of archaic, Eastern, and Western mystical experiences.

76. Born at Loyola in 1491, Ignatius had a romantic and adventurous youth. Gravely wounded during the Franco-Spanish War of 1521, he read several religious books, among which were the *Imitation of Christ* and the biographies of Saints Francis and Dominic. He decided to imitate them. On the occasion of his first pilgrimage to Montserrat, in March 1522, he made the vow at the altar of the Virgin to dedicate himself to the service of God. From then on, Ignatius led a life of extreme asceticism, fasting sometimes for an entire week, always going about on foot and in rags, and dedicating seven hours a day to prayer. After having learned Latin in an elementary school in Barcelona, he came to Paris in February 1528 and enrolled himself at the Collège Montaigu; he earned his licentiate in 1534. Ignatius obtained permission to establish, with nine companions, a new order, which was confirmed in 1540. At first limited to sixty members, the Society of Jesus counted more than a thousand at the time of Ignatius's death in 1556.

blind obedience to God's representative on earth betrays its mystical origin; one can compare it to the veneration of the Imâm in Shî'ism (§273) and of the spiritual master (*gurudev*) in Hinduism; there too, such veneration is justified by a mystical theology.

The religious genius of Ignatius of Loyola expresses itself above all, however, in his *Spiritual Exercises,* a short treatise which he began to write after his first mystical vision at Mannèse, near Montserrat. It is a practical manual, providing day by day indications of the prayers and meditations useful for one (not necessarily a member of the Society) who undertakes a four-week retreat. The work continues and prolongs an old Christian contemplative tradition. Even the celebrated exercise of the first week, involving the attempt of the imagination to compose in a concrete and living manner a landscape or an historical episode, has twelfth-century precedents. But Ignatius develops the method of this visualization with a rigor that recalls certain Indian meditative techniques. The retreatant learns to sacralize the space in which he finds himself by projecting it, through the force of the imagination, into a space where a sacred history *unfolds itself* (in the present!). He must *see* the old Jerusalem of Jesus, he must *follow with his own eyes* Joseph and the Virgin on the way towards Bethlehem. And so on. Even when he eats, he can see himself eating with the Apostles.

What must be emphasized here is the precision and severity of the *Spiritual Exercises;* every devotional impulse is carefully controlled. The retreatant's progressive purification prepares him for no *unio mystica.* The objective of the retreat is to form spiritual athletes—and to send them out into the world.

310. Humanism, Neoplatonism, and Hermeticism during the Renaissance

Having assembled manuscripts of Plato and Plotinus over a number of years, Cosimo de' Medici entrusted their translation to the great Florentine humanist Marsilio Ficino (1433–99). But around 1460, Cosimo obtained a manuscript of the *Corpus hermeticum* and asked Ficino to make him an immediate translation of it. At this period, Ficino had not yet begun his translation of Plato. But he nonetheless put the *Dialogues* aside and devoted himself with great urgency to the translation of the Hermetic treatises. In 1463, a year before Cosimo's death, these translations were completed. The *Corpus hermeticum* was thus the first Greek text to have been translated and published by Marsilio Ficino.[77] This demonstrates the prestige attached to the figure of Hermes Trismegistus, considered to be the author of the Hermetic treatises (cf. §209).

Ficino's Latin translations—above all the *Corpus hermeticum,* Plato, and Plotinus—played an important role in the religious history of the Renaissance: they enabled Neoplatonism to triumph at Florence, and aroused a passionate interest in Hermeticism all over Europe. The first Italian humanists—from Petrarch (1304–74) to Lorenzo Valla (ca. 1405–57)—had already inaugurated a new religious orientation by rejecting scholastic theology and returning to the Church Fathers. The humanists considered that as lay Christians and good classicists, they could study and understand better than the clergy the connections between Christianity on the one hand, and the pre-Christian conceptions concerning human nature and the divine on the other. As Charles Trinkaus has remarked, this new valorization of *Homo triumphans* is not necessarily of pagan origin; it is rather inspired by the patristic tradition.[78]

With the Neoplatonism inspired by Ficino, Pico della Mirandola (1463–94), and Egidio di Viterbo (1469–1532), the exaltation of the human condition gained a new dimension. But it did so without renouncing the Christian context. In creating the world, God granted man mastery of the Earth, and it was "through man's actions as a god on earth that the creative work of history and civilization was to be accomplished."[79] But the apotheosis of man, a tendency characteristic of the humanists, drew its inspiration more and more from a para-Christian Neoplatonism and from Hermeticism.

Ficino and Pico della Mirandola evidently had no doubt as to the orthodoxy of their faith. Already in the second century, the apologist Lactantius considered Hermes Trismegistus as a sage inspired by God,

---

77. Frances A. Yates, *Giordano Bruno and the Hermetic Tradition,* pp. 12–13. Until then, only one Hermetic treatise, the *Asclepius,* was accessible in Latin.

78. Cf. Charles Trinkaus, *"In Our Image and Likeness,"* 1, pp. xix ff., 41ff. (Petrarch), 150ff. (Lorenzo Valla); see above all the texts reproduced on pp. 341ff., 381ff. The full realization of the personality does not always imply an ideal borrowed from paganism; it is to be explained above all by the renewal of a theology of grace; cf. ibid., pp. xx, 46ff.

79. Ibid., p. xxii.

and he interpreted certain Hermetic prophesies as having been accomplished through the birth of Jesus Christ. This harmony between Hermeticism and Hermetic magic on the one hand, and Christianity on the other, was reaffirmed by Ficino.[80] Pico considered that *Magia* and *Cabala* confirmed the divinity of Christ.[81] The universal belief in a venerable *prisca theologia*[82] and in the famous "ancient theologians"—Zoroaster, Moses, Hermes Trismegistus, David, Orpheus, Pythagoras, Plato—knew now an exceptional vogue.

One can decipher in this phenomenon the profound dissatisfaction left by scholasticism and the medieval conceptions of man and the universe. It was a reaction against what one could call a "provincial" Christianity, that is, one that was purely *western,* as well as an aspiration to a universal, transhistorical, and "primordial" religion. Pico learned Hebrew to initiate himself into the Kabbala, a revelation which, according to him, preceded and explained the Old Testament. Pope Alexander VI commissioned at the Vatican a fresco swarming with Hermetic (that is, Egyptian) images and symbols. Ancient Egypt, the mythic Persia of Zoroaster, and the "secret doctrine" of Orpheus revealed "mysteries" that passed beyond the confines of Judeo-Christianity and the classical world recently rediscovered by the humanists. It was, in fact, a matter of certainty that one could rediscover the primordial revelations of Egypt and Asia, and demonstrate their common ground and their single source. (One meets the same enthusiasm and the same hope, although in more modest proportions, in the nineteenth century, after the "discovery" of Sanskrit and of the "primordiality" of the Vedas and Upanishads.)

For nearly two centuries, Hermeticism obsessed innumerable theologians and philosophers, believers no less than nonbelievers. If Giordano Bruno (1548–1600) greeted the discoveries of Copernicus with so much enthusiasm, it is because he thought that heliocentrism had a profound religious and magical significance. While he was in England, Bruno prophesied the imminent return of the magical religion

80. See, inter alia, D. P. Walker, *Spiritual and Demonic Magic: From Ficino to Campanella,* pp. 30ff.

81. Among the theses of Pico condemned by Innocent VII, one finds the celebrated affirmation: "Nulla est scientia que non magis certificet de divinitate Christi quam magia et cabala." Cf. Yates, *Giordano Bruno,* pp. 84ff.

82. Cf. D. P. Walker, *The Ancient Theology,* esp. pp. 22ff. ("Orpheus the Theologian").

of the ancient Egyptians such as it was described in the *Asclepius*. Giordano Bruno felt himself superior to Copernicus, for while the latter understood his theory only as a mathematician, Bruno could interpret the Copernican theory himself as the hieroglyph of divine mysteries.[83]

But Giordano Bruno pursued a different end: he had identified Hermes with Egyptian religion, which was considered to be the most ancient, and consequently he founded his religious universalism on the role of Egyptian magic. However, a number of sixteenth-century authors hesitated at resorting to Hermetic magic, which was now declared a heresy. Such is the case of Lefèvre d'Étaples (1460–1537), who introduced Hermeticism into France: he separated the bulk of the *Corpus Hermeticum* from the treatise *Asclepius*. The Neoplatonist Symphorien Champier (1472–1539) even tried to demonstrate that the author of the magical passages of the *Asclepius* was not Hermes but Apuleius.[84] In sixteenth-century France, as well as elsewhere in Europe, the exemplary value of Hermeticism derived, first and above all, from its religious universalism, a source for the restoration of peace and concord. Philippe de Mornay, a Protestant author, sought in Hermeticism a means to escape the terrors of the wars of religion. In his *De la vérité de la religion chrétienne* (1581), Mornay recalled that according to Hermes, "God is one . . . so that to Him alone belongs the name of Father and of Good. . . . Alone and himself All; without Name, and higher than any name."[85]

As J. Dagens has written, "this influence of Hermeticism touched the Protestants and the Catholics alike, favoring among both of them the most irenic tendencies."[86] The venerable religion revealed by Hermes and shared in the beginning by all humanity could, it was felt,

83. See Yates, *Giordano Bruno*, pp. 154ff. and passim. An erudite Hellenist, Isaac Casaubon, demonstrated in 1614 that the *Corpus Hermeticum* was a collection of quite late texts—not anterior to the second or third century of our era (cf. §209). But the fabulous prestige of the "Egyptian mysteries" continued to haunt the imagination of the European intelligentsia under a new form: the "mystery of hieroglyphics."

84. Yates, pp. 172ff. On Hermeticism in sixteenth-century France, see also Walker, *The Ancient Theology*, chap. 3.

85. Cited by Yates, p. 177 (in French). See also Walker, pp. 31–33, 64–67, etc. The Catholic Francesco Patrizi even believed that the study of the *Corpus Hermeticum* could convince the German Protestants to return to the Church; Yates, pp. 182ff.

86. "Hermétisme et cabale en France, de Lefèvre d'Étaples à Bossuet," p. 8; Yates, p. 180.

reestablish universal peace and accord between the diverse confessions. At the center of this revelation one finds the "divinity" of man. Man is the microcosm in whom all creation is synthesized. "The microcosm is the final goal of the macrocosm, while the macrocosm is the abode of the microcosm. . . . Macrocosm and microcosm are connected in such a manner that the one is always present in the other."[87]

The macrocosm-microcosm correspondence was known in China, ancient India, and in Greece. But it is above all in Paracelsus and his disciples that it regained a new vigor.[88] It is man who makes possible the communication between the celestial region and the sublunary world. In the sixteenth century, the interest in the *magia naturalis* represents a new attempt to work out a rapprochement between Nature and religion. In fact, the study of Nature constituted a quest for a better understanding of God. We will see the grandiose development of this conception.

311. New valorizations of alchemy: From Paracelsus to Newton

As we have already recalled (§283), the first Latin translations of alchemical works that had been conserved, or written, in Arabic date from the twelfth century. Among the most famous, the *Tabula Smaragdina,* attributed to Hermes, enjoys a considerable prestige. It is in this book that one finds the famous formula that illustrates the solidarity between Hermeticism and alchemy: "All that is above is like all that is below, all that is below is like all that is above, in order that the miracle of Unity be accomplished."

The western alchemists followed the scenario, known already in the Hellenistic period (cf. §211), of the four phases of the process of transmutation: that is, of the procurement of the Philosopher's Stone. The first phase (the *nigredo*)—the regression to the fluid state of matter—corresponds to the death of the alchemist. According to Paracelsus, "he who would enter the Kingdom of God must first enter with

---

87. Charles de Bouelles, cited by E. Garin, "Note sull'ermetismo del Rinascimento," p. 14.

88. Cf., inter alia, Alex Wayman, "The Human Body as Microcosm in India, Greek Cosmology, and Sixteenth-Century Europe"; Allen G. Debus, *Man and Nature in the Renaissance,* pp. 12ff., 26ff.

his body into his mother and there die.'' The ''mother'' is the *prima materia,* the *massa confusa,* the *abyssus.*[89] Certain texts emphasize the synchronism between the *opus alchymicum* and the intimate experience of the adept. ''Things are rendered perfect by their similars and that is why the operator must take part in the operation.''[90] ''Transform yourself from dead stones into living philosopher's stones,'' writes Dorn. According to Gichtel, ''we not only receive a new soul with this regeneration but also a new Body. The Body is extracted from the divine word or from the heavenly Sophia.'' That it is not solely a question of laboratory operations is proven by the insistence on the virtues and qualities of the alchemist: the latter must be healthy, humble, patient, chaste; he must be of free spirit and in harmony with his work; he must both work and meditate.

For our purposes, it will be unnecessary to summarize the other phases of the *opus.* Let us note, however, the paradoxical character of the *materia prima* and of the Philosopher's Stone. According to the alchemists, they both are to be found everywhere, and under all forms; and they are designated by hundreds of terms. To cite only a text of 1526, the Stone ''is familiar to all men, both young and old; it is found in the country, in the village, and in the town, in all things created by God; yet it is despised by all. Rich and poor handle it every day. It is thrown into the street by servant maids. Children play with it. Yet no one prizes it, though, next to the human soul, it is the most beautiful and most precious thing upon earth'' (*The Forge and the Crucible,* pp. 163–64). It is truly a question of a ''secret language'' that is at once both the expression of experiences otherwise intransmissible by the medium of ordinary language, and the cryptic communication of the hidden meaning of symbols.

The Stone makes possible the identification of opposites.[91] It pu-

---

89. Cf. Eliade, *The Forge and the Crucible,* pp. 154–55. See ibid, p. 155, for other citations on the ''philosophical incest.'' The acrostic constructed by Basil Valentine with the term *vitriol* underscores the implacable necessity of the *decensus ad inferos: Visita Interiora Terrae Rectificando Invenies Occultum Lapidem* (''Visit the interior of the Earth, and by purification you will find the secret Stone'').

90. *Liber Platonis quartorum* (of which the Arabic original cannot be later than the tenth century), cited in Eliade, *The Forge and the Crucible,* p. 158. One will find the same doctrine among the Chinese alchemists; cf. Eliade, *History of Religious Ideas,* vol. 2, pp. 37ff.

91. According to Basil Valentine, ''evil must become the same as good.'' Starkey describes the stone as ''the reconciliation of Contraries, a making of friendship between enemies''; *The Forge and the Crucible,* p. 166.

rifies and "perfects" the metals. It is the Arabic alchemists who imparted therapeutic virtues to the Stone, and it is through the intermediary of Arabic alchemy that the concept of the *Elixir vitae* arrived in the West.[92] Roger Bacon speaks of a "medicine which makes the impurities and all the corruptions of the most base metal disappear," and which can prolong human life for several centuries. According to Arnold of Villanova, the Stone cures all ills and makes the old young.

As regards the process for the transmutation of metals into gold, attested already in Chinese alchemy (§134), it accelerates the temporal rhythm and thus contributes to the work of nature. As is written in the *Summa Perfectionis,* an alchemical work of the sixteenth century, "what Nature cannot perfect in a vast space of time we can achieve in a short space of time by our art." The same idea is expounded by Ben Jonson in his play *The Alchemist* (Act 2, Scene 2). The alchemist affirms that "lead and other metals . . . would be gold if they had time"; and another character adds: "And that our art doth further."[93] In other words, the alchemist substitutes himself for Time.[94]

The principles of traditional alchemy—that is, the growth of minerals, the transmutation of metals, the Elixir, and the obligation to secrecy—were not contested in the period of the Renaissance and the Reformation.[95] However, the horizon of medieval alchemy was modified under the impact of Neoplatonism and Hermeticism. The certitude that alchemy can second the work of Nature received a christological significance. The alchemists now affirmed that just as Christ had redeemed humanity by his death and resurrection, so the *opus alchymicum* could assure the redemption of Nature. Heinrich Khunrath, a celebrated Hermeticist of the sixteenth century, identified the Philosopher's Stone with Jesus Christ, the "Son of the Macrocosm"; he thought besides that the discovery of the Stone would unveil the true

92. Cf. R. P. Multhauf, *The Origins of Chemistry,* pp. 135ff.

93. Cf. Eliade, *The Forge and the Crucible,* p. 51.

94. We have discussed the consequences of this Promethean gesture ibid., pp. 169ff.

95. Even in the eighteenth century, the learned did not question the growth of minerals. They asked themselves, however, whether alchemy could assist nature in this process, and above all whether "those alchemists who claimed to have done so already were honest men, fools, or impostors" (Betty Jo Teeter Dobbs, *The Foundations of Newton's Alchemy,* p. 44). Herman Boerhaave (1664–1739), considered the greatest "rationalist" chemist of his time and famous for his strictly empirical experiments, still believed in the transmutation of metals. And we will see the importance of alchemy in the scientific revolution accomplished by Newton.

nature of the macrocosm, in the same way that Christ had brought spiritual plenitude to man—that is, to the microcosm. The conviction that the *opus alchymicum* could save both man and Nature prolonged the nostalgia for a radical *renovatio,* a nostalgia which had haunted western Christianity since Joachim of Floris.

John Dee (born in 1527), the famous alchemist, mathematician, and encyclopedist, who had assured the Emperor Rudolf II that he possessed the secret of transmutation, estimated that a worldwide spiritual reform could be effected thanks to the forces unleashed by "occult operations," beginning with alchemical ones.[96] Similarly, the English alchemist Elias Ashmole saw in alchemy, astrology, and the *magia naturalis* the "Redeemer" of all the sciences. In effect, for the partisans of Paracelsus and Van Helmont, Nature could be understood only by the study of "chemical philosophy" (that is, the new alchemy) or the "true Medicine."[97] It was *chemistry* and not *astronomy* which provided the key to the decipherment of the secrets of Heaven and Earth. Since creation was explained as a chemical process, celestial and terrestrial phenomena could be interpreted in chemical terms. In taking into account the macrocosm-microcosm connections, the "philosopher-chemist" could apprehend the secrets of the Earth as well as those of the celestial bodies. Thus Robert Fludd could present a chemical description of the circulation of the blood modelled on the circular movement of the sun.[98]

Like a number of their contemporaries, the Hermeticists and philosopher-chemists expected—and some of them prepared for it feverishly—a general and radical reform of all religious, social, and cultural institutions. The first and most indispensable stage of this universal *renovatio* was the reform of learning. A new model of education was insisted upon in a small anonymous book, *Fama Fraternitatis,* published in 1614. The author revealed the existence of a secret society, that of the Rose Cross. Its founder, the legendary Christian Rosenkreuz, had mastered the "true secrets of medicine," and consequently all the other sciences as well. He had subsequently written a

96. Cf. Peter French, *John Dee: The World of an Elizabethan Magus;* R. J. W. Evans, *Rudolf II and His World: A Study of Intellectual History,* pp. 218–28. On John Dee's influence upon Khunrath, see Frances Yates, *The Rosicrucian Enlightenment,* pp. 37–38.
97. A. C. Debus, "Alchemy and the Historian of Science," p. 134.
98. A. C. Debus, *The Chemical Dream of the Renaissance,* pp. 7, 14–15.

certain number of books, but these works were accessible only and exclusively to members of the Rosicrucian order.[99] The author of the *Fama Fraternitatis* addressed himself to all the learned men of Europe, asking them to join the fraternity in order to accomplish the reform of knowledge. In other words, they were called upon to accelerate the *renovatio* of the Western world. This appeal provoked incomparable repercussions. In less than ten years, the program proposed by the mysterious society of Rosicrucians was discussed in several hundred books and brochures.

In 1619 Johann Valentin Andreae, whom some historians consider to be the author of the *Fama Fraternitatis,* published *Christianopolis.* The work probably influenced the *New Atlantis* of Bacon.[100] Andreae suggested the constitution of a new community of the learned in order to elaborate a new method of education founded on the "chemical philosophy." In the utopian *Christianopolis,* the center of studies was the laboratory: there "heaven and earth are married" and "the divine mysteries are discovered of which the surface of the land is the imprint."[101] Among the numerous admirers of the reform of knowledge demanded by the *Fama Fraternitatis* was Robert Fludd, a member of the Royal College of Physicians. Fludd was likewise a fervent adept of mystical alchemy. He maintained that it is impossible to master natural philosophy without a profound study of the occult sciences. For Fludd, the "true medicine" was the very foundation of natural philosophy. Knowledge of the microcosm—that is, of the human body—reveals to us the structure of the universe and leads us ultimately before the Creator. Moreover, the more one understands the universe, the more one advances in the knowledge of himself.[102]

Until recently, few were aware of Isaac Newton's role in this gener-

---

99. See, inter alia, ibid., pp. 17–18. Let us note in passing that at the beginning of the seventeenth century, one finds anew the old scenario so dear to Chinese, Tantric, and Hellenistic texts: a primordial revelation, recently rediscovered but solely reserved for initiates.

100. Cf. *Christianopolis, an Ideal State of the Seventeenth Century,* translated by Felix Held (New York and London, 1916). See also Yates, *The Rosicrucian Enlightenment,* pp. 145–46; Debus, *The Chemical Dream,* pp. 19–20.

101. *Christianopolis* (Held trans.), pp. 196–97.

102. Robert Fludd, *Apologia Compendiaris Fraternitatem de Rosea Cruce Suspicionis et Infamiae Maculis Aspersam, Veritatis quasi Fluctibus abluens et abstergens* (Leiden, 1616), pp. 88–93, 100–103, cited by Debus, *The Chemical Dream,* pp. 22–23.

al movement, whose goal was the *renovatio* of European religion and culture by means of an audacious synthesis of the occult traditions and the natural sciences. It is true that Newton never published the results of his alchemical experiments, although he declared that some of them were crowned with success. His innumerable alchemical manuscripts, ignored until 1940, have recently been meticulously analyzed by Betty Jo Teeter Dobbs in her book *The Foundations of Newton's Alchemy* (1975). Dobbs affirms that Newton experimented in his laboratory with the operations described in the immense alchemical literature, probing the latter "as it has never been probed before or since" (p. 88). With the aid of alchemy, Newton hoped to discover the structure of the microuniverse in order to homologize it with his cosmological system. The discovery of gravity, the force which keeps the planets in their orbits, did not completely satisfy him. But although he pursued the experiments indefatigably from 1669 to 1696, he did not succeed in identifying the forces which govern the corpuscles. Nevertheless, when he began to study the dynamics of orbital movement in 1679–80, he applied his "chemical" conceptions of attraction to the universe.[103]

As McGuire and Rattansi have shown, Newton was convinced that in the beginning, "God had imparted the secrets of natural philosophy and of true religion to a select few. The knowledge was subsequently lost but partially recovered later, at which time it was incorporated in fables and mythic formulations where it would remain hidden from the vulgar. In modern days it could be more fully recovered from experience."[104] For this reason, Newton examined the most esoteric sections of the alchemical literature, hoping that they would contain the true secrets. It is significant that the founder of modern mechanics did not reject the tradition of a primordial and secret revelation, just as he did not reject the principle of transmutation. As he wrote in his *Optics* (1704), "the change of Bodies into Light and of Light into Bodies is entirely in conformity with the Laws of Nature, for Nature seems ravished by Transmutation." According to Dobbs, "Newton's alchemical thoughts were so securely established that he never came to

103. Richard S. Westfall, "Newton and the Hermetic Tradition," esp. pp. 193–94; cf. Dobbs, *Foundations,* p. 211.

104. Dobbs, ibid., p. 90, citing the article of E. McGuire and P. M. Rattansi, "Newton and the 'Pipes of Pan,'" pp. 108–43.

deny their general validity, and in a sense the whole of his career after 1675 may be seen as one long attempt to integrate alchemy and the mechanical philosophy'' (*Foundations,* p. 230).

After the publication of the *Principia,* opponents declared that Newton's ''forces'' were in reality ''occult qualities.'' As Dobbs recognizes, in a certain sense these critics were right: ''Newton's forces were very much like the hidden sympathies and antipathies found in much of the occult literature of the Renaissance period. But Newton had given forces an ontological status equivalent to that of matter and motion. By so doing, and by quantifying the forces, he enabled the mechanical philosophies to rise above the level of imaginary impact mechanisms'' (p. 211). In analyzing the Newtonian conception of force, Richard Westfall arrives at the conclusion that modern science is *the result of the wedding of the Hermetic tradition with the mechanical philosophy.*[105]

In its spectacular flight, ''modern science'' has ignored, or rejected, the heritage of Hermeticism. Or to put it differently, the triumph of Newtonian mechanics has ended up by annihilating its own scientific ideal. In effect, Newton and his contemporaries expected a different type of scientific revolution. In prolonging and developing the hopes and objectives (the first among these being the redemption of Nature) of the neo-alchemist of the Renaissance, minds as different as those of Paracelsus, John Dee, Comenius, J. V. Andreae, Fludd, and Newton saw in alchemy the model for a no less ambitious enterprise: the perfection of man by a new method of knowledge. In their perspective, such a method had to integrate into a nonconfessional Christianity the Hermetic tradition and the natural sciences of medicine, astronomy, and mechanics. In fact, this synthesis constituted a new Christian creation, comparable to the brilliant results obtained by the earlier integrations of Platonism, Aristotelianism, and Neoplatonism. This type of ''knowledge,'' dreamed of and partially elaborated in the eighteenth century, represents the last enterprise of Christian Europe that was undertaken with the aim of obtaining a ''total knowledge.''

105. Richard S. Westfall, *Force in Newton's Physics: The Science of Dynamics in the Seventeenth Century,* pp. 377–91; Dobbs, ibid., p. 211.

39 Tibetan Religions

312. The "religion of men"

Tibetan religion, just like Hinduism and ancient and medieval Christianity, presents at its apogee a remarkable synthesis, the result of a long process of assimilation and syncretism. For several decades now, Western scholars, taking their lead from Tibetan authors, have interpreted the religious history of Tibet as a conflict between the autochthonous *Bon* religion and Indian Buddhism, the latter finally triumphing in the form of Lamaism. But recent studies, and above all the analysis of the documents found in the Tun Huang cave (eighth to tenth centuries), have revealed a more complex situation. For one thing, we must now take into account the importance and the coherence of an autochthonous religion which preceded the *Bon* and the first propagation of Buddhism. This traditional religion (called "the religion of men") is passed over in silence by the *Bon* authors no less than by the Buddhists.

Furthermore, we are beginning to get a better understanding of the exotic and syncretistic character of the *Bon,* and most notably of its Indian and Iranian sources. To be sure, the documents at our disposal are late (the Tibetan alphabet was created in the seventh century) and reflect the consequences of polemics and reciprocal borrowings between the *Bon* tradition and Buddhism. However, under the *Bon* and Lamaist veneer, one can decipher specific traits of the traditional religion. Tibetan historians distinguish the "religion of the gods" (*lha-chos*) from the "religion of men" (*mi-chos*); the first refers sometimes to the *Bon,* sometimes to Buddhism; the second designates the traditional religion.

One important source for information on the "religion of men"—

called *Gcug* (or *chos,* "custom")—is found in the "stories," that is, in the cosmogonic and genealogical myths. These "stories" were ritually narrated on such occasions as marriages, New Year festivals, and various competitions in honor of the gods of the soil. As in many archaic religions, the recitation of myths of origins—of the society itself, of a ritual or institution—reactualized continuity with the mythic time of "beginnings" and thereby assured the success of the various undertakings.[1] The correct narration of the myths of origins was "a religious act, necessary for upholding the order of the world and society."[2]

As one also finds elsewhere, the origin myths begin with the account of the cosmogony. The world was created by the celestial Phyva gods, imagined as being heavenly mountains. (We will return later to the religious importance and symbolism of mountains.) Certain of these mountain-gods descended to earth, bringing with them the animals, plants, and probably the first humans. This paradisal epoch, when men lived beside the gods, lasted a thousand years. A demon, enclosed under the ninth subterranean level, succeeded in escaping and spread evil on earth. The gods retired to the sky, and the world continued to degenerate for hundreds of millions of years. However, several men still practiced the *Gcug,* while awaiting the "age of impieties," following which a new world would appear, the gods would return to earth, and the dead would resuscitate.

This is clearly a version of the well-known myth of the "perfection of beginnings" followed by a progressive and universal degeneration. But one can equally suppose Indian influences (the cosmic cycles incorporating hundreds of millions of years) and Iranian ones (the demon who corrupts the creation).

The world has a tripartite structure: the Phyva gods reside above, the aquatic and subterranean divinities (*Klu*) below, and humans in the middle. The first king was a god who had descended to the earth and united himself with a mountain divinity; he thus instituted the model

1. See Eliade, *Myth and Reality,* pp. 21ff. See also G. Tucci, *Les religions du Tibet,* pp. 269ff.

2. R. A. Stein, *Tibetan Civilization,* trans., J. E. S. Driver, p. 195. "To ratify the group's relationship with the gods and ancestors, it is essential to go back in each recitation to the origin of such and such an institution, and the recitation must be absolutely authentic. This is the same even with Lamaist rituals, which always refer to the origin, the mystical precedent, that justifies each rite" (p. 198).

for the seven mythic sovereigns who followed him. The myths of the origin of the inhabited site—minor variants of the cosmogonic myth— speak sometimes of a conquered demon or dismembered animal, sometimes of a hierogamy between a god (mountain, rock, or tree) and a goddess (lake, spring, or river). "Each community inhabiting a given site thus finds its identity in its own ancestor and holy place."[3]

In the traditional religion, the role of the king was fundamental.[4] The sovereign's divine nature manifested itself in his "splendor" and in his magical powers. The first kings remained on earth only by day; at night they returned to heaven. They did not die in the ordinary sense, but at a certain moment made their definitive re-ascent to heaven on their magic rope, *mu* (or *dmu*). According to a *bonpo* chronicle, these first kings "had on the crown of their head a *mu* rope of light, a distant (or taut) rope, pale yellow (or brown) in colour. At the moment of their death they dissolved (like a rainbow) starting from their feet, and melted into the *mu* rope at the top of their head. The *mu* rope of light, in its turn, melted into the sky."[5] This is why there existed no royal tombs prior to the last sovereign of divine origin, Digun; proud and given to anger, the latter, during a duel, inadvertently severed his *mu* rope. Since then the bodies of kings have been buried; their tombs have been discovered and some of the funerary practices connected with them are known.[6] However, certain privileged beings—above all saints and magicians—still succeed in ascending to heaven by means of the *mu* rope.

313. Traditional conceptions: Cosmos, men, gods

The myth of the *mu* rope severed by Digun replicates, in another context, the story of the separation of men from the Phyva gods after the eruption of evil in the world. But its importance for the history of Tibetan religious thought is much greater than that. For one thing, the

3. Stein, ibid., p. 210.

4. See esp. A. Macdonald, "Une lecture des Pelliot tibétains . . . ," pp. 339ff. Cf. Erik Haarh, *The Yar Lun Dynasty*, pp. 126ff.

5. Stein, *Tibetan Civilization*, p. 224. Cf. Tucci, *Les religions du Tibet*, pp. 286ff. For comparative analysis of this mytheme, see our "Cordes et Marionettes" (= *The Two and the One*, pp. 160–88, esp. pp. 166–67).

6. See G. Tucci, *The Tombs of the Tibetan Kings*. Cf. Stein, pp. 201ff.

mu rope filled a cosmological function: it joined Earth and Heaven like an *axis mundi*. In addition, it played a central role in the cosmos–habitation–human-body system of homologies. Finally, after a certain moment that is difficult to pin down, one rediscovers the *mu* rope in the subtle physiology and in the rituals which assure liberation and the celestial ascent of the souls of the dead.

To be sure, Indian and *Bon* influences are evident. But the original character of the mythico-ritual complex and its symbolism are not subject to doubt. The cosmos–habitation–human-body homology is an archaic conception, abundantly widespread in Asia. Buddhism knew this homology, although it denied it salvific value (cf. §160).

The mountains are assimilated to the ladder or the *mu* rope of the first ancestor who descended to earth. The royal tombs are called "mountains."[7] Moreover, the sacred mountains—veritable "gods of the land" or "masters of the place"—are considered as "Pillars of the Sky" or "Pegs of the Earth," and "the same function can be taken on by pillars erected near tombs or temples."[8] Heaven and the subterranean world include stages to which access is made possible by a "Gate of Heaven" and a "Gate of the Earth." In the house, one communicates between stages by a ladder fashioned from a tree trunk. To the "Gate of Heaven" corresponds the roof hole, where light enters and smoke departs; to the "Gate of the Earth" corresponds the hearth.[9]

Just as the sacred mountain—the "god of the land"—is identified with the *mu* ladder that connects Heaven to Earth, so in the human body one of the protector gods, and precisely the one called "god of the land," is found on the top of the head, where the *mu* rope is attached (the "warrior god" and the "man's god" reside on the shoulders). The *mu* ladder is also called the "ladder of the wind." Now, the "horse of the wind" is a term used to represent a man's vitality. The "wind" is the vital principle analogous to the Indian *prāṇa*. "It is both the air we breathe, and a subtle fluid within the body."[10] The

7. The ancient kings' tombs and palaces would have been built "in the *mu* manner," even after Digun's severing of the rope; Stein, pp. 201–2.

8. Stein, p. 203. The sacred mountains are also warrior gods: they are addressed as "chief" or "king," and are linked from the beginning with the clan line; ibid, p. 207.

9. On the house's roof one finds the "gods of the summit" (represented by two stone altars and a flag); their cult is identical with the one performed on the mountains; cf. Stein, p. 222.

10. Stein, pp. 283–84.

"extension toward the top" is brought about by the *mu* rope. It is very likely that these conceptions were elaborated by Lamaist syncretism. In any case, the operation utilized by the lamas for the final deliverance of the soul recalls the manner by which the mythical kings dissolved themselves into the *mu* rope.[11] In other words, the saint is susceptible at the moment of his death to a repetition, *in spirit,* of the ascent which the mythical kings accomplished *in concreto* before the misadventure of Digun (itself a conception which recalls the north Asiatic myths about the "decadence" of contemporary shamanism: the first shamans ascended to heaven in flesh and bone; cf. §246).

We shall return to the role which light plays in Tibetan religions. Let us add for the moment that alongside the cosmos–habitation–human-body homology, which we have just observed, the traditional religion also implies a certain symmetry between man and gods. Sometimes "souls" (*bla*) are indistinguishable from "gods" (*lha*); since these two terms are pronounced alike, Tibetans often confuse them. One knows several exterior "souls" and "lives," which reside in trees, rocks, or objects inhabited by the gods.[12] Furthermore, as we have seen, the "gods of the land" and the warrior gods live as much in natural sites as in the human body.

To put it in different terms, *insofar as he is a spiritual being,* man partakes of a divine condition, and most notably of the function and destiny of the gods of the cosmic structure. It is this which explains the importance of the innumerable ritual competitions, from the horse races, athletic games, and diverse combats to the competitions in beauty, archery, and cattle-milking and the oratorical jousts. It is on the occasion of the New Year that these competitions take place. The essential theme of the New Year scenario is constituted by the struggle between the gods of heaven and the demons, represented by the mountains. As in other analogous scenarios, the victory of the gods assures the victory of the new life of the freshly beginning year. "The gods are present at the spectacle and laugh in common with men. The enigma contests and the recitation of stories, like that of the epic, have an effect on the harvest and the herds. Gods and men were reunited on the occasion of the great festivals, the social oppositions were affirmed but at the same time appeased. And the group, reuniting itself to its past

11. Syncretism is already found in the eleventh century. Milarepa speaks of the "cutting of the sealing rope of liberation (salvation)''; Stein, p. 224.

12. Ibid., p. 228.

(the origin of the world, or the ancestors) and to its habitat (the sacred ancestor-mountains), felt itself reinvigorated."[13]

The Iranian influences in the Tibetan New Year festival are evident, but the mythico-ritual scenario is archaic: one encounters it in numerous traditional religions. In a word, it is a conception, widely attested globally,[14] according to which the cosmos and life, and also the function of the gods and the human condition, are governed by the same cyclic rhythm, a rhythm that is constituted of mutually self-implying alternating and complementary polarities which periodically resolve themselves into a union-totality of the *coincidentia oppositorum* type. One could compare the Tibetan conception to the opposition of the *yang* and the *yin* and their rhythmic reintegration in the *tao* (cf. §132). In any case, the traditional religion which the first Buddhists encountered in Tibet was not "an amalgam of anarchical and dispersed magico-religious notions . . . , but a religion whose practices and rites were rooted in a structural system, founded on basic concepts radically opposed to those which sustained Buddhism."[15]

314. The *Bon:* Confrontations and syncretism

One may well ask oneself "for what reasons [Tibetan] historians were led to obliterate the ancient religion, whose name itself [*Gcug*] had disappeared, and to substitute for it a religion, the *Bon,* whose formation as a constituted religion must go back to the eleventh century. On the *bon-po*'s part, the matter is understandable: they were no doubt ready to support a version which augmented their prestige by assigning themselves the highest antiquity."[16] As for the Buddhist historians,

13. R. A. Stein, *Recherches sur l'épopée et le barde au Tibet*, pp. 440–41.

14. Cf. our study: "Remarques sur le dualisme religieux: dyades et polarités" (republished in *La nostalgie des origines*, pp. 231–311, and in *The Quest: History and Meaning in Religion*, pp. 127–75).

15. Cf. A. Macdonald, "Une lecteur," p. 367.

16. A. M. Blondeau, "Les religions du Tibet," p. 245. Moreover, Buddhism "could not condone animal sacrifice, much less human sacrifice. But above all, it was the conception of a god-king, one who maintained the order of the universe, and the belief in immortality—in a blessed afterlife that was conceived in the image of the terrestrial life and thus valorized the latter—that left no place for the fundamental principles of Buddhism: the impermanence of all existence; transmigration (*samsāra*); the ineluctable retribution for one's acts, exacted in this life or in another (*karman*). Furthermore, the ideal presented by the *Gcug* was an ideal of social justice, of human happiness, and not of moral perfection" (ibid.).

the bloody sacrifices and the eschatological conceptions of the autochthonous religions were deemed repugnant; as a result, they assimilated
them to *Bon* beliefs and magical practices.

It is difficult to describe the *Bon* without having first presented the
propagation of Buddhism to Tibet. These two religions clashed with
each other from the beginning, all the while influencing each other
reciprocally. They each had their turns being protected and then persecuted by the kings. Finally, from the eleventh century on, the "modified *Bon*" (*agyur Bon*) borrowed the doctrine, vocabulary, and
institutions of Lamaism. However, it is certain that *bon-po* ritualists,
diviners, and "sorcerers" operated in Tibet before the penetration of
Buddhist missionaries. Moreover, to present the *Bon* at this point of
our exposition allows us to appreciate the multiplicity and importance
of the foreign elements which contributed to the Tibetan religious syncretism. At least certain *bon-po* categories bear witness to an exotic
origin. According to the tradition, the "foreign *Bon*" had been introduced from Zhang-shung (southwestern Tibet) or from Tazig (Iran).
One can thus, on the one hand, account for the Iranian elements discernible in certain *Bon* conceptions and, on the other, advance the
probability of Indian influences (notably Śaivite) before the penetration of Buddhism.

The oldest documents speak of different classes of *bon-po:* ritualists, sacrificers, diviners, exorcists, magicians, etc. This is not to
imply, before the eleventh century, a unitary and well-articulated organization of all these "specialists of the sacred." Among their ritual
implements, let us note the scaffolds designed to capture demons and,
above all, the shamanic type of tambourine, which enabled the magicians to ascend to the sky. The woolen turban, the specific insignia of
the *bon-po*, served, according to the tradition, to conceal the ass's ears
of the legendary founder of the *Bon*, Shenrab ni bo (a precious detail,
since it betrays a Western origin; it is, in effect, a theme of Midas).[17]
Alongside other specialists in the sacred, the *bon-po* protected the sovereigns and the chiefs of the clans. They played an important role at
funerals (above all, at the royal funerals), guided the souls of the dead
to the other world, and were reputed to be capable of calling up the
dead and exorcising them.

Other documents, from a later period, present different cosmogonies

17. Cf. Stein, *Recherches sur l'épopée,* pp. 381ff.

and theologies as well: indeed, metaphysical speculations that were more or less systematized. Indian, and particularly Buddhist, influences are manifest. This does not imply that there was no prior ''theory''; it is very likely that ''speculative'' *bon-po* practitioners (genealogists, mythographers, theologians) had long coexisted with the ritualists and ''sorcerers.''

The later *bon-po* authors recounted their ''sacred history'' as follows: the founder of *Bon* was Shenrab ni bo (''the excellent man-priest-*shen*''). His birth and geography find their model in those of Sakyamuni and Padmasambhava (whom we will turn to shortly). Shenrab decided to take birth in a Western country (Zhang-shung or Iran). A ray of white light in the form of an arrow (image of the *semen virile*) penetrated the skullcap of his father, while a ray of red light (representing blood, the feminine element) entered the head of his mother. In another, more ancient, version, it is Shenrab himself who descends from the celestial palace in the form of five colors (that is, like a rainbow). Transformed into a bird, he perches on the head of his future mother, and two rays—one white, the other blue—issue from his genitals, entering the woman's body through the skull.[18] Once he comes to earth, Shenrab affronts the prince of demons, pursues him, and masters the demons he encounters by his magic powers. To guarantee their submission, the latter offer him objects and formulas containing the essence of their powers. Thus the demons are the guardians of the *Bon* doctrine and its techniques.[19] All of which amounts to saying that Shenrab reveals to the *bon-po* the prayers which they must address to the gods and the magical means of exorcising the demons. After having established the *Bon* in Tibet and China, Shenrab retires from the world, practices asceticism and, like the Buddha, attains Nirvana. But he leaves a son who, for three years, propagates the ensemble of the doctrine.

One must consider the legendary personage who is concealed under

18. Stein, *Tib. Civ.*, p. 242. According to Tibetans, at the moment of procreation, the soul of the child enters by the *sutura frontalis* into the mother's head, and it is through this same orifice that the soul leaves the body at the moment of death; cf. our study ''Spirit, Light, and Seed,'' p. 98 (in *Occultism, Witchcraft, and Cultural Fashions*).

19. See the texts summarized by Tucci, *Les religions du Tibet*, p. 304. The same motif is met in the legendary biography of Padmasambhava; this time, the Buddhist master subdues the *Bon* divinities.

the name of Shenrab as the creator of the doctrinal *Bon* system. To him is attributed the gathering and organizing of a considerable and contradictory mass of customs, rituals, mythological traditions, incantations, and magical formulas—"not so much the literary texts, for these, before his time, existed only in small numbers."[20] The *Bon* canon began to take shape in the eleventh century by a grouping of texts supposed to have been hidden during the persecutions by the Buddhist kings, and "rediscovered" later.[21] Its definitive form dates from the fifteenth century, at which point the texts attributed to Shenrab (reputed to have been translated from the language of Zhang-shung) had been brought together in the seventy-five volumes of the *Kanjur,* and their commentaries in the one hundred and thirty-one volumes of the *Tanjur.* The classification and the titles of these works are clearly borrowed from the Lamaist canon. The doctrine closcly followed that of Buddhism: "law of impermanence, of the bondage of acts which give rise to the cycle of *samsāra.* For the *Bon* also, the goal to attain is the Awakening, the state of the Buddha, or rather its Mahāyāna form, the state of Emptiness."[22] As among the Buddhist monks of the "old" school— that is, the disciples of Padmasambhava (see below §315), the *Bon* doctrine is articulated in nine "vehicles" (or "ways"). The last three vehicles are identical in the two religions. The first six present many common elements, but among the *bon-po* they also include a number of beliefs and original practices specific to the *Bon.*[23]

Several cosmogonies are attested in the *Bon* scriptures. Among the most important, let us cite the creation from a primordial egg, or from the members of an anthropomorphic Giant of the *Purusha* type (a theme conserved in the Gesar Epic), or, finally, as the indirect work of a *deus otiosus* from whom two radically opposed principles emerge. The Indian influence is evident in the first two of these cosmogonies.

20. Tucci, p. 305.

21. This is a mythic theme attested abundantly in the Near East and the Greco-Roman world of the Hellenistic period, in India, and in China. This does not, of course, exclude the possibility that a certain number of texts were really hidden and rediscovered after the persecutions.

22. Blondeau, "Les religions du Tibet," p. 310. Besides, the *Bon* borrowed the theory of Bodhisattvas and that of the Three Bodies of the Buddha. Despite the differences in names, the pantheon includes a "number of classes of gods and demons common to the two religions" (ibid.).

23. The most complete analysis has been made by D. Snellgrove, *The Nine Ways of Bon.* See also Tucci, pp. 291ff.; Blondeau, pp. 310ff.

According to the third, at the beginning there existed only a pure potentiality, between Being and Nonbeing, which nevertheless gives itself the name "Created, Master of Being." From the "Master" two lights emanate, one white and the other black, which engender two "men," also white and black. The latter, the "Black Hell," likened to a lance, is the incarnation of Nonbeing, the principle of negation, author of all evils and calamities. The white man, who proclaims himself "the Master who loves Existence," is the incarnation of Being and the principle of all that is good and creative in the world. Thanks to him, the gods are venerated by men and combat the demons and representatives of evil.[24] Such conceptions recall Zurvanite theology (cf. §213), and were probably transmitted by the Manichaeans of Central Asia.

Let us underline once again the syncretistic character of the *Bon,* as much in its traditional as in its "modified" forms. As we shall soon see, Lamaism takes up and undergoes the same development. In the historic period, syncretism seems to characterize the religious creativity of the Tibetan genius.

315. Formation and development of Lamaism

According to tradition, Buddhism would have been established in Tibet by King Srong-bstan sgam-po (620?–641), who came to be regarded later as an emanation of the Buddha Avalokiteshvara. But it is difficult to be precise on the contribution which this sovereign made to the propagation of the Law. One knows that he followed, at least in part, the ancient religious practices. On the other hand, it seems clear that the Buddhist message was known in certain regions of Tibet before the seventh century.

In its capacity as a state religion, Buddhism is attested for the first time in official documents under King Khri-ston lde-bcan (755–797?). The sovereign, proclaimed as the emanation of Mañjuśrī, invited the great Indian masters Śāntarakshita, Kamalashīla, and Padmasambhava to Tibet.[25] Two tendencies competed for the king's protection: the

24. See the sources summarized by Stein, *Tib. Civ.,* p. 246; Tucci, p. 273; cf. also pp. 280–88.

25. An entire mythology developed around this latter figure; to him is attributed the conversion of Tibet, and some consider him as the second Buddha; cf. the fabulous biography translated by C. Ch. Toussaint, *Le dict de Padma.*

"Indian school," teaching a gradual way of deliverance, and the "Chinese school," which proposed techniques whose aim was instantaneous illumination (ch'an; Japanese zen). After having presided over the presentation and defense of their respective methods (792–794), the king chose the Indian thesis. This famous controversy took place in the Bsam-yas monastery, founded by Khri-ston at the beginning of his reign. It was the first of a long series of monastic establishments which were constructed over ensuing centuries. It is Khri-ston who is repeatedly said to have conferred properties on the monasteries, thus inaugurating the developments which led to the Lamaist theocracy.

His successes reinforced Buddhism's status as an official religion. In the ninth century, the monks enjoyed a privileged situation in the political hierarchy, and always received the most important properties. King Ral-pa-čan (815–838), by his excess of zeal in favor of the monks, provoked the opposition of the nobles. He was assassinated, and his brother, who succeeded him (838–842), unleashed a violent persecution of the Buddhists: according to the later chronicles, this successor vigorously championed the Bon. But he was also assassinated, and after his death the country, fragmented into continually vying principalities, foundered into anarchy. For more than a century, Buddhism was prohibited. The temples were profaned, the monks were threatened with death, forced to marry or to embrace the Bon. The ecclesiastical institutions collapsed, the libraries were destroyed. However, a certain number of solitary monks survived, especially in the marginal provinces. This period of persecution and anarchy favored the diffusion of magic and Tantric practices of an orgiastic type.

At about 970, Ye-çes'od, a Buddhist king of western Tibet, sent Rin c'en bzan po (958–1055) to Kashmir to search for Indian masters. With him began the second diffusion of Buddhism. Rin c'en organized a school and proceeded to undertake the translation of canonical texts and the revision of earlier translations.[26] In 1042, a great Tantric master named Atīśa arrived in western Tibet. He initiated Rin c'en, already of advanced age, and his disciples. Among the latter, it was Brom-ston

---

26. He thus set forth the bases of the great corpus: the 100 volumes of the *Kanjur* (containing the Buddha's discourses) and the 225 volumes of the *Tanjur* (translations of commentaries and systematic treatises composed by Indian authors).

who became the most authoritative representative of the tradition taught by Atīśa. What transpired was a veritable reform aiming at the restoration of the original structures of Buddhism: strict moral conduct for the monks, celibacy, asceticism, traditional methods of meditation, and so on. The role of the *guru* (in Tibetan "lama," *bla-ma*), gained a considerable importance. This reform of Atīśa and his successors provided the basis for what later became the school of the "virtuous," the Gelugpa (*Dge-lugs-pa*). But a certain number of the religious, drawing upon teachings introduced by Padmasambhava, did not accept this reform. In time, they came to define themselves as the "Ancients," or Nyingmapa (*Rñin-ma-pa*).

Between the eleventh and fourteenth centuries a series of great spiritual masters intervened, creators of new "schools" and founders of monasteries that were to become highly celebrated. Tibetan monks traveled to India, Kashmir, and Nepal in search of renowned *gurus*, in the hope of being initiated into the mysteries (especially Tantric) of deliverance. This is the epoch of the famous yogins, mystics, and magicians Nāropa, Marpa, and Milarepa. They inspired and organized different "schools," of which some, in time, divided up into several branches. It is useless to enumerate them. Let it suffice to cite the name of Tsong-kha-pa (1359–1419), vigorous reformer in the line of Atīśa and founder of a school that would secure a most flourishing future, whose adepts received the name of the "New" or "Virtuous" (Gelugpa). The third successor of Tsong-kha-pa took the title of Dalai Lama (1578). Under the fifth Dalai Lama (1617–82), the Gelugpa achieved a definitive triumph. Since then, and down to today, the Dalai Lama is recognized as the sole religious and political leader of the country. The resources of the monasteries and the great number of monks, both lettered scholars and spiritual guides, have guaranteed the force and stability of the Lamaist theocracy.

As to the "Ancients," the Nyingmapas, beyond the uninterrupted oral transmission of the doctrine, they also recognized revelations obtained by the ecstatic inspiration of eminent religious personages, or conserved in books reputed to have been "hidden" during the persecutions and later "discovered." As among the *bon-po,* the great epoch of "discoveries" of texts extends, among the "Ancients," from the eleventh to the fourteenth century. One extremely gifted and enterprising monk, Klon-'chen (fourteenth century), organized the ensemble of Nyingmapa traditions into a well-articulated theoretical system. Paradoxically, the veritable renaissance of the "Ancients" begins in the seventeenth century. However, despite differences of a philosophic order and, above all, the variety of rituals, no true rupture took place between the "Ancients" and the "New" school of the Gelugpa. In the nineteenth century a movement of an eclectic type took shape, pursuing the integration of all the traditional Buddist schools.

316. Lamaist doctrines and practices

The Tibetans did not consider themselves innovators with regard to matters of doctrine. But one must recognize that "while Buddhism disappeared in India in the beginning of the thirteenth century, it continued to expand in Tibet as a vital tradition."[27] The first Buddhist missionaries had arrived after the triumph in India of the Great Vehicle (*Mahāyāna;* cf. §§187ff.). The dominant schools were the Mādhyamika, the "Middle Way" founded by Nāgārjuna (third century), the Yogācāra or Vijñānavāda established by Asanga (fourth to fifth century), and finally the Tantra or Vajrayāna (the "Diamond Vehicle"). During the following five centuries, all of these schools sent their representatives to Tibet, and contributed to the formation of Lamaism.

In simplest terms, one can say that the "reformed" Gelugpas followed the teaching of Nāgārjuna in utilizing logic and dialectic as the means of realizing Emptiness and thus obtaining salvation (cf. vol. 2, pp. 222ff.), whereas the "Ancients" gave priority to the tradition founded by Asanga, which accorded a decisive importance to yogic techniques of meditation. Let us insist, however, that this distinction does not imply any scorn of dialectic by the "Ancients" or absence of yoga in the teachings of the "Reformed." As to Tantric rituals, although practiced above all by the Nyingmapas, they were not neglected by the Gelugpas.

In short, the religious had a choice between an immediate way and a progressive way. But both presupposed that the Absolute (= Emptiness) could be grasped only by abolishing "dualities": subject (thinking)–object (thought), phenomenal world–ultimate reality, *samsāra–nirvāna*. According to Nāgārjuna, there are two kinds of truth: relative, conventional truth (*samvṛtti*), and absolute truth (*paramārtha*).

27. Blondeau, p. 271.

According to the first of these perspectives, the phenomenal world, although ontologically unreal, *exists* in an entirely convincing manner in the experience of the ordinary man. From the perspective of absolute truth, the mind discovers the unreality of all that seems to exist, but this revelation is verbally inexpressible. Such a distinction between the two truths—conventional and absolute—serves to preserve the value of moral conduct and the religious activity of the faithful laity.

The two kinds of truth correspond to different categories of human beings. To be sure, everyone possesses the buddha-nature in a virtual state, but the realization of buddhahood depends on the karmic equation of each individual, the result of innumerable previous existences. The faithful lay folk, condemned to the conventional truth, strive to accumulate merits by gifts to monks and to the poor, by numerous rituals and pilgrimages, by recitation of the formula *om mani padme hum*. For them, "it is the act of faith which chiefly counts in recitation; and this latter makes possible a species of meditation and an obliteration of the ego."[28] As for the religious, their situation differs according to the degree of their spiritual perfection. A certain number of monks still partake of the conventional-truth perspective. Others, by choosing the rapid method of illumination, exert themselves to realize the identification of the relative and the absolute, of *samsāra* and *nirvāna,* that is, to grasp in an experimental manner the ultimate reality, the Void. Some of these proclaim by their eccentric, and indeed aberrant, behavior that they have transcended the fallacious dualities of the conventional truth.

As in India (cf. §332), it is above all the various Tantric schools which apply, and transmit in the strictest secrecy, the techniques of meditation and the rituals aiming at the realization of the *coincidentia oppositorum* at all levels of existence. But all the Tibetan schools accept the fundamental concepts of Mahāyāna Buddhism, and in particular the idea that the High Science (*prajñā*), the feminine and passive principle, is intimately connected with the Practice or Means (*upāya*), the masculine and active principle. It is thanks to the "practice" that "wisdom" can manifest itself. Their union, obtained by the monk in the course of specific rituals and meditations, confers the Great Joy (*mahāsukha*).

---

28. Stein, *Tib. Civ.*, p. 174. Thanks to the merits accumulated during his life, the layman hopes for reincarnation in a superior state.

A characteristic trait of Lamaism is the capital importance of the *guru*. To be sure, in brahmanical and Hindu India, as well as in primitive Buddhism, the master was considered to be the spiritual father of the disciple. But Tibetan Buddhism elevates the *guru* to a nearly divine position: it is he who confers initiation upon the disciple, explains to him the esoteric meaning of the texts, and communicates to him a secret and all-powerful *mantra*. The master seeks first for the "dominant passion" of the novice, in order to discover who his tutelary divinity is, and thereby the kind of tantra appropriate to him.

As for the disciple, his faith in the *guru* must be absolute. "To venerate a single hair of one's teacher is a greater merit than to venerate all the Buddhas of the three times (past, present, and future)."[29] During meditation, the disciple identifies himself with his master, who is himself identified with the supreme divinity. The master submits his pupil to numerous tests in order to discover the quality and limits of his faith. Marpa pushes his disciple Milarepa to despair by humiliating, insulting, and beating him; but he does not succeed in shaking his faith. Irascible, unjust, and brutal, Marpa is so deeply moved by his disciple's faith that he frequently weeps in hiding.[30]

The religious activity of the monks consists essentially of a series of spiritual exercises of a yogico-tantric type, of which the most important is meditation.[31] The religious practitioners can utilize certain exterior objects as meditative supports: images of divinities, *maṇḍalas*, etc. But the divinities, as in India (and above all in Tantrism; see §333), must be interiorized, that is to say "created" and projected as onto a screen by the monk. One first grasps hold of "emptiness," from which, through a mystic syllable, the divinity emerges. The monk then identifies himself with this divinity. "He then has a luminous, empty, divine body; he is indissolubly merged with the deity, through whom he partakes of Emptiness." It is at this moment that the divinity is really present. "As proof of this it is related, for instance, that after a particular meditative evocation, the deities represented on the painting came out, walked around in a circle, and went back in: it was then noticeable that their clothes and appurtenances were out of

29. Text cited by Stein, ibid., p. 176.

30. See the admirable biography translated by J. Bacot, *Le poète tibétain Milarepa.*

31. Every monastery is provided with special cells for the retreat and meditation of the monks.

order on the picture. The master Bodhisattva's contemplation at Samyê was so intense that it rendered the divinities 'objectively' present before everyone's eyes: the statues came out of the temple, walked around it, and returned to their places."[32]

Certain meditations required the mastery of the techniques of Haṭha Yoga (§143); for example, the production of the heat (*gtum-mo*) which permits ascetics to pass winter nights drying out great numbers of wet sheets on their bodies while sitting naked in the falling snow.[33] Other meditations of the monks pursue the attainment of yogic powers (*siddhi;* cf. §195) of a fakiristic type; for example, the transfer of his "spirit" into a dead body, otherwise called the animation of the corpse. The most terrifying meditation, known as *gčod* ("to cut"), consists in offering one's own flesh to be devoured by demons. "The power of meditation gives rise to a goddess with saber aloft; she leaps at the head of the one who presents the sacrifice, she decapitates and dismembers him; then the demons and the wild beasts rush forward onto the quivering debris, devouring his flesh and drinking his blood. The words pronounced allude to certain *jātakas*, which tell how the Buddha, in the course of former incarnations, offered his own flesh to famished animals and anthropophagous demons."[34]

This meditation recalls the initiatic dismemberment of the future shaman by demons and the souls of ancestors. Nor is it the only example of the integration, within Lamaism, of shamanistic beliefs and techniques. Certain lama-sorcerers combat with each other by magical means, much as the Siberian shamans do. The lamas are masters of the atmosphere exactly like the shamans; they fly in the air, etc.[35] However, despite their shamanistic structure, the terrifying meditations of the Tibetan monks draw on spiritual meanings and values of an entirely

32. Stein, *Tib. Civ.*, pp. 182, 183.

33. One is dealing here with archaic techniques, already attested in ancient India (cf. *tapas*, §78) and specific to shamans; cf. Eliade, *Shamanism*, pp. 412ff., 434ff.; *Myths, Dreams, and Mysteries*, pp. 92ff., 146ff.

34. R. Bleichsteiner, *L'Église Jaune*, pp. 194–95; Eliade, *Shamanism*, p. 436. "The practice of *gčod* cannot be the result of a long spiritual preparation; psychologically speaking, it is reserved for the particularly strong disciple, lest, succumbing to the hallucinations which he himself provokes, he lose his mind. Despite the precautions taken by the masters, it would seem that this sometimes happens"; Blondeau, p. 284.

35. See Bleichsteiner, pp. 187ff., 224ff.; *Shamanism*, p. 438. The biography of Padmasambhava abounds in shamanistic features; cf. *Shamanism*, p. 434.

different order. The "contemplation of one's own skeleton," a specifically shamanic exercise, aims in Lamaism at the ecstatic experience of the unreality of the world and the self. To cite only one example, the monk must see himself as "a radiant white skeleton of enormous size, whence issueth flames so great that they fill the Void of the Universe."[36]

317. The ontology and mystical physiology of Light

This capacity to assimilate and revalorize diverse traditions, be they indigenous and archaic, or foreign and recent, characterizes the genius of Tibetan religion. One will be able to appreciate the results of such syncretism by examining certain conceptions and rituals connected with the phenomenon of Light. We have already remarked on the role of Light in discussing the myth of the *mu* cord and certain autochthonous cosmogonies of the *Bon*. Giuseppe Tucci considers the importance accorded to Light ("whether it be as generative principle, whether it be as symbol of the supreme reality, or as visible, perceptive revelation, of that light from which all issues and which is present in our self"),[37] as the fundamental characteristic of the Tibetan religious experience. For all the Lamaist schools, the Spirit (*sems*) is light, and this identity constitutes the base of the Tibetan soteriology.[38]

Let us recall, however, that in India, light was considered as the epiphany of the Spirit and of the creative energy at all levels. Indeed, such conceptions can be traced back to the Rig Veda (cf. §81). The homology—divinity, spirit, light, *semen virile*—is clearly articulated in the Brāhmaṇas and in the Upaniṣads.[39] When gods manifest themselves, and when a savior (Buddha, Mahāvīra) is born or enlightened, the event is attended by a profusion of supernatural light. For Mahāyāna Buddhism, the Spirit (= Thought) is "naturally luminous." On the other hand, we know the role which Light plays in Iranian

36. Lama Kasi Dawa Samdup and W. Y. Evans-Wentz, *Tibetan Yoga and Secret Doctrines*, p. 330.

37. Tucci, *Les religions du Tibet*, p. 97.

38. Ibid., p. 98; see also pp. 110ff., 125ff.

39. See our "Expérience de la lumière mystique" (republished in *The Two and the One*, pp. 19ff.).

theologies (cf. §215). We can thus presume that the identity between Spirit (*sems*) and Light, so important in Lamaism, would be derived from ideas that have entered Tibet from India and, indirectly, from Iran. We must, however, examine a pre-Buddhist myth about the origin of man from Light to see how this process of reinterpretation and revalorization has been accomplished within the very interior of Lamaism itself.

According to an ancient tradition, the White Light gave birth to an egg, from which emerged the primordial Man. A second version relates that the primordial Being took birth from the void and that he shone with light. Finally, another tradition explains how the passage from the Man-of-Light to actual human beings took place. In the beginning, men were asexual and without sexual desire; they had the light within themselves, and were radiant. The sun and moon did not exist. Then the sexual instinct awakened, the sexual organs appeared—and then sun and moon came forth in heaven. In the beginning, humans multiplied in the following fashion: the light which emanated from the body of the male penetrated, illuminated, and fecundated the womb of the female. The sexual instinct satisfied itself solely by light. But humans degenerated and began to touch each other with their hands, and finally they discovered sexual intercourse.[40]

According to these principles, Light and Sexuality are two antagonistic principles: when one of them dominates, the other cannot manifest itself, and the same inversely. This amounts to saying that Light is contained (or rather held captive) in the *semen virile*. As we have just recalled, the consubstantiality of the (divine) spirit, of light, and of the *semen virile* is clearly an Indo-Iranian conception. But the importance of Light in Tibetan mythology and theology (the *mu* cord, etc.) suggests an autochthonous origin of this anthropogonic theme—one, however, that does not exclude a later reinterpretation, probably under Manichaean influences.

According to Manichaeanism, the primordial Man, formed of five Lights, was conquered and devoured by the Demons of Darkness. Since then, it is in men, demonic creations, that the five Lights become captive, and particularly in the sperm (cf. §233). One meets the quintuple light again in an Indo-Tibetan interpretation of *maithuna*, the ritual union which imitates the divine "play," for it must not be con-

40. Ibid., pp. 47ff.

summated with a seminal emission (§334). Commenting on the *Guhyasamāja Tantra*, Candrakīrti and Ts'on Kapa insist on this detail: during *maithuna*, one consummates a union of a mystical order, as a result of which the couple obtains the nirvanic consciousness. For man, this nirvanic consciousness, called *bodhicitta*, the "Thought of Awakening," manifests itself by—and is in a certain sense identical with—a drop (*bindu*), which descends from the top of the head and fills the sexual organs with a jet of fivefold light. Candrakīrti prescribes: "During union, one must meditate on the *vajra* (*membrum virile*) and the *padma* (womb) as being filled, at their interior, with quintuple light."[41] The Manichaean influence seems evident in this five-light imagery. One also notes another analogy (not necessarily implying a borrowing) between the Tantric injunction to retain the sperm and the Manichaean safeguard against making the woman pregnant.

At the moment of death, the "soul" of the saint or yogin takes flight through the sinciput, like an arrow of light, and disappears through the "Smoke-hole of Heaven."[42] For the common man, the lama opens an orifice at the top of the head of the dying person in order to facilitate the release of the "soul." In the final phase of agony and for several days after the death, a lama reads on the departed's behalf the *Bardo Thödol* (*The Tibetan Book of the Dead*). The lama warns him that he will be abruptly awakened by a dazzling light: it is the encounter with his own self, which is at the same time the ultimate reality. The text enjoins the departed: "Be not daunted thereby, nor terrified, nor awed. That is the radiance of thine own true nature. Recognize it." Likewise, continues the text, the sounds of thunder and other terrifying phenomena "are . . . unable to harm thee: thou art incapable of dying. It is quite sufficient for thee to know that these apparitions are thine own thought-forms. Recognize this to be the *Bardo*."[43] But, conditioned

41. Texts cited by Tucci, "Some Glosses upon Guhyasamāja," p. 349. Let us recall that for the Mahāyāna, the cosmic elements—the *skandhas* or *dhātus*—are identified with the Tathāgatas. Now, the ultimate reality of the Tathāgatas is the differentially colored light. "All the Tathāgatas are five lights," writes Candrakīrti (Tucci, ibid., p. 348). Cf. on this problem, *The Two and the One*, pp. 37ff.; *Occultism, Witchcraft, and Cultural Fashions*, pp. 99ff.

42. This rite of the launching of the "soul" through the sinciput is still called "Opening of the Gate of Heaven"; Stein, "Architecture et pensée religieuse en Extrême-Orient," p. 184; cf. Eliade, "Briser le Toit de la Maison," pp. 136ff.

43. Evans-Wentz, *The Tibetan Book of the Dead*, p. 104.

by his karmic situation, the departed does not know how to put the lama's councils into practice. He perceives a succession of pure Lights—representing deliverance, the identification with the Buddha—but he allows himself to be drawn by impure Lights, symbolizing one after another form of post-existence or, in other words, return to the earth.[44]

Every man has his chance to attain liberation at the moment of his death: it suffices for him to recognize himself in the clear Light which he experiences at that very moment. The reading in a high voice of the *Book of the Dead* constitutes an ultimate appeal; but it is always the departed who decides his own fate. It is he who must have the will to choose the clear Light and the strength to resist the temptations of this afterlife existence. In other words, death offers a new possibility of being initiated, but this initiation, like every other, is a series of tests which the neophyte must confront and conquer. The experience of the postmortem Light constitutes the last, and perhaps the most difficult, initiatic trial.

318. Current interest in Tibetan religious creations

The *Bardo Thödol* is certainly the best-known Tibetan religious text in the Western world. Translated and published in English in 1928, it has become, especially since 1960, a sort of bedside reading for numerous young people. Such a phenomenon is significant for the history of contemporary Western spirituality. It is a profound and difficult text, unequalled in any other religious literature. The interest which it arouses, not only among the psychologists, historians, and artists, but above all among the young, is symptomatic: it indicates both the almost total desacralization of death in contemporary Western societies, and the restless inquiry and exasperated desire which seek to revalorize—religiously or philosophically—the act which terminates human existence.[45]

44. After the white and blue Lights, he will see yellow, red, and green Lights, and finally all the Lights together; ibid., pp. 110–30; cf. also pp. 173–77 and *Tibetan Yoga and Secret Doctrines,* pp. 237ff.

45. This success of an exotic "thanatology" in the contemporary Western world might be compared to the rapid diffusion of the dance of the skeletons which, according to B. Laufer, would be of Tibetan origin.

Of more modest but equally significant proportions is the growing popularity of Shambala, the mysterious land where, according to the tradition, the texts of the Kālacakra have been conserved.[46] There exist several guides to Shambala, drafted by lamas, but they are a mythical geography. In fact, the obstacles which the guides describe (mountains, rivers, lakes, deserts, diverse monsters) recall the itineraries toward fabulous lands which are spoken of in so many mythologies and folklores. What is more, certain Tibetan authors affirm that one can reach Shambala as the result of a voyage made in dreams or in ecstasies.[47] Here again, the fascination with this old myth of a land that is *paradisical* yet *real* discloses a characteristic nostalgia of desacralized Western societies. Let one recall the spectacular triumph of the mediocre novel *Lost Horizon,* and above all the film which it inspired.

After the *Bardo Thödol,* the only Tibetan work which has attained a certain success in the West has been the *Life of Milarepa,* composed at the end of the twelfth century and translated into French by J. Bacot (1925) and into English by Evans-Wentz (1938). Unfortunately, the poetic work of Milarepa (1052–1135) is hardly known. The first complete translation was published in 1962.[48] Both the life and poems of Milarepa are of exceptional interest. This magician, mystic, and poet admirably reveals the Tibetan religious genius. Milarepa begins by mastering magic in order to take revenge on his uncle; after his long and difficult apprenticeship under Marpa, he retires to a cave, attains sainthood, and experiences the beatitudes of one "delivered while alive." In his poems—which became celebrated when they were translated by poets—he renovated the Indian Tantric chanting technique (*doha*) and adapted it to indigenous chants. "He certainly did so from personal preference, but also with the idea of popularizing Buddhist thought and making it more familiar by putting it into folksongs."[49]

46. This Tantric school, still insufficiently studied, around 960 penetrated from central Asia to Bengal and to Kashmir. Sixty years later, the Kālacakra—literally "The Wheel of Time"—was introduced into Tibet conjointly with its specific system for measuring time and ascertaining its astrological implications. Cf. H. Hoffmann, *The Religions of Tibet,* pp. 126ff.; idem, "Kālacakra Studies I," passim.
47. Cf. Edwin Bernbaum, *The Way to Shambala,* pp. 205ff.
48. *The Hundred Thousand Songs of Milarepa,* trans. and annotated by Garma C. K. Chang.
49. Stein, *Tibetan Civilization,* p. 260.

Finally, it is likely that the Gesar Epic will soon be discovered, not only by comparativists but also by the cultivated public. Although the definitive redaction seems to have been achieved toward the end of the fourteenth century, the oldest epic cycle is attested three centuries earlier. The central theme builds upon the transformation of the hero. Through numerous tests, the ugly and wicked boy becomes an invincible warrior and finally the glorious sovereign Gesar, conqueror of demons and of the kings of the four directions of the world.[50]

If we have recalled the echoes which these several Tibetan religious creations have made in the West, it is because a great number of monks and erudite Tibetans find themselves, after the Chinese occupation, widely dispersed throughout the world. This diaspora may, with time, be able to radically modify, or even efface, the Tibetan religious tradition. But the oral teaching of the lamas may, on the other hand, have an effect in the West comparable to that of the exodus of the scholars of Byzantium charged with the saving of precious manuscripts after the fall of Constantinople.

The Tibetan religious synthesis presents a certain analogy with medieval Hinduism and with Christianity. In the three cases, it is a question of an encounter between a *traditional religion* (that is, a sacrality of cosmic structure), a *religion of salvation* (Buddhism, the Christian message, Vaishnavism), and an *esoteric* tradition (Tantrism, Gnosticism, magical techniques). The correspondence is still more striking between the medieval West, dominated by the Roman church, and the Lamaist theocracy.

50. Cf. Stein, ibid., pp. 276ff.; idem, *Recherches sur l'épopée*, pp. 345ff. and passim.

Abbreviations

ANET	J. B. Pritchard, *Ancient Near Eastern Texts Relating to the Old Testament* (Princeton, 1950; 2d ed., 1955)
Ar Or	*Archiv Orientálni* (Prague)
ARW	*Archiv für Religionswissenschaft* (Freiburg and Leipzig)
BEFEO	*Bulletin de l'Ecole française de l'Extrême-Orient* (Hanoi and Paris)
BJRL	*Bulletin of the John Rylands Library* (Manchester)
BSOAS	*Bulletin of the School of Oriental and African Studies* (London)
CA	*Current Anthropology* (Chicago)
HJAS	*Harvard Journal of Asiatic Studies* (Cambridge, Mass.)
HR	*History of Religions* (Chicago)
IIJ	*Indo-Iranian Journal* (The Hague)
JA	*Journal Asiatique* (Paris)
JAOS	*Journal of the American Oriental Society* (Baltimore)
JAS	*Journal of the Asiatic Society, Bombay Branch*
JIES	*Journal of Indo-European Studies* (Montana)
JNES	*Journal of Near Eastern Studies* (Chicago)
JRAS	*Journal of the Royal Asiatic Society* (London)
JSS	*Journal of Semitic Studies* (Manchester)
OLZ	*Orientalistische Literaturzeitung* (Berlin and Leipzig)
RB	*Revue Biblique* (Paris)

REG	*Revue des Etudes Grecques* (Paris)
RHPR	*Revue d'Histoire et de Philosophie religieuses* (Strasbourg)
RHR	*Revue de l'Histoire des Religions* (Paris)
SMSR	*Studi e Materiali di Storia delle Religioni* (Rome)
VT	*Vetus Testamentum* (Leiden)
WdM	*Wörterbuch der Mythologie* (Stuttgart)

Present Position of Studies: Problems and Progress. Critical Bibliographies

Chapter 31. The Religions of Ancient Eurasia

241. A good general introduction to the prehistory and protohistory of the religions of northern Eurasia has been written by Karl Jettmar in I. Paulson, A. Hultkrantz, and K. Jettmar, *Les religions arctiques et finnoises* (French ed., Paris, 1965; German ed., Stuttgart, 1962), pp. 289–340. For a historic presentation of central Asian cultures, see Mario Bussagli, *Culture e civiltà dell'Asia Centrale* (Rome, 1970), esp. pp. 27ff. (the origins of nomadic cultures), pp. 64ff. (the origins and character of the settled cultures), pp. 86ff. (the Scythic phase of the "Hunno-Sarmatic" period); this work contains excellent critical bibliographies. See also K. Jettmar, *Die frühen Steppenvölker* (Kunst der Welt, Baden-Baden, 1964); idem, "Mittelasien und Sibirien in vorturkischer Zeit," *Handbuch der Orientalistik*, i Abt. V, Bd. 5 (Leiden and Cologne, 1966), pp. 1–105; Sergei I. Rudenko, *Frozen Tombs of Siberia: The Pazyryk Burial of Iron Age Horsemen* (Los Angeles, 1970; Russian ed., 1953); E. Tryjarski, "On the Archaeological Traces of Old Turks in Mongolia," *East and West* (Rome, 1971); L. I. Albaum and R. Brentjes, *Wächter des Goldes: Zur Geschichte u. Kultur mittelasiatischer Völker vor dem Islam* (Berlin, 1972); Denis Sinor, *Introduction à l'étude de l'Eurasie Centrale* (Wiesbaden, 1963; with annotated bibliography).

The synthesis of René Grousset, *L'Empire des Steppes: Attila, Genghis-Khan, Tamerlan* (Paris, 1948), has not been surpassed. See also F. Altheim and R. Stiehl, *Geschichte Mittelasiens im Altertum* (Berlin, 1970); F. Altheim, *Attila und die Hunnen* Baden-Baden, 1951; French trans., 1953); idem, *Geschichte der Hunnen*, 1–4 (Berlin, 1959–62); E. A. Thompson, *A History of Attila and the Huns* (Oxford, 1948); Otto J. Maechen-Helfen, *The World of the Huns: Studies in Their History and Culture* (Berkeley, 1973; an important work, particularly for its use of archeological documents; extensive bibliography, pp. 486–578).

On the religious symbolism and the mythico-ritual scenarios involving the wolf (ritual transformation into a wild animal, myths of the descent of nomadic peoples from carnivores, etc.) see our study, "Les Daces et les loups" (1959; repub. in *De Zalmoxis à Genghis-Khan,* Paris, 1970, pp. 13–30; English ed., *Zalmoxis, the Vanishing God,* Chicago, 1972, pp. 12–20). "The first ancestor of Genghis Khan was a grey wolf sent from heaven, chosen by destiny; his spouse was a white hind." In this manner begins *L'Histoire secrète des Mongols.* The T'ou Kiue and the Uigurs maintain that their ancestor was a she-wolf (T'ou Kiue) or a wolf. According to Chinese sources, the Hsiung-nu are descended from a princess and a supernatural wolf. A similar myth is attested among the Kara-kirgises. (Several other versions—Tungus, Altaic, etc.—speak of the union of a princess and a dog.) See the sources cited by Freda Krestchmar, *Hundestammvater und Kerberos,* 1 (Stuttgart, 1938), pp. 3ff., 192ff. Cf. also Sir G. Clauson, "Turks and Wolves," *Studia Orientalia* (Helsinki, 1964), pp. 1–22; J.-P. Roux, *Faune et Flore sacrées dans les sociétés altaïques* (Paris, 1966), pp. 310ff.

It seems paradoxical that a wolf is united with a doe, the prey *par excellence* of the carnivores. But these myths of the foundation of a people, a nation, or a dynasty use the symbolism of the *coincidentia oppositorum* (thus the totality as the original unity) to emphasize that this is a matter of a new creation.

242.   The book by the Finnish scholar Uno Harva, *Die religiösen Vorstellungen der altaischen Völker,* FF Communications no. 125 (Helsinki, 1938), constitutes the best presentation on this subject (French trans., 1959). On the gods of the sky, see pp. 140–53; cf. also Eliade, *Traité d'histoire des religions,* §§17–18 (English ed., *Patterns in Comparative Religion,* New York, 1974, pp. 54–64). Extensive ethnographic documentation has been amassed by Wilhelm Schmidt in the last four volumes of his *Der Ursprung der Gottesidee,* vol. 9 (1949), Turks and Tatars; 10 (1952), Mongols, Tungus, Yukagirs; 11 (1954), Yakuts, Soyota, Karagas, Yenisei; 12 (1955), a synthetic view of the religions of the pastoralists of central Asia, pp. 1–613; a comparison with the African pastoralists, pp. 761–899. In using these documents, one must bear in mind the central thesis of R. P. Schmidt: the existence of an "Urmonotheismus." See idem, "Das Himmelsopfer bei den asiatischen Pferdezüchtern," *Ethnos* 7 (1942): 127–48.

On Tangri, see the monograph by Jean-Paul Roux, "Tängri: Essai sur le Ciel-Dieu des peuples altaïques," *RHR* 149 (1956): 49–82, 197–230; 150 (1957): 27–54, 173–212; "Notes additionnelles à Tängri, le Ciel-Dieu des peuples altaïques," *RHR* 154 (1958): 32–66. See also idem, "La religion des Turcs de l'Orkhon des VIIe et VIIIe siècles," *RHR* 160 (1962): 1–24.

On Turkic and Mongol religion, see now Jean-Paul Roux, *La religion des Turcs et des Mongols* (Paris, 1984). On the religion of the Mongols, consult

N. Pallisen, *Die alte Religion der Mongolischen Völker* (diss., Marburg, 1949), "Micro-Bibliotheca Anthropos" no. 7 (Freiburg, 1953). Walter Heissig, "La religion de la Mongolie," in G. Tucci and W. Heissig, *Les religions du Tibet et de la Mongolie* (French ed., Paris, 1973), pp. 340–490, presents popular religion and Lamaism among the Mongols. The author cites profusely from the edited texts and translations of his own important work: *Mongolische volksreligiöse und folkloristische Texte* (Wiesbaden, 1966).

On the religion of the Huns, see finally Otto J. Maenchen-Helfen, *The World of the Huns*, pp. 259–96, esp. pp. 267ff. (shamans and visionaries), pp. 280ff. (masks and amulets).

243. On the cosmology, see Uno Harva, *Die religiöse Vorstellungen*, pp. 20–88; M. Eliade, *Le chamanisme et les techniques archaïques de l'extase* (2d edition, 1968), pp. 211–22 (English ed., *Shamanism, Archaic Techniques of Ecstasy*, Princeton, 1972, pp. 259–79); I. Paulson, in *Les religions arctiques et finnoises*, pp. 37–46, 202–29; J. P. Roux, "Les astres chez les Turcs et les Mongols," *RHR* (1979): 153–92 (prayers toward the sun, pp. 163ff.).

As a divinity, the Earth does not seem to have played an important role: it was not represented by idols, and sacrifices were not addressed to it (cf. Harva, pp. 243–49). Among the Mongols, the Earth goddess Ötügen originally designated the first homeland of the Mongols (ibid., p. 243). See also E. Lot-Falck, "A propos d'Atüngän, déesse mongole de la terre," *RHR* 149 (1956): 157–96; W. Heissig, "Les religions de la Mongolie," pp. 470–80 ("Culte de la Terre et culte des hauteurs").

244. On the myth of the "cosmogonic dive," see our study "The Devil and God," in *Zalmoxis*, pp. 76–130. The versions of the Eurasian peoples have been presented and analyzed by W. Schmidt in vols. 9–12 of his *Ursprung der Gottesidee;* cf. his synthetic essay, vol. 12, pp. 115–73. It should be added that we are not always in agreement with this author's historical analysis and conclusions.

On Erlik, the god of death in the Paleo-Turkic inscriptions, see Annemarie v. Gabain, "Inhalt und magische Bedeutung der alttürkischen Inschriften," *Anthropos* 48 (1953): 537–56, esp. pp. 540ff.

245. On the different shamanisms—in northern and central Asia, in North and South America, in southeast Asia and Oceania, in Tibet, in China, and among the Indo-Europeans—see our *Shamanism*. The first six chapters are devoted to the shamanism of central Asia and Siberia (pp. 3–215). Among the important works published after this book's appearance, let us single out V. Dioszegi, ed., *Glaubenswelt und Folklore der sibirischen Völker* (Budapest,

1963), nine studies on shamanism; Carl-Martin Edsman, ed., *Studies in Shamanism* (Stockholm, 1967); Anna-Leena Siikala, *The Rite Technique of the Siberian Shaman*, FF Communications no. 220 (Helsinki, 1978).

For a general exposition, see Harva, *Rel. Vorstell.*, pp. 449–561. Wilhelm Schmidt sums up his ideas on the shamanism of central Asian pastoralists in *Ursprung d. Gottesidee*, vol. 12 (1955), pp. 615–759. See also J.-P. Roux, "Le nom du chaman dans les textes turco-mongols," *Anthropos* 53 (1958): 133–42; idem, "Éléments chamaniques dans les textes pré-mongols," ibid., pp. 440–56; Walter Heissig, *Zur Frage der Homogenität des ostomongolischen Schamanismus* (Collectanea Mongolica, Wiesbaden, 1966); idem, "Chamanisme des Mongols," in *Les religions de la Mongolie*, pp. 351–72; "Le repression lamaïque du chamanisme," ibid., pp. 387–400.

On the diseases and initiatory dreams of future shamans, see Eliade, *Shamanism*, pp. 33ff.; idem, *Mythes, rêves et mystères* (Paris, 1957), pp. 110ff. (English ed., *Myths, Dreams, and Mysteries*, New York, 1975, pp. 73ff.). Far from being neurotics (as a number of scholars, from Krivushapkin in 1861 to Ohlmarks in 1939, have maintained), the shamans appear superior to their milieu in intellectual terms. "They are the principal custodians of the rich oral literature: the poetic vocabulary of a Yakut shaman comprises some 12,000 words, whilst his ordinary speech—all that is known to the rest of the community—consists of only 4,000. . . . The shamans exhibit powers of memory and self-control well above the average. They can perform their ecstatic dance in the very restricted space in the middle of a yurt crowded with spectators; and this without touching or hurting anyone, though they are wearing costumes loaded with from thirty to forty pounds of iron in the form of discs and other objects" (*Myths, Dreams, and Mysteries*, p. 78).

G. V. Ksenofontov's book has been translated into German by A. Friedrich and G. Buddruss, *Schamanengeschichten aus Sibirien* (Munich, 1956).

On the public initiation of the Buryat shamans, see the sources cited and summarized in *Shamanism*, pp. 115–22 (p. 115, n. 15, bibliography).

246. On the myths of origins of the shamans, see L. Steinberg, "Divine Election in Primitive Religions" (*Congrès International des Américanistes*, session 21, pt. 2 [1924], Göteborg, 1925), pp. 472–512, esp. pp. 474ff.; Eliade, *Shamanism*, pp. 68ff.

On the Altaic horse sacrifice, see W. Radlov, *Aus Sibirien: lose Blätter aus dem Tagebuche eines reisenden Linguisten* (Leipzig, 1884), vol. 2, pp. 20–50, summarized in *Shamanism*, pp. 190–98. See ibid., pp. 198–200, for the historical analysis of the connections between Tengere Kaira kan, Bai Ulgän, and the shamanic horse sacrifice.

On ecstatic descents into Hell, see *Shamanism*, pp. 200–224. Cf. Jean-Paul Roux, *La mort chez les peuples altaïques anciens et médiévaux* (Paris, 1963);

idem, "Les chiffres symboliques 7 et 9 chez les Turcs non musulmans," *RHR* 168 (1965): 29–53.

Among certain peoples, the division of "white" and "black" shamans is known, although it is not always easy to define the opposition. Among the Buryats, the innumerable class of demigods is subdivided into black Khans served by the "black shamans," and the white Khans, protectors of the "white shamans." This situation is not, however, primitive; according to the myths, the first shaman was "white"; the "black" one did not appear until later; cf. Garma Sandschejew, "Weltanschauung und Schamanismus der Alaren-Burjaten," *Anthropos* 27 (1927–28): 933–55; 28 (1928): 538–60, 967–86, esp. p. 976. On the morphology and origin of this dualistic division, see *Shamanism*, pp. 184–89. See also J.-P. Roux, "Les Etres intermédiares chez les peuples altaïques," in *Génies, Anges et Démons*, Sources Orientales, 8 (Paris, 1971), pp. 215–56; idem, "La danse chamanique de l'Asie centrale," in *Les Danses Sacrées*, Sources Orientales, 6 (Paris, 1963), pp. 281–314.

247. On the symbolism of the shaman's costume and drum, see *Shamanism*, pp. 145–80.

On the formation of North Asian shamanism, see ibid., pp. 288–300. On the role of shamanism in religion and culture, see ibid., pp. 508–11.

248. To the Paleo-Siberian linguistic group belong the Yukagirs, Chukchees, Koryaks, and Gilyaks. The Uralian languages are spoken by the Samoyeds, Ostyaks, and Voguls. The Finno-Ugrians include the Finns, Cheremis, Votyaks, Hungarians, etc.

Uno Harva's *Die Religion der Tscheremissen*, FF Communications no. 61 (Poorvo, 1926), merits special mention. A general presentation of the "Religions des Asiates septentrionaux (tribus de Sibérie)" and the "Religions des peuples finnois" has been given by Ivan Paulson in *Les religions arctiques et finnoises*, pp. 15–136, 147–261 (excellent bibliographies).

On the celestial god Num, see M. Castrén, *Reiseerinnerung aus den Jahren 1838–44*, 1 (St. Petersburg, 1853), pp. 250ff.; Paulson, "Les religions des Asiates septentrionaux," pp. 61ff.; R. Pettazzoni, *L'onniscienza di Dio* (Turin, 1955), pp. 379ff.

On the myth of the cosmogonic dive, see Eliade, *Zalmoxis*, pp. 76ff.

On Ugrian shamanism, see Eliade, *Shamanism*, pp. 220ff.; among Estonians, cf. Oskar Loorits, *Grundzüge des estnischen Volksglauben*, 1 (Lund, 1949), pp. 259ff.; 2 (1951), pp. 459ff. On Lapp shamanism, see Louise Backman and Ake Hultkrantz, *Studies in Lapp Shamanism* (Stockholm, 1978).

On the "shamanic" origins of Väinämöinen and other heroes of the *Ka-*

levala, see Martti Haavio, *Väinämöinen, Eternal Sage,* FF Communications no. 144 (Helsinki, 1952).

On the Master of the Animals and guardian spirits, protectors of game, see Ivan Paulson, *Schutzgeister und Gottheiten des Wildes (der Jagdiere und Fische) in Nordeurasien: Eine religionsethnographische u. religions-phänomenologische Untersuchung jägerischer Glaubensvorstellungen* (Stockholm, 1961). See idem, "Les religions des Asiates septentrionaux (tribus de Sibérie)," pp. 70–102; "Les religions des peuples finnois," pp. 170–87; "The Animal Guardian: A Critical and Synthetic Review," *HR* 3 (1964): 202–19. One finds the same ideas among the primitive hunters of North and South America, Africa, the Caucasus, etc.; cf. the bibliography recorded by Paulson, "The Animal Guardian," nn. 1–12.

249. The written sources have been edited by C. Clemen, *Fontes historiae religionum primitivarum, praeindogermanicarum, indogermanicarum minus notarum* (Bonn, 1936): A. Mierzynski, *Mythologiae lituanicae monumenta,* 1–2 (Varsovie, 1892–95), presents and studies the sources up to the middle of the fifteenth century. On the position of studies up to 1952, see Haralds Biezais, "Die Religionsquellen der baltischen Völker und die Ergebnisse der bisherigen Forschungen," *Arv* 9 (1953): 65–128.

A comprehensive study of Baltic religion is given by Haralds Biezais in Ake V. Ström and Biezais, *Germanische und baltische Religion* (Stuttgart, 1975). One finds general presentations, written from different perspectives, in V. Pisani, "La religione dei Balti," in Tacchi Venturi, *Storia delle Religioni,* 6th ed. (Turin, 1971), vol. 2, pp. 407–61; Marija Gimbutas, *The Balts* (London and New York, 1963), pp. 179–204; Jonas Balys and Haralds Biezais, "Baltische Mythologie," in *WdM* 1 (1965): 375–454.

Considerable documentation, especially on the folklore and ethnography, with extensive bibliographies, can be found in the works of Haralds Biezais, *Die Gottesgestalt der Lettischen Volksreligion* (Stockholm, 1961) and *Die himmlische Götterfamilie der alten Letten* (Uppsala, 1972). See also H. Usener, *Götternamen,* 3d ed. (Frankfurt am Main, 1948), pp. 79–122, 280–83; W. C. Jaskiewicz, "A Study in Lithuanian Mythology: Juan Lasicki's Samogitian Gods," *Studi Baltici* 9 (1952): 65–106.

On Dievs, cf. Biezais, *WdM* 1 (1965): 403–5; idem, "Gott der Götter," in *Acta Academia Aboensis,* Ser. A., Humaniora, vol. 40, no. 2 (Abo, 1971).

Perkūnas, Lettish Pērkons, Old Prussian Percunis, derive from a Balto-Slavic form *Perqūnos (cf. Old Slavic Perunu) and are related to the Vedic Parjanya, the Albanian Perën-di, and the Germanic Fjorgyn. On Perkūnas, see J. Balys in *WdM* 1 (1965): 431–34, and the bibliography cited therein, p. 434. On Pērkons, see Biezais, *Die himmlische Götterfamilie der alten Letten,* pp. 92–179 (pp. 169ff., a comparative study of Indo-European storm gods).

The Baltic cosmogonic myths are not known. There is a Tree of the Sun

(= Cosmic Tree) in the middle of the Ocean or toward the West; the setting Sun hangs its belt there before going to its repose.

On the Goddess of the Sun, Saule, and her sons and daughters, and the celestial weddings, see Biezais, *Die himmlische Götterfamilie der alten Letten,* pp. 183–538. Saule's daughters are similar to the Indo-European goddesses of the dawn.

On Laima, see Biezais, *Die Hauptgöttinen der alten Letten* (Uppsala, 1955), pp. 119ff. (her connections with fortune and misfortune), pp. 139ff. (her relations with God), pp. 158ff. (with the Sun). As the goddess of destiny, Laima rules over birth, marriage, abundance of harvests, and the well-being of animals (pp. 179–275). Biezais's interpretation has been accepted by a number of Balticists (cf. the review by Alfred Gaters in *Deutsche Literaturzeitung* 78, 9 Sept. 1957), but has been rejected by the Estonian scholar Oskar Loorits; cf. "Zum Problem der lettischen Schicksalsgöttinen," *Zeitschrift für slavische Philologie* 26 (1957): 78–103. The central problem is the following: in what measure do the folksongs (*daina*) represent authentic documents of ancient Lettish paganism? According to Pēteris Šmits, the *daina* would have flourished between the twelfth and sixteenth centuries. On the contrary, Biezais estimates that the *daina* have preserved much more ancient religious traditions; the "flowering" in the sixteenth century only reflects a new epoch in popular poetic creativity (*Die Hauptgöttinen,* pp. 31ff., 48ff.). Other scholars are equally insistent that the *daina* are susceptible to continual self-renewal (cf. Antanas Maceina in *Commentationes Balticae,* 2, 1965). But Oskar Loorits estimates that the *dainas* are relatively too recent for Laima to have been an ancient divinity of Indo-European origin; her function as divinity of destiny is secondary (p. 82); Laima is an "inferior" divinity, her role being limited, according to Loorits, to aiding in childbirth and blessing the newborn (p. 93); in short, Laima is a secondary manifestation of a syncretic type, much like the figure of the Virgin Mary in Lettish religious folklore (pp. 90ff.).

Let us recall, however, that the chronological criterion no longer imposes itself when it is a matter of evaluating not the age of the *oral literary expression of a belief, but its religious content.* The patron goddesses of childbirth and the newborn have an archaic structure; see, inter alia, Momolina Marconi, *Riflessi mediterranei nella più antica religione laziale* (Milan, 1939); G. Rank, "Lappe Female Deities of the Madder-akka Group," *Studia Septentrionalia,* 6 (Oslo, 1955), pp. 7–79. It is difficult to believe that the popular Baltic feminine deities or semideities—Laima, etc.—have been fabricated after the model of the Virgin Mary. More likely, Mary replaces the ancient pagan divinities, or again these latter, after the Christianization of the Balts, have borrowed traits from the mythology and cult of the Virgin.

On lycanthropy toward "positive" ends, affirmed by an old Lett of the eighteenth century, see the text of the trial published by Otto Höfler,

Kultische Geheimbünde der Germanen, 1 (Frankfurt am Main, 1934), pp. 345–51, and summarized in our *Occultism, Witchcraft, and Cultural Fashions* (Chicago, 1978), pp. 77–78. Cf. ibid., pp. 73ff., 78ff., the analysis of several analogous phenomena (the *benandanti* of Aquileia, the Romanian *strigoï,* etc.).

On the archaism of Baltic folklore, see also Marija Gimbutas, "The Ancient Religion of the Balts," *Lituanus* 4 (1962): 97–108. Light has also been shed on other Indo-European survivals; cf. Jaan Puhvel, "Indo-European Structure of the Baltic Pantheon," in *Myth in Indo-European Antiquity,* ed. G. J. Larson (Berkeley, 1974), pp. 75–85; Marija Gimbutas, "The Lithuanian God Velnias," in Larson, ed., pp. 87–92. See also Robert L. Fischer, Jr., "Indo-European Elements in Baltic and Slavic Chronicles," in *Myth and Law among the Indo-Europeans,* Jaan Puhvel, ed. (Berkeley, 1970), pp. 147–58.

250.   For a clear and concise presentation of the origin and ancient history of the Slavs, see Marija Gimbutas, *The Slavs* (London and New York, 1971); cf. also V. Pisani, "Baltico, slavo, iranico," *Ricerche Slavistiche* 15 (1967): 3–24.

The Greek and Latin texts on the religion have been edited by C. H. Meyer, *Fontes historiae religionis slavicae* (Berlin, 1931). In the same volume are found the Icelandic text and Latin translation of the *Knytlingasaga,* and the Arabic documents in German translation. The most important sources have been translated by A. Brückner, *Die Slawen,* Religionsgeschichtliches Lesebuch, vol. 3 (Tübingen, 1926), pp. 1–17. The sources concerning the eastern Slavs have been published and abundantly annotated by V. J. Mansikka, *Die Religion der Ostslaven,* 1 (Helsinki, 1922).

There is no comprehensive work on the religious history of the Slavs. For a general presentation, see L. Niederle, *Manuel de l'antiquité slave,* vol. 2 (Paris 1926), pp. 126–68; B. O. Unbegaun, *La religion des anciens Slaves* (*Mana,* vol. 3 [Paris, 1948]), pp. 389–445 (rich bibliography); Marija Gimbutas, *The Slavs,* pp. 151–70.

On the mythology, see Aleksander Brückner, *La mitologia slava,* trans. from the Polish by Julia Dicksteinówna (Bologna, 1923); R. Jakobson, "Slavic Mythology," in Funk and Wagnalls' *Dictionary of Folklore, Mythology, and Legend* (New York, 1950), vol. 2, pp. 1025–28; N. Reiter, "Mythology der alten Slaven," *WdM* 1, 6 (Stuttgart, 1964): 165–208 (with bibliography).

On the religion of the western Slavs, see Th. Palm, *Wendische Kultstätten* (Lund, 1937); E. Wienecke, *Untersuchungen zur Religion der Westslawen* (Leipzig, 1940); R. Pettazzoni, *L'onniscienza di Dio,* pp. 334–72 ("Divinità policefale").

On the conception of divinity among the Slavs, see Bruno Merriggi, "Il concetto del Dio nelle religioni dei popoli slavi," *Ricerche Slavistiche* 1 (1952): 148–76; cf. also Alois Schmaus, "Zur altslawischen Religionsgeschichte," *Saeculum* 4 (1953): 206–30.

A very rich comparative study of the ethnology and folklore of the Slavs has been completed by Evel Gasparini, *Il Matriarcato Slavo: Antropologia dei Protoslavi* (Florence, 1973), with an extensive bibliography (pp. 710–46). Certain of the author's conclusions are subject to caution, but his documentation is invaluable; cf. our observations in *HR* 14 (1974): 74–78. The work of F. Haase, *Volksglaube und Brauchtum der Ostslawen* (Breslau, 1939), is still very useful. See also Vladimir Propp, *Feste agrarie russe* (Bari, 1978).

The *Chronica Slavorum* of Helmold (approximately 1108–77) has been edited in *Monumenta Germaniae historica,* vol. 21 (Hannover, 1869). The passages concerning religion have been reproduced by V. J. Mansikka, *Die Religion der Ostslaven,* 1, and by Aleksander Brückner, *Die Slawen,* pp. 4–7. On the *Chronicle of Nestor,* see Brückner, *Mitologia Slava,* pp. 242–43; idem, *Die Slawen,* pp. 16–17.

Of the rich bibliography on Perun, it suffices to mention Brückner, *Mitologia Slava,* pp. 55–80 (hypercritical); R. Jakobson, "Slavic Mythology," p. 1026; Gasparini, *Matriarcato Slavo,* pp. 537–42. Certain authors have seen in Perun "the supreme God, the master of the thunderbolt," of whom the Byzantine historian Procopius speaks. But the celestial god, distant and indifferent, evoked by Helmold, is by his very structure different from the gods of the storm. On the value of Procopius's testimony, see R. Benedicty, "Prokopios Berichte über die slawische Vorzeit," *Jahrbuch der Oesterreichischen Byzantinischen Gesellschaft* (1965), pp. 51–78.

On Volos/Veles, see Brückner, *Mitologia Slava,* pp. 119–40; R. Jakobson, "Slavic Mythology," p. 1027; idem, "The Slavic God 'Veles' and His Indo-European Cognates," *Studi Linguistici in Onore di Vittore Pisani* (Brescia, 1969), pp. 579–99; Jaan Puhvel, "Indo-European Structures of the Baltic Pantheon," in *Myth in Indo-European Antiquity,* ed. G. I. Larson (Berkeley and Los Angeles, 1974), pp. 75–89, esp. pp. 88–89; Marija Gimbutas, "The Lithuanian God Veles," in Larson, pp. 87–92.

On Simarglŭ, see Jakobson, "Slavic Mythology," p. 1027. On Mokosh, see Brückner, *Mitologia Slava,* pp. 141ff. On Dazhbog, see Brückner, *Mitologia Slava,* pp. 96ff.; Jakobson, "Slavic Mythology," p. 1027 (the two works contain a rich bibliography).

On Rod and *rozhenitsa,* see Brückner, *Mitologia Slava,* pp. 166ff. On Matisyra zemlja, see Gimbutas, *The Slavs,* p. 169. Her principal feast, *Kupala* (from *kupati,* "to bathe"), took place at the summer solstice, and included a ritual lighting of fires and a collective bath. An idol was made of straw, *kupala,* dressed as a woman, and was placed under a tree trunk that was cut, stripped of its branches, and crammed into the earth. Among the

Baltic Slavs, the women alone cut and prepared the sacred tree (a birch) and offered it sacrifices. The birch represented the Cosmic Tree which connects the Earth to the Sky (Gimbutas, p. 169).

On the Baltic gods, see the works of Th. Palm and E. Wienecke cited above, and the critical remarks of Pettazzoni, *L'onniscienza di Dio,* pp. 562ff.

The Germanic sources and the *Knytlinga Saga* (written in Old Icelandic in the thirteenth century) supply certain important information on the sanctuaries and cult of Rüggen. The wooden idols, decorated with metal, had three, four, or more heads. At Stettin, a temple was dedicated to Triglav, the tricephalic "Summus Deus." The statue of Sventovit at Arkona had four heads. Other idols had still more; Rugevit presented seven faces on a single head.

On Svantovit, see Reiter, "Mythology der alten Slaven," pp. 195–96; V. Machek, "Die Stellung des Gottes Svantovit in der altslavischen Religion," in *Orbis Scriptus* (Munich, 1966), pp. 491–97.

251. For the spirits of the forest (*leshy,* etc.), see the documentation in Gasparini, *Il Matriarcato Slavo,* pp. 494ff. For the *demovoi,* see ibid., pp. 503ff.

For the different versions of the myth of the cosmogonic dive, see chap. 3 of our *Zalmoxis,* pp. 76–131.

On Bogomilism, see the bibliography cited in §293, below.

On Slavic "dualism," see the bibliography cited in *Zalmoxis,* pp. 91–92, nn. 34–36.

Chapter 32. The Christian Churches up to the Iconoclastic Crisis

252. Let us mention several recent syntheses on the end of antiquity: S. Mazzarino, *The End of the Ancient World* (London, 1966), presents and analyzes the hypotheses advanced by modern historians; Peter Brown, *The World of Late Antiquity* (London, 1971), to this day, the best introduction to the subject; Hugh Trevor-Roper, *The Rise of Christian Europe* (New York, 1965), esp. pp. 9–70. The book of Johannes Geffcken, *Der Ausgang des grieschisch-römischen Heidentums,* 2d ed. (Heidelberg, 1929), has not been surpassed. Among the more detailed works, let us cite Ferdinand Lot, *La fin du monde antique et le début du Moyen Age* (Paris, 1951); Michael Rostovtzeff, *Social and Economic History of the Roman Empire,* 2d ed., vols. 1–2 (Oxford, 1957); Ernst Stein, *Histoire du Bas Empire,* 1–2 (Brussels, 1949, 1959); Lucien Musset, *Les invasions: les vagues germaniques* (Paris, 1965; 2d rev. ed., 1969); idem, *Les invasions: le second assaut contre l'Europe chrétienne: VII-XIe siècles* (1966). See also the studies of the different scholars in A. Momigliano, ed., *The Conflict between Paganism and Christianity in the Fourth Century* (1963), above all Momigliano, "Pagan and Christian Historiography in the Fourth Century," ibid., pp. 79–99. Cf. Peter Brown, *The Making of Late Antiquity* (Cambridge, Mass., 1978).

On the reaction of the pagan elites, see P. de Labriolle, *La réaction païenne: Etude sur la polémique anti-chrétienne du Ier au VIe siècle* (new ed., Paris, 1950), and above all Walter Emil Kaegi, *Byzantium and the Decline of Rome* (Princeton, 1968), esp. pp. 59–145.

The most recent (and the best) edition and critical translation of *The City of God* is the *La Cité de Dieu* of the *Etudes Augustiniennes,* in five volumes, edited by B. Dombart and A. Kalb and translated by G. Combès (Paris, 1959–60).

On the preparation and the structure of *The City of God,* see Peter Brown, *Augustine of Hippo: A Biography* (Berkeley and Los Angeles, 1967), pp. 299–329. See also J. Claude Guy, *Unité et structure logique de la "Cité de Dieu" de saint Augustin* (Paris, 1961). It may seem paradoxical that Saint Augustine does not discuss contemporary religious expressions (the Mysteries, Eastern religions, Mithraism, etc.), but rather an archaic paganism which, according to Peter Brown, "existed solely in the libraries." But by the fifth century, the pagan elites were enthusiastic over the *litterata vetustas*— the immemorial tradition conserved by the classical writers (Brown, p. 305).

On the cyclical conception in Greek and Roman historiography, as well as in Judaism and Christianity, see G. W. Trompf, *The Idea of Historical Recurrence in Western Thought: From Antiquity to the Reformation* (Berkeley and Los Angeles, 1979), esp. pp. 185ff.

253. Of the enormous critical literature on Saint Augustine, let us cite: H. I. Marrou, *S. Augustin et la fin de la culture antique* (1938; 2d ed., 1949), and Peter Brown, *Augustine of Hippo* (these two works include the richest bibliographies). See also Etienne Gilson, *Introduction à l'étude de saint Augustin,* 2d ed. (Paris, 1943); idem, *La philosophie au moyen âge* (Paris, 1944), pp. 125ff.; P. Borgomeo, *L'Eglise de ce temps dans la prédication de saint Augustin* (Paris, 1972); E. Lamirande, *L'Eglise céleste selon saint Augustin* (1963); Roy W. Battenhouse, ed., *A Companion to the Study of St. Augustine* (Oxford, 1955).

254. On the Fathers of the Church, see J. Quasten, *The Golden Age of Greek Patristic Literature from the Council of Nicaea to the Council of Chalcedon* (Utrecht, 1960); H. A. Wolfson, *The Philosophy of the Church Fathers,* vols. 1–2 (Cambridge, Mass., 1956); J. Plagnieux, *Saint Grégoire de Nazianze théologien* (Paris, 1952); J. Daniélou, *Platonisme et théologie mystique: Essai sur la doctrine spirituelle de saint Grégoire de Nysse,* 2d ed. (Paris, 1954); O. Chadwick, *John Cassian: A Study in Primitive Monasticism*

(Cambridge, 1950); J. R. Palanque, *Saint Ambroise et l'empire romain* (Paris, 1933); P. Antin, *Essai sur saint Jérôme* (Paris, 1951).

On Origen, see Eugène de Faye, *Origène, sa vie, son oeuvre, sa pensée*, 1–3 (Paris, 1923–28), and, above all, Pierre Nautin, *Origène: Sa vie et son oeuvre* (Paris, 1977). Nautin carefully analyzes all the accessible sources to establish the biography and reconstruct, at least in its main lines, Origen's thought. On the biography written by Eusebius in his *Ecclesiastical History* (on which see Nautin, pp. 19–98), see Robert Grant, *Eusebius as Church Historian* (Oxford, 1980), pp. 77–83.

Nautin justly remarks that Origen "failed in his death. If he had perished in his dungeon, the title of martyr would have protected his memory from the attacks which were levelled at him for several centuries. He had, however, desired martyrdom his entire life: he wished to throw himself into it following his father under Septimius Severus; he was again ready for it under Maximin of Thrace when he wrote the *Exhortation to Martyrdom;* he submitted to its sufferings under Decius, but he did not earn its glory in the eyes of posterity" (p. 441).

The treatise *De principiis,* the complete text of which is found only in the Latin version of Rufinus, has been translated into English by G. W. Butterworth, *On First Principles* (London, 1936), and into French by Henri Crouzel and Manlio Simonetti, *Traité des Principes,* "Sources Chrétiennes," 4 vols. (1978–80). The fourth book of the *De principiis,* together with the *Exhortation to Martyrdom, The Prayer,* the prologue to the commentary on the Song of Songs, and *Homily XXVII on Martyrs,* have been translated by Rowan A. Greer, *Origen* (New York, 1979). See also *Commentaire sur saint Jean,* "Sources Chrétiennes," 3 vols. (1966–75), ed. and trans. by Cécile Blanc; *Contre Celse,* 5 vols. (1967–76), ed. and trans. by Marcel Borret; *Commentaire sur L'Evangile selon Matthieu* (Paris, 1970), ed. and trans. by Marcel Girot; *Les Homélies sur les Nombres,* trans. A. Méhat (Paris, 1951); and the *Homélies sur Jérémie,* ed. and trans. by P. Nautin (Paris, 1976–77).

On the formation of the *Hexaples,* see Nautin, *Origène,* pp. 333–61.

On Origen's theology, see H. de Lubac, *Histoire et esprit: L'Intelligence de l'Écriture d'après Origène* (Paris, 1950); H. Crouzel, *Théologie de l'image de Dieu chez Origène* (Paris, 1956); B. Drewery, *Origen on the Doctrine of Grace* (London, 1960); M. Harl, *Origène et la fonction révélatrice du Verbe Incarné* (Paris, 1958).

Origen's adversaries often accused him of supporting metempsychosis in his treatise *De principiis* (*Peri Archon*). See the critical analysis of Claude Tresmontant, *La métaphysique du christianisme et la naissance de la philosophie chrétienne* (Paris, 1961), pp. 395–518. However, Pierre Nautin observes that Origen himself "had always energetically rejected this accusation. His hypothesis allowed for only one incarnation of the soul in each world:

there was no metensomatosis (= metempsychosis) but simply ensomatosis''
(Nautin, p. 126).

255. The best edition and translation of the *Confessions* is that of A. Soli-
gnac, E. Tréhorel, and G. Bouissou, *Oeuvres de saint Augustin*, vols. 13–14
(1961–62). See P. Courcelle, *Les "Confessions" de saint Augustin dans la
tradition littéraire: Antécédents et postérité* (Paris, 1963).

On Manichaeanism in Roman Africa and Saint Augustine, see F. Decret,
L'Afrique manichéenne (IV–Vᵉ siècles): Étude historique et doctrinale, 2
vols. (1978); idem, *Aspects du manichéisme dans l'Afrique romaine: Les con-
troverses de Fortunatus, Faustus et Felix avec saint Augustin* (1970).

Fragments of Augustine's anti-Manichaean treatises (notably *Acta contra
Fortunatum Manichaeum*, written in 392, *De Genesi contra Manichaeos*,
388, and *De natura boni contra Manichaeos*, 398–99) are reproduced and
commented upon by Claude Tresmontant, *La métaphysique du Christianisme*,
pp. 528–49.

On Donatus and Donatism, see W. H. C. Frend, *The Donatist Church*
(Oxford, 1952); G. Willis, *Saint Augustine and the Donatist Controversy*
(London, 1950).

On Pelagius and Pelagianism, see G. de Plinval, *Pélage: Ses écrits, sa vie
et sa réforme* (Lausanne, 1943); J. Fergusson, *Pelagius* (Cambridge, 1956); S.
Prete, Pelagio e il Pelagianesimo (1961). Cf. also Peter Brown, *Augustine of
Hippo*, pp. 340–75.

Augustine's texts on the origin of the soul, original sin, and predestination
are cited and discussed by Claude Tresmontant, *La métaphysique*, pp. 588–
612.

On the theology of Nature and Grace, especially in Saint Augustine, see A.
Mandouze, *Saint Augustin: L'aventure de la raison et de la grâce* (Paris,
1968), and, more definitively, Jaroslav Pelikan, *The Emergence of the Catholic Tradition, 100–600* (Chicago, 1971), pp. 278–331.

256. On the evolution of Saint Augustine's opinions concerning the cult of
martyrs, see, finally, Victor Saxer, *Morts, martyrs, reliques en Afrique chrétienne aux premiers siècles* (Paris, 1980), pp. 191–280.

On the cult of the saints and the religious exaltation of relics in the Western
Church, see the fundamental works of H. Delehaye, *"Sanctus," essai sur le
culte des saints dans l'antiquité* (Brussels, 1927); *Les origines du culte des
martyrs*, 2d ed. (Brussels, 1933); *Les légendes hagiographiques*, 4th ed.
(Brussels, 1955). The little book of Peter Brown, *The Cult of the Saints: Its
Rise and Function in Latin Christianity* (Chicago, 1980), returns to the problem and in good part replaces the earlier literature on the subject.

On the *martyria*, the work of André Grabar, *Martyrium, recherches sur le*

culte des reliques et l'art chrétien antique, 1–2 (Paris, 1946), remains fundamental. Cf. also E. Baldwin Smith, *The Dome: A Study in the History of Ideas*
(Princeton, 1950).

On the sale of relics in the High Middle Ages, see, finally, Patrick J.
Geary, "The Ninth-Century Relic Trade: A Response to Popular Piety?" in
James Obelkevich, ed., *Religion and the People, 800–1700* (Chapel Hill,
1979), pp. 8–19.

On the pilgrimage, see B. Kötting, *Peregrinatio religiosa: Wallfahrten in
der Antiken und das Pilgerwesen in der alten Kirche* (Münster, 1950).

An exemplary monograph on the genesis and development of the legends of
Saint Nicholas, perhaps the most popular saint, has been written by Charles
W. Jones, *Saint Nicholas of Myra, Bari, and Manhattan: Biography of a
Legend* (Chicago, 1978).

257.   For a general introduction, see J. Daniélou, *Message évangélique et
culture hellénistique* (Paris, 1961); Jaroslav Pelikan, *The Spirit of Eastern
Christendom* (Chicago, 1974); Hans-George Beck, *Kirche u. theologische
Literatur im byzantinischen Reich* (Munich, 1959); D. Obolensky, *The By-
zantine Commonwealth: Eastern Europe, 500–1454* (London, 1971); Francis
Dvornik, *The Idea of Apostolicity in Byzantium and the Legend of the Apostle
Andrew* (Cambridge, Mass., 1958); Olivier Clément, *L'essor du chris-
tianisme oriental* (Paris, 1967).

The history and consequences of the Council of Chalcedon have been presented by R. V. Sellers, *The Council of Chalcedon* (London, 1953), and in
detail in the studies assembled by Aloys Grillmeier and Heinrich Bacht, *Das
Konzil von Chalkedon: Geschichte und Gegenwart,* 3 vols. (Würzburg,
1951–52).

On Monophysitism, see W. H. C. Frend, *The Rise of the Monophysite
Movement: Chapters in the History of the Church in the Fifth and Sixth Centuries* (Cambridge, 1972).

On the Byzantine liturgy, see N. M. D. R. Boulet, *Eucharistie ou la Messe
dans ses variétés, son histoire et ses origines* (Paris, 1953); Jean Hani, *La
divine liturgie: Aperçus sur la Messe* (Paris, 1981). On Romanos Melodus,
see E. Wellecz, *A History of Byzantine Music and Hymnography* (Oxford, 1949).

On the symbolism of the Byzantine church, see H. Sedlmayr, *Die Entstehung der Kathedrale* (Zurich, 1950); Jean Hani, *Le symbolisme du temple
chrétien,* 2d ed. (Paris, 1978).

On *theosis* ("divinization"), see Jules Cross, *La divinisation du chrétien
d'après les Pères grecs: Contribution historique à la doctrine de la grâce*
(Paris, 1938); Pelikan, *The Spirit of Eastern Christendom,* pp. 10–36.

On Maximus the Confessor, see Hans Urs von Balthasar, *Kosmische Litur-*

gie (Freiburg, 1941); Lars Thunberg, *Microcosm and Mediator: The Theological Anthropology of Maximus the Confessor* (Lund, 1965); Irénée Hausherr, *Philautie: De la tendresse pour soi à la charité, selon saint Maxime le Confesseur* (Rome, 1952).

The best French translation of Dionysius the (Pseudo-) Areopagite is that of Maurice de Gandillac (Paris, 1942). On the influence of Maximus the Confessor in the West, through the Latin translation of Dionysius, see Deno John Geanakoplos, *Interaction of the 'Sibling' Byzantine and Western Cultures in the Middle Ages and the Italian Renaissance, 330–1600* (Yale, 1976), pp. 133–45.

258. The iconoclastic movement had two phases: the first from 726 to 787, the second between 813 and 843. In 726, the Emperor Leo III promulgated an edict against the use of icons, and his son, Constantine V (745–775), continued the same policy. Constantine V also rejected the cult of the saints and even that of the Virgin; he prohibited the terms "saint" and *theotokos:* "if someone makes an image of Christ, . . . he has not really penetrated the depths of the dogma of the inseparable union of the two natures of Christ" (text cited by Pelikan, *The Spirit of Eastern Christendom,* p. 116).

The Council of Hierea in 754 unanimously condemned the cult of images. However, in 787 the widow of Leo III and the Patriarch of Constantinople convoked the Seventh Ecumenical Council at Nicaea. Iconoclasm was declared anathema, but it was reintroduced in 815 by Emperor Leo V. It was not until 843 that the Synod called by the Empress Theodora definitively reestablished the cult of the icons.

Let us add that the iconoclasts destroyed all the icons they were able to find, and that the second Council of Nicaea (783) ordered the confiscation of all iconoclastic literature; no original text has come down to us.

On the origin of the cult of the icons, see A. Grabar, *L'iconoclasme byzantin, dossier archéologique* (Paris, 1957), pp. 13–91; E. Kitzinger, "The Cult of Images in the Age before Iconoclasm," *Dumbarton Oaks Papers* 8 (1954): 83–159.

For a comparative study, see Edwin Bevan, *Holy Images: An Inquiry into Idolatry and Image-Worship in Ancient Paganism and Christianity* (London, 1940).

On the history of the controversy, see N. Iorga, *Histoire de la vie byzantine: Empire et civilisation d'après les sources* (Bucharest, 1934), 2, pp. 30ff., 65ff.; E. I. Matin, *A History of the Iconoclastic Controversy* (New York, n. d.); Stephen Gero, *Byzantine Iconoclasm during the Reign of Constantine V* (Louvain, 1977); Paul J. Alexander, *The Patriarch Nicephorus of Constantinople: Ecclesiastical Policy and Image Worship in the Byzantine Empire* (Oxford, 1958); Norman Baynes, "The Icons before Iconoclasm,"

Harvard Theological Review 44 (1955): 93–106; idem, "Idolatry and the Early Church," *Byzantine Studies and Other Essays* (London, 1960), pp. 116–43; Gerhart B. Ladner, "The Concept of the Image in the Greek Fathers and the Byzantine Iconoclastic Controversy," *Dumbarton Oaks Papers* 7 (1953): 1–34; Milton Anastos, "The Argument for Iconoclasm as Presented by the Iconoclasts in 754 and 815," *Dumbarton Oaks Papers* 7 (1953): 35–54. See also George Florovsky, "Origen, Eusebius and the Iconoclastic Controversy," *Church History* 19 (1956): 77–96; Peter Brown, "A Dark-Age Crisis: Aspects of the Iconoclastic Controversy," first published in *English Historical Review* 88 (1973): 1–34; now in Brown, *Society and the Holy in Late Antiquity* (Berkeley and Los Angeles, 1982), pp. 251–301.

On the aesthetics of the icons and their theological presuppositions, see Gervase Mathew, *Byzantine Aesthetics* (New York, 1963), esp. pp. 98–107; E. Kissinger, "Byzantine Art in the Period between Justinian and Iconoclasm," in *Berichte zum XI. Internationalen Byzantinisten-Kongress* (Munich, 1958), pp. 1–56; Cyril Mango, *The Art of the Byzantine Empire, 312–1453* (Englewood Cliffs, 1972), pp. 21–148; Fernanda de Maffei, *Icona, pittore e arte al Concilio Niceno II* (Rome, 1974).

The hypothesis of Islamic influences has been reexamined by G. E. von Grunebaum, "Byzantine Iconoclasm and the Influence of the Islamic Environment," *HR* 2 (1962): 1–10.

Chapter 33. Muhammad and the Unfolding of Islam

259. On the history and cultures of Arabia before Islam, a short and clear exposé is provided by Irfan Shahîd in *The Cambridge History of Islam*, 1 (1970), pp. 3–29. See also H. Lammens, *Le berceau de l'Islam* (Rome, 1914); idem, *L'Arabie occidentale avant l'Hégire* (Beirut, 1928); W. Coskel, *Die Bedeutung der Beduinen in der Geschichte der Araber* (Cologne, 1953); F. Gabrielli, ed., *L'antica società beduina* (Rome, 1959); F. Altheim and R. Stiehl, *Die Araber in der alten Welt*, 1–4 (Berlin, 1964–68); M. Guidi, *Storia e cultura degli Arabi fino alla morte di Maometto* (Florence, 1951); J. Ryckmans, *L'institution monarchique en Arabie méridionale avant l'Islam* (Louvain, 1951).

On the religions of pre-Islamic Arabia, see J. Wellhausen, *Reste arabischen Heidentums*, 3d ed. (Berlin, 1961); G. Ryckmans, *Les religions arabes préislamiques*, 2d ed. (Louvain, 1951); A. Jamme, "Le panthéon sudarabe préislamique d'après les sources épigraphiques," *Le Muséon* 60 (1947): 57–147; J. Henninger, "La religion bédouine préislamique," in *L'antica società beduina*, pp. 115–40; Maria Höfner, "Die vorislamischen Religionen

Arabiens," in H. Gese, M. Höfner, K. Rudolph, *Die Religionen Altsyriens, Altararabiens und der Mandäer* (Stuttgart, 1970), pp. 233–402. The inscriptions and monuments of southern Arabia have been edited and analyzed in the *Corpus des inscriptions et antiquités sud-arabes,* Académie des Inscriptions et des Belles Lettres (Louvain, 1977).

On the beliefs in the spirits, cf. J. Henninger, "Geisterglaube bei den vorislamischen Araben," *Festschrift für P. J. Schebesta* (Freiburg, 1963), pp. 279–316.

On the three goddesses—Allāt, Manāt, and al-'Uzzā—see M. Höfner, "Die vorislamischen Religionen," pp. 361ff., 370ff.; and J. Henninger, "Ueber Stenkunde u. Sternkult in Nord- und Zentralarabien," *Ziet. f. Ethnologie* 79 (1954): 82–117, esp. pp. 99ff.

On the structure and pre-Islamic cult of Allah, see *Shorter Encyclopedia of Islam,* H. A. R. Gibb and J. H. Kramers, eds. (Leiden, 1961), p. 33; M. Höfner, "Die vorislamischen Religionen," pp. 357ff.; idem, in *WdM* 1 (1965): 420ff. J. Chelhoud has written two important contributions on the religiosity of the Arabs, before and after Islam: *Le sacrifice chez les Arabes* (Paris, 1955); *Les structures du sacré chez les Arabes* (1965).

On the sacrifices of the firstfruits, see Joseph Henninger, *Les fêtes de printemps chez les Sémites et la Pâque israélite* (Paris, 1975), pp. 37–50, with an exhaustive bibliography. See also idem, "Zum Verbot des Knochenzerbrechens bei den Semiten," *Studi . . . Giorgio Levi della Vida* (Rome, 1956), pp. 448–59; idem. "Menschenopfer bei den Araber," *Anthropos* 53 (1958): 721–805. The general theory of sacrifice among the ancient Semites, worked out by W. Robertson Smith and illustrated by an account of Saint Nilus concerning the pre-Islamic Arabs, has been discussed by Karl Heussi, *Das Nilusproblem* (Leipzig, 1921), and by J. Henninger, "Ist der sogenannte Nilus-Bericht eine brauchbare religionsgeschichtliche Quelle?" *Anthropos* 50 (1955): 81–148.

On the cult of the Moon in ancient Arabia and in Islam, see Maxime Rodinson in *La Lune: Mythes et Rites,* Sources Orientales 5 (Paris, 1962), pp. 153–214 (rich bibliography).

On the pilgrimage to Mecca in pre-Islamic antiquity and Islam, see J. Gaudefroy-Demombynes, *Le Pèlerinage à la Mecque* (Paris, 1923); Muhammad Hamidullah, in *Les Pèlerinages,* Sources Orientales 3 (1960), pp. 87ff.; J. Henninger, "Pèlerinages dans l'ancien Orient," *Suppl. au Dictionnaire de la Bible,* vol. 7, fasc. 38, cols. 567–84 (Paris, 1963).

On the Ka'ba, see the succinct account of M. Höfner, "Die vorislamischen Religionen," pp. 360ff., and the article s.v. "Ka'ba" in the *Shorter Encyclopedia of Islam,* pp. 192–98. See also the bibliography provided below in §263.

The interest in these cults, symbols, and mythologies of ancient Arabia resides above all in their later revalorizations by the popular mythologizing piety and imagination.

The primary sources on the life and activity of Muhammad are first of all the Quran and the oldest biographies written on the basis of oral traditions by Ibn-Ishâk (d. 768), *Shîrah* ("Life"), abridged and edited by Ibn-Hisham (d. 822), and *Maghâzi* ("Expeditions") by al-Wâqidî (d. 822). The first, which is the most important, has been translated by Alfred Guillaume, *The Life of Muhammad: A Translation of (Ibn) Ishâq's "Sîrat Rasûl Allâh"* (London, 1955). One must specify, however, that a number of episodes seem legendary; for example, Muhammad's caravan journeys in Syria, his encounters with Christian monks, etc.

Among the more recent and the best biographies of Muhammad, special mention is merited for Tor Andrae, *Mohammad, the Man and His Faith* (London, 1936; repr., New York, 1960); this work insists on the eschatological elements in the Prophet's prophecy; Régis Blachère, *Le problème de Mahomet: Essai de biographie critique du fondateur de l'Islam* (1952), shows the lacunae in our information; W. Montgomery Watt, *Muhammad at Mecca* (Oxford, 1953); idem, *Muhammad at Medina* (Oxford, 1956), examines in detail the social and political implications of Muhammad's preaching and indicates his political genius; idem, *Muhammad: Prophet and Statesman* (Oxford, 1961), condenses the two above-mentioned volumes; Maurice Gaudefroy-Demombynes, *Mahomet* (Paris, 1957), a learned work, reflecting the positivist historiography of the end of the nineteenth century; Maxime Rodinson, *Mahomet* (1965; 2d ed., revised and augmented, 1969); idem, "The Life of Muhammad and the Sociological Problem of the Beginnings of Islam," *Diogenes* no. 20 (1957), pp. 28–51. See now also Martin Lings, *Muhammad: His Life Based on the Earliest Sources* (New York, 1983). The two volumes by Muhammad Hamidullah, *Le Prophète de l'Islam. 1: Sa Vie. 2: Son Oeuvre* (Paris, 1959), despite their rich documentation, are unusable.

The Quran has been translated several times into the most important European languages. We have consulted the following: Arthur J. Arberry, *The Koran Interpreted*, 2 vols. (London, 1955), the translation considered as the most successful from a literary perspective, although it distorts archaisms; Richard Bell, *The Qur'an*, 2 vols. (Edinburgh, 1937–39), gives a more exact version, but it is rather difficult to read; Régis Blachère, *Le Coran: Traduction selon un essai de reclassement des sourates*, 2 vols. (Paris, 1947–50), the first volume of which has been republished under the title *Introduction au Coran* (Paris, 1959), and the translation was republished, with a reduced number of notes, in 1957 as *Le Coran*. The entire work has been received enthusiastically by a large number of Orientalists, French and foreign. Cf. also the translation by D. Masson (Paris, 1967), from which quotations in the

French edition were taken. English citations are from Arberry, but we have always consulted the versions of R. Blachère and Bell as well.

The revelations learned by heart by the first believers were fixed in writing during Muhammad's lifetime. But the reunion of the suras into a "Book" was effected under the order of the third caliph, Uthman, son-in-law of the Prophet (644–55). The order of the suras is not chronological; the longest ones have been placed at the beginning and the shortest ones at the end.

On the elaboration of the Quranic text, see A. Jeffrey, *Materials for the History of the Text of the Qur'an* (Leiden, 1937); R. Blachère, *Introduction au Coran,* passim; John Burton, *The Collection of the Quran* (Cambridge, 1977); John Wansbrough, *Quranic Studies: Sources and Methods of Scriptural Interpretation* (Oxford, 1977).

On Muhammad's first ecstatic experiences, see the texts cited and analyzed by Tor Andrae, *Mohammed,* pp. 34ff.; Watts, *Muhammad at Mecca,* pp. 39ff.; Arthur Jeffrey, *Islam: Muhammad and His Religion* (New York, 1958), pp. 15–21.

The angel Gabriel is not mentioned in the suras composed before Medina. It is possible that Muhammad believed in the beginning that he had had a vision of God Himself; cf. Watts, p. 42. The ecstatic experiences of Muhammad were different from those of the "seers" (*kâhin*). However, like the *kâhin,* Muhammad covered his head with his mantle whenever he expected a revelation; cf. Quran 73:1; 74:1. Moreover, it is a matter of ritual behavior characteristic of several types of Eastern and Mediterranean manticism.

On the *hanîfs,* see Tor Andrae, *Les Origines de l'Islam et le Christianisme* (trans. from German, Paris, 1955), pp. 39–65; N. A. Faris and H. W. Glidden, "The Development of the Meaning of the Koranic Hânif," *Journal of the Palestine Oriental Society* 19 (1930): 1–13; Watts, *Muhammad at Mecca,* pp. 28ff., 96, 162–64.

260. On the monotheistic tendencies of the Arabs, see J. Wellhausen, *Reste arabischen Heidentums,* pp. 215ff.

On the different phases of Muhammad's monotheism, see C. Brockelmann, "Allah und die Götzen, der Ursprung des islamischen Monotheismus," *ARW* 21 (1922): 99ff.; Watt, *Muhammad at Mecca,* pp. 63ff.

On the order to make his revelations public, see the suras cited and commented upon by Watt, *Muhammad at Mecca,* pp. 48ff.

On Christianity in Arabia and the eventual influences on Muhammad, see Richard Bell, *The Origin of Islam in Its Christian Environment* (London, 1926); Tor Andrae, *Les Origines de l'Islam et le Christianisme,* pp. 15–38, 105–12, 201–11; Joseph Henninger, *Spuren christlicher Glaubenswahrheiten im Koran* (Schöneck, 1951); J. Ryckmans, "Le Christianisme en Arabie du Sud préislamique," in *Atti del Convegno Internazionale sul tema: L'Oriente cristiano nella storia della civiltà* (Rome, 1964).

On the eschatology preached by Muhammad, see Paul Casanova, *Mohammad et la Fin du Monde: Étude critique sur l'Islam primitif* (Paris, 1911–12), used for the rich documentation, but the author's thesis has not been accepted; Tor Andrae, *Mohammed*, esp. pp. 53ff. On the conception of death, the afterlife, and resurrection, see Thomas O'Shaughnessy, *Muhammad's Thoughts on Death: A Thematic Study of the Qur'anic Data* (Leiden, 1969); Ragnar Eklund, *Life between Death and Resurrection according to Islam*, diss. (Uppsala, 1941); M. Gaudefroy-Demombynes, *Mahomet*, pp. 443ff.; Alford T. Welch, "Death and Dying in the Qur'an," in Frank E. Reynolds and Earle H. Waugh, eds., *Religious Encounters with Death* (University Park and London, 1977), pp. 183–99.

On the abrogation of the verses on the three goddesses, cf. Watt, *Muhammad at Mecca*, pp. 103ff. The abrogation gave rise later to a special doctrine of dogmatic theology; see several texts in Jeffrey, *Islam*, pp. 66–68.

261.   On the mythico-ritual scenario of the celestial ascension of a Messenger (= Apostle) in order to bring back the "Holy Book," see G. Widengren, *The Ascension of the Apostle and the Heavenly Book* (Uppsala, 1950); idem, *Muhammad: The Apostle of God and His Ascension* (Uppsala, 1955).

On the *mî'râj* (a significant term originally signifying "stairway" and later "ascension," in particular the ascension of Muhammad), see s.v. "mî'râj" in *Shorter Encyclopedia of Islam*, pp. 381–84; Widengren, *Muhammad: The Apostle of God*, pp. 76ff.; Alexander Altman, *Studies in Religious Philosophy and Mysticism* (Ithaca, 1969), pp. 41–72 ("The Ladder of Ascension").

On Muslim eschatology and its eventual influences on Dante, see Miguel Asín Palaciós, *La escatología musulmana e la Divina Commedia*, 2d ed. (Madrid, 1941); E. Cerulli, *Il "Libro della Scala" e la questione delle fonte arabo-spagnole della Divina Commedia*, Studi e Testi 150 (Vatican City, 1949); idem, *Nuove ricerche sul "Libro della Scala" e la conoscenza dell'Islam in Occidente*, Studi e Testi 271 (Vatican City, 1972).

After Geo Widengren, Alessandro Bausani has highlighted other Iranian elements in the Quran; see his *Persia Religiosa* (Milan, 1959), pp. 136ff. Let us recall the most important: the two Quranic angels of music, Harut and Marut (Quran 2:102), derive from the two Mazdaean Amesha Spentas, Haurvatât and Ameretât (the hypothesis, advanced by Lagarde, has been confirmed by G. Dumézil, *Naissances d'Archanges* [Paris, 1945], pp. 158ff.); the argument concerning the resurrection of the body (29:19–20) is also found in the Pahlavi texts (e.g., *Zâtspram*, chap. 34); the image of the shooting stars flung against the demons who try to conquer heaven (Quran 15:17–18; 37:79; etc.) has parallels in the *Mênôkê Khrat* (chap. 44); the expression "the unction [tincture] of God" (2:138) recalls a passage from the *Dênkart:* "Ohrmazd the Creator tinted Time with colors," etc. These Iranian elements have been diffused by the medium of gnoses and syncretistic mythologies of Judaism, late Christianity, and Manichaeanism (Bausani, p. 144).

262–63. On the persecution of the faithful in Mecca, see Watt, *Muhammad at Mecca,* pp. 177ff.; on the causes of the emigration of a group of Muslims into Abyssinia, see ibid., pp. 115ff.

On the Prophet's relations with the Jews of Medina, see Gaudefroy-Demombynes, *Mahomet,* pp. 119ff., 152ff.; Watt, *Muhammad at Medina,* pp. 192ff. (with bibliography); idem, *Muhammad, Prophet and Statesman,* pp. 166ff. On Jewish influences, see A. J. Wensinck, *Mohammed en de Joden te Medina* (Leiden, 1928; partially translated by G. H. Bousquet and G. W. Bousquet-Mirandolle under the title: "L'influence juive sur les origines du culte musulman," *Revue Africaine* 98 [154]: 85–112); Tor Andrae, *Les origines de l'Islam,* pp. 100ff.; Abraham I. Katsh, *Judaism in Islam* (New York, 1954).

On the Prophet's activities in Medina, see Gaudefroy-Demombynes, *Mahomet,* pp. 110–226; Watt, *Muhammad at Medina,* passim; *Shorter Encyclopedia of Islam,* s.v. "al-Madina," pp. 291–98.

On the *ummah,* see *Shorter Encyclopedia of Islam,* s.v., pp. 603–4; Marshall Hodgson, *The Venture of Islam,* vol. 1, pp. 172–93; F. M. Denny, "The Meaning of *Ummah* in the Qur'ân," *HR* 15 (1975): 34–70. Let us add that, despite its religious structure, the *ummah* still conserved certain tribal customs.

On Abraham in the Quran, see *Shorter Encyclopedia,* s.v. "Ibrahim," pp. 254–55 (bibliography); Yonakim Moubarac, *Abraham dans le Coran: L'histoire d'Abraham dans le Coran et la naissance de l'Islam* (Paris, 1957).

The *Ka'ba* was a very ancient ceremonial center; Muhammad proclaimed that it was erected by Abraham and his son Ishmael; see *Shorter Encyclopedia,* s.v., pp. 181–89 (rich bibliography). The symbolism of the "Center of the World," implicit in every archaic ceremonial center, is developed later according to the Jewish model of Jerusalem; cf. A. J. Wensinck, *The Ideas of the Western Semites concerning the Navel of the Earth* (Amsterdam, 1916; reissued, New York, 1978), pp. 11–20, 48ff., 52ff. The Ka'ba was created 2,000 years before the creation of the world; Adam was moulded near Mecca; the substance of the body of Muhammad was gathered in the "navel of the Earth," which is found at Mecca, etc. (pp. 18ff.). The symbolism of the Ka'ba has been abundantly reinterpreted by Muslim mystics and theosophers; see, inter alia, Henry Corbin, "La configuration du Temple de la Ka'ba comme secret de la vie spirituelle," *Eranos-Jahrbuch* 34 (1965): 79–166.

264. For quite a long time, Muhammad showed a certain sympathy toward the Christians: " 'We are Christians,' that, because some of them are priests and monks, and they wax not proud, and when they hear what has been sent down to the Messenger, thou seest their eyes overflow with tears because of the truth, they recognize. They say: 'Our Lord, we believe, so do Thou write us down among the witnesses' " (5:85–90).

It was only after the conquest of Mecca, when he clashed with the resistance of the Syrian Christians, that Muhammad changed his attitude; cf. 9:29–35 ("They have taken their rabbis and their monks as lords apart from God and the Messiah, Mary's son—and they were commanded to serve but One God" [9:31]).

On the relations between Christian beliefs (especially those of the Nestorians and certain Judaeo-Christian Gnostic sects) and the theology of Muhammad, see Tor Andrae, *Les Origines de l'Islam*, esp. pp. 105ff.; D. Masson, *Le Coran et la révélation judéo-chrétienne: Études comparées* (Paris, 1958); and the bibliography provided in §260.

It is significant that certain Gnostic doctrines, above all the idea that Jesus was not crucified and did not know death, doctrines which, following the polemics and persecutions of the Church, barely survived into the seventh century, regained their currency thanks to Muhammad and the spread of Islam. On the other hand, it is likely that certain antitrinitarian Christians were attracted by the absolute monotheism preached by Muhammad and were among the first to embrace Islam.

There is an immense literature on Quranic theology. The best introductions are the articles on Allah by D. B. Macdonald (*Shorter Encyclopedia of Islam*) and Louis Gardet (*Encyclopédie de l'Islam*, new ed., 1956). See also A. J. Wensinck, *The Muslim Creed* (Cambridge, 1932); A. S. Triton, *Muslim Theology* (London, 1947); L. Gardet and M. M. Anawati, *Introduction à la Théologie musulmane* (Paris, 1948); Gaudefroy-Demombynes, *Mahomet*, pp. 261–497; Fazlur Rahman, *Islam* (London and New York, 1966), pp. 30–66, 85–116; F. M. Pareja, *Islamologia*, pp. 374–91, 445–92 (with bibliographies).

On the evolution of the legend of Muhammad and the veneration of the Prophet as a superhuman being, see Pareja, pp. 553–54 (p. 554, bibliography).

For an analytic account of several interpretations of Islam by Western Orientalists—notably I. Goldziher, C. Snouck Hurgronje, C. H. Becker, D. B. Macdonald, and Louis Massignon—see Jean-Jacques Waardenburg, *L'Islam dans le miroir de l'Occident* (Paris and The Hague, 1963), with an important bibliography, pp. 331–51.

265. The history of the first forty years after the Hijra is meticulously presented (with the translation of the principal sources) by Leone Caetani, *Annali dell'Islam*, 10 vols. (Milan and Rome, 1905–26); but his interpretations are frequently subject to caution.

Marshall G. S. Hodgson has presented a general history of Islam in the three volumes of his posthumous work, *The Venture of Islam: Conscience and History of a World Civilization* (Chicago, 1974); vol. 1, *The Classical Age of Islam;* vol. 2, *The Expansion of Islam in the Middle Periods;* vol. 3, *The Gunpowder Empires and Modern Times*. Only the first volume relates to the problems discussed in this chapter; see most especially pp. 146–280.

Islamologia, the encyclopedic work of F. M. Pareja with the collaboration of A. Bausani and L. Hertling (Rome, 1951), contains several chapters on religious institutions and the caliphate (pp. 73ff., 392ff.).

On the history of the first caliphs and the Umayyad dynasty, see in the *Cambridge History of Islam*, vol. 1 (1970), the exposition of the whole by Laura Veccia Vaglieri and D. Sourdel, pp. 57–139, and the bibliographies recorded on pp. 739–40; see also F. Gabrielli, *Muhammad and the Conquests of Islam* (London, 1968); H. Lammens, *Etudes sur le siècle des Omayyades* (Beirut, 1930); A. A. Vasiliev, *Byzance et les Arabes*, vols. 1–3 (Brussels, 1935–68); B. Spuler, *The Muslim World: A Historical Survey*, vol. 1, *The Age of the Caliphs* (Leiden, 1960; translated from German).

On the Abbasid dynasty, see finally M. A. Shaban, *The Abbasid Revolution* (Cambridge, 1978).

On the relations between Mu'âwiya and 'Alî, see E. L. Petersen, *Alî and Mu'âwiya in Early Arabic Tradition* (Copenhagen, 1964).

On Shî'ism and Ismailism, see chapter 35 of this work and the bibliographies assembled in §§273-74.

On the religious ceremonies commemorating the murder of Husayn, see lastly Earle H. Waugh, "Muharram Rites: Community Death and Rebirth," in Frank Reynolds and Earle H. Waugh, eds., *Religious Encounters with Death* (University Park and London, 1977), pp. 200–213.

On the influences of Christian religious architecture, see E. Baldwin Smith, *The Dome: A Study in the History of Ideas* (Princeton, 1950), pp. 41ff. and passim.

On the continuity of Oriental and Mediterranean ideas and artistic techniques in Islamic culture, see Ugo Monneret de Villard, *Introduzione allo studio dell' archeologia islamic* (Venice, 1960), pp. 89ff. and passim.

On the establishment of Baghdad by the Caliph al-Mansûr and its simultaneously cosmological and imperial symbolism (of Sassanid origin), see Charles Wendell, "Baghdād: *Imago mundi*, and Other Foundation-Lore," *International Journal of Middle East Studies* 2 (1971): 99–128.

Chapter 34. Western Catholicism from Charlemagne to Joachim of Floris

266. For a universal history of the Middle Ages, including also the Near East and Asia, see the work directed by Edouard Perroy, *Le Moyen Age: L'expansion de l'Orient et la naissance de la civilisation occidentale* (Paris, 1955; 5th ed., revised 1967). An alert and personal presentation of the history, and of Western culture during the Middle Ages, has been given by Friedrich Heer, *The Medieval World: Europe 1100–1350* (London, 1962; the German original appeared in 1961). See also R. Morghen, *Medioevo cristiano,* 2d ed. (Bari, 1958).

On the passage from antiquity to the Middle Ages, see Hugh Trevor-Roper, *The Rise of Christian Europe* (London and New York, 1965); William Carroll Park, *Origins of the Medieval World* (Stanford, 1958); H. I. Marrou, *Décadence romaine ou antiquité tardive? III–VIe siècle* (Paris, 1977) and the collective anthology *Il passaggio dell'antichità al medioevo in Occidente* (Spoleto, 1962).

The bibliography of criticism of Henri Pirenne's *Mahomet and Charlemagne* (1937) has been gathered together by Park, pp. 114–24.

On Christianity in the Carolingian Age, see K. F. Morrison, *The Two Kingdoms: Ecclesiology in Carolingian Political Thought* (Princeton, 1964); E. Patzelt, *Die Karolingische Renaissance* (Graz, 1965).

On Pope Gregory VII and his reform of the Church, see A. Fliche, *La réforme grégorienne,* vols. 1–3 (Paris, 1924–37). In 1074, one year after his election, Gregory VII decreed the dismissal of simoniac priests and those who were married or had concubines. In 1075 he published a collection of twenty-seven propositions, the *Dictatus Papae,* in which he proclaimed the independence of the papacy and the Church vis-à-vis lay powers, offering "to establish a pontifical theocracy" (Jacques Le Goff, in *Histoire des Religions,* 1972, vol. 2, p. 813). We cite the most audacious propositions: "1: The Roman Church has been founded by the Lord alone. 2: Only the Roman pontiff is justly called universal. 12: It is permitted to him to depose emperors. 19: He cannot be judged by anyone" (ibid., p. 814). The high clergy, the princes, and especially the emperor Henry IV received the *Dictatus Papae* poorly. But in 1075, Gregory VII "excommunicated the Emperor, deposed him and released his subjects from their oath of allegiance. The Emperor extricated himself by his penitence at Canossa (1077), which disarmed the Pope" (ibid.). Canossa "contains at one and the same time the origins of secularization and the weakening of the humbled empire, and the demonstration of the fundamental impossibility of putting into effect a pontifical theocracy" (J. Chelini, cited by Le Goff, p. 814).

See also R. Folz, *L'idée d'Empire en Occident du Ve au XIVe siècle* (Paris, 1953); M. D. Chenu, *La théologie au douzième siècle* (Paris, 1957).

On apocalyptic themes in the Middle Ages, see Norman Cohn, *The Pursuit of the Millennium* (new rev. and augmented ed., Oxford, 1970), pp. 29ff. and passim; Bernard McGinn, *Visions of the End: Apocalyptic Traditions in the Middle Ages* (New York, 1979). On the theme of the ''Emperor of the Last Days,'' see Marjorie Reeves, *The Influence of Prophecy in the Later Middle Ages* (Oxford, 1969), pp. 293ff.

In his book *L'An Mil* (Paris, 1980), Georges Duby presented and brilliantly analyzed a selection of texts on terrors and prodigies of the millennium.

267. On sacred royalty among the ancient Germans, see the bibliography provided in vol. 2 of this work, pp. 478–79. On the survival of this conception after the conversion to Christianity, see Marc Bloch, *Les rois thaumaturges* (Strasbourg, 1922); William A. Chaney, *The Cult of Kingship in Anglo-Saxon England: The Transition from Paganism to Christianity* (Berkeley and Los Angeles, 1970). Cf. also Gale R. Owen, *Rites and Religions of the Anglo-Saxons* (London, 1981).

On chivalry and feudalism, see S. Painter, *French Chivalry* (Baltimore, 1940); Carl Stephenson, *Mediaeval Feudalism* (Ithaca, N.Y., 1942; excellent introduction; see esp. pp. 40ff.); Gustave Cohen, *Histoire de la chevalerie en France au Moyen Age* (Paris, 1949). The dubbing ceremony is well analyzed by Philippe du Puy de Clinchamps, *La chevalerie* (Paris, 1961), pp. 37ff.

268. In the abundant recent bibliographies on the Crusades, see esp. René Grousset, *L'Epopée des Croisades* (Paris, 1939); Steven Runciman, *History of the Crusades,* vols. 1–3 (Cambridge, 1951–54); Adolf Waas, *Geschichte der Kreuzzüge,* vols. 1–2 (Freiburg i. B., 1956); Paul Alphandéry and Alphonse Dupront, *La chrétienté et l'idée de Croisade,* vols. 1–2 (Paris, 1958–59); K. Setton, *A History of the Crusades,* vols. 1–2 (Philadelphia, 1958, 1962); J. A. Brundage, *The Crusades* (Milwaukee, 1962). See also the studies collected in the volume *L'idée de Croisade* (= X Congresso Intern. di Scienze storiche, Rome, 1955, Relazzioni III, Florence, 1955), esp. P. Lemerle, ''Byzance et la Croisade,'' and A. Cahen, ''L'Islam et la Croisade.''

A selection of Arabic sources have been translated into Italian by Francesco Gabrielli, *Storici Arabi delle Crociate* (Turin, 1957); there is also an English translation, *Arab Historians of the Crusades* (Berkeley and Los Angeles, 1969).

On the eschatological and millenarian elements, see A. Dupront, ''Croisades et eschatologie,'' in E. Castelli, ed., *Umanesimo e esoterismo* (Padua, 1960). pp. 175–98; Norman Cohn, *The Pursuit of the Millennium* (rev. and augmented ed., Oxford, 1970), pp. 61ff., 98ff.

See also F. Cardini, *La Crociate fra il mito e la storia* (Rome, 1971).

269. On the first monastic orders founded at the end of the eleventh century, see J. B. Mahn, *L'ordre cistercien,* 2d ed. (Paris, 1951); J. Leclercq, *Saint Bernard et l'esprit cistercien* (Paris, 1966).

On the three classes of medieval Western society, see J. Le Goff, *Pour un autre Moyen Âge: Travail et culture en Occident: 18 essais* (Paris, 1977), pp. 80–90; G. Duby, *Les trois ordres ou l'imaginaire du féodalisme* (Paris, 1978).

On the symbolism of cathedrals, see Hans Sedlmayr, *Die Entstehung der Kathedrale* (Zurich, 1950); Otto von Simpson, *The Gothic Cathedral* (New York, 1956); Marie-Madeleine Davy, *Initiation à la symbolique romane* (Paris, 1964); Aurelia Stappert, *L'Ange roman, dans la pensée et dans l'art* (Paris, 1975), esp. pp. 149ff., 440ff. (abundant bibliography; excellent iconography); Erwin Panofsky, *Gothic Architecture and Scholasticism* (New York, 1976).

On Eleanor of Aquitaine and her influence, see F. Heer, *The Medieval World,* pp. 157ff.; cf. also A. Kelly, *Eleanor of Aquitaine and the Four Kings* (Cambridge, Mass., 1952).

On courtly literature, see A. Jeanroy, *La poésie lyrique des troubadours* (Toulouse and Paris, 1934); R. R. Bezzola, *Les origines et la formation de la littérature courtoise en Occident, 500–1200* (Paris, 1944); P. Zumthor, *Histoire littéraire de la France médiévale, V–XIVᵉ siècle* (Paris, 1954); J. Lafitte-Houssat, *Troubadours et Cours d' Amour* (Paris, 1960), excellent overview; contains a translation of some "judgments" rendered by the Court of the Ladies, pp. 49–63; Moshé Lazar, *Amour courtois et "Fin Amors" dans la littérature du XIIᵉ siècle* (Paris, 1964).

270. On the religious valorization of the feminine principle, see the texts cited by Elaine Pagels, *The Gnostic Gospels* (New York, 1979), pp. 57ff. The treatise *Le Tonnerre, Esprit Parfait* has been translated by George W. Mac-Rae, *The Nag Hammadi Library* (James M. Robinson, ed., New York and San Francisco, 1977), pp. 271–77. Cf. ibid., pp. 461–70, the translation by John Turner of another important treatise, *Trimorphic Protennoia.*

The problem of the influence of lyric and Hispano-Arabic poetry on the poetry of Spain and Provence has given rise to an abundant critical literature. See Menéndez Pidal, *Poesía árabe y poesía europea* (Madrid, 1950); Emilio Garcia Gómez, *Poemas arábigo-andaluces* (new ed., Madrid, 1940); idem, "La lírica hispano-arabe y la aparición de la lírica romance," *Al Andalus 21* (1956): 310ff.; Claudio Sanchez Albornoz, "El Islam de España y el Occidente," in *L'Occidente e l'Islam, Atti della XIIa settimana di studio di Spoleto,* 2–8 April 1964 (Spoleto, 1965), vol. 1, pp. 149–308, esp. pp. 177ff.; S. M. Stern, "Esistono dei rapporti letterari tra il mondo islamico e l'Europa occidentale nell'alto medio evo?," ibid., 2:631–65.

On the secret language of the *Fedeli d'Amore*, see R. Ricolfi, *Studi su i "Fedeli d'Amore,"* vol. 1 (Milan, 1933); cf. Mircea Eliade, *Naissances mystiques* (Paris, 1959), pp. 267ff.

From the enormous critical literature on the romances of the Arthurian cycle, let us single out the following: Roger S. Loomis, ed., *Arthurian Literature in the Middle Ages* (Oxford, 1959); idem, *The Development of Arthurian Romance* (London, 1963); Jean Marx, *La légende arthurienne et le Graal* (Paris, 1952); idem, *Nouvelles recherches sur la légende arthurienne* (Paris, 1965); R. W. Barber, *Arthur of Albion: An Introduction to the Arthurian Literature and Legends in England* (London, 1961): T. B. Grant et al., eds., *The Legend of Arthur in the Middle Ages* (Cambridge, 1983). See also the collective work *La Lumière du Graal* ("Cahiers du Sud," 1951), especially the article by J. Vendryès, "Le Graal dans le cycle breton," pp. 73ff., and the proceedings of the Colloque International: *Les Romans du Graal aux XIIe et XIIIe siècles* (Paris, 1956; edition of the C.N.R.S.).

On the initiatory elements in the romances of the Arthurian cycle, see Eliade, *Naissances mystiques*, pp. 264ff.; see also Antoinette Fiers-Monnier, *Initiation und Wandlung: Zur Geschichte des altfranzösischen Romans im XII. Jahrhundert*, Studiorum Romanorum, vol. 5 (Berne, 1951).

On the Oriental elements in the *Parzival*, see Hermann Goetz, "Der Orient der Kreuzzüge in Wolframs *Parzival*," *Archiv für Kulturgeschichte*, vol. 2, pp. 1–42. Cf. also the erudite and suggestive work of Helen Adolf, *Visio Pacis: Holy City and Grail* (Pennsylvania State University Press, 1960; excellent documentation, pp. 179–207).

On the Hermetic influence on Wolfram von Eschenbach's *Parzival*, see Henry and Renée Kahane, *The Krater and the Grail: Hermetic Sources of the Parzival* (Urbana, 1965), an interpretation accepted by H. Corbin, *En Islam iranien* (1971), vol. 2, pp. 143–54. The etymology of three enigmatic personages is significant: Kiot would be the very cultivated Count Guillaume de Tudèle; Flégétanis seems to involve a reference to a Kabbalistic work of the twelfth century, *Falakath Thani*, "the second Heaven," whose title was interpreted as the name of a philosopher (H. Kolb, cited by Goetz, pp. 2ff.); Trevrizent, according to Henry and Renée Kahane, derives from *Trible Escient* (triple wisdom), in other words from Hermes Trismegistus (cf. *The Krater and the Grail*, pp. 59ff.). See also Paulette Duval, *La Pensée alchimique et le conte du Graal* (Paris, 1979).

On the relationship between chivalry and the mythico-ritual scenario of the Grail, see J. Frappier, "Le Graal et la Chevalerie," *Romania* 75 (1954): 165–210.

On the analogies with Iran, see Sir Jahangîr C. Coyajee, "The Legend of the Holy Grail: Its Iranian and Indian Analogues," *Journal of the K. R. Cama Oriental Institute*, Bombay (1939), pp. 37–126; "The Round Table of King

Kai Khusraun," ibid., pp. 127–94; H. Corbin, *En Islam iranien*, vol. 2, pp. 155–88.

271.   To the three treatises of Joachim of Floris cited in n. 70, one should add the *Tractatus super Quattuor Evangelia*, Ernesto Buonaiuti, ed. (Rome, 1930), and the *Liber Figurarum*, L. Tondelli, ed. (*Il Libro delle Figure dell'Abate Gioacchino da Fiore*, 2d ed., Turin, 1954); on this work, see also Marjorie Reeves and Beatrice Hirsch-Reich, *The Figurae of Joachim of Fiore* (Oxford, 1972). The pseudo-Joachimite writings are cited by Marjorie Reeves, *The Influence of Prophecy in the Later Middle Ages: A Study in Joachimism* (Oxford, 1969), pp. 512–18, 541–42. A selection of Joachim's texts, translated with commentary, is found in B. McGinn, *Apocalyptic Spirituality* (New York, 1979), pp. 97–148, 289–97.

On Joachim of Floris, see above all H. Grundmann, *Studien über Joachim von Floris* (Leipzig, 1927); idem, *Neue Forschungen über Joachim von Floris* (Freiburg i. B., 1950); idem, "Zur Biographie Joachims von Fiore und Rainers von Ponza," *Deutsches Archiv für Erforschung des Mittelalters* 16 (1960): 437–546; E. Buonaiuti, *Gioacchino da Fiore, i tempi, la vita, il messaggio* (Rome, 1931); A. Crocco, *Gioacchino da Fiore* (Naples, 1960); Marjorie Reeves, *The Influence of Prophecy;* H. Mottu, *La manifestation de l'Esprit selon Joachim de Fiore* (Neuchâtel and Paris, 1977); Bernard McGinn, *Visions of the End: Apocalyptic Traditions in the Middle Ages* (New York, 1979), pp. 126–41, 313–18. McGinn has given an excellent critical review of the recent research on Joachim and Joachimism in "Apocalypticism in the Middle Ages: An Historiographical Approach," *Mediaeval Studies* 37 (1975): 252–86. See also Henri de Lubac, *La postérité spirituelle de Joachim de Flore*, vols. 1–2 (Paris, 1979, 1981).

On the House of Corazzo, see F. Russo, *Gioacchino da Fiore e le fondazioni florensi in Calabria* (Naples, 1958).

On the biblical origins of Joachim's symbolism, see B. McGinn, "Symbolism in the Thought of Joachim of Fiore," in *Prophecy and Millenarianism: Essays in Honor of Marjorie Reeves* (London, 1980), pp. 143–64.

Chapter 35. Muslim Theologies and Mystical Traditions

272.   Let us first indicate several general presentations: H. A. R. Gibb, *Mohammedanism: An Historical Survey* (Oxford, 1949; 2d ed., 1961); Fazlur Rahman, *Islam* (Chicago, 1966; 2d ed., 1979); Toufic Fahd, "L'Islam et les sectes islamiques," *Histoire des Religions*, under the direction of Henri Charles Puech (Paris, 1977), vol. 3, pp. 3–177; A. Bausani, *L'Islam* (Milan, 1980). See also the bibliographies cited above, §§264–65.

Indispensable for its richness, at once both a general introduction to the history of Islam and a reference work, is Henri Laoust, *Les schismes dans l'Islam* (Paris, 1965).

Gustave E. von Grunebaum has given a presentation of medieval culture and spirituality in *Medieval Islam* (Chicago, 1946; 2d ed. revised and enlarged, 1953). See also the collective work *Islam and Cultural Change in the Middle Ages* (Wiesbaden, 1975), and the articles of A. H. Hourani, S. M. Stern, S. A. El-Ali, and N. Elisséeff, in A. H. Hourani and S. M. Stern, eds., *The Islamic City* (Oxford, 1970).

On the Sunni *Kalâm,* see the clear account of Henry Corbin, *Histoire de la philosophie islamique* (Paris, 1964), vol. 1, pp. 125–78; L. Gardet and M. M. Anawati, *Introduction à la théologie musulmane* (Paris, 1948); A. N. Nader, *Le système philosophique des Mo'tazilites* (Beirut, 1956); A. J. Arberry, *Revelation and Reason in Islam* (London, 1957); H. A. Wolfson, *The Philosophy of the Kalam* (Cambridge, Mass., 1976), a fundamental work. See also F. Rahman, *Prophecy in Islam: Philosophy and Orthodoxy* (London, 1958); S. H. Nasr, *An Introduction to Muslim Cosmological Doctrines* (Cambridge, Mass., 1964); Daniel Gimaret, *Théories de l'acte humain en théologie musulmane* (Louvain, 1980).

On al-Ash'arî and Asharism, see W. C. Klein, *The Elucidation of Islam's Foundation* (New Haven, 1940; English trans. of the *Kitab al-Ibâna* of al-Ash'arî); W. W. Watt, *Free Will and Predestination in Early Islam* (London, 1948).

273. On the history of Shî'ism. see Henri Laoust, *Les schismes dans l'Islam,* pp. 25ff., 98ff., 181ff. An exhaustive interpretation of Shî'ite thought and spiritual techniques has been presented for the first time by Henry Corbin in a large number of studies published in the *Eranos-Jahrbücher* and in several books. One will find a useful synthesis in his *Histoire de la philosophie islamique,* vol. 1, pp. 41–150 (cf. p. 350, a bibliography of his articles up to 1964). See also *Terre céleste et corps de résurrection: de l'Iran mazdéen à l'Iran shî'ite* (Paris, 1961), containing the translation of eleven authors, and *En Islam iranien,* vols. 1–2 (Paris, 1971–72), s.v. "shî'isme," "shî'ites."

274. On Ismailism, see W. Ivanow, *Studies in Early Persian Ismaelism* (Bombay, 1955); Henry Corbin, "Épiphanie divine et naissance spirituelle dans la Gnose ismaélienne," *Eranos-Jahrbuch* 23 (1955); idem, *Trilogie ismaélienne* (translation with commentary of three treatises; Paris, 1961); idem, *Histoire de la philosophie islamique,* pp. 110–48, 351 (bibliography).

In the oldest conserved Ismaili work, one notices the reminiscences of the apocryphal *Infancy Gospel,* certain themes of the mystical science of numbers (of Gnostic origin), the pentades, which play a role in cosmology and which betray a Manichaean influence (for example, the seven combats of Salman against the Antagonist, etc.); cf. Corbin, *Histoire*, p. 11.

On the myth of the Mahdî, see *Shorter Encyclopedia of Islam*, pp. 310–13; Ibn Khaldûn, *The Muqaddimah, An Introduction to History*, vols. 1–3, trans. by Franz Rosenthal (New York, 1958), pp. 156–200 (see also pp. 186ff., Sufi opinions on the Mahdî).

On the reformed Ismailism of Alamût, see Marshall G. S. Hodgson, *The Order of the Assassins: The Struggle of the Early Isma'îlîs against the Islamic World* (The Hague, 1955).

On the "Old Man of the Mountain," see C. E. Nowell, "The Old Man of the Mountain," *Speculum* 22 (1947): 497ff.; idem, "The Sources of the History of the Syrian Assassins," *Speculum* 27 (1952): 875ff.; W. Fleischhauer, "The Old Man of the Mountain: The Growth of a Legend," *Symposium* 9 (1955): 76ff. On the account of Marco Polo, see Leonardo Olschki, *Marco Polo's Asia* (Berkeley and Los Angeles, 1960), pp. 362–81.

275. There is a considerable literature on Sufism in the principal European languages. Let us single out several important works: Reynold A. Nicholson, *Studies in Islamic Mysticism* (Cambridge, 1921; new ed., 1967); A. J. Arberry, *Sufism: An Account of the Mystics of Islam* (London, 1950); Marijan Molé, *Les mystiques musulmans* (Paris, 1965; excellent introduction); G. C. Anawati and Louis Gardet, *Mystique musulmane: Aspects et tendances, expériences et techniques* (Paris, 1961; contains a large number of translated texts with commentary): Fritz Meier, *Vom Wesen der islamischen Mystik* (Basel 1943; insists upon the initiation of disciples); Seyyed Hossein Nasr, *Sufi Essais* (London, 1972); Anne-Marie Schimmel, *Mystical Dimensions of Islam* (Chapel Hill, 1975; one of the best works on Sufism, with bibliographies).

For a history of Sufi studies in the West, see A. J. Arberry, *An Introduction to the History of Sufism* (London, 1942). Among the anthologies of translated texts, let us cite Margaret Smith, *Readings from the Mystics of Islam* (London, 1950); idem, *The Sufi Path of Love* (London, 1954); Martino Mario Moreno, *Antologia della Mistica Arabo-Persiana* (Bari, 1951).

For an analysis of Sufi language, see Louis Massignon, *Essai sur les origines du lexique technique de la mystique musulmane* (Paris, 1922; new ed., 1968); Paul Nwyia, *Exégèse coranique et langage mystique* (Beirut, 1970).

On the first mystics, see L. Massignon, "Salmân Pâk et les prémices spirituelles de l'Islam iranien," *Société des Études Iraniennes* 7 (1934); Margaret Smith, *Râbi'a the Mystic and Her Fellow Saints in Islam* (Cambridge, 1928).

On the relations between Shî'ism and Sufism, see H. Corbin, *Histoire de la philosophie islamique*, pp. 262ff.; S. H. Nasr, *Sufi Essais*, pp. 97–103; John

B. Taylor, "Ja'far al Sâdiq, Spiritual Forebear of the Sufis" *Islamic Culture,* vol. 40, no. 2, pp. 97ff.; Nasr, *Sufi Essais,* pp. 104ff.

Let us cite a passage from al-Qushairî on the radical differences between the Law and the divine Reality sought after by the Sufis: "The *Sharî'a* is concerned with the observance of rites and acts of devotion; while the Reality (*Haqîqa*) is preoccupied with the interior vision of divine power. Every rite not animated by the spirit of Reality is without value, and every spirit of Reality not structured by the Law is incomplete. The Law exists in order to govern humanity, while Reality makes known to us the dispositions of God. The Law exists for the service of God, while Reality exists for His contemplation. The Law exists for the obedience to what He has prescribed, while Reality is to comprehend His commandment: the one is the exterior, the other the interior" (*Rîsâlat,* French translation by Eva de Vitray-Meyerovitch, *Rûmî et le soufisme,* Paris, 1977, p. 80).

276. On Dhû'l Nûn, see Margaret Smith, Readings from the *Mystics of Islam,* no. 20; A.-M. Schimmel, *Mystical Dimensions,* pp. 42ff.

On Bistâmî, see M. Molé, *Les mystiques musulmans,* pp. 53ff.; A.-M. Schimmel, pp. 47ff.; cf. the references cited in nn. 32–34.

On Junayd, see A. H. Abdel Kader, *The Life, Personality and Writings of al-Junayd* (London, 1962); R. C. Zaehner, *Hindu and Muslim Mysticism,* pp. 135–161; M. Molé, pp. 61ff.; Schimmel, pp. 57ff.

On Tirmidhî, see Schimmel, pp. 56–57 and the bibliography cited in nn. 35–36; H. Corbin, *Histoire,* pp. 273–75.

On the Sufi doctrine of *qutb,* see M. Molé, pp. 79ff.

277. On al-Hallâj, it suffices to recall the works of Louis Massignon, above all *La Passion d'al-Husayn-ibn-Mansûr al-Hallâj, martyr mystique de l'Islam, exécuté à Bagdad le 26 Mars 922,* 2 vols. (Paris, 1955; new edition corrected and augmented, 4 vols., Paris, 1975). Massignon's works on Hallâj are indicated in the bibliography, vol. 4, pp. 101–8.

Hallâj's life and martyrdom are admirably presented and interpreted by Massignon in the first volume of *La Passion.* On Hallâj's works (the catalogue of his works, edited sixty years after his death, contains 46 titles), see ibid., vol. 3, pp. 286ff. Massignon indicates that more than 350 isolated citations of works by Hallâj entered the classical repertoire of Muslim mysticism in the course of the fourth/ninth century; cf. ibid., pp. 296ff. See also Massignon's new translation of the *Diwân* ("Documents Spirituels," vol. 10, Paris, 1955).

On the *malâmatîya,* see Alessandro Bausani, "Note sul 'Pazzo sacro' nell' Islam," *SMSR* 29 (1958): 93–107; M. Molé, *Les mystiques musulmans,* pp.

72ff., and the bibliography provided by Schimmel, *Mystical Dimensions*, p. 86, n. 59.

On the "fools for Christ," analogues of the *malâmatîya*, see V. Roshcau, "Saint Siméon Salos, ermite palestinien et prototype des "Fous-pour-le-Christ," *Proche-Orient Chrétien* 28 (1978): 209–19; idem, "Que savons-nous des Fous-pour-le-Christ?" *Irénikon* 53 (1980): 341–53, 501–12.

278.   On Shiblî and Niffarî, see Schimmel, *Mystical Dimensions*, pp.77–82, and n. 46 (bibliography).

On the theories and practices of classical Sufism, see G. C. Anawati and L. Gardet, *Mystique musalmane*, pp. 41ff., 77ff., 147ff.; Schimmel, pp. 89ff. (with bibliographies).

On Ghazzâlî, see Miguel Asin y Palacios, *Espiritualidad de Algazel y su sentido cristiano*, vols. 1–4 (Madrid and Granada, 1934–41); W. Montgomery Watt, *Muslim Intellectual: A Study of Al-Ghazzâlî* (Edinburgh, 1963) and the bibliography noted by Schimmel, p. 92, n. 66.

On the translations of Ghazzâlî's works, see the bibliography in Schimmel, pp. 92–95, nn. 67, 71, 72. Let us mention those which bear directly upon our interests: W. H. Temple Gairdner, *Al-Ghazzâlî's The Niche for Lights* (London, 1915); W. M. Watt, *The Faith and Practice of Al-Ghazzâlî* (London, 1952; translation of the treatise "The Liberator of Errors"); G. H. Bousquet, *Ih' yâ' oulum al-dîn' ou Vivification des Sciences de la Foi* (Paris, 1955; containing the summary of four chapters).

279.   The best exposition of the ensemble is Henry Corbin, *Histoire de la philosophie islamique* (Paris, 1964). See ibid., pp. 348ff. (elements of bibliography).

On al-Kindî, see ibid., pp. 217–22, 355 (bibliography).

On al-Fârâbî, see ibid., pp. 222ff.; D. M. Dunlop, *The Fusul al-Madanî: Aphorisms of the Statesman al-Fârâbî* (text and translation, Cambridge, 1961); Muhsin Mahdi, trans., *Alfarabi's Philosophy of Plato and Aristotle* (Glencoe, Ill., 1962). On the doctrine of prophecy in al-Fârâbî, see F. Rahman, *Prophecy in Islam: Philosophy and Orthodoxy* (London, 1958), pp. 11–29.

On Avicenna, see A. M. Goichon, *La distinction de l'essence et de l'existence d'après Ibn Sina* (Paris, 1937); Louis Gardet, *La pensée religieuse d'Avicenne* (Paris, 1951); F. Rahman, *Avicenna's Psychology* (London, 1952); S. M. Afnan, *Avicenna, His Life and Works* (London, 1958); Henry Corbin, *Avicenne et le récit visionnaire: Étude sur le cycle des récits avicenniens* (Paris and Teheran, 1954; 2d ed. Paris, 1979); S. H. Nasr, *Three Muslim Sages* (Cambridge, Mass., 1963), pp. 9–51.

Let us also mention some recent translations: A. M. Goichon, trans., *Livres des Directives et Remarques* (Paris, 1952); M. Anawati, trans., *La Méta-physique du Shifâ* (Quebec, 1952); M. Achena and H. Massé, trans., *Le Livre de Science,* 2 vols. (Paris, 1955); cf. the bibliography supplied by Corbin, pp. 357–58.

On the philosophy and theology of Muslims in Spain, see the exposition of the ensemble in Corbin, *Histoire,* pp. 305–42, 361–63 (bibliography).

On Ibn Massara, see Miguel Asin Palacios, *Ibn Massara y su escuela: Origines de la filosofia hispana-musulmana,* 2d ed. (Madrid, 1946).

On Ibn Hazm, see A. R. Nykl, *A Book Containing the Risâla Known as "The Dove's Neck Ring about Love and Lovers"* (Paris, 1932); idem, *His-pano-Arabic Poetry and Its Relations with the Old Provençal Troubadors* (Baltimore, 1946).

On Avempace, see M. Asin Palacios, ed. and trans., *Avempace: El regimen del solitario* (Madrid and Granada, 1946).

On Ibn Tofail, see Léon Gauthier, *Ibn Thofail, sa vie, ses oeuvres* (Paris, 1909); idem, *Hayy ibn Yaqdhan, roman philosophique d'Ibn Thofail* (text and translation, 2d ed., Paris, 1936).

280. Let us mention several recent translations of Averroës: L. Gauthier, trans., *Traité décisif (Façî al-maqâl) sur l'accord de la religion et de la philo-sophie,* 3d ed. (Algiers, 1948); S. Van der Bergh, trans., *Averroes' Tahâfut al-Tahâfut (The Incoherence of the Incoherence),* 2 vols. (Oxford, 1954); G. F. Hourani, trans., *On the Harmony of Religion and Philosophy* (London, 1954).

The critical literature is considerable. Let us mention: L. Gauthier, *Ibn Rochd (Averroës)* (Paris, 1948); M. Horten, *Die Metaphysik des Averroes* (Halle, 1912); see also the synthetic presentations in the *Histoires* of medieval philosophy by Etienne Gilson, H. Corbin, and Julius R. Weinberg.

On the works of Ibn Arabî accessible in translation, see R. W. J. Austin, *Ibn al'Arabî: The Bezels of Wisdom* (New York, 1980), p. 12. Let us single out: Titus Burckardt, *La Sagesse des Prophètes* (Paris, 1956), a partial trans-lation of the *Pearl Necklace,* and Austin, *The Bezels of Wisdom,* an integral translation with abundant commentary. The autobiographic writings of Ibn Arabî have been translated by Austin in his *Sufis of Andalusia* (London, 1971).

The essentials of the critical bibliography are provided by Austin, *The Bezels,* p. 13. Special mention must be made of: Izutsu, *Comparative Study of Key Philosophical Concepts in Sufism and Taoism,* part 1 (Tokyo, 1966); Henry Corbin, *L'imagination créatrice dans le soufisme d'Ibn Arabî* (Paris, 1958); and S. A. Q. Husaini, *The Pantheistic Monism of Ibn al-Arabî* (Lahore, 1970).

281. Henry Corbin has edited the first two volumes of the *Oeuvres philo-*

sophiques et mystiques de Sohrawardî (Istanbul and Leipzig, 1945; Teheran and Paris, 1952). It is again Henry Corbin who has elaborated the most penetrating exegesis of Sohrawardî; see, above all, his *En Islam iranien*, vol. 2: *Sohrawardî et des Platoniciens de Perse* (Paris, 1971); *Histoire de la philosophie islamique*, pp. 285–304; *L'Archange empourpré: Quinze traités et récits mystiques traduits du persan et de l'arabe* (Paris, 1976).

It is difficult to specify to what degree Sohrawardî knew, from oral or written sources, the Mazdaean tradition. (Beyond Corbin's contributions, let us mention A. Bausani, *Persia Religiosa*, pp. 181ff., and J. Duchesne-Guillemin, *La Religion de l'Iran Ancien*, pp. 363ff.). In any case, Soharawardî draws upon the Persian tradition as well as upon Neoplatonic theology. Let us recall that under the Sassanid dynasty (226–635), Mazdaism became the official Church of the Empire, although Zurvanism (§213) did not lose its adherents. The great priest Kartêr, who succeeded in bringing about the condemnation of Mani (§231), was the architect of Mazdaean orthodoxy. It is equally under the Sassanids that interest in the mythology and ideology of royalty underwent a major intensification (cf. G. Widengren, *Les religions de l'Iran*, pp. 343ff.).

On the religious and political plane, the sole important event prior to the Muslim conquest had been the revolution of Mazdak, favored by King Kavâd (488–531). Mazdak affirmed that social inequality was the cause of Evil and suffering; as a result, he proposed the distribution of goods and women. But the lay and religious aristocracy succeeded in convincing King Kavâd otherwise, and in 528–529 the latter organized a great massacre of the Mazdakites. It is significant that it is the troubles provoked by Mazdak "that set in motion the last redaction of the Avesta and the victory of the Zoroastrian State Church" (Widengren, p. 343). A short while after (in 635), Persia was conquered by the Muslims. But Mazdaism, isolated in the southern parts of the country, underwent a veritable renaissance in the ninth century (the period of the redaction of the principal works in Pahlavi, the *Bundahishn*, *Dênkart*, etc.; Duchesne-Guillemin, pp. 365ff.). However, the hope of shaking off the yoke of the Caliphs and of restoring the Zoroastrian state was destroyed by the Turks of the Ghaznavid and Seljuk dynasties, implacable adversaries of the religious tradition and of the political autonomy of the Iranian people.

It is in such an ideological context, unfortunately still little known, that one must situate the nostalgia for ancient Persia felt by Sohrawardî and so many other Iranian poets and mystics.

282. The *Mathnawî* has been edited and translated into English by Reynold A. Nicholson, 8 vols. (London, 1925–40); see the list of other partial translations in A. M. Schimmel, *Mystical Dimensions of Islam*, p. 310, n. 24. Selections of the *Dîvân-i Shams-i Tabriz* have been translated into English by R. A.

Nicholson (1898; new ed., Cambridge, 1961) and into French (under the title *Odes mystiques*) by E. de Vitray-Meyerovitch (Paris, 1973); for other European-language translations, see Schimmel, p. 310, n. 25.

On Rûmî, see A. M. Schimmel, *The Triumphal Sun: A Study of Mewlana Rûmî's Life and Work* (London and The Hague, 1978); idem, *Mystical Dimensions*, pp. 309–28; E. de Vitray-Meyerovitch, *Rûmî et le soufisme* (1970; idem, *Mystique et poésie en Islam: Djalâlud-Dîn Rûmî et les derviches tourneurs*, 2d ed. (Paris, 1973); R. A. Nicholson, *Rûmî, Poet and Mystic* (London, 1950); William C. Chittick, *The Sufi Path of Love: The Spiritual Teachings of Rûmî* (Albany, 1983); cf. also the bibliographies provided by de Vitray-Meyerovitch, *Rûmî*, p. 188, and Schimmel, *Mystical Dimensions*, p. 311, nn. 25, 26; p. 316, nn. 28–31.

On the religious music and dance, see Marijan Molé, "La Danse extatique en Islam," in *Les Danses Sacrées*, "Sources Orientales," vol. 4 (Paris 1963), pp. 145–280. On the dance of the Dervishes, see Fritz Meier, "Der Derwischtanz: Versuch eines Ueberblicks," *Asiatische Studien* 8 (1954): 107–36. On the *mawlawi* dance, see Hellmut Ritter, "Der Reigen der tanzenden Derwische," *Zeitschrift für vergleichende Musikwissenschaft* 1 (1933): 28–42.

283. On the *dhikr*, see Louis Gardet, "La mention du nom divin (*dhikr*) en mystique musulmane," *Revue Thomiste* (1952): 642–79; (1953): 197–216; idem, *Mystique musulmane*, pp. 187–258; M. Eliade, *Yoga*, pp. 216–19; 408 (bibliography).

On the origin of alchemy, see the bibliography provided in volume 2 of the present work, pp. 481ff.; cf. also M. Eliade, *Forgerons et alchimistes*, 2d ed., corrected and augmented (Paris, 1977), pp. 173ff. (English trans., *The Forge and the Crucible* [New York 1962], pp. 179ff.).

On the history of Arabic alchemy, see the bibliography in Eliade, *Forgerons*, pp. 175ff. (*The Forge and the Crucible*, pp. 195ff.). See, above all, Paul Kraus, *Jabîr ibn Hayyân, contribution à l'histoire des idées scientifiques dans l'Islam*, vols. 1–2 (Cairo, 1942–43); H. Corbin, "Le Livre du Glorieux de Jabîr ibn Hayyân, Alchimie et Archétypes," *Eranos-Jahrbuch* 18 (Zurich, 1950): 47–114. Cf. also the translation by Stéphane Ruspoli of a small treatise by ibn Arabî, *L'alchimie du bonheur parfait* (Paris, 1981).

Chapter 36. Judaism from the Bar Kokhba Revolt to Hasidism

284. On R. Yohanan ben Zakkai and the consequences of the destruction of the temple, see the bibliography cited at §224 (vol. 2, p. 538).

The history of the Jews from the end of antiquity to the Middle Ages has been presented in magisterial manner by Salo W. Baron, *A Social and Religious History of the Jews*, vols. 3–4 (New York, new. ed., 1950–58).

On the Sanhedrin, see Hugo Mantel, *Studies in the History of the Sanhedrin* (Cambridge, Mass., 1961).

The book of George Foote Moore, *Judaism in the First Centuries of the Christian Era: The Age of the Tannaim*, vols. 1–2 (Cambridge, Mass., 1927; with numerous reprintings), still retains its full value. (One must, however, take into account the observations of Porter, recalled and discussed by Jacob Neusner, *Judaism*, pp. 5–14.)

On the Mishnah, one now has at one's disposal the clear and vigorous exposition of Jacob Neusner, *Judaism: The Evidence of the Mishnah* (Chicago, 1981), a synthesis of Neusner's numerous earlier publications. Let us cite the most important for an understanding of the Mishnah: *The Idea of Purity in Ancient Judaism* (Leiden, 1973); *A History of the Mishnaic Law of Purities*, vols. 1–22 (Leiden, 1974–77); *The Modern Study of the Mishnah* (Leiden, 1973); *A History of the Mishnaic Law of Holy Things*, vols. 1–6 (Leiden, 1978–79); *Form-Analysis and Exegesis: A Fresh Approach to the Interpretation of Mishnah* (Minneapolis, 1980).

One will find an essential bibliography in Neusner's *Judaism*, pp. 381–403.

285. Among the translations of the Babylonian Talmud, one can consult the new edition, reviewed and corrected by I. M. Weiss (Boston, 1918), of the version of M. L. Rodkinson (New York, 1896–1910; 10 vols.). The translation carried out by several scholars, under the direction of I. Epstein and J. H. Hertz, appeared in London (1935ff.) in 35 volumes. Let us also mention several anthologies: A. Cohen, *Everyman's Talmud* (London, 1932, repr. 1949); C. Montefiore and C. G. Loewe, *Rabbinic Anthology, Selected and Arranged with Comments and Introduction* (London, 1938; repr. New York, 1960); G. Goldin, *The Living Talmud* (Chicago and London, 1958).

From the rich critical literature, let us note: Solomon Schechter, *Aspects of Rabbinic Theology* (New York, 1909; repr. 1961 with an introduction by Louis Finkelstein); G. F. Moore, *Judaism in the First Centuries of the Christian Era*, vol. 1, pp. 173ff.; David Goodblatt, "The Babylonian Talmud," in *Aufstieg und Niedergang der römischen Welt* (Berlin, 1972), vol. 1, pp. 257–336; J. Neusner, ed., *Understanding Rabbinic Judaism: From Talmudic to Modern Times* (New York, 1974), and cf. David Goodblatt, "Bibliography on Rabbinic Judaism," ibid., pp. 383–402; Joseph Heinemann, *Prayer in Talmud: Forms and Patterns*, Richard Sarason, trans. (Berlin, 1977); Jacob Neusner, *The Formation of the Babylonian Talmud* (Leiden, 1970); Gerd A. Wewers, *Geheimnis und Geheimhaltung im rabbinischen Judentum* (Berlin and New York, 1975); J. Neusner, "The History of Earlier Rabbinic Judaism: Some New Approaches," *HR* (1977): 216–36.

On the Karaites, see L. Nemoy, *Karaite Anthology* (New Haven, 1952); D. Sidersky, "Le Caraïsme et ses doctrines," *RHR* 114 (1936): 197–221; Z. Cahn, *The Rise of the Karaite Sect: A New Light on the Halakah and the Origin of the Karaites* (Philadelphia, 1937); A. Paul, *Recherches sur l'origine du Qaraïsme* (Paris, 1970).

On connections with the sectarians of Qumran, see N. Wieder, *The Judaean Scrolls and the Karaites* (London, 1962).

286. On medieval Jewish philosophy, see G. Vajda, *Introduction à la pensée juive du Moyen Age* (Paris, 1947); Isaac Husik, *A History of Medieval Jewish Philosophy* (New York, 1916; repr. 1958); Julius Guttmann, *Die Philosophie des Judentums* (Munich, 1933; English trans. *Philosophies of Judaism,* New York, 1964). A brilliant and original exposition of the whole is André Neher, "Philosophie Juive médiévale," in *Histoire de la Philosophie,* Encyclopédie de la Pléiade, vol. 1 (Paris, 1969), pp. 1006–47.

An annotated selection of Philo's texts has been published by Nahum Glatzer, *The Essential Philo* (1971), and David Winston, *Philo of Alexandria: The Contemplative Life, The Giants and Selections* (New York, 1981). The complete works are in the process of being translated by R. Arnaldez, J. Pouilloux, and Mondésert (Paris, 1961 and ff.; 36 volumes have appeared by 1980). The best work on Philo is V. Nikiprowetzky, *Le commentaire de l'Ecriture chez Philon d'Alexandrie* (Leiden, 1977).

On the influence of Philo, both direct and indirect, on medieval Christian thought, see H. A. Wolfson, *Philo,* vols. 1–2 (Cambridge, Mass., 1847); on the state of the question, cf. ibid., vol. 2, pp. 158ff.

The first Jewish philosopher is Isaac Israeli (ca. 855–955), who lived and died in Egypt. His writings are a compilation of different sources, but, translated into Latin, they were utilized by the Christian Scholastics in the thirteenth century. Certain fragments have been translated and commented upon in A. Altmann and S. Stern, *Isaac Israeli* (London, 1959).

The complete translation of the work of Saadia has been carried out by S. Rosenblatt, *The Book of Beliefs and Opinions* (New Haven, 1948). See also M. Ventura, *La Philosophie de Saadia Gaon* (Paris, 1934); H. A. Wolfson, *Kalam Arguments for Creation in Saadia, Averroes, Maimonides and St. Thomas* (Saadia Anniversary volume, New York, 1943), pp. 197ff.

On Ibn Gabirol, see above all S. Munk, *Mélanges,* pp. 151–306; J. Guttmann, *Die Philosophie des Judentums,* pp. 102–19; Isaac Husik, *A History of Medieval Jewish Philosophy* (New York, 1916), pp. 59–80; Julius R. Weinburg, *A Short History of Medieval Philosophy* (Princeton, 1964), pp. 146–49.

The treatise of Bahya ibn Paqûda, *Introduction aux devoirs des coeurs,* has been translated by A. Chouraqui (Paris, 1950). There is also the English translation by Edwin Collins, *The Duties of the Heart* (London, 1909).

The work of Judah Halevi has been translated and annotated by Hartwig Hirschfeld, *Book of Kuzari* (New York, 1946). See also Isaac Husik, *Three Jewish Philosophers: Philo, Saadia Gaon, Jehuda Halevi,* trans. from the Hebrew by Hans Lewy, A. Altmann, and I. Heinemann (New York, 1965; selections with commentary).

287. An excellent anthology of the texts of Maimonides has been drawn together by Isadore Twersky, *A Maimonides Reader: Edited with an Introduction and Notes* (New York, 1972). It contains long extracts from the treatise *Mishneh Torah* (pp. 35–227), an important selection from the *Guide for the Perplexed* (pp. 231–358), and several smaller works and letters that are difficult to get hold of in translation (pp. 361–482). See also Arthur Cohen, *Teachings of Maimonides,* Prolegomena by Marvin Fox (New York, 1968). Among the translations of the *Moreh Nevukhim,* we have used the latest: Shlomo Pines, trans., *The Guide for the Perplexed* (Chicago, 1963). Translations of the *Mishneh Torah* are indicated in *Maimonides Reader,* p. 484, and in David Hartmann, *Maimonides: Torah and Philosophic Quest* (Philadelphia, 1976), pp. 269–72. The works of Shlomo Pines (pp. 484–90) and David Hartmann (pp. 272–88) include rich bibliographies.

Among the most exhaustive presentations, one should mention Salo W. Baron, *A Social and Religious History of the Jews,* vol. 8 (New York, 1958), pp. 55–138; Joseph Sarachek, *Faith and Reason: The Conflict over the Rationalism of Maimonides* (New York, 1970). See also Daniel Y. Silver, *Maimonidean Criticism and the Maimonidean Controversy: 1180–1240* (Leiden, 1965); Harry A. Wolfson, "Maimonides on the Unity and Incorporeality of God," *Jewish Quarterly Review* 56 (1965): 112–36; Alexander Altmann, "Essence and Existence in Maimonides," in *Studies in Religious Philosophy and Mysticism* (Ithaca, 1969), pp. 108–27; "Free Will and Predestination in Saadia, Bahya, and Maimonides," in *Essays in Jewish Intellectual History* (Hannover and London, 1981), pp. 35–64; "Maimonides 'Four Perfections,'" ibid., pp. 65–76; "Maimonides and Thomas Aquinas: Natural or Divine Prophecy?" ibid., pp. 77–96.

The work of David Hartmann is precious above all for the numerous texts illustrating the continuity between the *Mishneh Torah* and the *Moreh Nevukhim;* see his *Maimonides: Torah and Philosophic Quest,* pp. 102ff. Contrary opinions have been set forth by Isaac Husik, *A History of Medieval Jewish Philosophy* (repr. New York, 1958), p. 5, and Leo Strauss, *Persecution and the Art of Writing* (Chicago, 1952), pp. 38–95: "The Literary Character of the *Guide for the Perplexed*"; idem, "Notes on Maimonides' Book of Knowledge," in *Studies . . . Presented to Gershom Scholem* (Jerusalem, 1967), pp. 269–85.

288. The only essential and exclusive work on the history of Jewish mysticism, from its origins to Hasidism, is Gershom Scholem, *Major Trends in Jewish Mysticism* (New York, 1946); we have utilized the fourth edition, revised and augmented with supplementary bibliographies. See also the French translation, *Les grands courants de la mystique juive* (Paris, 1950). Let us also cite the same author's *Les origines de la Kabbale* (Paris, 1966; German ed., *Ursprung und Anfänge der Kabbala,* Berlin, 1962); *On the Kabbalah and Its Symbolism* (New York, 1965; German ed., Zurich, 1960); *The Messianic Idea in Judaism and Other Essays on Jewish Spirituality* (New York, 1971; collection of articles published between 1937 and 1970).

A brief general introduction, including the translation of several significant texts, has been published by Guy Casaril, *Rabbi Siméon bar Yochaï et la Kabbale* (Paris, 1961, collection "Maîtres Spirituels"). The book of Paul Vuilliaud, *La Kabbale Juive: Histoire et Doctrine: Essai critique,* 2 vols. (Paris, 1923), has been severely criticized by Scholem. Still useful, above all for the post-Renaissance Christian Kabbalists, is the work of A. E. Waite, *The Holy Kabbalah: A Study of the Secret Traditions of Israel* (London, 1929). On Jewish esotericism and the Kabbalah, see G. Vajda, "Recherches récentes sur l'esotérisme juif (1947–53)," *RHR* 147 (1955): 62–92; idem, "Recherches récentes . . . (1954–62)," *RHR* 164 (1963): 39–86, 191–212; *RHR* 165 (1964): 49–78; idem, *L'amour de Dieu dans la théologie juive du Moyen Âge* (Paris, 1957); idem, *Recherches sur la philosophie et la Kabbale dans la pensée juive du Moyen Âge* (Leiden, 1969).

On the *Merkabah,* see Scholem, *Major Trends,* pp. 40–79; idem, *Jewish Gnosticism, Merkabah Mysticism and Talmudic Tradition* (New York, 1960), passim; idem, *Les Origines de la Kabbale,* pp. 27–33, 118–122, 128–138, 153–160, etc. See also Ithamar Gruenwald, *Apocalyptic and Merkawah Mysticism* (Leiden, 1979).

On *Shi'ur Qoma,* see also Alexander Altmann, "'Moses Narboni's 'Epistle on Shi'ur Qoma,'" in *Studies in Religious Philosophy and Mysticism* (Ithaca, 1969), pp. 180–209.

On the *Sefer Yetsira,* see Scholem, *Major Trends,* pp. 84 ff., 126ff., 367ff.; idem, *Les Origines de la Kabbale,* pp. 31ff. The most recent translation is that of Guy Casaril, pp. 41–48. See also G. Vajda, "Le Commentaire de Saadia sur le *Sepher Yetsira,*" *Revue des Études Juives* 56 (1945): 64–86.

On the Hasids of Germany, see Scholem, *Major Trends,* pp. 80–118. On the mythology of the Golem and its origins, cf. Scholem, "The Idea of the Golem," in *On the Kabbalah and Its Symbolism,* pp. 158–204.

289. On the reactualization of certain mythological themes in the Kabbalah, see G. Scholem, "Kabbalah and Myth," in *On the Kabbalah and Its Symbolism,* pp. 87–117.

The *Bahir* has been translated into German and commented upon by Scholem, *Das Buch Bahir* (Leipzig, 1923); see also *Major Trends,* pp. 74ff., 229ff.; *Origines de la Kabbale,* pp. 78–107, 164–94, 211ff.

On *devekuth,* see G. Scholem, "*Devekut,* or Communion with God," in *The Messianic Idea in Judaism,* pp. 203–26 (article published in 1950).

On Abraham Abulafia, see Scholem, *Major Trends* pp. 119–55 (and the bibliographical notes, pp. 398ff.). Cf. Guy Casaril, pp. 66ff. There is a nearly complete translation of the *Zohar* by Sperling and Maurice Simon, *The Zohar,* 5 vols. (London, 1931–34, re-edition 1955); see also David Chanan Matt, *Zohar: The Book of Enlightenment,* translation and introduction (New York, 1983). See above all G. Scholem, *Die Geheimnisse Sohar* (Berlin, 1935), and *Zohar: Book of Splendor* (selections and commentary). The best presentation remains, as always, Scholem, *Major Trends,* pp. 156–243 (and the critical notes, pp. 385–407). See also Ariel Bension, *The Zohar in Moslem and Christian Spain* (London, 1932); F. Secret, *Le Zohar chez les kabbalistes chrétiens de la Renaissance* (Paris and The Hague, 1958).

On the history of the concept of the *Shekinah,* see G. Scholem, "Zur Entwicklungsgeschichte der kabbalistischen Konzeption der Schekinah," *Eranos-Jahrbuch* 21 (Zurich, 1952): 45–107. On the transmigration of souls, see Scholem, *Major Trends,* pp. 241ff.; idem, "The Messianic Idea in Kabbalism" (in *The Messianic Idea in Judaism,* pp. 37–48), pp. 46ff.; idem, "Seelenwanderung und Sympathie der Seelen in der jüdischen Mystik," *Eranos-Jahrbuch* 24 (1955): 55–118.

290.   An excellent presentation of the spriritual life at Safed in the sixteenth century has been given by R. J. Zwi Werblowsky, *Joseph Karo, Lawyer and Mystic* (Oxford, 1962; repr. Philadelphia, 1977), pp. 38–83. See ibid., pp. 84–168 (R. Joseph Karo's bibliography); pp. 169–286 (analysis of Karo's mystical experiences and theology).

On Isaac Luria and his school, see Scholem, *Major Trends,* pp. 244–86, 407–15.

When one of his disciples asked him why he did not express his ideas in the form of a book, Luria answered him: "It is impossible, because all things are interrelated. I can hardly open my mouth to speak without feeling as though the sea burst its dams and overflowed. How then shall I express what my soul has received; and how can I put it down in a book?" Cited by Scholem, *Major Trends,* p. 254.

Isaac Luria claimed to be the only Kabbalist after Nahmanides to have learned the secret doctrine directly from the prophet Elijah.

The diffusion of his ideas was almost entirely the work of Israel Sarug, who between 1592 and 1598 propagated them among the Kabbalists of Italy. However, Sarug knew Luria's ideas only through the writings of Vital. On certain points he radically reinterpreted the master's doctrine; he provided him with a quasi-philosophical base by introducing a sort of Platonism—which in the last analysis explains his success; Scholem, *Major Trends,* pp. 257–58.

291. On Sabbatai Zwi and Sabbatianism, see Scholem, *Major Trends,* pp. 286–324; idem, "Redemption through Sin," in *The Messianic Idea in Judaism,* pp. 78–141 (this article first appeared in Hebrew in 1937); idem, "The Crypto-Jewish Sect of the Donmeh (Sabbatianism) in Turkey," in *The Messianic Idea,* pp. 142–66; and especially Scholem's magnum opus, translated from the Hebrew by R. J. Zwi Werblowsky, *Sabbatai Sevi, the Mystical Messiah* (Princeton, 1973; this is a revised and augmented version of the original, which was published in Tel Aviv in 1957). See also Yosef Hayim Yerushalmi, *From Spanish Court to Italian Ghetto* (New York, 1971; repr. Seattle and London, 1981), pp. 313–49. The great majority of the theological and historical documents have been destroyed. However, the moderate forms of Sabbatianism, in which orthodox piety and heretical beliefs coexisted, survived for quite a long time; see Scholem, *Major Trends,* pp. 299ff.

292. On Hasidism, see Scholem, *Major Trends,* pp. 325–50 (cf. the bibliographies provided on pp. 436–38, 445–46); idem, "The Neutralization of the Messianic Element in Early Hassidism," in *The Messianic Idea in Judaism,* pp. 176–202; Martin Buber, *Die chassidischen Bücher* (Hellerau, 1928; numerous reprintings); idem, *Jewish Mysticism and the Legend of Baal Shem* (London, 1931); idem, *Deutung des Chassidismus* (Berlin, 1935); idem, *Hassidism* (New York, 1948); idem, *The Origin and Meaning of Hassidism,* Maurice Friedman, ed. (New York, 1960); Arnold Mandel, *La Voie du Hassidisme* (Paris, 1963); Elie Wiesel, *Célébration hassidique* (Paris, 1972); idem, *Les récits hassidiques,* trans. A. Guerne (Paris, 1961).

On Rabbi Shneur Zalman of Ladi and the *Habad,* see Scholem, *Major Trends,* pp. 340ff.; Guy Casaril, *Rabbi Simeon bar Yochai,* pp. 166ff. On *Habad,* see also Dov Baer of Lubavitch, *Lettre aux hassidim sur l'extase* (French version by Georges Levitte, Paris, 1975; English translation, with introduction and notes, by Louis Jacobs: Dobh Baer, *Tract on Ecstasy* [London, 1963; reprinted as *On Ecstasy: A Tract,* Chappaqua, N. Y., 1983]).

Chapter 37. Religious Movements in Europe

293. On Bogomilism, see the rich bibliography in Dimitri Obolensky, *The Bogomils: A Study in Balkan Neo-Manicheism* (Cambridge, 1948), pp. 290–

304, to be supplemented by the works mentioned in our "The Devil and God" (*Zalmoxis, the Vanishing God*, Chicago, 1972, pp. 76–130), pp. 89–90, n. 26; see also Arno Borst, *Les Cathares* (French trans., Paris, 1974), pp. 55ff., useful above all for the bibliographical citations. Outside of Obolensky's monograph, the best presentation of the whole remains Steven Runciman, *The Medieval Manichee: A Study of the Christian Dualist Heresy* (Cambridge, 1947; French trans., Paris, 1949; *Le manichéisme médiéval*).

The most important sources are Cosmas the Priest, *Le Traité contre les Bogomiles*, translated with commentary by H. Ch. Puech and A. Vaillant (Paris, 1945), and the *Dogmatic Panoply* of Euthymius Zigabenus (in Migne, *Patrologia Graeca*, vol. 130). See the analysis of these two texts in Runciman, pp. 73ff.

The book of Jordan Ivanov, *Bogomilski Knigi i legendy* (Sophia, 1925), has been translated by Monette Ribeyrol, *Livres et légendes bogomiles* (Paris, 1976; pp. 381–90, recent bibliography, provided by D. Angelov).

Among the recent contributions on the history of the heresy and on the survivals of Bogomilism in the Balkan peninsula and in Romania, see Robert Browning, *Byzantium and Bulgaria: A Comparative Study across the Early Medieval Frontier* (London, Berkeley, and Los Angeles, 1975), pp. 163ff.; Răzvan Theodorescu, *Bizant, Balcani, Occident la începuturile culturii medievale românesti, secolele X–XIV* (Bucharest, 1974), pp. 341ff.; M. Lambert, *Medieval Heresy: Popular Movements from Bogomil to Hus* (1977); G. Cantacuzino, "Les tombes de Bogomiles découvertes en Roumanie et leurs rapports avec les communautés hérétiques byzantines et balkaniques" *Acts of the Fourteenth International Congress of Byzantine Studies* (Bucharest, 1975), vol. 2, pp. 515–28; Anton Balotă, "Bogomilismul şi cultura maselor populare în Bulgarie şi în Tările Române," *Romanoslavica* 10 (Bucharest, 1964): 14–69.

On the Apocrypha and their Bogomil reinterpretation, see E. Turdeanu, "Apocryphes bogomiles et apocryphes pseudo-bogomiles," *RHR* 138 (1950): 22–52, 176–218. On the history of the circulation of the apocryphal *The Wood of the Cross*, see N. Cartojan, *Cărtile populare în literatura românească*, 2d ed. (Bucharest, 1974), vol. 1, pp. 155ff.; Esther Casier Quinn, *The Quest of Seth for the Oil of Life* (Chicago, 1962), pp. 49ff. On the *Interrogatio Johannis* see Edina Bozóky, ed., trans., and comm., *Le Livre Secret des Cathares: Interrogatio Iohannis, Apocryphe d'origine bogomile* (Paris, 1980).

294.   On the Cathars, see the general presentations of Steven Runciman, *The Medieval Manichee*, pp. 116–70, and of Arno Borst, *Les Cathares*, esp. pp. 79–196 (with a very rich bibliography). Cf. also H. Ch. Puech, "Catharisme médiéval et bogomilisme," in *Oriente ed Occidente nel Medio Evo* (Rome. 1957), pp. 56–84; reprinted in *Sur le manichéisme et autres essais* (Paris, 1979), pp. 395–427.

The Cathar texts, small in number, have been edited and translated by A. Dondaine, *Le "Liber de duobus principiis" suivi d'un fragment de rituel cathare* (Rome, 1932); C. Thouzellier, *Un traité cathare inédit du début du XIIIᵉ siècle* (Louvain, 1961); *Une somme anticathare* (Louvain, 1964); and René Nelli, *Écritures Cathares* (Paris, 1968). See also Edina Bozóky, *Le Livre Secret des Cathares: Interrogatio Iohannis, Apocryphe d'origine bogomile* (Paris, 1980).

On the Albigensian Crusade, see P. Belperron, *La Croisade contre les Albigeois et l' union du Languedoc à la France* (Paris, 1943; 2d ed. 1948).

On the Inquisition, see J. Guiraud, *Histoire de l'Inquisition au Moyen Âge*. Vol. 1, *Cathares et vaudois*. Vol. 2, *L'Inquisition au XIIIᵉ siècle en France, en Espagne et en Italie* (Paris, 1935, 1938). The recent bibliography has been provided by H. Grundmann in Jacques Le Goff, ed., *Hérésies et sociétés dans l'Europe pré-industrielle* (Paris and The Hague, 1968), pp. 425–31.

For the historical context, see Friedrich Heer, *The Medieval World* (London and New York, 1962), pp. 197ff.

295. For the religious valorization of poverty, see Jeffrey B. Russell, *Religious Dissent in the Middle Ages* (New York, 1971), pp. 41ff.

The best biography of Saint Francis is that of Omer Englebert, *Vie de Saint François* (Paris, 1947; abundant bibliography, pp. 396–426). The essentials are presented by Ivan Gobry, *Saint François et l'esprit franciscain* (Paris, 1957; including also a selection of Saint Francis's writings, pp. 119–52). See also Lawrence Cunningham, ed., *Brother Francis: An Anthology of Writings by and about Saint Francis of Assisi* (New York, 1972), and, above all, *François d'Assise: Écrits* (Latin text and translation, "Sources chrétiennes," 285, Paris, 1981).

On the Order of Friars Minor, see John Moorman, *A History of the Franciscan Order* (Oxford, 1968); Cagetan Esser, O.F.M., *Origins of the Franciscan Order* (Chicago, 1970); Malcolm D. Lambert, *Franciscan Poverty: The Doctrine of the Absolute Poverty of Christ and the Apostles in the Franciscan Order, 1210–1323* (London, 1961); *S. Francesco nella ricerca storica degli ultimi ottanta anni*, Convegni del Centro di Studi sulla spiritualità medioevale, 9 (Todi, 1971).

296. The only complete edition of the works of Saint Bonaventure is that published in nine in-folio volumes by the Franciscan fathers of Quaracchi. French translations are listed by J. G. Bougerol, *Saint Bonaventure et la* *sagesse chrétienne* (Paris, 1963), pp. 180–82. For a selection of works translated into English, see Ewert H. Cousins, trans. with introduction, *Bonaventure, Classics of Western Spirituality* (New York, 1978).

Among recent monographs dedicated to Saint Bonaventure's thought, let us cite Etienne Gilson, *La philosophie de Saint Bonaventure,* 2d ed. (Paris, 1943); J. G. Bougerol, *Introduction to the Works of Bonaventure,* trans. Jose de Vinck (New York, 1964); idem, *Introduction à l'étude de saint Bonaventure* (Tournai, 1961); John Quinn, *The Historical Constitution of Saint Bonaventure's Philosophy* (Toronto, 1973); Ewert H. Cousins, *Bonaventure and the Coincidence of Opposites* (Chicago, 1978).

On the symbolism of the ladder and of mystical ascension, see Dom Anselme Stolz, *Théologie de la mystique,* 2d ed. (Chèvetogne, 1947), pp. 117–45; Alexander Altmann, *Studies in Religious Philosophy and Mysticism* (Ithaca, 1949); cf. the bibliography recorded in Eliade, *Shamanism,* pp. 487ff.

297. The editions of the works of Albertus Magnus, Saint Thomas Aquinas, and other scholastic authors are provided in Etienne Gilson, *La philosophie au Moyen Âge* (Paris, 1947). In the same work, one will also find an essential critical bibliography of the authors discussed. See also E. Gilson, *Le thomisme,* 2d ed. (Paris, 1952); F. Copleston, *Aquinas* (Harmondsworth, 1955; p. 265 lists English translations of Saint Thomas's works); M. D. Chenu, *Introduction à l'étude de saint Thomas d'Aquin* (Montreal, 1950); idem, *La théologie comme science au XIIIe siècle* (Paris, 1957); idem, *Toward Understanding Saint Thomas* (Chicago, 1964).

For a different interpretation of Scholasticism, see Steven Ozment, *The Age of Reform, 1250–1550: An Intellectual and Religious History of Late Medieval and Reformation Europe* (New Haven, 1980; on Thomas Aquinas, see pp. 9ff., 60ff.; on Ockham, see pp. 35ff., etc.). Ozment also presents the most recent critical literature.

On Duns Scotus, see Effren Bettoni, *Duns Scotus: The Basic Principles of His Philosophy* (Washington, 1961).

On Ockham, see Gordon Leff, *William of Ockham: The Metamorphosis of Scholastic Discourse* (Manchester, 1975); idem, *The Dissolution of the Medieval Outlook: An Essay on Intellectual and Spiritual Change in the Fourteenth Century* (New York, 1976).

On Scholasticism, see also F. van Steenberghen, *Aristotle in the West: The Origins of Latin Aristotelianism* (Louvain, 1955); idem, *The Philosophical Movement of the Thirteenth Century* (Edinburgh, 1955); Gordon Leff, *Medieval Thought: St. Augustine to Ockham* (Baltimore, 1962).

One finds a synthetic view in H. A. Oberman, *The Harvest of Medieval Theology* (Cambridge, Mass., 1963).

298. The critical edition of the works of Meister Eckhart is in the course of publication: *Die deutsche Werke,* vols. 1–5 (Stuttgart, 1938ff.), and *Die lateinische Werke,* vols. 1–5 (1938ff.). One will find a brief history of the various editions that have preceded this enterprise of the Deutsche Forschungsgemeinschaft in ''A Note on Eckhart's Works'' in Edmund Colledge and Bernard McGinn, *Meister Eckhart: The Essential Sermons, Commentaries, Treatises and Defense* (New York, 1981), pp. 62ff. The translations into various European languages undertaken before the critical edition must be approached with caution; such is the case, for example, with C. de B. Evans, *Meister Eckhart,* vols. 1–2 (London, 1924, 1931). Among the English translations, the most useful are Armand Maurer, *Master Eckhart: Parisian Questions and Prologues* (Toronto, 1974); Reiner Schurmann, *Meister Eckhart: Mystic and Philosopher* (Bloomington, 1978; containing the translation of eight German sermons and an important study of Eckhart's thought); and above all the translations of Edmund Colledge and Bernard McGinn. The best German translation has been achieved by Josef Quint, *Deutsche Predigten und Traktate* (Munich, 1955, also reproducing original texts in Middle High German). There is also a French translation of the German work: Paul Petit, *Oeuvres de Maître Eckhart: Sermons-Traités* (Paris, 1942). See also the translations of Jeanne Ancelet-Hustache, *Maître Eckhart et la mystique rhénane* (Paris, 1956), pp. 77–119.

Of the rich critical bibliography, let us note Vladimir Lossky, *Théologie négative et connaissance de Dieu chez Maître Eckhart* (Paris, 1960; an important work); C. F. Kelley, *Meister Eckhart on Divine Knowledge* (New Haven and London, 1977); Bernard Welte, *Meister Eckhart: Gedanken zu seinen Gedanken* (Freiburg, 1979; a new interpretation); M. de Gandillac, ''La 'dialectique' de Maître Eckhart,'' in *La mystique rhénane,* Colloque de Strassbourg, 1961 (Paris, 1961), pp. 59–94 See also the bibliography provided by Colledge and McGinn, pp. 349–53.

On medieval mysticism as a whole, the best exposition is J. Leclercq, F. Vandenbroucke, and L. Bouyer, *La spiritualité du Moyen Âge* (Paris, 1961). See also *L'Attesa dell'età nuova nella spiritualità della fine del Medio Evo,* Convegni del Centro di Studi sulla spiritualità medioevale, 3 (Todi, 1963).

299. On the heretical religious movements (or those accused of heresy) in the Middle Ages, see M. D. Lambert, *Medieval Heresy: Popular Movements from Bogomil to Hus* (London, 1977); Jacques Le Goff, ed., *Hérésies et sociétés dans l'Europe pré-industrielle, XIᵉ–XVIIᵉ siècles,* Colloque de Royaumont (Paris, 1968); *Movimenti religiosi populari ed eresie del medioevo,* in *X Congresso Internazionale di Scienze Storiche, Relazioni,* vol. 3 (Rome, 1955); Gordon Leff, *Heresy in the Later Middle Ages,* vols. 1–2 (Manchester and New York, 1967).

An abundantly documented analysis of several radical eleventh-century ascetic attitudes—above all those of Peter Damien and Anselm of Canterbury—has been given by Robert Bultot, *La doctrine du mépris du monde: Le XIe siècle*, vols. 1–2 (Louvain and Paris, 1963–64).

On the Beguines and Beghards, see E. W. McDonnell, *The Beguines and Beghards in Medieval Culture* (New Brunswick, 1954; rich documentation); Gordon Leff, *Heresy in the Later Middle Ages*, vol. 1, pp. 195ff.; Ozment, *The Age of Reform*, pp. 91ff.

On Mechthilde of Magdeburg, see Lucy Menzies, *The Revelations of Mechthilde of Magdebourg* (London, 1953); on the Flemish Beguine Hadewich, see Mother Columbia Hart, O.S.B., trans. with introduction, *The Complete Works* (New York, 1980).

On the movement of the Free Spirit, see G. Leff, vol. 1, pp. 310–407; Robert E. Lerner, *The Heresy of the Free Spirit in the Later Middle Ages* (Berkeley, 1972); H. Grundmann, *Religiöse Bewegungen im Mittelalter*, 2d ed. (Darmstadt, 1961), pp. 355–436.

On Marguerite Poret's *Le miroir des simples âmes* and the literature of the pseudo-Eckhart, see the analysis in Lerner, pp. 200ff.

See also Caroline Walker Bynum, *Jesus as Mother: Studies in the Spirituality of the High Middle Ages* (Berkeley and Los Angeles, 1982).

300.   On the ecclesiastical crisis of the fourteenth century, see the recent analyses of the state of the question in the works of Steven Ozment, *The Age of Reform*, pp. 135–81, and Francis Oakley, *The Western Church in the Late Middle Ages* (Ithaca and London, 1979), pp. 25–80, 131–74.

On the Flagellants, see Gordon Leff, *Heresy in the Later Middle Ages*, vol. 2, pp. 485–93 (rich documentation).

On the obsession with death in the Middle Ages, see T. S. R. Boase, *Death in the Middle Ages* (New York, 1972; excellent on iconography); E. Dubruck, *The Theme of Death in French Poetry of the Middle Ages and the Renaissance* (The Hague, 1964); F. Oakley, pp. 116ff. Cf. *Il dolore e la morte nella spiritualità dei secoli XII–XIII*, Convegni del Centro di Studi della spiritualità medioevale, 5 (Todi, 1967).

On the *danse macabre*, see J. M. Clark, *The Dance of Death in the Middle Ages and the Renaissance* (1950); Jurgís Baltrušaitis, *Le Moyen Âge fantastique* (Paris, 1955), pp. 235ff. (rich bibliography, pp. 258ff., esp. n. 15); Norman Cohn, *The Pursuit of the Millennium*, rev. ed. (London, 1970), pp. 130ff.

On the history of the doctrine of Purgatory, see now the definitive work of Jacques Le Goff, *La naissance du Purgatoire* (Paris, 1982), esp. pp. 177ff., 236ff., 357ff., 383ff.

French translations of Tauler and Suso are provided in Jeanne Ancelet-Hustache, *Maître Eckhart et la mystique rhénane*, pp. 190–91.

For the most important translations of Ruysbroeck, we have utilized Eric Colledge, *The Spiritual Espousals* (London, 1952), and C. A. Wynschenk and Evelyn Underhill, *John of Ruysbroeck: The Adornment of the Spiritual Marriage; The Sparkling Stone; The Book of Supreme Truth* (London, 1951); see also Kay C. Petry, ed., *Late Medieval Mysticism* (Philadelphia, 1957), pp. 285ff.

It is very likely that Gerson attacked Ruysbroeck on the basis of a quite erroneous Latin translation of his writings written in Flemish. See André Combes, *Essai sur la critique de Ruysbroeck par Gerson,* 3 vols. (Paris, 1945–59).

On G. Groote and the *devotio moderna,* see the well-documented work of R. R. Post, *The Modern Devotion: Confrontation with Reformation and Humanism* (Leiden, 1968).

301. The critical edition of the works of Nicholas of Cusa—*Nicolai de Cusa Opera Omnia*—is in course of publication under the care of the Academy of Letters of Heidelberg (Leipzig, 1932ff.).

Among the French translations, let us cite M. de Gandillac, *Oeuvres choisies* (Paris, 1942); L. Moulinier, *De la Docte Ignorance* (Paris, 1930); E. Vansteenberghe, *Traité de la vision de Dieu* (Louvain, 1925). For a general presentation, see E. Vansteenberghe, *Le cardinal de Cues* (Paris, 1920); P. Rotta, *Il cardinale Nicola da Cusa* (Milan, 1928).

The best monograph remains as always M. de Gandillac, *La philosophie de Nicolas de Cues* (Paris, 1941). See also Ernst Cassirer, *The Individual and the Cosmos in Renaissance Philosophy* (New York, 1963; the German original was published in 1927 in *Studien der Bibliothek Marburg,* 10, Leipzig and Berlin), chapters 1 and 2 (pp. 7–72); Paul E. Sigmund, *Nicholas of Cusa and Medieval Political Thought* (Cambridge, Mass., 1963); E. Hoffmann, *Universum des Nicolaus von Cues* (Heidelberg, 1930); idem, *Die Vorgeschichte der cusanischen Coincidentia oppositorum* (introduction to the translation of the treatise *De Beryllo,* Leipzig, 1938); G. Saitta, *Nicola da Cusa e l'umanesimo italiano* (Bologna, 1957); Jaroslav Pelikan, "Negative Theology and Positive Religion: A Study of Nicholas Cusanus *De pace fidei,*" in *Prudentia,* Supplementary Number, 1981: *The Via Negativa,* pp. 61–77.

On the theology of John Hus, see M. Spinka, *John Hus at the Council of Constance* (New York, 1966).

On the history of the conflict between the *sacerdotium* and *regnum* and the developments concerning the political theology of the origin and structure of royalty, see Ernst H. Kantorowitz, *The King's Two Bodies: A Study of Medieval Political Theology* (Princeton, 1957), pp. 193ff.

302. For a rapid introduction, see Olivier Clément, *L'essor du christianisme oriental* (Paris, 1964); idem, *Byzance et le christianisme* (Paris, 1964). Cf.

also Steven Runciman, *The Eastern Schism* (Oxford, 1955); P. Sherrard, *The Greek East and the Latin West* (New York, 1959); and, above all, D. Obolensky, *The Byzantine Commonwealth, Eastern Europe, 500–1453* (New York, 1971), and A. Toynbee, *Constantine Porphyrogenitus and His World* (London, 1973).

A clear and penetrating exposition has been given by Jaroslav Pelikan, *The Spirit of Eastern Christendom, 600–1700* (Chicago, 1974), pp. 146–98 (pp. 308–10, critical bibliography). See also Francis Dvornik, *The Photian Schism: History and Legend* (Cambridge, 1948); idem, *Byzantium and the Roman Primacy* (New York, 1966); idem, *Byzantine Mission among the Slavs: SS. Constantine-Cyril and Methodius* (New Brunswick, 1970).

The relations between the two churches—and the two cultures—have been admirably analyzed by Deno John Geanakoplos, *Byzantine East and Latin West* (New York, 1966); idem, *Interaction of the "Sibling" Byzantine and Western Culture in the Middle Ages and the Renaissance* (New Haven and London, 1976), esp. pp. 3–94.

303. Let us first of all cite several recent works on Eastern theology: V. Lossky, *Essai sur la théologie mystique de l'Église d'Orient,* 2d ed. (Paris, 1960); idem, *A l'image et à la ressemblance de Dieu* (Paris, 1967); M. Lot-Borodine, *La déification de l'homme* (Paris, 1970); J. Meyendorff, *Le Christ dans la théologie byzantine* (Paris, 1969); L. Ouspensky, *Essai sur la théologie de l'icône dans l'Eglise orthodoxe* (Paris, 1960).

On Simeon, see J. Darrouzès, trans., *Siméon le nouveau théologien, chapitres théologiques, gnostiques et pratiques,* Sources Chrétiennes, vol. 51 (Paris, 1951). Cf. also Hermegild Maria Biedermann, *Das Menschenbild bei Symeon dem Jüngerem dem Theologen* (Würzburg, 1949).

On the "prayer of the heart," cf. Jean Gouillard, *Petite Philocalie de la Prière du Coeur* (Paris, 1953; new ed., 1968).

On John Climacus, see Colm Luibheid and Norman Russell, trans., *John Climacus, The Ladder of Divine Ascent* (New York, 1982, with a long and erudite introduction by Kallistos Ware).

On Hesychasm, see Irénée Hausherr, *La Méthode d'oraison hésychaste* (Rome, 1927, Orientalia Christiana IX, 2); idem, "L'Hésychasme, étude de spiritualité," *Orientalia Christiana Periodica* 22 (1956): 5–40, 247–85.

Jean Meyendorff has contributed greatly to the rediscovery of Gregory Palamas. Let us cite above all his edition and translation of the *Triades pour la défense des saints Hésychastes* (Louvain, 1959); *Introduction à l'étude de Grégoire Palamas* (Paris, 1959; containing a complete exposition of the published and unpublished works of Palamas, pp. 331–400); *Saint Grégoire Palamas et la mystique orthodoxe* (Paris, 1959). See also Leonidas C. Coutos, *The Concept of Theosis in Saint Gregory Palamas: With Critical Text of the "Contra Akindynum,"* 2 vols. (Los Angeles, 1963); Jaroslav Pelikan, *The*

Spirit of Eastern Christendom (Chicago, 1974), pp. 261ff.; Vladimir Lossky, "La Théologie de la Lumière chez Grégoire Palamas de Thessalonique," *Dieu Vivant* 1 (1945): 93–118.

For a comparative presentation of the experience of the mystical light, see M. Eliade, *The Two and the One* (Chicago, 1966), pp. 19–77.

A clear and rapid overview of Nicholas Cabasilas is given in Olivier Clément, *Byzance et le christianisme oriental* (Paris, 1964), pp. 50–73.

Chapter 38. Religion, Magic, and Hermetic Traditions

304. In his work *La religion populaire au Moyen Age: Problèmes de méthode et d'histoire* (Montreal and Paris, 1975), Raoul Manselli brings into relief the "osmosis which has achieved a rapport of exchange between two civilizations" (p. 20), "paganism" and Christianity.

The homologization of regional mythologies to Christian "sacred history" does not constitute a "succession," as Paul Saintyves interprets it in his *Les Saints successeurs des dieux* (Paris, 1907). See the observations of E. Vacandart, *Études de critique et d'histoire religieuses,* 3d Series (Paris, 1912), pp. 59–212: "Origines du culte des saints. Les saints sont-ils successeurs des dieux?"

It is not necessary to recall the survival, under more or less Christianized forms, of certain mythico-symbolic complexes abundantly diffused throughout the world: for example, the Cosmic Tree, the Bridge, the Ladder, Hell and Paradise, etc. It will be enough for us to mention the persistence of the very old scenario of the eschatological Bridge (cf. Eliade, *Shamanism,* pp. 386ff., 492ff.) as it is elaborated in the Middle Ages (cf. Peter Dinzelbacher, *Die Jenseitsbrücke im Mittelalter,* Vienna, 1973) and down to our own day (cf. Luigi M. Lombardi Satriani and Mariano Meligrana, *Il Ponte di San Giacomo: L'ideologia della morte nella società contadina del Sud,* Milan, 1982, pp. 121ff.).

We have left aside ceremonies and customs linked with the fairground and the public square of the city—for example, the Feast of Fools, celebrated on New Year's Day, when the faithful, masked and costumed, entered the cathedral, led by a bishop of Fools, and were allowed all sorts of liberties. In Normandy, the deacons played dice and cards on the altar, all the while eating sausages. See also the analyses of Mikhail Bakhtine, *L'oeuvre de François Rabelais et la culture populaire au Moyen Age et sous la Renaissance* (French translation, Paris, 1970).

On pagan survivals in Greece, see J. C. Lawson, *Modern Greek Folklore and Ancient Greek Religion* (Cambridge, 1910; re-ed. New York, 1964); Georges Dumézil, *Le problème des Centaures* (Paris, 1929), pp. 155–93; C. A. Romaios, *Cultes populaires de Thrace: Les Anasténaria; la cérémonie du lundi pur* (Athens, 1949); Basil Makrakis, *Fire Dances in Greece* (Heraklion, 1982). For Paul Friedrich, the study of certain groups in rural Greece helps one to clarify the structures of Homeric society, and the cult of the Virgin Mary can better aid us to understand Demeter; cf. Friedrich, *The Meaning of Aphrodite* (Chicago, 1978), p. 55. Cf. also C. Poghirc, "Homère et la ballade populaire roumaine," *Actes du IIIe Congrès international du Sud-Est européen* (Bucharest, 1974); Leopold Schmidt, *Gestaltheiligkeit im bäuerlichen Arbeitsmythos: Studien zu den Ernteschnitzgeräten und ihre Stellung im europäischen Volksglauben und Volksbrauch* (Vienna, 1952); M. Eliade, "History of Religions and 'Popular' Cultures," *HR* 20 (1980): 1–26, esp. 5ff.

A considerable literature exists on the *Colinde* (see our "History of Religions and 'Popular' Cultures," p. 11, n. 29. Let us only recall the works we have cited: Al. Rosetti, *Colindele religioase la Români* (Bucharest, 1920); P. Caraman, "Substratul mitologic al sărbătorilor de iarnă la Români şi Slavi," *Arhiva* 38 (Iaşi, 1931): 358–447; Ovidiu Bîrlea, "Colindatul în Transilvania," *Anuarul Muzeului Etnografic al Transilvaniei pe anii 1965–67* (Cluj, 1969), pp. 247–304; Monica Bratulescu, *Colinda Românească* (Bucharest, 1981); idem, "Ceata feminină—încercare de reconstituire a unei instituţii tradiţionale româneşti," *Revista de Etnografie şi Folclor* 23 (Bucharest, 1978): 37–60; Petru Caraman, "Descolindatul în sud-estul Europei" (part 1), *Annarul de Folclor* 2 (Cluj-Napoca, 1981): 57–94.

On the initiatory structures still discernible in the organization and instruction of the *colindători*, see Traian Herseni, *Forme străvechi de cultură populară românească* (Cluj-Napoca, 1977), pp. 160ff.

305. See M. Eliade, "Notes on the *Căluşari*," in *The Gaster Festschrift: Journal of the Ancient Near Eastern Society of Columbia University* 5 (1973): 109ff.; idem, "History of Religions and 'Popular' Cultures," pp. 17ff.

The most important documentary sources on the organization of the *căluşari* are in Tudor Pamfile, *Sărbătorile de vară la Români* (Bucharest, 1910), pp. 54–75; Theodor T. Burada, *Istoria teatrului în Moldova*, 2 vols. (Jassy, 1905), vol. 1, pp. 62–70. Numerous materials are presented by Mihai Pop, "Consideratii etnografice şi medicale asupra căluşului oltenesc," *Despre medicina populară românească* (Bucharest, 1970), pp. 213–22; Gheorghe Vrabie, *Folclorul* (Bucharest, 1970), pp. 511–31; Horia Barbu Oprişan, *Căluşari* (Bucharest, 1960), and above all Gayle Kligman, *Căluş* (Chicago, 1981). Cf. also R. Vuia, "Originea jocului de căluşari," *Dacoromania* 2 (Cluj, 1922): 215–54; Eliade, "Notes," pp. 120ff.

On *Männerbund* initiations, see Eliade, *Initiation, rites, sociétés secrètes* (= *Naissances mystiques*), pp. 185ff., and the bibliographies indicated ibid., nn. 6–66.

306. From the immense bibliography on European witchcraft, let us retain the following: H. R. Trevor-Roper, *The European Witch-Craze of the Sixteenth and Seventeenth Centuries* (New York, 1969; see also chaps. 1–4 of his *The Crisis of the Seventeenth Century: Religion, the Reformation and Social Change,* 1968); Alan Macfarlane, *Witchcraft in Tudor and Stuart England* (New York, 1970); Jeffrey Burton Russell, *Witchcraft in the Middle Ages* (Ithaca, 1972; with a rich bibliography, pp. 350–77); Keith Thomas, *Religion and the Decline of Magic* (New York, 1971); Norman Cohn, *Europe's Inner Demons* (New York, 1975; French trans., *Démonolâtrie et sorcellerie au Moyen Age,* Paris, 1982); F. E. Lorint and J. Bernabé, *La sorcellerie paysanne* (Brussels, 1977); Robert Mandrou, *Possession et Sorcellerie au XVIIIᵉ siècle: Textes inédits* (Paris, 1979); E. William Monter, *Witchcraft in France and Switzerland: The Borderlands during the Renaissance* (Ithaca, 1976).

Extracts from sources are found in E. William Monter, *European Witchcraft* (New York, 1969); Barbara Rosen, *Witchcraft* (London, 1970); Max Marwick, ed., *Witchcraft and Society* (Baltimore, 1970); and above all Alan C. Kors and Edward Peters, *Witchcraft in Europe, 1100–1700: A Documentary History* (Philadelphia, 1972). Cf. H. C. Erik Midelfort, *Witch Hunting in Southwestern Germany, 1562–1684: The Social and Intellectual Foundations* (Stanford, 1972), esp. pp. 30ff., 193ff. This work sheds light on the differences between the "witch hunts" of the Catholics and the Protestants.

See also the works written from the perspective of the history of medicine: Gregory Zilboorg, *The Medieval Man and the Witch during the Renaissance* (Baltimore, 1935); Thomas R. Forbes, *The Midwife and the Witch* (New York, 1966).

Cf. E. W. Monter, "The Historiography of European Witchcraft: Progress and Prospects," *Journal of Interdisciplinary History* 2 (1972): 435–51; M. Eliade, "Some Observations on European Witchcraft," *HR* 14 (1975): 149–72 (= *Occultism, Witchcraft, and Cultural Fashions,* pp. 69–92); Richard A. Horsley, "Further Reflections on Witchcraft and European Folk Religion," *HR* (1979): 71–95.

On the *benandanti,* the best source remains the work of Carlo Ginzburg, *I Benandanti: Ricerche sulla stregoneria e sui culti agrari tra cinquecento e seicento* (Turin, 1966).

One will find a rich bibliography on beliefs and rites concerning the caul in Thomas R. Forbes, "The Social History of the Caul," *Yale Journal of Biology and Medicine* 25 (1953): 495–508.

On the *Wilde Heer,* see Victor Waschnitius, *Perht, Holda und verwandte Gestalten: Ein Beitrag zur deutschen Religionsgeschichte* (Vienna, 1914), esp. pp. 173ff.; Otto Höffler, *Kultische Geheimbünde der Germanen,* vol. 1, pp. 68ff.; idem, *Verwandlungskulte,* pp. 78ff.; Waldemar Liungmann, *Tradi-*

tionswanderungen: Euphrat-Rhein, Folklore Fellows Communication, 118 (Helsinki, 1937), pp. 596 ff.; R. Bernheimer, *Wild Men in the Middle Ages* (Cambridge, Mass., 1952), pp. 79ff., 132; C. Ginzburg, *I Benandanti,* pp. 48ff.

On the etymology of *zîna* (< Diana) and *zînatec* (< Latin *dianaticus*), see the critical bibliography in Alejandro Cioranescu, *Diccionario etimologico Rumano* (Universidad de la Laguna, 1961), p. 915; Al. Rosetti, *Istoria limbii române* (Bucharest, 1968), pp. 367–95.

On *zîne* and *iele,* see, inter alia, Aurel Candrea, *Folclorul românesc comparat* (Bucharest, 1944), pp. 156ff.; I. Muşlea and O. Bîrlea, *Tipologia folclorului,* pp. 206ff.

307. Of the considerable number of biographies of Martin Luther and works on his period, let us call attention to some recent contributions: R. H. Bainton, *Here I Stand* (New York and Nashville, 1950); Erik Erikson, *Young Man Luther* (1958; a brilliant but controversial interpretation; see the criticism in Ozment, *The Age of Reform,* pp. 223–31); E. G. Schwiebert, *Luther and His Times; The Reformation from a New Perspective* (St. Louis, 1950); R. H. Fife, *The Revolt of Martin Luther* (New York, 1957); Richard Stauffer, *La Réforme, 1517–1564* (Paris, 1970); J. Pelikan, *Luther the Expositor* (St. Louis, 1959); H. G. Haile, *Luther: An Experiment in Biography* (New York, 1980; precious above all on Luther's last years).

On the history of indulgences, see J. E. Campbell, *Indulgences* (Ottawa, 1953); P. F. Palmer, ed., *Sacraments and Forgiveness* (Westminster, 1960).

See also Arthur Rühl, *Der Einfluss der Mystik auf Denken und Entwicklung des jungen Luthers* (Oberhessen, 1960); J. Pelikan, ed., *Interpreters of Luther: Essays in Honor of Wilhelm Pauck* (Philadelphia, 1968); Steven Ozment, *Homo Spiritualis: A Comparative Study of the Anthropology of Johannes Tauler, Jean Gerson and Martin Luther in the Context of Their Theological Thought* (Leiden, 1968); F. E. Cranz, *An Essay on the Development of Luther's Thought on Justice, Law and Society* (Cambridge, Mass., 1959); S. Ozment, ed., *The Reformation in Medieval Perspective* (Chicago, 1971). See also the bibliography provided in §308.

308. We have availed ourselves of the most recent translations of the works of Martin Luther, published under the direction of J. Pelikan and H. T. Lehman, *Works,* 58 vols. (St. Louis, 1955ff.); see especially vol. 25 (Lessons on the Epistle to the Romans), vol. 38 (Word and Sacrament), and vols. 42–43 (devotional writings). We have also consulted Bertram Lee Woolf, trans. with commentary, *Reformation Writings* (London, 1959). See also Bengt Hoffman, trans. with commentary, *The Theologia Germanica of Martin Luther* (New York, 1980).

Among recent expositions of Luther's theology, let us mention especially John Dillenberger, *God Hidden and Revealed: The Interpretation of Luther's deus absconditus and Its Significance for Religious Thought* (Philadelphia, 1953); R. Prentor, *Spiritus Creator* (Philadelphia, 1953); Bengt Hägglund, *Theologie und Philosophie bei Luther und in der occamistischen Tradition* (Lund, 1955); B. A. Gerrish, *Grace and Reason: A Study in the Theology of Luther* (Oxford, 1952; important); H. A. Oberman, ed., *Luther and the Dawn of the Modern Era* (Leiden, 1974).

On Erasmus, the biography by J. Huizinga, *Erasmus of Rotterdam* (English trans. 1924), still keeps all its freshness. Roland H. Bainton, *Erasmus of Christendom* (New York, 1969), is precious above all for the numerous fragments of letters and lesser-known works of Erasmus which it contains (excellent bibliography, pp. 285–99). See also John C. Olin, ed., *Erasmus: Christian Humanism and the Reformation, Selected Writings* (New York, 1965).

On Erasmus's work and thought, see Louis Bouyer, *Autour d'Erasme* (Paris, 1955); Peter G. Bietenholz, *History and Biography in the Work of Erasmus* (Geneva, 1966); Ernst Wilhelm Kohls, *Die Theologie des Erasmus*, vols. 1–2 (Basle, 1966); Jean-Claude Margolin, *Erasme par lui-même* (Paris, 1965); Margaret M. Phillips, *Erasmus and the Northern Renaissance* (London, 1949); A. Renaudet, *Erasme et l'Italie* (Geneva, 1954). See also Richard L. De Molens, ed., *Essays on the Works of Erasmus* (New Haven and London, 1978), above all De Molen's "Opera Omnia Desiderii Erasmi" (pp. 1–50), and B. A. Gerrish, "Erasmus on Piety, Theology and the Lutheran Dogma" (pp. 187–209).

There are numerous editions and translations of *De Libero Arbitrio* and of *De Servo Arbitrio*. We have made use of the most recent and most complete: E. Gordon Rupp and Philip S. Watson, trans. with commentary, *Luther and Erasmus: Free Will and Salvation* (Philadelphia, 1969).

309. On the life and thought of Zwingli, see lastly Fritz Büsser, *Huldrych Zwingli: Reformation als prophetischen Auftrag* (Zurich, 1973); G. H. Potter, *Zwingli* (Cambridge, 1976); W. H. Neuser, *Die reformatorische Wende bei Zwingli* (Neukirchen-Vluyn, 1976). An excellent selections of the writings of Zwingli and Bullinger is given in G. W. Bromiley, *Zwingli and Bullinger: Selected Translations with Introduction and Notes* (Philadelphia, 1953).

On the Anabaptists and other movements of the "Radical Reformation," see above all G. H. Williams, *The Radical Reformation* (Philadelphia, 1962; cf. ibid., pp. 118–20, the history of the first Anabaptists in Switzerland, southern Germany, and Austria); see also G. H. Williams and A. Mergal, eds., *Spiritual and Anabaptist Writers* (Philadelphia, 1957); G. Hershberger, ed., *The Recovery of the Anabaptist Vision* (Scottsdale, Pa., 1957).

One of the best introductions to the thought and work of Calvin is that of A. M. Schmidt, *Jean Calvin et la tradition calvinienne* (Paris, 1956). The first biography, that written by Calvin's contemporary, Theodore Beza, *La Vie de Calvin* (English trans., Philadelphia, 1836), constitutes the principal source of all the later biographies. See above all Alexandre Ganoczi, *Le jeune Calvin: Genèse et évolution de sa vocation réformatrice* (Wiesbaden, 1966).

We have utilized the text of the first French edition (1541) of the *Institutions de la religion chrétienne,* edited by A. Lefranc, J. Pannier, and H. Chatelain (Paris, 1911 ff., repr. 1978) and the translation with commentary of the last Latin edition (1559) by John T. McNeill and F. L. Battles, *Institutes of the Christian Religion,* 2 vols. (Philadelphia, 1960); this work has the merit of having taken into account all the editions—Latin and French—of the *Institutes.*

On Calvin's theology, see John T. McNeill, *The History and Character of Calvinism* (New York, 1957); Quirinus Breen, *John Calvin: A Study in French Humanism,* 2d ed. (Grand Rapids, 1968); E. W. Monter, *Calvin's Geneva* (New York, 1967); Rudolf Pfister, *Kirchengeschichte der Schweiz,* vol. 2 (Zurich, 1974); Emile G. Léonard, *Histoire générale du protestantisme,* 1–2 (Paris, 1961); Dewey D. Wallace, Jr., *Puritans and Predestination: Grace in English Protestant Theology, 1525–1695* (Chapel Hill, 1982).

On Servetus, see Roland H. Bainton, *Hunted Heretic: The Life and Death of Michael Servetus, 1511–1553* (Boston, 1960).

On the conflict with the Anabaptists, see Willem Balke, *Calvin and the Anabaptist Radicals,* trans. William J. Heynen (Grand Rapids, 1981).

On the Catholic Reformation, see Léon Cristiani, *L'Eglise à l'époque du concile de Trente* (Paris, 1948); Hubert Jedin, *Geschichte des Konzils von Trient,* 1–2 (Freiburg i. B., 1949–57; English trans., St. Louis, 1957–62); Hermann Tüchler, C. A. Bouman, and Jacques Le Brun, *Réforme et Contre-Réforme* (Paris, 1968); Marvin R. O'Connell, *The Counter Reformation, 1599–1610* (New York, 1974).

On Ignatius of Loyola, see Alain Guillermou, *Saint Ignace de Loyola et la Compagnie de Jésus* (Paris, 1960; clear and lively introduction, with excellent iconography; cf. ibid., p. 187, the bibliography of the texts of Ignatius of Loyola translated into French). See also Henry Dwight Sedgwick, *Ignatius Loyola: An Attempt at an Impartial Biography* (New York, 1923; work by a nonspecialist, but well informed); Alexandre Brou, S.J., *Ignatius' Methods of Prayer* (Milwaukee, 1947; useful above all for the great number of texts cited and commented upon, situating the *Exercises* in the history of Christian spirituality); James Broderick, S.J., *The Origins of the Jesuits* (London and New York, 1940; Saint Ignatius' biography in relation to the history of the Order).

310.   On the Christianity of the Italian humanists, see Charles Trinkaus, *"In Our Image and Likeness": Humanity and Divinity in Italian Humanist Thought,* 2 vols. (Chicago, 1970; an indispensable work, precious also for the texts it includes, pp. 325–457, 778–885). See also Gioacchino Paparelli, *Feritas, Humanitas, Divinitas: Le componenti dell'Umanesimo* (Messina and

Florence, 1960); Paul Oskar Kristeller, *Renaissance Thought: The Classic, Scholastic and Humanistic Strains* (New York, 1961); Wallace K. Ferguson, ed., *Renaissance Studies* (New York, 1963); John W. O'Malley, *Giles of Viterbo on Church and Reform: A Study in Renaissance Thought* (Leiden, 1968); Franco Gaeta, *Lorenzo Valla: Filologia e storia nell' umanesimo italiano* (Naples, 1955).

For interpretations of religion in the Renaissance, see Carlo Angeleri, *Il problema religioso del Rinascimento: Storia della critica e bibliografia* (Florence, 1952). See also Giovanni di Napoli, *Studi sul Rinascimento* (Naples, 1973), pp. 1–84.

On Marsilio Ficino, see above all P. O. Kristeller, *Il pensiero filosofico di Marsilio Ficino* (Florence, 1953; a translation with additions from the English original of 1943); Giuseppe Saitta, *Marsilio Ficino e la filosofia dell' Umanesimo*, 3d ed., enlarged (Bologna, 1954); E. Garin, *L'umanesimo italiano*, 2d ed. (Bari, 1958); Raymond Marcel, *Marsile Ficin* (Paris, 1958).

On Pico della Mirandola, see Eugenio Garin, *Giovanni Pico della Mirandola* (Florence, 1937); Engelbert Monnerjahn, *Giovanni Pico della Mirandola: Ein Beitrag zur philosophichen Theologie des italienischen Humanismus* (Wiesbaden, 1960); Giovanni di Napoli, *G. Pico della Mirandola e la problematica dottrinale del suo tempo* (Rome, 1963).

On Renaissance Hermeticism, see above all Frances Yates, *Giordano Bruno and the Hermetic Tradition* (London and Chicago, 1964). On the *prisca theologia*, see D. P. Walker, *The Ancient Theology* (London, 1972). On magic in the Renaissance period, see D. P. Walker, *Spiritual and Demonic Magic, from Ficino to Campanella* (London, 1958; new ed. Notre Dame and London, 1975); Edgar Wind, *Pagan Mysteries in the Renaissance* (enlarged ed., London, 1967; esp. pp. 1–16, 218–35); Ioan P. Culiano, *Eros et Magie* (in press).

On esotericism, see E. Garin, ''Note sull'ermetismo del Rinascimento,'' in E. Castelli, ed., *Testi umanistici dell' Ermetismo* (Rome, 1955), pp. 8–19; E. Castelli, ed., *Umanesimo e esoterismo* (Padua, 1969; above all the studies of Maurice de Gandillac, Cesare Vasoli, and François Secret). See also J. Dagens, ''Hermétisme et cabale en France de Lefèvre d'Étaples à Bossuet,'' *Revue de Littérature Comparée* (January–March, 1961), pp. 3ff.

On the Christian Kabbalists, see F. Secret, *Les Kabbalistes chrétiens de la Renaissance* (Paris, 1964), and the studies brought together in *Kabbalistes chrétiens,* Cahiers de l'Hermétisme, 5 (Paris, 1979).

On the macro-microcosm homology, see Leonard Barkan, *Nature's Work of Art: The Human Body as the Image of the World* (New Haven, 1977); Alex Wayman, ''The Human Body as Microcosm in India, Greek Cosmology, and Sixteenth-Century Europe,'' *HR* 32 (1982): 172–90; Allen G. Debus, *Man and Nature in the Renaissance* (Cambridge, 1978), pp. 26ff.

311. For a brief presentation of alchemy and its relations with the mythologies of metallurgy, see our *The Forge and the Crucible* (1962; cf. also the enlarged French ed., *Forgerons et alchimistes* [Paris, 1977]). Cf. also R. P. Multhauf, *The Origins of Chemistry* (London, 1966); Allan G. Debus, "The Significance of the History of Early Chemistry," *Cahiers d'histoire mondiale* 9, no. 2 (1965): 37–58; John Read, *Through Alchemy to Chemistry* (New York, 1956).

On medieval alchemy, see the literature cited in *The Forge and the Crucible*, pp. 197–98; *Forgerons et alchimistes*, pp. 175–76. On alchemy in the period of the Renaissance and Reformation, see the bibliography gathered in the same two titles, pp. 198–99 and 176–77. Cf. above all Walter Pagel, *Paracelsus: An Introduction to Philosophical Medicine in the Era of the Renaissance* (Basel and New York, 1958; French trans., 1963); Allan G. Debus, *The English Paracelsians* (London, 1965); idem, *The Chemical Dream of the Renaissance* (Cambridge, 1968); idem, "The Chemical Philosophers: Chemical Medicine from Paracelsus to van Helmond," *History of Science* 2 (1974): 235–59; idem, *Man and Nature in the Renaissance* (Cambridge, 1978); Peter French, *John Dee: The World of an Elizabethan Magus* (London, 1972); R. J. W. Evans, *Rudolf II and His World* (Oxford, 1973).

For the revalorization of alchemy in the era of Newton, see Betty Jo Teeter Dobbs, *The Foundations of Newton's Alchemy* (Cambridge, 1975); Frances Yates, *The Rosicrucian Enlightenment* (London, 1972); Richard S. Westfall, *Force in Newton's Physics* (London and New York, 1971); idem, "Newton and the Hermetic Tradition," in *Science, Medicine and Society in the Renaissance: Essays to Honor Walter Pagel* (New York, 1972), vol. 2, pp. 183–98.

On J. V. Andreae, see J. W. Montgomery, *Cross and Crucible: Johann Valentin Andreae (1586–1654), Phoenix of the Theologians,* 1–2 (The Hague, 1973).

The *Fama Fraternitatis* has been reproduced in the work of Frances Yates, *The Rosicrucian Enlightenment*, pp. 238–51. Bernard Gorceix in his *Bible des Rose-Croix* has given a French translation of the *Fama,* of the *Confessio Fraternitatis R. C.* (1615), and of the *Noces Chimiques* of Christian Rosenkreutz.

Jean-Jacques Mathé provides a critical bibliography of the French works published from 1954 to 1977 in his *Alchimie, Cahiers de l'Hermétisme* (Paris, 1978), pp. 191–212. See in the same collective work the contributions by Antoine Faivre and Bernard Husson.

Chapter 39. Tibetan Religions

312. On the history and civilization of Tibet, see R. A. Stein, *Tibetan Civilization* (Stanford, 1972; translation of *La civilisation tibétaine*, Paris, 1962);

G. Tucci, *Tibet, Land of Snow* (London, 1967); D. Snellgrove and H. Richardson, *A Cultural History of Tibet* (New York, 1968).

Among the general works on Tibetan religion, let us cite the following: Charles Bell, *The Religion of Tibet* (Oxford, 1931; dated, but still useful for the author's first-hand information); R. B. Ekvall, *Religious Observances in Tibet: Patterns and Functions* (Chicago, 1964; presents the author's observations in western Tibet); H. Hoffmann, *Die Religionen Tibets* (Freiburg i. Breisgau, 1956; English trans., *The Religions of Tibet,* London, 1961); Marcelle Lalou, *Les religions du Tibet* (Paris, 1957); G. Tucci and W. Heissig, *Die Religionen Tibets und der Mongolie* (Stuttgart, 1970; French trans., *Les Religions du Tibet et de Mongolie,* Paris, 1973), pp. 13–336 (the most complete exposition of the whole of Tibetan religions). Excellent general presentations are found in R. A. Stein, *Tibetan Civilization,* pp. 164–247; Anne-Marie Blondeau, "Religions du Tibet," in *Histoire des Religions* (under the direction of Henri-Charles Puech), vol. 3 (1976), pp. 233–329.

The prehistory is still little known; cf. Paul Aufschneiter, "Prehistoric Regions Discovered in Inhabited Tibet," *East and West* 7 (1956): 74–88. Attention has been called to several megalithic monuments, and some have tried to decipher the traces of a megalithic culture in certain constructions and customs: cf. A. W. Macdonald, "Une note sur les mégalithes tibétains," *JA* (1963): 63–76; S. Hummel, "Die Steinreihen des tibetischen Megalithikums und die Ge-sar-sage," *Anthropos* 60 (1965): 933–88 (with references to the author's earlier works on this problem).

On the traditional religion, see A. Macdonald, "Une lecture des Pelliot tibétains 1286, 1287, 1038, 1047 and 1290: Essai sur la formation et l'emploi des mythes politiques dans la religion royale de Sron-bcan rgam-po," in *Études tibétaines dédiées à la mémoire de Marcelle Lalou* (Paris, 1971), pp. 190–391 (insightful analysis of the Tun-huang manuscripts, which alter the interpretation of pre-Buddhist traditions; the results are presented briefly in A. M. Blondeau, pp. 236–45); R. A. Stein, "Du récit au rituel dans les manuscrits tibétains de Touen-houang," in *Études tibétaines . . . Marcelle Lalou,* pp. 479–547; idem, *Tibetan Civilization,* pp. 191–229; F. W. Thomas, *Ancient Folk-literature from North-Eastern Tibet* (Berlin, 1957; includes edited and translated versions of several divination manuals and their myths of origins, found at Tun-huang). It is still unknown why a considerable number of manuscripts were hidden in a walled-up cave at Tun-huang (Kan-su province) between the seventh and tenth centuries.

On the Phyva gods, see A. Macdonald, "Une lecture des Pelliot tibétains," pp. 291ff.; on the "good religion of Gcug," see ibid., pp. 341ff.; on the temporal cycles, pp. 364ff.

Several fragments of cosmogonic myths are translated by Macdonald in *L'Origine du Monde,* Sources Orientales, 1 (Paris, 1959), pp. 422ff.; see also the beginnings of the origin myths published and translated by E. Haarh, *The*

Yar-lun Dynasty (Copenhagen, 1969), pp. 134ff. The myth which explains the origin of the world from an egg probably reflects a *Bon* tradition influenced by India; cf. Stein, *Tibetan Civilization,* pp. 194–95.

The origin myths of the first kings are presented and discussed in Haarh, *The Yar-lun Dynasty,* pp. 126ff. and passim; A. Macdonald, "Une lecture," pp. 202ff.; J. Russell Kirkland, "The Spirit of the Mountain: Myth and State in pre-Buddhist Tibet," *HR* 21 (1982): 257–71; Manabu Waida, "Symbolism of 'Descent' in Tibetan Sacred Kingship and Some East Asian Parallels," *Numen* 20 (1973): 60–78.

The myth of the descent of the first kings from Heaven and their reascent at death is attested among the Sumerians; see §17 and the bibliography cited in vol. 1, p. 392. On the luminosity of the Babylonian gods, cf. the bibliography in vol. 1, p. 395. The Tibetan royal tombs have been identified by Giuseppe Tucci, *The Tombs of the Tibetan Kings* (Rome, 1950); they have been violated since the fall of the monarchy. We have just begun, thanks to recent works, to understand the funerary conceptions and the sacrifices around the royal tombs. Inhumation was generally practiced, since there was belief in the resurrection of the body: the souls of the deceased awaited the event in two different regions, one a sort of "paradise" and the other a sort of "hell"; cf. A. Macdonald, pp. 365ff.; R. A. Stein, *Tibetan Civilization,* pp. 200–202; A. M. Blondeau, pp. 243–45.

On the *mu* rope of the first mythic kings, see G. Tucci, *Les religions du Tibet,* pp. 286ff., 301ff. (the sacrality of the king); E. Haarh, pp. 28ff., 177ff.; Eliade, *The Two and the One,* pp. 166–67.

On the preeminent role of the sovereigns in the traditional religion, see A. Macdonald, pp. 376ff. and passim.

313. On the cosmos–house–human-body homology, see M. Eliade, "Centre du Monde, Temple, Maison," in *Le Symbolisme cosmique des monuments religieux* (Rome, 1957), pp. 57–82; idem, "Briser le toit de la maison: Symbolisme architectonique et physiologie subtile," in *Studies in Mysticism and Religion, Presented to Gershom G. Scholem* (Jerusalem, 1967), pp. 131–39; R. A. Stein, "Architecture et pensée religieuse en Extrême-Orient," *Arts Asiatiques* 4 (1957), pp. 163–86; idem, "L'habitat, le monde et le corps humain en Extrême-Orient et en Haute-Asie," *JA* (1957): 37–74.

The warrior character of the holy mountains is illustrated by the festivals which are consecrated to them: various competitions; dances by groups of warriors, each group singing alternately, etc.; cf. Stein, *Tibetan Civilization,* p. 210.

The "warrior god" and the "man's god," who reside on the shoulders, "related man to his group in space and time: in space, because identical with those controlling the physical environment, house, or country; in time, because they preside over the fortunes of the line, from ancestors to descendants. For man himself, in whom all these relationships intersect, his gods guarantee—if all goes well—life-force, power, longevity and success" (Stein, *Tibetan Civilization,* p. 222, J. E. Stapleton Driver, trans.).

On the plurality of souls, cf. Stein, *Tibetan Civilization,* pp. 226ff. On the ritual competitions, see Stein, *Recherches sur l'épopée et le barde au Tibet* (Paris, 1959), pp. 437ff.; idem, *Tibetan Civilization,* pp. 212ff. On Iranian influences, cf. idem, *Recherches,* p. 296.

We have analyzed the mythico-ritual complex of antagonisms and competitions in our "Remarques sur le dualisme religieux" (1967), republished in *La Nostalgie des Origines* (1971); cf. above all pp. 284ff.; in English, see Eliade, *The Quest: History and Meaning in Religion* (Chicago, 1969), pp. 126–75 ("Prolegomenon to Religious Dualism: Dyads and Polarities," esp. pp. 159ff. on Indonesian, Tibetan, and Indian myths and rituals).

314. On the *Bon,* see G. Tucci, *Les religions du Tibet,* pp. 271ff.; Helmut Hoffmann, *Quellen zur Geschichte der tibetischen Bon-Religion* (Wiesbaden, 1950; the author primarily uses Buddhist sources); Marcelle Lalou, "Tibétain ancien Bod/Bon," *JA* 246 (1958): 157–268; D. L. Snellgrove, *The Nine Ways of Bon* (London, 1967); S. G. Karmay, *The Treasury of Good Sayings: A Tibetan History of Bon* (London, 1972); P. Kvaerne, "Bonpo Studies: The A-Khrid System of Meditation," *Kailash* 1 (1973): 19–50, 248–322; idem, "The Canon of the Tibetan Bonpos," *IIJ* 16 (1974): 18–56, 96–144.

On the analogies between certain *Bon* practices and shamanism, see M. Eliade, *Shamanism,* pp. 431ff.; cf. also H. Hoffmann, *Symbolik der tibetischen Religionen und des Schamanismus* (Stuttgart, 1967), pp. 67–141.

On Bon-po funerals, see M. Lalou, "Rituel Bon-Po des funérailles royales," *JA* 249 (1952): 339–62; idem, "Le chemin des morts dans les croyances de Haute Asie," *RHR* 135 (1949): 42–48; R. A. Stein, "Du récit au rituel," *Études tibétaines . . . Marcelle Lalou,* pp. 479–547 (the role of origin myths recited in the funerary rituals).

On the relationships among spirit, light, and the *semen virile,* see Eliade, *Occultism, Witchcraft, and Cultural Fashions,* pp. 93–119.

315. On the history of Buddhism in Tibet, see H. Hoffmann, *The Religions of Tibet,* pp. 28–83, 111–80; G. Tucci, *Les religions du Tibet,* pp. 29–54; P. Demiéville, *Le Concile de Lhasa* (Paris, 1952; the controversy between the representatives of Indian and Chinese Buddhism); D. S. Ruegg, "Sur les rapports entre le Bouddhisme et le 'substrat religieux' indien et tibétain," *JA* (1964): 77–95.

On Atīśa, see A Chattopadhyaya, *Atīśa and Tibet* (Calcutta, 1967); on Padmasambhava, see C. C. Toussaint, *Le dict de Padma* (1933); A. M. Blon-

deau, "le Lha-'dre bka'-than," in *Études tibétaines . . . Marcelle Lalou,* pp.
29–126 (translation of a text that was hidden and rediscovered, concerning
the submission of the gods and demons by Padmasambhava); on Naropa, see
H. Guenther, *The Life and Teachings of Naropa* (Oxford, 1963); on Marpa,
see J. Bacot, *La vie de Marpa le "traducteur"* (1937); on Milarepa, see
below, §317.

On Tsong-kha-pa, see E. Obermiller, "Con-kha-pa le Pandit," *Mélanges
chinois et bouddhiques* 3 (1934–35): 319–338; R. Kaschewsky, *Das Leben
des lamaistischen Heilige Tsongkhapa* (Wiesbaden, 1971). See also C.
Schulemann, *Die Geschichte der Dalai-Lamas* (Heidelberg, 1911).

316. On the doctrines and practices of Lamaism, see R. Stein, *Tibetan Civilization,* pp. 164–91; Tucci, *Les religions du Tibet,* pp. 55–210; R. Bleichsteiner, *Die Gelbe Kirche* (1936; French trans., *L'Église jaune,* 1937); H. V.
Guenther, *sGam-po-pa, The Jewel Ornament of Liberation* (London, 1959);
idem, *Buddhist Philosophy in Theory and Practice* (London, 1972); F. Lessing and A. Wayman, *Mkhas grub rje's Fundamentals of Buddhist Tantras*
(The Hague, 1968; Tibetan text and annotated translation); Eva M. Dargyay,
The Rise of Esoteric Buddhism in Tibet (Delhi, 1977).

One should consult the works of G. Tucci, *Indo-Tibetica,* 7 vols. (Rome
1932–41); *Tibetan Painted Scrolls,* 2 vols. (Rome, 1949); *The Theory and·
Practice of the Mandala* (London, 1961). On certain "popular" aspects of
Lamaism, see R. Nebesky-Wojkovitz, *Oracles and Demons of Tibet* (The
Hague, 1956); Stephen Beyer, *The Cult of Tārā: Magic and Ritual in Tibet*
(Berkeley and Los Angeles, 1973).

On iconography, see W. E. Clark, *Two Lamaistic Pantheons* (New York,
1937); A. K. Gordon, *The Iconography of Tibetan Lamaism* (Tokyo, 1959).
On the iconography of the "magicians," see T. Schmid, *The Eighty-Five
Siddhas* (Stockholm, 1958).

On the *gčod,* see R. Bleichsteiner, *L'Église jaune,* pp. 194ff.; Alexandra
David-Neel, *With Mystics and Magicians in Tibet* (London, 1931; originally
Mystiques et Magiciens du Thibet, Paris, 1929), pp. 126ff.; Eliade, *Shaman-
ism,* pp. 436–37.

On shamanism in Tibet and among the Mo-so, see Eliade, *Shamanism,* pp.
436ff., 444ff.

317. On the morphology and meanings of light, see Eliade, "Expérience de
la lumière mystique" (1957), republished in *The Two and the One,* pp. 19–
77; idem, "Spirit, Light, and Seed" (1971), republished in *Occultism,
Witchcraft, and Cultural Fashions,* pp. 93–119.

On the symbolism of the soul-light penetrating and leaving the human body
in the form of an arrow or ray, see Eliade, "Briser le toit de la maison," and the

two studies of R. A. Stein, "Architecture et pensée religieuse"; idem, "L'habitat, le monde et le corps humain" (cited above, §313).

The texts of Candrakīrti and Tsong-kha-pa have been translated by G. Tucci, "Some Glosses upon Guhyasamāja," *Mélanges chinois et bouddhiques* 3 (1934–35): 339–53. See now Alex Wayman, *Yoga of the Guhyasamājatantra* (Delhi and Benares, 1977).

The *Bardo Thödol* has been translated by Lama Kazi Dawa-Samdup and W. Y. Evans-Wentz, *The Tibetan Book of the Dead* (Oxford, 1927; numerous re-editions; French version, 1958); by Francesca Fremantle and Chögyam Trungpa, *The Tibetan Book of the Dead* (Berkeley and London, 1975); and by Giuseppe Tucci, *Il Libro Tibetano dei morti* (Milan, 1949). See also D. M. Back, *Eine buddhistische Jenseitsreise: Das sogenannte "Totenbuch der Tibeter" aus philologischer Sicht* (Wiesbaden, 1979); Dawa-Samdup and Evans-Wentz, *Tibetan Yoga and Secret Doctrines* (Oxford, 1935), pp. 223ff.

318. The Tantric Kālacakra system was introduced into Tibet in the first quarter of the eleventh century. It presents, among other innovations, an astrological interpretation of temporal cycles. The Tibetan calendar begins with the year 1026, the date of the official adoption of the Kālacakra. The doctrines and history of this last expression of the Mahāyāna are still little studied. See George Roerich, "Studies in the Kālacakra," *Journal of Urusvati Himalayan Research Institute of the Roerich Museum* 2 (1931): 11–22; H. Hoffmann, "Kālacakra Studies, I: Manichaeism, Christianity and Islam in Kālacakra Tantra," *Central Asiatic Journal* 13 (1969): 52–75; idem, *The Religions of Tibet*, pp. 126ff.

According to Tibetan traditions, the Kālacakra was elaborated and conserved in a mysterious land called Shambhala, situated to the north of Tibet; some scholars have located it near Khotan (Laufer, Pelliot), others in Bactria (Sarat Chandra Das) or in Central Asia. One will find the history of the controversy, as well as the diverse symbolic interpretations of Shambhala, in Edwin Bernbaum, *The Way to Shambhala: A Search for the Mythical Kingdom beyond the Himalayas* (New York, 1980; cf. the bibliographical citations, pp. 269–87).

Among the partial translations of Milarepa, the most suitable are Berthold Laufer, *Milaraspa: Tibetische Texte in Auswahl übertragen* (Hagen i. W. and Darmstadt, 1922); H. Hoffmann, *Mi-la ras-pa: Sieben Legenden* (Munich and Planegg, 1950); Sir Humphrey Clarke, *The Message of Milarepa* (London, 1958). Cf. also the new translation of Lobsang P. Lhalungpa, *The Life of Milarepa* (New York, 1977).

The first complete translation is that by Garma C. C. Chang, *The Hundred Thousand Songs of Milarepa*, 2 vols. (New York, 1962). See the severe review of this work by D. Snellgrove, *Asia Major* 10 (1963): 302–10; cf. also de Jong, *IIJ* 10 (1967): 204–12, who takes pains to bring out "the good side of the work" (p. 205); ibid., 211–12, the complete list of translations.

On the iconography, see T. Schmid, *The Cotton-clad Mila: The Tibetan Poet-Saint's Life in Pictures* (Stockholm, 1958).

On the Gesar epic, see Alexandra David-Neel and Lama Yongden, *The Superhuman Life of Gesar of Ling* (London, 1933; = *La vie surhumaine de Guésar de Ling,* Paris, 1931: general presentation of the epic and partial translation); R. A. Stein, *L'épopée tibétaine de Gesar dans sa version lamaïque de Ling* (1956); idem, "Peintures tibétaines de la Vie de Gesar," *Arts Asiatiques* 5 (1958): 243–71; idem, *Recherches sur l'épopée et le barde au Tibet* (1959; the definitive work); idem, "Une source ancienne pour l'histoire de l'épopée tibétaine," *JA* (1963): 77–105; M. Hermanns, *Der National-Epos der Tibeter: Gling König Ge sar* (Regensburg, 1965; an erudite and thick work of more than 1000 pages; to be consulted with care).

Index